Black
Literature
and
Literary
Theory

Republic of Literature w/ citizens of
literature — invokes belief that
we may all participate
in formation of a cannon, especially
crucial when we know develop. of
a cannon "a national literature"
has historically been work of white
western men. 'Non-canonical' critc
barely contain happiness that
Repub. of literature is experiencing alterations,
accomodating historically disenfranchised.

— reading blk. texts as simply political
has historically been case
" one more slave narrative "
— avoids discussing literary traditions though
myths, signs, language, art, religion
seeing these, blk. texts echo, revise, + extend w.
canon

Edited by Henry Louis Gates, Jr

BLACK LITERATURE AND LITERARY THEORY

Methuen   New York and London

First published in 1984 by
Methuen, Inc.
733 Third Avenue, New York, NY 10017

Published in Great Britain by
Methuen & Co. Ltd
11 New Fetter Lane,
London EC4P 4EE

This collection © 1984 Methuen, Inc., and
Methuen & Co. Ltd

© 1984 'Criticism in the jungle'
Henry Louis Gates, Jr

Typeset in Great Britain by
Nene Phototypesetters Ltd
and printed in the United States of America

Library of Congress Cataloging in
Publication Data

Main entry under title:
Black literature and literary theory.
Includes index.
1. American fiction – Afro-American authors –
History and criticism – Addresses, essays, lectures.
2. African fiction (English) – Black authors –
History and criticism – Addresses, essays, lectures.
3. Caribbean fiction (English) – Black authors –
History and criticism – Addresses, essays, lectures.
4. Literature – History and criticism – Theory, etc. –
Addresses, essays, lectures.   5. Criticism –
Addresses, essays, lectures.   I. Gates, Henry Louis.
PS153.N5B555   1984   813'.009'896073
84–6636

ISBN 0–416–37230–9
ISBN 0–416–37240–6 (pbk.)

British Library Cataloguing in Publication
Data

Black literature and literary theory.
1. English literature – Black authors – History and
criticism   2. English literature – 20th century –
History and criticism
I. Gates, Henry Louis
820.9'896   PR478.B5

ISBN 0–416–37230–9
ISBN 0–416–37240–6 Pbk

For
Charles T. Davis
and Paul de Man,
in memoriam

[The slaves] would compose and sing as they went along, consulting neither time nor tune. The thought that came up, came out – if not in the word, in the sound; – and as frequently in the one as in the other. They would sometimes sing the most pathetic sentiment in the most rapturous tone, and the most rapturous sentiment in the most pathetic tone. . . . This they would sing, as a chorus, to words which to many would seem unmeaning jargon, but which, nevertheless, were full of meaning to themselves. . . .

I did not, when a slave, understand the deep meaning of those rude and apparently incoherent songs. I was myself within the circle; so that I neither saw nor heard as those without might see or hear.   (Frederick Douglass, 1845)

It is one thing for a race to produce artistic material; it is quite another thing for it to produce the ability to interpret and criticize this material.

(W. E. B. DuBois, 1925)

Contents

Part II Practice

Notes on the contributors

Sunday O. Anozie is Professor of English and Comparative Literature at the University of Port-Harcourt, Nigeria, a fellow of the Rockefeller Foundation Humanities Program, and founder, editor and publisher of *The Conch* – a sociological journal of African literatures and cultures. He is the author of *Sociologie du roman africain* (1970), *Christopher Okigbo: Creative Rhetoric* (1972), *Structural Models and African Poetics* (1981) and *Deconstruction and Politics: Language, Criticism and the Speakerly Text* (1984). The books he has edited include *Structuralism and African Folklore* (1971), *Language Systems in Africa* (1973) and *Phenomenology in Modern African Studies* (1982).

Anthony Appiah is an Assistant Professor of Afro-American Studies and Philosophy at Yale University, and a member of the Council on African Studies. He has taught at the University of Ghana and at Clare College, Cambridge, England. He is currently writing a book on those aspects of the philosophy of mind most relevant to the interpretation of language, as well as editing and analysing some 7000 Twi proverbs from Asante in Ghana, and working on philosophical problems relating to traditional religion in West Africa.

Houston A. Baker, Jr, is the Albert M. Greenfield Professor of Human Relations at the University of Pennsylvania. He has published numerous essays, books and reviews in the general area of Afro-American literary and cultural study. He is also a poet, whose third volume, *Blues Journeys Home*, mines the agrarian blues tradition so familiar to black expressive culture in the United States.

Kimberly W. Benston is an Associate Professor of English at Haverford College. He is the author of *Baraka: The Renegade and the Mask* (1976) and has edited *Critical Essays on Amiri Baraka* (1978) and *The Language of Blackness* (1984). He is currently working on a book about modern drama.

Barbara E. Bowen is an Assistant Professor of English at Wellesley College. She has published a study of the poetry of Gwendolyn Brooks and is completing a dissertation begun at Yale University on the problem of representation in language, economics, politics and dramatic structure in Shakespeare's plays.

Jay Edwards is an Associate Professor of Anthropology at Louisiana State University. He has conducted research, and written a number of articles, on the vernacular architecture of the Caribbean and French Louisiana, on the Creole English of the West Indies, and on oral literature in Afro-American communities. He is the author of *The Afro-American Trickster Tale: A Structural Analysis* (1978) and a forthcoming two-volume study of the *Vernacular Architecture of French Louisiana*.

Henry Louis Gates, Jr, is an Associate Professor in the English and Afro-American Studies departments at Yale University, where he teaches courses in literary theory and in African and Afro-American literature. He has edited *Black is the Color of the Cosmos: Charles T. Davis's Essays on Black Literature and Culture* (1982), *Our Nig; or, Sketches From the Life of a Free Black* (1983) and *The Slave's Narrative* (1984). He has written two books, *Figures in Black: Words, Signs, and the Racial Self* and *The Signifying Monkey* (both forthcoming). In 1981 he was selected as one of the first MacArthur Prize Fellows.

Barbara Johnson is Professor of Romance Languages and Literatures at Harvard University. She has written *Défigurations du langage poétique* (1979) and *The Critical Difference* (1980), translated Jacques Derrida's *Dissemination* (1981) and edited *The Pedagogical Imperative: Teaching as a Literary Genre* (1982). She is currently working on a book on Zora Neale Hurston.

James A. Snead is an Assistant Professor of English and Comparative Literature at Yale University. He has written widely in the field of twentieth-century American, English and German literature, particularly on the writings of Faulkner, Joyce and Mann. Forthcoming books include a study of rhetoric and the self in Faulkner's major novels, and an analysis of linearity versus cyclicality in the structure of modern prose fiction.

Wole Soyinka, who is internationally acclaimed as a playwright, poet, novelist and critic, is currently Professor of Comparative Literature at the University of Ife, Nigeria. He holds an honorary Doctorate of Letters from Yale University and has been accorded major literary prizes in England, including the John Whiting Award. His previous works published in America include his *Collected Plays* (1973 and 1975), a memoir, *The Man Died* (1973), a critical study, *Myth, Literature and the African World* (1978), and an autobiography, *Ake* (1981).

Robert B. Stepto is an Associate Professor of English, Afro-American Studies and American Studies at Yale University. His previous publications include *From Behind the Veil: A Study of Afro-American Narrative* (1979) and two edited volumes – (with Michael S. Harper) *Chant of Saints: A Gathering of Afro-American Literature, Art, and Scholarship* (1979) and (with Dexter Fisher) *Afro-American Literature: The Reconstruction of Instruction* (1979).

Mary Helen Washington is an Associate Professor of English at the University of Massachusetts at Boston. She is the author of numerous essays on black literature and feminist theory and has published two books, *Black-Eyed Susans: Classic Stories by and about Black Women* (1975) and *Midnight Birds: Stories of Contemporary Black Women Writers* (1980). In 1974 she received the Richard Wright Award for Literary Criticism.

Susan Willis defines herself as an Americanist on a hemispheric plane. Her teaching and writing embrace Latin American, Caribbean and American literary traditions. She is currently writing a book of literary criticism from this hemispheric point of view, as well as another book on the development of American popular culture. Her current spot in the universe is the University of California, Santa Cruz.

Acknowledgements

The editor and publisher would like to thank the following for permission to reproduce copyright material:

Wole Soyinka and Indiana State University, Chapter 1, first appeared as 'The critic and society: Barthes, leftocracy, and other mythologies', *Black American Literature Forum*, 15, 4 (1981); James A. Snead and Indiana State University, Chapter 2, first appeared as 'On repetition in black culture', *Black American Literature Forum*, 15, 4 (1981); Jay Edwards and Indiana State University, Chapter 3, 'Structural analysis of the Afro-American trickster tale', *Black American Literature Forum*, 15, 4 (1981); Sunday O. Anozie and Indiana State University, Chapter 4, first appeared in America as 'Negritude and structuralism', *Black American Literature Forum*, 15, 4 (1981); Anthony Appiah and Indiana State University, Chapter 5, first appeared as 'Structural criticism and African fiction: an analytical critique', *Black American Literature Forum*, 15, 4 (1981); Kimberly W. Benston and Indiana State University, Chapter 6, first appeared as '"I yam what I am": naming and unnaming in Afro-American literature', *Black American Literature Forum*, 16, 1 (1982); Robert B. Stepto and the University of Georgia, Chapter 7, 'Storytelling in early Afro-American fiction: Frederick Douglass's "The Heroic Slave"', *The Georgia Review* (1982); Barbara E. Bowen and Indiana State University, Chapter 8, 'Untroubled voice: call and response in *Cane*', *Black American Literature Forum*, 16, 1 (1982); Barbara Johnson, Chapter 9, 'Metaphor, metonymy and voice in *Their Eyes Were Watching God*'; Houston A. Baker and the Modern Language Association of America, Chapter 10, first appeared as 'To move without moving: an analysis of creativity and commerce in Ralph Ellison's Trueblood episode', *PMLA*, 98 (1983); Mary Helen Washington and the University of Massachusetts, Chapter 11,

'"Taming all that anger down": rage and silence in Gwendolyn Brooks's *Maud Martha*', *The Massachusetts Review*, Winter, (1983); Susan Willis and Indiana State University, Chapter 12, 'Eruptions of funk: historicizing Toni Morrison', *Black American Literature Forum*, 16, 1 (1982); the University of Chicago, Chapter 13, 'The blackness of blackness: a critique of the sign and the Signifying Monkey', *Critical Inquiry*, 9, 4 (1983).

Henry Louis Gates, Jr

Criticism in the jungle

Son, these niggers writing. Profaning our
sacred words. Taking them from us and
beating them on the anvil of Boogie-
Woogie, putting their black hands on them
so that they shine like burnished amulets.
Taking our words, son, these filthy niggers
and using them like they were their god-
given pussy. Why ... why 1 of them dared
to interpret, critically mind you, the great
Herman Melville's *Moby Dick!*

(Ishmael Reed, *Mumbo Jumbo*)

The canons are falling
One by one
(John Ashbery,
'The Tomb of
Stuart Merrill')

I

My first epigraph, from *Mumbo Jumbo*, refers to the splendid work of criticism that
C. L. R. James wrote while unlawfully imprisoned in 1952 on Ellis Island. James's
work, *Mariners, Renegades, and Castaways: The Story of Herman Melville and the World We
Live In*, which he published himself at New York in 1953, is an explication of
Moby-Dick and *Pierre*, read as allegories of the fascist years in the post-war United
States, of which Senator Joseph McCarthy remains only a convenient sign. 'I pub-
lish [my] protest [against racism and fascism]', writes the critic, 'with the book on
Melville.' One of the few other literary events in the black tradition that strikes
me with such poignancy is the publication of *Madmen and Specialists*, an allegorical

play that Wole Soyinka wrote after emerging from twenty-seven months of imprisonment in Nigeria, twenty-four of which he was forced to spend in solitary confinement. Not once does Soyinka indict his captors, except by the deafening silence he creates by the absence of the certain indictment that it was his to pronounce upon those who tortured and tried to murder him. Rather, the playwright creates the enigmatic 'cult of As', an extended signifyin(g) riff upon Wallace Stevens's 'An Ordinary Evening in New Haven' ('As it is, in the intricate evasions of as . . .').

Who among us dares to claim to have made a critical gesture as subtle or as poignant as those of Soyinka and James? Who, indeed? The act of writing, for James and Soyinka, was no idle matter; it represented a profound definition and defense of the critical self: in an act of self-defense, the writer asserts the integrity of the self through the device of displacement; through the very forces of displacement, the self is both distanced and affirmed. For James, this 'act' assumed the form of a searching critical engagement with the complexities of a fascistic America signified most aptly in the synecdoche of Ahab's crew, comprised of 'meanest mariners, and renegades and castaways'. For Soyinka, the first words written by the protagonist emerging from his willed trek across the abyss (Ogun's role, in Soyinka's revision of classical Yoruba mythology) engage, of all texts, Stevens's canonical 'An Ordinary Evening in New Haven'. Trinidadian and Nigerian; one imprisoned by white aliens, the other twenty-five years later by his black countrymen: both chose to write their way out of the prison-house of experience by engaging canonical Western texts.

I have chosen my second epigraph, taken from Ashbery's 'The Tomb of Stuart Merrill', as a gloss upon the first. Reed's character, a parody of the 'canonical critic', grows ever more hysterical as he wonders aloud about the dangers inherent in 'niggers writing', 'Profaning our sacred words', 'Taking our words, son, . . . and using them'. We overhear the voice of the critic who speaks the word 'canon' to invoke a closed set of texts written mostly by men who are Western and white; a most useful organizing concept for pedagogy becomes another mechanism for political control. The sheer chaos created by texts emerging from national literatures of the black cultures, euphemistically dismissed as somehow 'Third' World – texts like James's and Soyinka's, determined to revise antecedent, 'canonical' texts – is signified upon by Reed's novel. For, if James can reread Moby-Dick and Soyinka rewrite Stevens (and, for that matter, Euripides, Sophocles, Shakespeare and Brecht), then none of 'our sacred words' is safe from profane 'black hands'. As Ashbery laments, 'The canons are falling / one by one.' Whereas Reed's canonical critic can barely contain his hysteria at the threat to the sanctity of the canon, then the 'non-canonical' critic can barely contain her or his elation at the faint hope that the republic of 'literature' is experiencing alterations which can, at last, enable it to accommodate even those citizens historically disenfranchised by the critic's version of the 'grandfather clause'.

The essays collected in Black Literature and Literary Theory are concerned with the question of the formal relation between 'black' (African, Caribbean, Afro-American) literatures and Western literatures. What is the status of the black literary work of art? How do canonical texts in the black traditions relate to canonical texts of the Western traditions? As if these questions were not problematic enough, how are we to read black texts? Can the methods of explication developed in Western criticism be 'translated' into the black idiom? How 'text-specific' is literary theory, and how 'universal' are rhetorical strategies? If every black canonical text is, as I shall argue, 'two-toned' or 'double-voiced', how do we explicate the signifyin(g) black difference that makes black literature 'black'? And what do we make of the relation between the black vernacular tradition and the black formal tradition, as these inform the shape of a black text? Do we have to 'invent' validly 'black' critical theory and methodologies? Once fully addressed, the answers to these questions will help us to understand more broadly and convincingly the nature of the constituencies which comprise the republic of literature.

Black Literature and Literary Theory is not a programmatic manifesto announcing a unified set of responses to these questions. Indeed, I have edited it carefully to reveal the diversity of the criticism practiced by these citizens of literature, with essays such as Soyinka's, Anozie's, Edwards's and Appiah's engaging each other precisely at points of divergence. Nor do the essays merely 'repeat' or 'apply' a mode of reading that is 'formalist', 'Marxist', 'structuralist' or 'post-structuralist', borrowed whole from the Western tradition. Rather, these critics – while unarguably sharing with Western critics certain presuppositions about the study and status of literature – adapt and thereby question received theories of literature. Ours is repetition, but repetition with a difference, a signifying black difference.

If Western literature has a canon, then so does Western literary criticism. If the relation of black texts to Western texts is problematic, then what relationship obtains between (Western) theories of (Western) 'literature' and its 'criticism' and what the critic of black literature *does* and reflects upon? This book attempts to address these questions and to answer, implicitly, how 'applicable' is contemporary literary theory to the reading of the African, Caribbean and Afro-American literary traditions. A few of the difficulties of such a task may perhaps be illustrated by a short account of my own struggles to respond to shaping by a 'classical' English education, the rigors of contemporary literary theory, and a desire for precise definitions and close, sensitive readings of Afro-American texts. My own works of criticism have tried to draw upon contemporary theories of reading, both to explicate discrete black texts and to define the precise structure of the Afro-American literary tradition itself by attempting to link, in Geoffrey Hartman's phrase, 'the form of art and the form of its historical consciousness'. I have been concerned, in other words, with that complex relationship between what it is useful to call 'the representative' in black letters and its modes of 'representation', of mimesis. To explore this relation, moreover, I have attempted, with varying degrees of success, to 'read' the black tradition closely, drawing rather eclectically upon the activity of reading as practiced by critics outside the black literary traditions.

This has been no easy task. Difficulty has arisen, not because of the supposed subtleties of literary-theoretical discourse, but because of the very question of the so-called 'translatability' of these theories to the reading of works outside what Hartman calls their 'text-milieu'. Theory, like words in a poem, does not 'translate' in a one-to-one relationship of reference. Indeed, I have found that, in the 'application' of a mode of reading to black texts, the critic, by definition, transforms the theory and, I might add, transforms received readings of the text into something different, a construct neither exactly 'like' its antecedents nor entirely new. I have tried to take from contemporary Western critical theory that which enables me, in some way, to respond to the signifying structures that a sensitive reading should produce in the texts of the black canon. Key texts, signposts of the tradition, seem to demand to be read in certain ways. If theory and practice from formalism, structuralism or post-structuralism aid the critic in responding to the multifarious demands of the texts of our tradition, then the critic must embark upon their mastery. How can it be otherwise?

Who would seek to deny us our complexity? Who, indeed? Wole Soyinka, whose vast corpus of works is perhaps the most sustained and challenging in the African canon, has reflected upon this question, which is a profound reformulation of the question of the relation the individual talent bears to tradition(s); in the case of the writer of African descent, her or his texts occupy spaces in at least two traditions: a European or American literary tradition, and one of the several related but distinct black traditions. The 'heritage' of each black text written in a Western language is, then, a double heritage, two-toned, as it were. Its visual tones are white and black, and its aural tones are standard and vernacular.

Soyinka's recapitulation of this relation between the individual black talent and Western traditions is an enterprising one: 'A ò lè b'ara ni tan, k'á f'ara wa n'itan ya. A free translation would read: 'Kinship does not insist that, because we are entwined, we thereby rip off each other's thigh. The man who, because of ideological kinship, tries to sever my being from its self-apprehension is not merely culturally but politically hostile.' We could just as well substitute 'critical' for 'ideological'. The 'textual' tradition in evidence here is one broadly defined, including as it does both the imaginative and the political text. We, the critics of black literary traditions, owe it to those traditions to bring to bear upon their readings any 'tool' which helps us to elucidate, which enables us to see more clearly, the complexities of figuration peculiar to our literary traditions. Close reading of any critical complexion is what this volume advocates; there can be no compromise here.

By definition, the medium in which the critical activity is engaged is language, spoken and written words. The ways in which language and literature mediate between 'reality' (defined variously) and its reflections are both complex and subtle. Any meaningful effort to shorten this distance between text and 'reality' is especially difficult for the critic because a text is a coded structure which must somehow be decoded; its structures of signification can never be what they appear to be, or might be in a discourse such as mathematics. Even to achieve a grasp of a text's reduced 'meaning' presupposes and demands mastery of the several modes of explication with which we are satisfactorily able to produce a reading. For all sorts of complex historical reasons, the very act of writing has been a 'political' act for the black author. Even our most solipsistic texts, at least since the Enlightenment in Europe, have been treated as political evidence of one sort or another, both implicitly and explicitly. And, because our life in the West has been one political struggle after another, our literature has been defined from without, and rather often from within, as primarily just one more polemic in those struggles. The black literary tradition now demands, for sustenance and for growth, the sorts of reading which it is the especial province of the literary critic to render; and these sorts of reading all share a fundamental concern with the nature and functions of figurative language as manifested in specific texts. No matter to what ends we put our readings, we can never lose sight of the fact that a text is not a fixed 'thing' but a rhetorical structure which functions in response to a complex set of rules. It can never be related satisfactorily to a reality outside itself merely in a one-to-one relation.

If Euro-Americans have used the creative writing of Afro-Americans primarily as evidence of the blacks' mental or social 'perfectibility' or as a measure of the blacks' 'racial' psychology or sociology, then they have used African literature as evidence of African 'anthropology', of traditional and modern African customs and beliefs. Chinua Achebe, more often than not, is taught in anthropology classes in America; at Cambridge in 1973, Wole Soyinka was neatly shunted away from the Faculty of English and appointed instead to the Faculty of Social Anthropology! If we were forced to compile a list of the received critical 'fallacies' that we wish to avoid in the analysis of black literature, the 'anthropology' fallacy* would most certainly stand near the top of our list, perhaps just beneath the 'perfectibility' fallacy and the 'sociology' fallacy (that is, that blacks create literature primarily to demonstrate their intellectual equality with whites, or else to repudiate racism). The anthropology fallacy, moreover, can be divided into its two components, the 'collective' and 'functional' fallacies. ('All African art is collective and functional', whatever this is supposed to mean.) Our list could be extended to include all sorts of concerns with the possible functions of black texts in 'non-literary' arenas rather than with their internal structures as acts of language or their formal status as works of art.

Because of this curious valorization of the social and polemical functions of black literature, the structure of the black text has been *repressed* and treated as if it

---

* I wish to stress the difference between the use of black literature as anthropological data and Houston Baker's important theory of reading black texts, which (in a signifyin(g) riff) he calls 'the anthropology of art'.

were *transparent*. The black literary work of art has stood at the center of a triangle of relations (M. H. Abrams's 'universe', 'artist' and 'audience'), but as the very thing *not* to be explained, as if it were invisible, or literal, or a one-dimensional document. The relation of the black text to its 'universes', its author, and its various readerships has been of such intense interest to critics that close or practical criticism has until recently been the exception rather than the rule. Accordingly, mimetic and expressive theories of black literature continue to predominate over the sorts of theories concerned with discrete uses of figurative language.

The essays collected in *Black Literature and Literary Theory* share a concern with the nature of the figure, with the distinctively 'black' uses of our English and French language and literature. The essayists here explore, in several ways, what we might think of as 'black' uses of figurative language. We are concerned to turn critical attention, in other words, to that which has been most repressed: the language of the black text. Rather than with the imitation of what the black Brazilian symbolist poet Joao da Cruz e Souza ('the Black Swan') called 'white Forms', the critics collected here seek to define *black Forms*, forms of language and literature peculiar to the black tradition, traditions of language-use related to, but distinct from, Western literary traditions. Canonical Western texts are to be digested rather than regurgitated, but digested along with canonical black formal and vernacular texts. The result, in work such as that by Aimé Césaire, Nicolás Guillén, Ralph Ellison and Soyinka, is a literature 'like' its French or Spanish, American or English antecedents, yet differently 'black'.

How 'black' is figuration? Given the obvious political intent of so much of our literary traditions, is it not somewhat wistful to be concerned with the intricacies of the figure? The Afro-American tradition has been figurative from its beginnings. How could it have survived otherwise? I need not here trace the elaborate modes of signification implicit in black mythic and religious traditions, in ritual rhetorical structures such as 'signifying' and 'the dozens'. Black people have always been masters of the figurative: saying one thing to mean something quite other has been basic to black survival in oppressive Western cultures. Misreading signs could be, and indeed often was, fatal. 'Reading', in this sense, was not play; it was an essential aspect of the 'literacy' training of a child. This sort of metaphorical literacy, the learning to decipher complex codes, is just about the blackest aspect of the black tradition. If, as is said in the epigraph I cite in my essay printed below, 'Signification is the nigger's occupation', then we may also say rightfully that 'Figuration is the nigger's occupation.' For a critic of black literature to be unaware of the black tradition of figuration and its bearing upon a discrete black text is as serious a flaw as for that critic to be unaware of the texts in the Western tradition which the black text echoes, revises and extends. Hartman's definition of 'text-milieu' ('how theory depends on a canon, on a limited group of texts, often culture-specific or national') does not break down in the context of the black traditions; it must, however, be modified, since the texts of the black canon occupy a rhetorical space in at least two canons, as does black literary theory. The sharing of common texts does allow for enhanced dialogue between critics; but the sharing of a more or less compatible critical approach also allows for a dialogue between two critics of two different canons whose knowledge of the other's text is less than ideal. The black text-milieu is 'extra-territorial', as George Steiner might put it.

The black critic must face squarely another quandary, of a more subtle and therefore more profoundly trying nature. For the question of 'blackness' inhabits the subject, as well as the object, of our criticism. As Barbara Johnson puts it, 'an inquiry that attempts to study an object by means of that very object is open to certain analyzable aberrations' ('this pertains', she continues, 'to virtually all important investigations: the self analyzing itself, man studying man, thought thinking about thought, language speaking about language, etc.'). The problem, for us, can perhaps be usefully stated in the irony implicit in the attempt to posit a 'black self' in the very Western languages in which blackness itself is a figure of absence, a negation. Ethnocentrism and 'logocentrism' are profoundly inter-related in Western discourse as old as the Phaedrus of Plato, in which one finds one of the earliest figures of blackness as an absence, a figure of negation. If Keats called the Enlightenment in Europe 'the grand march of intellect', then logo-centrism and ethnocentrism marched together in an attempt to deprive the black human being of even the potential to create art, to imagine a world and to figure it. A study of the so-called arbitrariness of the sign, of the ways in which concepts divide reality arbitrarily, and of the relation between a sign, such as blackness, and its referent, such as absence, can help us to engage in more sophisticated readings of black texts. But it can also help to explain the figuration of blackness in Western texts.

In the final essay of this book, on the Signifying Monkey and on Mumbo Jumbo, I attempt to combine an analysis of what I call 'race and superstructure' criticism with an analysis of the idea of a transcendent signified, a belief in an essence called 'blackness', a presence which our tradition has tried of late to will into being, in order to negate two and a half millennia of its figuration as an absence. As healthy politically as such a gesture was, as revealing as it was (in this country and abroad) of the very arbitrariness of the received sign of blackness itself, we must also criticize the idealism, the notion of essence, implicit in even this gesture. To think oneself free simply because one can claim – can utter – the negation of an assertion is not to think deeply enough. Negritude already constituted such a claim of blackness as a transcendent signified, of a full and sufficient presence; but to make such a claim, to feel the necessity to make such a claim, is already to reveal too much about perceived absence and desire. It is to take the terms of one's assertion from a discourse determined by an Other. Even the terms of one's so-called 'spontaneous' desire have been presupposed by the Other. I render this critique of blackness as a transcendent signified in order to help to break through the enclosure of negation.

The enclosure of negation is only one trap. That sort of intellectual indenture, which we might call, after Jean Price-Mars, 'bovarysme collectif', is quite another, and equally deadly, trap. Jules de Gaultier, expanding upon Price-Mars, defines 'bovarysm' as the phenomenon of being 'fated to obey the suggestion of an external milieu, for lack of an auto-suggestion from within'. The challenge of black literary criticism is to derive principles of literary criticism from the black tradition itself, as defined in the idiom of critical theory but also in the idiom which constitutes the 'language of blackness', the signifyin(g) difference which makes the black tradition our very own. To borrow mindlessly, or to vulgarize, a critical theory from another tradition is to satisfy de Gaultier's definition of 'bovarysm'; but it is also to satisfy, in the black idiom, Ishmael Reed's definition of 'The Talking Android'. The sign of the successful negotiation of this precipice of indenture, of slavish imitation, is that the black critical essay refers to two contexts, two traditions – the Western and the black. Each utterance, then, is double-voiced.

In a 1925 review of James Weldon Johnson's *The Book of American Negro Spirituals*, W. E. B. DuBois argued that evidence of critical activity is a sign of a tradition's sophistication, since criticism implies an awareness of the process of art itself and is a second-order reflection upon those primary texts that define a tradition and its canon. Insofar as we, critics of the black tradition, master our craft, we serve both to preserve our own traditions and to shape their direction. All great writers demand great critics. The imperatives of our task are clear.

The essays collected here, ranging from theoretical to practical criticism, exemplify various modes of reading. The black literary and critical traditions need all sorts of close readings; the body of practical criticism which enabled new theories of reading to emerge in the Western tradition is still being created in the black traditions. The tradition needs readings of several kinds, before it can 'move' into the mainstream of critical debate in the profession. Such a move, it seems to me, is a desirable one, since ultimately our subject is literary discourse, and not the blackness of blackness. Nevertheless, I am not advocating a new form of de Gaultier's 'bovarysm', in which we seek to imitate, from the critics with whom we have an affinity, 'all that can be imitated, everything exterior, appearance, gesture, intonation, and dress'. To do so would be to repeat the mistake of a neo-Romantic poet, such as Countee Cullen, for whom 'form' was a container into which he could pour a precious and black content. Rather than proselytizing for one warring faction of criticism or another, or vulgarizing this or that theory by reducing it to 'summary' or 'method', this book seeks to encourage a plurality of readings, as various as the discrete texts in our literary tradition, and as black. These essays address issues fundamental to critical theory *and* to the nature of black literary discourse. Our subject is the discipline of literature and its criticism.

In an essay called 'For Whom Does One Write?' (collected in *What is Literature?*) Jean-Paul Sartre asks none too rhetorically, 'To whom does Richard Wright address himself?' Sartre's answer helps us to answer our own central question: for whom does the critic of black literature write?

each of Wright's works contains what Baudelaire would have called 'a double simultaneous postulation'; each word refers to two contexts; two forces are applied simultaneously to each phrase and determine the incomparable tension of his tale. Had he spoken to the whites alone, he might have turned out to be more prolix, more didactic, and more abusive; to the negroes alone, still more elliptical, more of a confederate and more elegiac. In the first case, his work might have come close to satire; in the second, to prophetic lamentations. Jeremiah spoke only to the Jews. But Wright, a writer for a split public, has been able both to maintain and go beyond this split. He has made it the pretext for a work of art.

How does this split readership affect the work of criticism? The most obvious way, it seems to me, is in exactly what one can take for granted. While a reader from within the black traditions might need no footnote on Èṣù, Josephine Baker or 'signifying', that same reader might need data about *The Lyrical Ballads*, 'East Coker' or John Donne. The problem is compounded by the need one often feels to establish the very texts one explicates, to make available to the reader our text-milieu. Only footnoting and extensive quotation can do this; 'pinpoint' quotation is effective only where readers share familiarity with a common body of texts. Not even other critics of black texts share the sort of familiarity we assume when interpreting 'canonical' texts; we are still in the process of establishing the texts in the tradition, a process necessarily preceding canon formation.

What we are able to assume about our readers is related to the matter of 'originality'. How 'original' is the use of contemporary theory to read black texts? Only critics who are familiar with black texts can ascertain this, since only they understand the received interpretations that serve as discourse on these texts. What is 'original' about Edward Said's use of post-structuralist theory to analyze representations of 'the Oriental' is his 'application'; indeed, the 'application' of a mode of reading to explicate a black text changes both the received theory and received ideas about the text. When this occurs, the results are 'original'.

We write, it seems to me, primarily for other critics of literature. Through shared theoretical presuppositions, the arduous process of 'cultural translation', if not resolved, is most certainly not hindered. To 'maintain' yet 'go beyond this split' text-milieu is our curse and, of course, our challenge, as is the fact that we must often resurrect the texts in our tradition before we can begin to explicate them. To render major contributions to contemporary theory's quest to 'save the text', in Barthes's phrase, is our splendid opportunity. Unlike critics in almost every other literary tradition, much of what we have to say about our literature is new. What critics of the Western tradition can make an even remotely similar claim? Jeremiah could speak only to the Jews; we, however, must address two audiences, the Jews and the Babylonians, whose interests are distinct yet overlapping in the manner of interlocking sets. The challenge of our endeavor is to bring together, in a new fused form, the concepts of critical theory and the idiom of the Afro-American and African literary traditions. To undertake this complex process, we use Western critical theories to read black texts. The obvious question about such an intellectual activity, however, is this: does the critic of black literature acquire his or her identity parodically, as it were, in the manner of the parrot, as David Hume alleged of Francis Williams's Latin odes?

I would say that the methodological assumption shared in this book is that one 'repeats', as it were, in order to produce *difference*. As Said argues in 'On Repetition' about Marx's narrative strategy in the *Eighteenth Brumaire of Louis Bonaparte*, he repeats 'not to validate Bonaparte's claims but to give facts by emending their apparent direction.' We are able to achieve difference through repetition: as Ralph Ellison puts it, we 'change the joke and slip the yoke'. Marx himself in *Eighteenth Brumaire* states the process in this way:

> the beginner who has learned a new language always retranslates it into his mother tongue: he can only be said to have appropriated the spirit of the new language and to be able to express himself in it freely when he can manipulate it without reference to the old, and when he forgets his original language while using the new one.

Does this sort of repetition, Said asks at the end of his essay, 'enhance or degrade a fact'? His creative response bears repeating here: 'But the question brings forth consciousness of two where there had been repose in one; and such knowledge of course, like procreation, cannot really be reversed. Thereafter the problems multiply. Naturally or not, filiatively or affiliatively, is the question.' The speculative and interpretative essays of this book chart our critics' adventures through the jungle of criticism, as we wrestle with that dense and compelling terrain, and with Said's rhetorical question.

II

If the contributors to this collection do not speak with one critical voice, they do share certain basic assumptions about the relation between 'Western literature' and 'black literature'. Since all of our essays, except for Sunday Anozie's consideration of 'Negritude, structuralism, deconstruction', analyze black literature in English, we may think of this matter in terms of either the place of black literature in the English department, or the place of English literature in a comparative (black) literature department, or even the place of literature(s) in English in a truly comparative literature department. Are we forced to advocate the 'abolition of the English department', as happened at the University of Nairobi in 1968, to achieve a truly integrated notion of the canon of literature in English? Perhaps it will be useful to summarize the terms of debate at the University of Nairobi, and its creative resolution.

My understanding of the events at Nairobi stems from the account rendered by Ngugi Wa Thiong'o in *Homecoming: Essays on African and Caribbean Literature, Culture and Politics* (1972). Ngugi's essay, 'On the Abolition of the English Department', states in its title the debate's resolution. Since such a resolution will strike even many of the essayists in this book as extreme, it is interesting to outline the argument set forth by Ngugi, Henry Owuor-Anyumba and Taban Lo Liyong.

The three lecturers in English were responding to a paper 'presented by the Acting Head of the English Department at the University of Nairobi to the 42nd meeting of the Arts Faculty on the 20th September, 1968'. The acting department head's paper attempted to define the ideal relation in the university of the teaching of modern languages (especially French) and African languages (especially Swahili) to a new Department of Linguistics and Languages, and its relation to the Department of English. The solution proffered by the acting head was to establish a Department of Linguistics and Languages, 'to be closely related to English', and perhaps a Department either of African Literature or of African Literature and Culture. The lecturers, Ngugi informs us, 'questioned the validity of an English department, the only department concerned with literary studies, which continued teaching only British literature in the heart of independent Africa'. Such a practice, the lecturers argued, was 'chauvinistic' and a 'basically colonial approach' to the study of both literature and the humanities.

In response to the argument that the English department be retained, if modified somewhat 'to become less "British" [and] more open to other writing in English (American, Caribbean, African, Commonwealth) and also to continental writing, for comparative purposes', Ngugi and his co-authors made three points which proved telling to their colleagues at Nairobi:

1 Underlying [this] suggestion is a basic assumption that the English tradition and the emergence of the modern west is the central root of our [black] consciousness and cultural heritage. Africa becomes an extension of the west. . .

2 If there is need for a 'study of the historic continuity of a single culture', why can't this be African? Why can't African literature be at the centre so that we can view other cultures in relationship to it?

   This is not mere rhetoric: already African writing, with the sister connections in the Caribbean and the Afro-American literatures, has played an important role in the African renaissance. . . . Just because for reasons of political expediency we have kept English as our official language, there is no need to substitute a study of English culture for our own. We reject the primacy of English language and literature.

3 The aim, in short, should be to orient ourselves towards placing Kenya, East Africa, and then Africa in the centre. All other things are to be considered in their relevance to our situation, and their contribution towards understanding ourselves. (My emphasis)

The arguments of Ngugi, Owuor-Anyumba and Lo Liyong resulted in the abolition of the English department and in the establishment of two departments: one of languages, the other of literature.

Since all but one of the contributors to this book teach in traditionally designated English, French (or Romance language) or comparative literature departments, and all but two of us teach in the United States, I would imagine that few, if any, of us would advocate the abolition of the English department in our university.* Our presences in these faculties would suggest that such an alternative was not necessary to effect even a rudimentary redefinition of what it means to 'teach literature' at our respective institutions.

What is of interest here, however, is what Ngugi calls the 'source of influence' on the forms of African, Caribbean and Afro-American literatures by non-black literatures, and what this sort of formal influence implies about the status of the black work of art, received ideas of 'the' canon, and even the criticism of the black text. Ngugi maintains, correctly, that 'European literatures constitute one source of influence on modern African literatures in English, French, and Portuguese'. But there are other, equally telling, 'sources of influence' as well, including 'Swahili, Arabic, and Asian literatures', and, 'the most significant, the African [oral or vernacular] tradition', which he later labels 'our primary root'. Oral literature is of such import because in it is to be located what I have called 'the signifyin(g) black difference', the very difference, in Ngugi's words, which enables the black writer to 'transcend "fixed literary patterns" and what that implies – the preconceived ranking of art forms'. Black oral literary forms, in other words, can merge with received (European) 'literary' forms to create new (and distinctively black) genres of literature.

Ngugi cites Abiola Irele, now the Professor of French at the University of Ibadan, on the exciting implications of this formal fusion:

one may note that African literature in the European languages lays claim to being differentiated from the metropolitan literatures not only in its content but also to some extent in its form. Its originality comes from the recourse made by our writers not only to African themes and subjects, and to elements of folklore, but also to stylistic innovations derived from the formal features of traditional African literature.

The black formal difference, in other words, is inscribed in black vernacular literatures still alive and dynamic in contemporary African, Caribbean and Afro-American cultures. The 'two-toned', or 'double-voiced', metaphor of the black text's antecedents, then, can be drawn as follows:

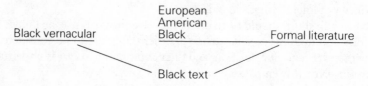

* The University of Ife, at which Wole Soyinka is Professor of Comparative Literature, renamed the Department of English the Department of Literature.

Restoring the study of the black vernacular literatures to the teaching of 'literature' in the university, then, is central to the full explication of even the canonical black text, whether the text be one created by Césaire, Guillén, Ellison or Soyinka.

Finally, Ngugi concludes, the substitution of a truly comparative Department of Literature for the Department of English entails a fundamental reorientation of our received ideas about the question of *value*, which have led more often than not to the relegation of vernacular literatures (and often even formal black literature) to anthropology, sociology or linguistics departments in the West and even in colonial and 'neo-colonial' Africa. It is the question of value – its nature and function – Ngugi insists, which demanded the abolition of the received structures through which students at Nairobi studied 'English':

> One of the things which has been hindering a radical outlook in our study of literature in Africa is the question of literary excellence; that only works of undisputed literary excellence should be offered. (In this case it meant virtually the study of disputable 'peaks' of English literature.) *The question of literary excellence implies a value judgement as to what is excellence, and from whose point of view.* (My emphasis)

To circumvent that curious matter of what we might think of as the 'politics' of normative judgment – that is, of the problematic status of 'universal' norms of beauty and excellence, and their implicit connection with relations of political and economic power – Ngugi and his colleagues abolished the Department of English, so that they might radically *decenter* the place of English language and literature in the study of the larger institution of 'literature'. What Ngugi's faculty did is somewhat analogous to the innovation in cartography effected by the editors of The Times Atlas of the World, by placing each country analyzed at the very center of the globe, so that the reader sees, say, the United Kingdom as it might appear from, say, the Republic of Kenya. Ngugi summarizes this intention aptly:

> after we have examined ourselves, we radiate outwards and discover peoples and worlds around us. With Africa at the centre of things, not existing as an appendix or a satellite of other countries and literatures, things must be seen from the African perspective. The dominant object in that perspective is African literature.

If the critics gathered in this volume would not abolish their English or Romance language departments, they would at least, I believe, argue for a critical perspective and a definition of a canon of literature that accounted for 'the African [or black] perspective'. Indeed, it is safe to say that we take it for granted that the canon of literature in English, for example, is a 'genetic' mulatto, and that the criticism of black texts, precisely because of their curiously complex antecedents, must draw upon, and simultaneously diverge from, the methodologies of close reading practiced by contemporary literary theorists.

III

How are these abstract concerns to redefine and to *revitalize* the study of 'literature' made concrete in the essays in this collection? Let me outline the import of each, as these are arranged in the pages that follow. Let me add first, however, that the essays published here (except for those by Baker, Johnson, Stepto, Washington and myself) were published initially in America in two special issues of the *Black American Literature Forum*, of which I served as a guest editor. Johnson's essay appears here for the first time, while those by Baker, Stepto, Washington and myself are reprinted from the *PMLA*, *The Georgia Review*, *The Massachusetts Review* and *Critical Inquiry*, respectively.

In 'The critic and society: Barthes, leftocracy and other mythologies', Wole Soyinka uses the occasion of Roland Barthes's untimely death (which occurred while Soyinka happened to be visiting London) to reacquaint himself with Barthes's theoretical work, and to consider the nature of the curious relation between African literature and European literary criticism. For anyone even vaguely familiar with Soyinka's corpus of poetry, drama and criticism, or with the recent and often strident Nigerian Marxist critiques of Soyinka's work, Soyinka's concerns come as no surprise.

Soyinka's creative works, particularly his tragedies, straddle with no apparent strain two literary traditions: the Western and the Yoruba. In a language densely metaphorical and compellingly lyrical, Soyinka has managed to redefine our very concept of 'modern tragedy' by creating a unique synthesis of classical and vernacular Yoruba and Western tragic forms. Soyinka's idea and practice of tragedy are similar to his belief that black critical practice must account for the *specificity* of the language of the text *and*, as it were, its *historical unconscious*.

Soyinka, reacting to a group of critics who have stridently urged him to diminish the distance between his 'meaning' and a hypothetical African pro-letarian readership by eschewing figurative language, asks his critics: 'for whom does the *critic* write [my italics]? For Mr Dele Bus-Stop of Idi-Oro? Or for the Appointments and Promotions Committee and the Learned Journals Inter-national Syndicate of Berne, Harvard, Nairobi, Oxford or Prague?' We would do well to think of Soyinka's rhetorical questions as epigraphs to this book. Soyinka uses Barthes's demystification of French bourgeois culture (which, like all bourgeois culture, is passed off as 'universal') to challenge African critics to stop 'transposing the petit-bourgeois signs and iconography of their mentor culture into a universal culture'. While his specific example is 'the radical, socially committed critic of today's African intelligentsia', Soyinka's dictum applies to the black critical activity as a whole.

James Snead, in 'Repetition as a figure of black culture', uses the existence of the 'cut' in black culture to turn Hegel's unfortunately racist strictures on the African on their head: Hegel, Snead argues, could not have guessed 'that in his very criticism of [black culture] he had almost perfectly described the "there" to which European culture was "headed".' Snead, a novelist and a musician as well as a literary critic, distinguishes black forms of repetition from European repetition by the difference between circulation and flow, on one hand, and accumulation and growth, on the other. In black culture, he argues, 'the thing . . . is "there for you to pick it up when you come back to get it".' Goals, or ends, are 'always deferred'. Snead uses this remarkably useful distinction between the black and the European modes of repetition to trace discrete forms of repetition through an impressively broad array of media, ranging from the rhythm-and-blues music of James Brown to the *Götterdämmerung*. Having traced the distinction in careful detail, however, Snead then shows how modern developments in European music and literature (notably, Stravinsky, Joyce, Stoppard) signify the foregrounding of repetition and of the 'cut', revealing that Europeans are imitating a mode of repetition which is traditionally black, and for which Hegel censured the African, relegating him or her to a category beneath the civilized. The import of Snead's ironic and subtle reading of Hegel and the nice distinctions he draws in practical examples of repetition are perhaps best summarized in the black maxim that 'what goes around comes around'. Snead's brief but provocative readings of Ralph Ellison's 'sermon', the 'Blackness of Blackness', and of Ishmael Reed's *Mumbo Jumbo* prefigure issues that I address at greater length in my own essay.

Jay Edwards's 'Structural analysis of the Afro-American trickster tale' is as concerned to argue for the use of 'structural models [of] the African-based folk-tale' as to explicate closely the continuities of 'structuration' that obtain – remarkably – between African and Afro-American vernacular forms. Long a matter of polemical dispute, Edwards's book, *The Afro-American Trickster Tale*, demonstrates convincingly that black cultures separated by vast expanses of time and space share patterns of figuration, offering perhaps the long-sought-for evidence of a proverbial 'unbroken arc' of shared language-use in cultures seemingly as unlike as the Asante of Ghana and the Creole French of Louisiana. In his essay printed here, Edwards proffers a critique of both the syntagmatic models of folktale deep structure developed by Propp, Paulme and Bremond, and Lévi-Strauss's 'superstructural formula'. Edwards argues for a new structural model of the folktale, one which accounts for 'the role of semantics', 'the place of transformational rules', and 'the problem of culture-specific metaphoric formulations of structural elements'. Edwards, in other words, is as determined to present a new theory of the trickster tale as he is to explicate a signal example of that tale.

If Edwards seeks to challenge and revise received structural models of the folk-tale, then Sunday O. Anozie's 'Negritude, structuralism, deconstruction' first charts analogues and points of agreement between Senghor's 'romantic black-ness' and Lévi-Strauss's romantic musings about Indians and the marvels of speech, then uses a deconstructive turn to unravel 'old myths and metaphysics about, as well as in, Africa'. Anozie, no one will dispute, is Africa's first and principal structuralist, a veritable sub-Saharan Roland Barthes. Anozie brought African criticism to Europe, and to the second half of the twentieth century. His role is that of the pioneer, a role not without its dangers. His work has been subjected to heated and sometimes hysterical review, especially by Africans who obviously respect the man's mind, if not his methods. But Anozie teaches us about African literature, about how it is *put together*. His value to black criticism, to our concern with contemporary theory, is difficult to estimate. But Anozie also teaches us about the theories we imitate, and how to revise them, how to make a hybrid that accounts for black language-use. Anozie, while a careful reader and a diligent pupil, still manages to modify the themes at hand, 'nationalizing' them, as it were. Anozie's use of deconstructive theory is no exception, and also exemplifies the dynamic and flexible nature of that critic's endeavor.

If Anozie more often than not elicits the hysterical response, then Anthony Appiah's reading of structuralist poetics generally, and of Anozie's work specifically, is an example of an intelligent way for us to disagree. Appiah, an analytic philosopher, admits his presuppositions: 'everything in my training, my thought and my culture resists the desire, which pervades much of con-temporary American culture, to be Derridian'. Despite this admission, however, Appiah presents one of the most cogent accounts that I have encountered of the premises upon which 'structuralism' rests, then considers these premises from the stance of an analytic philosopher. Appiah, I think it safe to say, objects most strenuously to Anozie's apparent belief in transcendent 'African' conceptual systems; 'an' African anything, for Appiah, is a highly dubious claim. Because there are thousands of African languages 'with their associated conceptual systems', and only a tiny number of systematic analyses of these conceptual systems, Appiah argues that to generalize about 'an African' this or that is somewhat akin to myth-making, blind faith or bad faith. Appiah protests against any theory of literature which does not account for African differences – not merely how 'Africa' differs from Europe, but how the Yoruba differ from the Asante.

But Appiah has other things to say about the endeavor which Black Literature and Literary Theory presupposes. This he calls the problem of mediation between Europe and Africa. I can do no better than to quote him:

> It is not that a structuralist poetics is inapplicable in Africa because struc-turalism is European; so far as it is successful in general, it seems to me as applicable to African literary material as to any other. But we should not expect the transfer of a method to a new set of texts to lead to exactly the same results ... indeed, this would surely *show* that there was something wrong with the method.

Appiah protests that to attempt to 'embed' Africa in European culture – that is, to attempt to take whole a European theory of criticism and place it like a grid upon an African text – is an example of what he calls 'the Naipaul fallacy', 'a post-colonial inferiority complex', wherein we feel it necessary to *explain* 'Africa' to Europeans, to justify who we are and what we do in the language of the colonizer. 'African novels do not need justification,' Appiah argues; 'they need ... reading.' Appiah is concerned that we 'locate' our works of art for an alien readership by explaining these not in terms that perhaps reflect neo-colonial (conceptual) power relations, but in terms that, first, arise from *within* these African conceptual systems. If we then wish to ground these terms in analogies familiar to a European reader, then so much the better. Appiah, as it were, 'deconstructs' the premises upon which Anozie's use of structuralism rests, though Appiah would say that he has merely *read* Anozie. Appiah would agree with Soyinka's admonition that the black interpreter should 'be careful. When you create your own myth don't carelessly promote another's, and perhaps a more harmful one.'

Kimberly W. Benston's 'I yam what I am: the topos of (un)naming in Afro-American literature' functions in this volume as an essay of transition. Whereas the preoccupation of the book's first five essays is with literary theory as a mediation between Europe and Africa – which Appiah emblematizes in the 'O' in Sunday O. Anozie's name – Benston's essay introduces the reader to a series of close readings of canonical texts in the Afro-American literary tradition. Benston tropes Appiah's passing nod to the (non)mediating 'O' in Anozie's name by focusing his attention upon the 'singular "X" ' that the Black Muslims employed as a complex 'variable', 'a symbol not of something unnamable but of something unknowable – the inaugural African identity that was usurped during Middle Passage.' Malcolm's 'X' constitutes an 'unnaming of American heritage', an ironic modernist revision of all those imposed and borrowed designations spawned by slavery and its aftermath.

By (re)naming themselves at their emancipation, the black slaves 'unnamed' 'the immediate [imposed] past', to symbolize 'the long-unacknowledged, nascent selfhood that had survived and transcended slavery.' Whereas James Snead's careful study of tropes of repetition demonstrates a subtle example of difference in the 'texts' of Africa and Europe, Benston's essay traces relentlessly how a cultural practice adopted by the slaves becomes a trope of the Otherness of the hyphenated Afro-American. (Un)naming is the unspeakable figure of an unnamable African linguistic difference, the visual sign of which is an unadulterated blackness. Because of this peculiar mode of marginality, blacks (un)name 'the white name for the blackness of blackness, . . . a name for difference'. Every black act of naming, then, is simultaneously an act of (un)naming, an act of ~Audre Lorde~ linguistic appropriation. Benston sees (un)naming as the fundamental topos of the black tradition, as central to black discourse as is topos repetition.

To illustrate his thesis, Benston explicates this ironic trope in an impressive assortment of black canonical texts. While grounding his readings with references to the peculiarly American preoccupation with names, Benston shows how this topos functions *within* the tradition; his essay reveals how the tradition *names* itself. Accordingly, his essay constitutes a major definition of the Afro-American canon and argues for a basis upon which to construct that very canon. Unlike the essays by Soyinka, Snead, Edwards and Appiah, which seek to mediate between European and black theories of literature, Benston's is an engagement with the turn of the black tradition *inward*, upon itself. Benston shows how a *topos*, a commonplace of the tradition, has been transformed into its central *trope*. Black texts, he argues cogently, speak primarily to other black texts, naming and (un)naming even these. 'All of Afro-American literature', he concludes, 'may be seen as one vast genealogical poem that attempts to restore continuity to the ruptures or discontinuities imposed by the history of black presence in America.' This is so, he reasons, because 'For the Afro-American . . . self-creation and reformation of a fragmented familial past are endlessly interwoven: naming is inevitably genealogical revisionism.' Benston makes explicit that which the tradition enunciates implicitly; his theory of the canon emerges from the canon itself, rather than from Europe. His is a mapping of the Afro-American textual terrain.

Benston's essay ends the book's theoretical section and introduces seven essays of practical criticism. These essays explore in even more careful detail several of the black canonical texts to which Benston refers. What I have called Benston's 'turn inward', his sense of the shape (and shaping) of a literary tradition, is pursued at length in the seven essays that comprise the second section of *Black Literature and Literary Theory*. While we are still in the process of assigning texts to our canon, it is perhaps not rash to say that the fictions of Frederick Douglass, Jean Toomer, Zora Neale Hurston, Ralph Ellison, Gwendolyn Brooks, Toni Morrison and Ishmael Reed occupy places in the black canon.

Robert B. Stepto's 'Storytelling in early Afro-American fiction: Frederick Douglass's "The Heroic Slave"' is a close reading of the tradition's first novella, and Douglass's only fiction. While Douglass's *Narrative of the Life* (1845) is perhaps our most carefully explicated slave narrative, 'The Heroic Slave' (1853) has yet to receive the attention it deserves. Stepto argues that 'The Heroic Slave' represents 'a first step, albeit a small one, toward the creation of an Afro-American fiction based upon the conventions of the slave narratives.' Stepto seeks here to establish formal echoing and revision as a basis to define what he elsewhere has called the 'idea' of a literary tradition. As he concludes perceptively about the manner in which signal *topoi* repeat in our canonical texts,

stories of immersion in and ascent from a kind of limbo are central to the history of Afro-American letters, chiefly because they so conspicuously prefigure the trope of hibernation . . . in Ralph Ellison's *Invisible Man*, published almost exactly one hundred years later. Madison Washington's cave in the realm between the plantation and the world beyond . . . anticipates the Invisible Man's hole in the region between black and white Manhattan. Once

Washington's wolf and bear become, in the mind's eye, Brer Wolf and Brer Bear, this particular contour in Afro-American literary history is visible and complete.

No critic of Afro-American literature has done more to establish formal principles of canon formation than has Robert Stepto.

Barbara E. Bowen's close reading of Jean Toomer's *Cane* (1923) exemplifies a remarkably successful attempt to read a black text in terms generated from within the Afro-American tradition. Bowen explicates Toomer's text by tracing his use of the Afro-American trope of antiphony, 'call and response', a mode as central to black art as is repetition; indeed, the two figures are related. Bowen argues that the concept of voice ('finding authority to speak') – who speaks, and to whom or what – signifies the difference between the Anglo- and the Afro-American traditions: 'For Romantic poets, response from nature assures the continuity that empowers voice; for Afro-American poets, the empowering response is from their people.' Call and response, Bowen concludes, always re-enacts the 'drama of finding authority through *communal* voice' (my emphasis).

By structuring *Cane* around this traditional black rhetorical pattern, Toomer 'has enabled the creation of a distinctively Afro-American literary form'. For Bowen, then, Toomer's significance, in large part, lay in his capacity to 'translate' a mode of musical composition and oratory into a lyrical form of narration. Bowen's essay locates what I have been calling 'the signifyin(g) black difference' in discrete uses of literary language, uses peculiar to the Afro-American tradition, uses that signify 'a new cultural myth': 'While the American poet seeks the authority to speak by trying to recover an unfallen continuity of language and nature, the Afro-American poet seeks authority by trying to recover an unexiled continuity of speaker and listener.' Bowen takes her terms of analysis from black culture, and reads the text in these very terms. Hers is an excellent example of a meaningful engagement between the form of a text and the form of its cultural consciousness.

Barabara Johnson's reading of metaphor and metonymy in Zora Neale Hurston's *Their Eyes Were Watching God* (1937) 'deconstructs' the received (Western-male) concept of voice in the text as an impulse to 'unification and simplification' (Auerbach) and reveals that, in the black and feminist tradition, 'The sign of an authentic voice is ... not self-identity but self-difference.' Moreover,

> If 'unification and simplification' is the privilege and province of the male, it is also, in America, the privilege and province of the white. If the woman's voice, to be authentic, must incorporate and articulate division and self-difference, so, too, has Afro-American literature always had to assume its double-voicedness.

Janie, Hurston's protagonist, learns to speak in public only after she has learned to name, to figure, her 'inside and outside' and mastered the fine art of keeping them separate. Johnson's reading of Janie's enunciation of difference (narrated in 'two figural mini-narratives' and the chiasmus that obtains between them: 'a metaphorically grounded metonymy' and 'a metonymically grounded metaphor') resolves a heated debate among contemporary black critics about the concept of voice and its relation to identity represented in *Their Eyes*. But her reading also demonstrates the ideal relation that obtains between the (white) universal (theory) and the (black) particular, the text explicated. Johnson, with a certain rhetorical flair and boldness for which she is widely acclaimed, shows that the chiastic relation between Hurston's two mini-narratives clarifies and refines the classic opposition between metaphor and metonymy, which for convenience she analyzes in Roman Jakobson's seminal essay, 'Two Aspects of Language and Two Types of Aphasic Disturbances'. Johnson reads Jakobson's opposition *through* Hurston's text, rather than attempting to 'apply' Jakobson's distinction *to* the text, as if it were a grid. She shows that the most profound, if largely unrecognized, distinction made in Jakobson's article is that between speech and aphasia, 'between silence and the capacity to articulate one's own voice'. Just as Janie's articulation of her sense of self is absolutely dependent upon recognizing and *maintaining* 'the necessity of [both poles] of figurative language', so, too, must critical theories not 'privilege *either* metaphor or metonymy'. To do so is 'to run the risk of producing an increasingly aphasic *critical* discourse.'

Johnson's achievement in this essay is quite remarkable: rather than to 'use' European theory to explicate a black text, she theorizes about a central problem in literary theory through a close reading of the black text. Johnson eschews asking or answering the question of the 'applicability' of 'contemporary theory' as an appropriate tool to read 'non-canonical' literature. Instead, she explicates *theory* through the prism of *Their Eyes Were Watching God*. Johnson inverts the power relation, the relation of dominance, that generally figures into discussions of the asserted or denied 'universality' of theories of criticism by reading the Western theoretical tradition *against* the actual practice of Hurston's text. Rather than (re)colonizing the black text through the imposition of Western theory, she deconstructs Western theory by re-reading it through the canonical black text. This gesture represents a major departure in contemporary black criticism, one potentially able to redefine the terms of the power relation that is thought to obtain between what Chinweizu calls 'the West and the rest of us'. Johnson's international reputation as one of the few 'second-generation' deconstructive readers who has been able to retain a certain lucidity *and* profoundly revise deconstructive theories is well deserved. Her forthcoming book on Zora Neale Hurston, of which this essay is a chapter, promises to perform for the criticism of black and feminist texts that function which she has performed with such suppleness and grace for post-structural criticism.

Houston A. Baker, Jr, in a definitive and dazzling reading of the Trueblood episode of Ralph Ellison's *Invisible Man* (1952), draws upon post-structural theory and Marxist criticism to explicate Ellison's theory of the black vernacular. Baker, one of the most prolific and versatile critics of Afro-American literature, redefines post-structural and ideological analysis by filtering both through the medium of the blues. Baker, using Ellison's 'blues praxis' in Trueblood's multi-vocal narrative(s) of incest to read Ellison's theory of black vernacular discourse, argues implicitly that Afro-American culture *theorizes* about itself in its vernacular forms. A cultural self-reflexivity, he argues, is inscribed in modes of discourse such as the blues and signifyin(g). Baker uses the blues both as *topos* and trope, not only to explicate Ellison's text of many canons, but to make theory *usable* in this reading of the black text.

Baker's deft mastery of contemporary theories of close reading enables him to draw upon Freud, Clifford Geertz, Victor Turner, Fredric Jameson and Hayden White to teach even the seasoned reader of Ellison's text just how complex the dialogical structure of Trueblood's narrative indeed is. Baker's reading of Trueblood's dream narrative (one of several of his embedded narratives) is exemplary of his fresh insights:

Trueblood's dream and subsequent incest seem to represent, where Freud's speculations are concerned, a historical regression. The sharecropper's dreamed violations of southern social and sexual taboos are equivalent to a slaughter of the white patriarch represented by Mr Broadnax, who does, indeed, control the 'fat' and 'fat meat' of the land. To eat 'fat meat' is to partake of the totemic animal. And, having run backward in time through the grandfather clock, Trueblood becomes the primal father, assuming all sexual prerogatives unto himself.

Baker, in these few sentences, has shown that even the tradition's 'most read' text remains to be explicated closely using the tools of contemporary criticism.

But Baker also shows how 'Trueblood finds, in the system of the blues, the meet symbolic code for expressing the negativity of his own act.' Trueblood becomes a master teller of his own tale, a black and blues artist, who narrates his tales-within-a-tale in exchange for money. Narrative, for Trueblood, performs a commodity function. Moreover, he must market 'an image of himself that is itself a *product* . . . a bizarre product' of the slave trade, an image of himself as a double sign of negation, (black) minstrel man in black face. Not content merely to borrow Marxist categories of analysis through which to read Trueblood's commodity function, Baker turns to the black tradition to explain the complex phenomenon of which Trueblood is an emblem:

The act of 'commodifying' expressiveness for blacks, therefore, is not simply a gesture in a bourgeois economics of art. Rather, it is a crucial move in a somewhat limited repertoire of black survival motions in the United States. . . . Afro-America's exchange power has always been coextensive with its stock of expressive resources.

Baker, finally, uses his remarkably insightful reading of Trueblood's 'redundancy of structure' to read Ellison's theory of Afro-American vernacular discourse. For Baker, Freudian and Marxian criticism are most useful to black criticism if 'sung' through the language of the blues.

Mary Helen Washington's feminist reading of Gwendolyn Brooks's *Maud Martha* (1953) turns on an opposition between 'rage and silence', on one hand, and the ability to speak, on the other. Washington's oppositions call to mind those that Barbara Johnson analyzes in *Their Eyes Were Watching God*. Hurston's and Brooks's texts, Washington makes abundantly clear, are connected by Brooks's act of repetition and revision, arguing dramatically for a formal basis of the black woman's literary tradition.

Washington shows that *Maud Martha* thematizes the relation between repressed rage and silences. 'Maud Martha rarely speaks aloud to anyone else. She has learned to conceal her feelings behind a mask of gentility, to make her hate silent and cold, expressed only in the most manipulative and deceptive ways.' *Maud Martha*, then, not only is about the absence of spoken thought; it is also about the relation between masking and narration, the same relation that Baker explores in his essay on Trueblood. Washington demonstrates how the novel's rhetorical strategies, and especially its *grammar*, 'enact Maud Martha's silence':

> Ranging in length from one and a half pages to eighteen pages, these tightly controlled chapters withhold information about Maud, just as she withholds her feelings; they leave her frozen in an arrested moment so that we are left without the reactions that are crucial to our understanding of her. With no continuity between one chapter and the next, the flow of Maud's life is checked just as powerfully as she checks her own anger. The short, declarative sentences, with few modifiers and little elaboration, are as stiff, unyielding and tight-lipped as Maud Martha herself.

Washington shows us how rhetoric, grammar and theme tightly interweave in Brooks's long-ignored but brilliantly crafted novel.

Washington contrasts the remarkable degree of 'double-consciousness' expressed in the text's passages of free indirect discourse (*style indirect libre*) with what she calls, after Anna Julia Cooper, Maud's 'broken utterances', grammatical 'evidence of a woman denied expression of powerful feelings'. Even when Maud speaks, Washington reveals with great precision, her rhetoric undermines her intent: 'The words she uses to refashion herself – *white, princess, wavy, lily* – all suggest how complete a transformation she imagines she needs in order to be accepted.' Her most striking revelation of self, moreover, is rendered in free indirect discourse, when she fantasizes about Paul's negative feelings towards her as they encounter strangers along the street. Washington calls this 'a grotesque act of double-consciousness', which reminds us of Johnson's convincing thesis that free indirect discourse is the narrative mode of irreconcilable division. We are not surprised, then, to learn that 'Shortly after the birth of her child, Maud speaks aloud the longest set of consecutive sentences she has so far uttered', because

birth not only represents a *process* of division, but is the *sign* of division itself. Having her baby connects 'Maud to some power in herself, some power to speak, to be heard, to articulate feelings'. Maud Martha's capacity to 'speak herself free', as David Ruggles put it, turns upon her capacity to narrate her own division.

If Johnson and Washington seek to explicate difference in a rhetoric of division, then Susan Willis suggests that Toni Morrison's fictions seek to repair the alienation of the (black) self from its culture and ruptures of culture transmission and continuity through tropes that Morrison calls 'eruptions of funk'. Willis explains that Morrison's tropes of funk 'include metaphors drawn from past moments of sensual fulfillment as well as the use of lack, deformity and self-mutilation as figures for liberation.' Using these eruptions of funk – 'the intrusion of the past in the present' – Morrison posits an alternative social world, one in which '"otherness" no longer functions as an extension of domination (as it does when blackness is beheld from . . . racist bourgeois society, or when the crippled, blind and deformed are compared to the terrorizing totality of a whole, and therefore "perfect", body).' Instead, the worlds of otherness that Morrison weaves permit 'a reversal of domination' and transform 'what was once perceived from without as "other" into the explosive image of a utopian mode.' These utopian worlds, Willis shows, are figured in three-woman households, Morrison's signifyin(g) revision of the *dystopian* three-woman household in Faulkner's *Absalom! Absalom!*

Willis's close reading of Morrison's canon reveals that Morrison's 'highly sensual descriptions' function to 'explode the effects of alienation and repression and stave off the advent of reification', because 'sensuality is embedded in a past which is inaccessible to sexual repression and bourgeois culture.' Morrison's lyrical language, in other words, reinscribes a sexuality fundamental to the text of the Afro-American past. This linguistic 'retrieval of sensuality allows an alternative social mode and historical period to be envisioned.' Black utopia, then, can be summoned to being by a black and sensual language, a language 'prior to the advent of capitalism and bourgeois society', a language similar in function to black song, 'the unwritten text of history and culture'.

Willis shows how geographic or physical spaces function in Morrison's work as figures of history, a transfer that is 'symptomatic of a time when a people's past no longer forms a continuity with the present.' It is this gesture which ties Morrison's work, especially *Song of Solomon*, to the great Latin American modernist novels, such as *La casa verde*. Willis argues that the matter of discontinuity and rupture of the self from its cultural traditions is 'resolved' through a trick of structure similar to the effect that mythic structure has upon otherwise irreconcilably opposed forces. As Willis concludes,

> the synchronic relationship defined in geographic space stands for a diachronic relationship. The most interesting feature about these modernist

texts is that, in reading them, the reader, like Milkman, restores diachrony to the text; and, in so doing, realizes the historical dialectic which the text presents as inaccessible.

Morrison's figure of history, of 'the descent into the past', allows her characters to step 'out of reified and fetishized relationships', into a black, as it were, underground community of restored, integral relationships.

In 'The blackness of blackness', I have tried to find both a metaphor and a ritual rhetorical act which could be used to account for patterns of formal revision that define the relation between texts in the Afro-American tradition. To do so, I trace the descent of the Signifying Monkey from the Pan-African trickster figure, Èṣù-Ẹlẹ́gbára, then attempt to show how canonical black texts 'signify upon' each other's tropes and *topoi*. Finally, I explicate Ishmael Reed's *Mumbo Jumbo* (1972), applying to its reading the principles of interpretation derived from the black vernacular tradition.

The movement of this book, then, is from theory to interpretation. Each of the contributors is as desirous of 'opening up the canon', in Houston Baker's and Leslie Fiedler's apt phrase, as of revealing the shape of our own black literary and critical traditions. I would hope that this collection helps to address both ends, since our purpose is to address two audiences, one seeking to learn about contemporary theory, the other seeking to learn about the nature and function of black writing.

Part I

Theory: on structuralism and post-structuralism

1   Wole Soyinka

The critic and society: Barthes, leftocracy and other mythologies*

Roland Barthes is not a familiar name to academia or the general reader in Africa. He died in March 1980. The usual obituary notices appeared in the literary columns of European journals, and brought back to mind instantly, in total recall, the picture of a plump, untidy don at Leeds University where I was a student. As he lectured, his plain academic gown fell constantly off his shoulders from wild Gallic gesticulations meant to propel forward certain ideas on fiction and reality. They were a drastic departure from our normal fare of fiction criticism. No, the figure was not that of the critic himself: I never met him. The speaker was a visiting academic who had come to spread the gospel of the New Fiction from across the Channel to conservative England. We were part bemused, part fascinated; here was the plain old novel being unnecessarily complicated, and words that were once simply words being turned into signs. A totally new language of reality was introduced by this visitation, and the theories of Saussure and Barthes which were seminal influences on the New Fiction entered – at least peripherally, and with resentment – our intellectual baggage of fact and fiction.

Browsing in Dillon's bookshop in London some days after Barthes's death, I was drawn again towards his writings. There was a volume of essays I had not encountered until then, being belated translations – some of them as recent as 1977 – of his commentaries on the development of new mythologies, linguistic-semiological shorthands of the old, which were created by the European (French) bourgeoisie. They involved, more importantly, a socially directed

---

* From the inaugural lecture delivered at the University of Ife, Nigeria, in November 1982.

investigation of the operations of myth on the daily sensibilities of social man – and of a particular class: the bourgeoisie. Increasingly engaged, I parted reluctantly with some precious pounds and took away the paperback. It did not take long for me to realize that I had stumbled on a perfect paradigm for the social reality of the radical shift in critical language in my own African community: and that is the genesis of the elaboration in the title of this essay.

I also recalled as a student providing my own private syntax for the semantic codes of the then newly introduced Saussurean linguistics – a very simple one, in fact, created through my extremely rudimentary knowledge not even of the French language but of a few French expressions. I shall occasionally draw on it for specific purposes, so I must explain it here. The specialist terms – *langue, parole,* etc. – will be very sparingly used; when they are, the context will be so clear as to require no elaboration. I propose to stick to familiar semantic units and clusters such as language, meaning, vocabulary, syntax, and so on, in their most ordinary usage. But the word 'language' can hardly ever be used in any ordinary sense; indeed, it obviously shed all ordinary sense after its first paradoxical employment as a description of its own system – that is, a system of socially agreed significations. For language does not operate simply as communication but as matrices of discrete activities including, of course, those of articulation and meaning. And when we talk about the language of literature or criticism we assume multiple levels of internal operations of basic cognitives and their triggering social agencies, a matrix of latent and activated meanings which add to our problems of apprehension by acting in a self-constitutive way. To differentiate this particular activity, the socially constituting activity, I recall that I found it useful to devise a simple phonetic pun on the French *langage*, that word being *l'engage:*[1] the operation of social cogs within the code of meanings; the engagement of gears within a cluster of codes, shifting the actual intent of language from one matrix and coupling it to another in social operation. The French *langage* will continue to stand for the totality of options in a system; *l'engage* indicates the selective operation within the *langue*, engaging the differential to deliver a socially active meaning. This last is the context of my basic interest and will be what is signified, unless otherwise stated, when the plain 'language' is used for convenience, in relation to what the critic or the creative artist actually does with the system. In short, *langage* is the cold topography before the linguist; *l'engage* or language is the actual course being mapped by you and me.

And now to the critics, pausing only to state from the outset that their understanding of my own work will not be avoided in this essay. After all, their preoccupations in recent times have tended to suggest that there are no other African authors on the bookshelves or, if there are, that their study is incomplete unless Mr Wole Soyinka is roped in somewhere. This is not an egotistical claim but a statistical fact. From an objective sense of proportion, it is necessary that this inert material return the compliment, manifesting its own critical voice just once in a while. No occasion could be more appropriate than this.

To my knowledge, very few attempts have been made to study the critic as a socially situated producer, and therefore as a creature of social conditioning. Such social conditioning in fact offers no certitudes about the nature of critics' commitment to the subject that engages them, about their motivations, indeed, about the very nature of their social existence. About the writer, on the other hand, we are traditionally over-informed – which is to say, ingenuously disinformed, since nothing but selective information, censored, even distorted to suit the critic's thesis, ever survives the pages in the direction of the reader. But, although readers have at least some measure of fact, fiction and speculation about the writer to engage their interest, regarding the critic they have none. And then, of course, what society? What is the critic's society? Is it, for instance, a society that we may describe as International Academia? Or is it Ipetumodu? The distinction is crucial. There is a world of difference in the social situation of any critic – either as an exploiter of language for the weekly or twice-weekly seminars of the University of Nsukka, Ibadan or Maiduguri; or as a critic who is profoundly angry that the writer has never even recognized the existence of the social anomalies within Ipetumodu, Abakaliki or Koton Karfi in his or her writings.

We are familiar, probably even excruciatingly bored, with the question: for whom does the writer write? Very rarely, however, is the same degree of social *Angst* encountered in the case of the critic. Indeed, the question is very rarely posed: for whom does the critic write? For Mr Dele Bus-Stop of Idi-Oro? Or for the Appointments and Promotions Committee and the Learned Journals International Syndicate of Berne, Harvard, Nairobi, Oxford or Prague? Unquestionably there is an intellectual cop-out in the career of any critics who cover reams of paper with unceasing lament over the failure of this or that writer to write for the masses of the people, when they themselves assiduously engage – with a remorseless exclusivity – only the incestuous productivity of their own academic, bourgeois-situated literature. It is a very convenient case of having one's cake and eating it, of feeding on yet damning the output of producers of literature in one's community – often in the most scabrous, dismissive language – continually treading the same grooves, looking for something new to say and never finding it, pouncing on the latest product of the same pariah writer like a famished voyager, building up c.v.s at the expense of the condemned productivity (the genuine productivity, not the parasitic kind which is the critic's) of the handful of literary workers in the same ossified community. 'Reactionary', 'élitist', 'privileged', 'a splurge of romantic decadence', 'articulator of the neo-colonial agent class' . . . well, then, what is the critic doing?

But this is, of course, a very one-sided, partial view. It is true that the critics with whom we are here concerned do venture from time to time into the field of popular literature, popular theatre, popular music – in short, the so-called proletarian art. But, we must ask, in what language? What *langue* is deployed in this great, generous excursion into non-bourgeois art? When the 'committed' critic unwraps the poetry of the 'ewi' specialist Lanrewaju Adepoju, the earthy Majority Music Club under Professor alias Majority, the exotic Dan Maraya, whose *langue* does the critic speak and, therefore, to what society does he address himself? Is he speaking back to Dan Maraya or the 'Waka Queen', Salawa?[2] Can they penetrate the critic's *parole* to commence a genuine engagement with language? Is this proletarian art returned to its producers, or is it merely refurbished in the *langue* of the assessors of the Appointments and Promotions Committee or of the learned journals? In short, is the excursion into Onitsha Market Literature or alias Majority music ever different from opportunism, an appropriation of proletarian production by a member of the bourgeoisie for its small erudite coterie?

I experience in this, naturally, some embarrassment, for when speaking of such a society I equally indict myself. An additional embarrassment, even inhibition, stems from the fact that one of the favourite fodders for the 'commitment machine' of these critics happens to be none other than the present writer. However, this is one debate which this essay must initiate: in *what* society is the African critic situated? The stridency of recent criticism makes such a debate inevitable, for criticism has lately outstripped creativity in quantity – at least in Nigeria. I intend to introduce the discussion with an extreme example of the resultant language of alienation – not, however, from papers of the Department of Literature or Drama or Philosophy or African Languages and Literature, but from a popular journal. Indeed, the subject is not even literature at all but a simple social phenomenon: violence. I propose wherever possible to employ the methodology of oblique references, just to widen the area of discussion and provide analogies in related social concerns.

Let us begin with an obviously concerned social critic. He is *motivated* – shall we concede? – by the phenomenon of violence in society. The journal in which the following passage appears is not even a learned journal; it is the Lagos *Sunday Times*.[3] The immediate cause of the article is a report of student violence at the University of Ibadan. Now nothing can be more proletarian than violence: violence, we know, is one of the few universal commodities; unlike rice, it cannot be placed under licence.[4] Even so, I wish to stress that violence has to be *produced*. When offered, it is a product that has involved both risk and labour, and a level of commitment. In a sense, this present act of criticism falls automatically within the same system of appropriation which I am about to address. In other words, what is my purpose? What is the end of attempting to prove that one critic has appropriated the violence of a group of students and converted it to neutral ends? If I were writing in support of, or in criticism of, the act of the students, I could claim that my motives were nobler; I would remain within the immediate cause-and-effect nexus of the originating event, possibly even initiating a movement towards redress. But here I am concerned only to buttress, by a slant of objectives, my contention that academic writers, when they move into the arena of proletarian production, adopt the conversion language of a particular class, the bourgeois intelligentsia. The commodity can be a piece of sculpture, a hunter's traditional chant, Ladi Kwale's pottery or Baba Sala's Comic

Muse, a workers' strike or student violence. And the language is indisputably the language of alienation, even deliberately so, as the following illustrates:

Some University of Ibadan students were some time ago reported as having physically affronted laboratory equipment. In the process the University and the entire Nigerian community lost invaluable science equipment.

Predictably the reactions to the incident followed two lines. On the one hand, there were those who splotch [sic] the students as overfed, over-pampered and overpetted marginal adults who should be called to order. . . . On the other hand there were those who glorified and lionized the students . . .

Beyond the queer semantic cluster 'physically affronted laboratory equipment', we are not yet irretrievably in the terrain of alienation. The field appears to be declared open, however clumsily – any intelligent member of society must know that there would be those two camps, so why tell us? However, there is a promise here of something akin to motivation. Whatever the writer has done, he has succeeded in engaging us, within the matrix of contending forces, in the prospects of his own position, and the options are three: for, against, or an arbitrating neutral between the two positions. Alas – and this is where we come to the crunch – there is a *fourth* position. What is *signified* turns out to be a confidence trick; the writer has no interest whatsoever in that physical confrontation, nor in its consequences for the rest of society. His sociology would help us, but we have no facts, only a name below the article; but the sign is beginning to come out strongly, barely three paragraphs later. We realize then that we are being moved from the field of 'physically affronted laboratory equipment' to the operational field of seminars at the University of Lagos or Maiduguri, into the structure of the seminar paper where the subject serves only the linguistic ritual. Let us spend a little more time probing this intellectual tumour through all its tissues: I believe that the exercise is long overdue and may prove salutary.

There are two equally tenable and plausible positions on one and the same issue. And philosophy, as a professional discipline, begins where two extreme but equally plausible propositions are asserted on one and the same event, topic or concept. This is true whether the concept in question, say 'violence' in this instance, is obviously philosophical or not. But things are made easy in this context because the term 'violence' happens to be a moral concept.

Questions asking for explications and elucidations of the causes of violence and questions about the role of violence in a nation's consciousness and culture are legitimate and will be treated as cognates of the distinctively philosophical question: 'What is violence?'

There are three ways by which it is possible to gain an insight into this question. The first is etymological, the second is definitional, and the third is distinctional. Concerning the etymology of the word 'violence'. . .

Need one go on? This is language which has not even arrived at the edges of social topography, much less *l'engage* of social signification. The contemporaneous *langage* is this: heads are now being 'physically affronted', arrests were being made, detentions in police cells for students and workers... This is the indicative of the language-in-the-making of any projected resolution, from the obscured *langage* of police slaughter of unarmed students (in Zaria, if you recall), to the insolently corrupt findings of judicial inquiries, the police siege of campuses, loss of employment for staff, rustication of students, prohibition of unions, round-the-clock surveillance of suspected activists, seizure of passports, etc. etc. This was the 'total language' of violence out of which was carved the burning of laboratory equipment in Ibadan as sign. But the essayist of the *Sunday Times* would have us believe that this event is best apprehended through the definitions of violence and opinions held by Professor Gaiver, Professor Robert Audi, 'whose article on violence earned him an award of the American Council for Philosophical Studies', Heraclitus, Hegel, Machiavelli, Rousseau, Engels, Lenin (at least, their followers); Hitler, Heinrich von Treitschke, 'himself a brilliant Nazi theoretician' ... I believe that exhausts the list. And so a particular purposeful act – damn it or laud it – with its own finite, unambiguous, risk-committed clarity has been converted to the seminarist language with its infinite discursiveness, submerging, distorting and finally appropriating the original commodity in its quotational garrulity.

The annotations are bewildering. We understand why it is that this essayist needs to confer upon us the honour of listening to the opinions of Professor Robert Audi – thus the c.v. extract which narrates his credentials on the subject of violence – 'whose article on violence earned him an award of the American Council for Philosophical Studies'. Reader, the author thus informs you and me, you are in the presence of a man who knows what the subject is about! But, by contrast, does it matter in the least at what point of Greek philosophy – or indeed any school of philosophy – Heraclitus emerged in this context? 'Heraclitus,' introduces Dr Momoh, 'a pre-Socratic philosopher'. Does it matter in the slightest if Heraclitus was a neo-Stoic sybarite or an Aeolian rhapsodist? The signification of that 'pre-Socratic' bunting is, of course, only an academic symbol, an iconic sign, *à la* Barthes. The matrix of Greek philosophy, history, the patina of antiquarian scrolls have all been gratuitously introduced in order to distance the event of a contemporary gesture at least, act at best, a signification of urgent social import. To summarize: the author here is not addressing the specific issue of one act of violence, not even violence in general; he is not addressing the issue of violence in his society; he is not even condescending to address his society, but is primarily, secondarily and ultimately engaged in the act of appropriating a harsh reality to a *langue* of 'scholarship' – and one, incidentally, of the superficial catalogue variety. I have already stated that it is an extreme case. Nevertheless, anyone who believes that it is singularly atypical is recommended to make a sample study of seminar, conference and learned-journal sociological papers on any one social problem from violence to pacific alcoholism.[5]

That task over, such a sceptic is perhaps more readily prepared to understand the mechanics of the appropriation of direct products of intellectual labour – such as the artistic and literary. Just as violence is a value produced towards the attainment of a concrete expectation, a settlement to be concluded in social terms, so is a work of art – in whatever language – a value of labour, one which, curiously, without any self-criticism, the critic appropriates to ends other than the ends for which the work is produced and marketed. A mystique is created by the appropriator about the 'availability' of art, one which grants it the special status of victim that cannot question, in its turn, the status of the appropriator in the value scale of (1) the readership for whom the work is intended and (2) the production intent and delimited goals of the commodity. No, the appropriator assumes and asserts ends, failure to attain which constitutes a crime against the critic's calling.

Now Roland Barthes is a rare breed of academic worker who has tried to explore, in very concrete terms, the social situation of the critic/teacher in relation to the practice of his profession. I have described him as an academic worker because this is the very image he appears to strive towards. It is part of the engaging honesty of Barthes that he admits that in the first and final analysis he is not, and cannot become, a *worker* in the historical sense of the word. Roland Barthes is, I repeat, a rare exegetist in the world of the intellect because he does not merely debate; he acts out, almost by perverse example, the best and the worst of the paradox of the leftist scholar, a would-be academic popularizer who, however, does not employ a 'popular' *langue*. Indeed, it is not so much what Barthes says but his *l'engage*, the social tension of his discourse, which makes him an obvious example for the radical, socially committed critic of today's African intelligentsia.

Barthes is no friend of the bourgeoisie, and we can usefully begin by examining how this detestation manifests itself in the attempt to prune language of bourgeois accretions, to expose the bourgeois mythology that lies beneath, sustains and is indeed the very foundation of linguistic and imagic signifiers which society takes so much for granted. Like the group of academics who, we have suggested, occasionally attempt to enter proletarian art and relations, Barthes proves himself an obsessive leveller. What really lies beneath the *geste*? Within what code does a seemingly straightforward signifier transmit or trigger into public consciousness the real message, the signified, converting it into a neo-mythology, a semiograph if you prefer, establishing an autonomy of bourgeois values? To this end, Barthes focused his attention on what he appropriately labels the so-called mass-culture: professional wrestling, cinema stereotypes, the detective story, tourist guides, advertisements, soap powders and detergents, Charlie Chaplin, steak and chips, Greta Grabo, ornamental cookery, French toys, plastic technology, and so on. Barthes, in his preface to the

1970 edition of *Mythologies*,[6] reminds his society that the 'essential enemy' is still the bourgeois norm and recalls that part of his hopes with the collection of essays is that, by treating 'collective representations as sign-systems, one might hope to go further than the pious show of unmasking them and account in *detail* for the mystification which transforms petit-bourgeois culture into a universal culture'. I suggest that special attention be paid to that last phrase – the problem of the 'mystification which transforms petit-bourgeois culture into a universal culture'. Along the way we may have cause to suspect that undiscriminating African critics have been trapped into transposing the petit-bourgeois signs and iconography of their mentor culture into a universal culture.

Barthes himself provides the simple explanation for this transformation, one we have already dealt with above – the phenomenon of class appropriation. Petit-bourgeois criticism, even when it is very much of the Left as it gropingly is these days in sections of our own academia, simply appropriates the object of criticism into the *langue* of its own class. Every essay in Barthes's collection, *Mythologies*, is an ironic repetition of the process, an unconscious act of linguistic vengefulness: even as language takes off the mask of petit-bourgeois mythology of objects and activities, it clothes them anew in the garb of bourgeois intellectualism. Roland Barthes – an honest intellectual, as I have already stated – is compelled to concede this much in *Image–Music–Text*,[7] in the final essay in that collection, entitled 'Writers, Intellectuals, Teachers': a must, I seriously suggest, for every single leftocrat still remaining if ever a genuine proletarian revolution is to overtake our universities. This overt act of grace does not, however, come remotely close in self-revelation to Barthes's direct appropriation, in the socio-linguistic context, of the mass-culture, on behalf of the minority class to which he, Roland Barthes, belongs.

Fortunately television has been with us awhile, and *Wrestling from Chicago* is, I believe, still staple diet to many addicts and even non-addicts of television in Nigeria. It would be most instructive to find what such consumers make of the following passage from Barthes's semiological analysis of these sweat-and-groan artists of muscular repulsion:

> In other words, wrestling is a sum of spectacles, of which no single one is a function: each moment imposes the total knowledge of a passion which rises erect and alone, without ever extending to the crowning moment of a result.

Or try this one:

> Each moment in wrestling is therefore like an algebra which instantaneously unveils the relationship between a cause and its represented effect.

Just one final, irresistible quote:

> Armund Mazaud, a wrestler of an arrogant and ridiculous character (as one says that Harpagon is a character), always delights the audience by the mathematical rigour of his transcriptions, carrying the form of his gestures to

the furthest reaches of their meaning, and giving to his manner of fighting the kind of vehemence and precision found in a great scholastic disputation, in which what is at stake is at once the triumph of pride and the formal concern with truth.[8]

I confess that I also have watched wrestling, both in the flesh and on the television screen. I have never seen more than two oversized, consciously theatrical monstrosities earning fair wages in return for sending a matinee audience hysterical with vicarious sadism. Nothing that I saw at any time recalled any scholastic disputation or brought regrets for my failings in school as an algebraic hope. Nevertheless, Barthes's purpose is manifest: wrestling is a mere input into the structuralist-semiotic computer program which then emits a Barthes-specific *langue*. If I were an addictive econo-leftocrat, I would, in accents of gravely committed proletariat empathy, accuse Roland Barthes of failing to relate the wrestling spectacle to the economic contradictions of his social situation and his performers' social situating. I would in fact demand that his treatment of wrestling should lead into the sort of socio-political coda he inserts in some of his other essays such as 'Wine and Milk', where, after a totemistic exposition of wine in the life of the Frenchman, he concludes:

> There are thus very engaging myths which are however not innocent. And the characteristic of our current alienation is precisely that wine cannot be an unalloyedly blissful substance, except if we wrongfully forget that it is also the product of an expropriation.[9]

Thus is the radical conscience saved – by a double appropriation of the labour of the Algerian worker: first converting his labour into the language exchange of the intellectual class, then crediting this act with a basic political consciousness. Neither achieves anything concrete for the expropriated Algerian worker. The essay on wrestling is, in the end, more intellectually humble, for it pretends to nothing but the attempted transmission of the ontology of the game – in the language of the intellectual.

There is, however, more serious matter in that essay. The summative passage has a suspiciously essentialist tone:

> In wrestling, nothing exists except in the absolute, there is no symbol, no allusion, everything is presented exhaustively. Leaving nothing in the shade, each action discards all parasitic meanings and ceremonially offers to the public a pure and full signification, rounded like Nature. This grandiloquence is nothing but the popular and age-old image of the perfect intelligibility of reality. What is portrayed by wrestling is therefore an ideal understanding of things; it is the euphoria of men raised for a while above the constitutive ambiguity of everyday situations and placed before the panoramic view of a univocal Nature, in which signs at last correspond to causes, without obstacle, without evasion, without contradiction.[10]

And yet I cannot pretend not to understand Barthes or pretend that I have not endorsed in personal experience his re-creation of the physical moment in seemingly incongruous matrices – mathematical, musical, architectural and, of course, linguistic. One need not go as far as Norman Mailer, whose floridly purple passages, especially commissioned by Life magazine,[11] celebrated the first advent of man into space in a linguistic extravaganza which, in a rather impoverished way, anticipated the time-out and spaced-out collaboration of the composer Richard Strauss, the philosopher Nietzsche and the film maker Stanley Kubrick in the unfinished space classic 2001: A Space Odyssey. The film Star Wars and its follow-up The Empire Strikes Back are, in a comparative sense, the literal completion of the symbolic, mythological 2001: A Space Odyssey. Constructed frankly on technological gadgetry and spectacle, these later epics make no attempt at mystery and mythology and would therefore have provided, speculatively, more likely material for Roland Barthes than 2001. The speculation, based on Barthes's own 'The World of Wrestling', is: would the language of Barthes not have appropriated them into the 'bourgeois' linguistic field of 2001, into that timeless mythological symbiosis of Thus Spake Zarathustra, Austrian nineteenth-century Romantic music and the entire Wagnerian mythopoeic construct of Kubrick's film? We have seen that the critic, even at his most consciously leftocratic, cannot escape his bourgeois linguistic situations. Remote and mysterious though space appears, the cult of space has been a mass one, resulting in the popular mythographic language of Star Trek. When Mailer undertook his mission to play tourist guide to the millions who could not be present at Cape Canaveral, he could have chosen the direct langue of the gladiatorial fanfare, the popular fiestas. Instead his choice was, predictably perhaps, a 1960s bourgeois-literati langue. Barthes similarly succeeds in appropriating the modern gladiatorial arena of wrestling into a langue not of wrestling but of letters. The linguistic rocket that launched the first spaceman into the galaxy is structurally identical with the Barthesian semiotic transfiguration of two sweat-and-groan artists into a mystic paradox of Essence withdrawn and eternalized through unchanging Reality.

The writings of Roland Barthes of course constitute a paradox, which is perhaps why he lends himself so readily to being conscripted into the role of critical paradigm for the new Left-leaning African, especially the Nigerian critic. And a basic divergence of one from the other is that this academic is not only conscious of but takes great pains to particularize his social situation. I have to insist that the majority of our academics do not. The traps into which they fall arise very simply from this fact, and their extremisms arise from the failure to understand that the language of criticism is socially situated. The leftocracy would, of course, deny it, but here is a typical failure, conveniently located in the realm of language. Writing on Opera Wonyosi, Yemi Ogunbiyi makes the following statement:

In Soyinka's version of Macheath's opening piece, he refers to the Igbeti marble which led to the mysterious disappearance of enquiring citizens about the marble deposits. He, however, concludes in the cynically ironic tone which runs through the play that little can be done in the circumstances of Igbeti situation.

'For it takes more than the darkness
To protect one beast of prey
When there's interest joined to interest
All we can do is pray.'[12]

Translated back into the contextual language of the dramatis personae, that last, offending line would read, 'Adura lo ku' or 'gba'. Any critic who succeeded in making that language leap, of situating himself and the action in the realistic environment of the *parole*, would recognize that this is a simple standard figure of speech, connoting by no stretch of the imagination a decision to leave everything in the hands of God. Is it really necessary to particularize to this critic the fact that when human throats were being meticulously cut during the northern pogrom of 1966 the pious liturgy which was monotonously recited over the prone victim was 'Bismillahi' ('With the name of God')? The question he should ask in order to penetrate this specific *parole* is: do the characters in the play *act* pious resignation? When, to a standard greeting of 'How are things?', an acquaintance responds 'Anbe'lorun' ('We are pleading with God'), do you really conclude that he is just getting up from his knees? Ogunbiyi's reading of this line, as of so many other lines, is a wholly alienated reading. Revolutionary aspirations, and the wish to see such aspirations clothed in a language of action, cannot eliminate the fact of the existence of tension within used, seemingly inert syntax.[13]

My experience in Nigeria alone, to go no further, is that in times of social confrontation language is often used as a holding device, a massed coil before the release of the spring. But then the worker in language grasps both the sound of meaning and the meaning of sound within the mere gesture of articulation. What is even more strange is the fact that there are clues to this understanding to be followed by the willing critic. Ogunbiyi recognizes them but chooses to corral them into an alternative which is merely convenient for an *a priori* thesis: the thesis of ambiguity in Soyinka which is much favoured by leftocratic criticism. Take the message of Anikura's song which follows almost immediately after the quoted passage:

But look, one day you will find
That pus-covered mask hides a mind
And then – boom! *Oga sah* [Yes, massa]
What's that blur? – *oga sa!* [Massa, turn tail]
With a red flame fanning his behind.

Ogunbiyi's footnote 12, commenting on the two verses quoted above, reads:

'The kind of ambiguity I refer to here relates to that statement or statements so fundamentally contradictory that they reveal a basic division or even contradiction in the author's mind.' Our critic resolves, in that last-quoted section, that the author of the play – again to use his own words – 'concludes [that] . . . little can be done in the circumstances of Igbeti situation.' This is a very large claim to the state of mind of the playwright, and one that is founded on a deliberate linguistic fragmentation. It removes the employment of a particular typology of *langue* from a real milieu and turns it *parole*-wise literal, leaving us with a *signified* which has been plucked from a lingual matrix whose sole claim to compatibility is simplistically grammarian.

Ambiguity levelled at the writer is very often a cover for the critic's own social evasion. Ogunbiyi again finds that a problem of ambiguity has been raised because the playwright has satirized the buffoon figure of Emperor Bokassa, preening himself as a Marxist. He quotes from Bokassa's monologue: 'Now a revolutionary dance must possess what we Marxists call social reality. So we are going to adapt this dance to the social reality of our progressive Centrafrique Social Experiment.'[14] The socially situated responsibility which Ogunbiyi evades here is that of information. He fails to inform his readers that the object of satire here is the opportunistic ploy notoriously adopted on this continent by nearly every reactionary dictator: the ploy of assuming poses of radicalism, revolution, even Marxism. Idi Amin, Mobutu Sese Seko, Léopold Senghor, Bokassa, Macias Nguema, and so on: each one, at one time or the other, has presented himself on the podium of power as the heir of Marx and Lenin – with a significant, often deadly qualification. Ogunbiyi's stance towards the playwright therefore becomes charitable criticism – in favour of the fascist leaders, at the expense of the satirist.[15] It could be, of course, that the critic here considers the audiences of *Opera Wonyosi* to be in mortal peril of mistaking the barb for reality; if so, such criticism should be properly addressed to the sociology of the specific audience. Yet even that would require a thorough social situating of the critic, which is precisely what this brand of criticism lacks. There is yet further proof.

Footnote 7 deals with the danger that the ingredients of theatrical pleasure – melodies, costuming, dance, witty dialogue, etc. – might become counter-productive to the aims of a work of social criticism. Drawing on an experience of the original production of Brecht's *The Threepenny Opera*, on which *Opera Wonyosi* is based, Ogunbiyi recalls that Lotte Lenya (who acted in the original production) narrated how

> Berlin was gripped by a *Threepenny Opera* fever. Everywhere, even in the streets, the tunes were whistled – a Threepenny Bar was opened where no other music was played. . . . Once when I was walking down the Tiergarten I passed a blind beggar. He called after me: 'Fräulein Lenya, you only have time for blind beggars on the stage eh?'[16]

Now this of course is a very sobering piece of theatrical sociology, one which has always raised profound questions about the very activity of art; it hankers back to what we have already described as the appropriation of the masses by the class of artists and intellectuals even down to their rags, their violence and misery. It is a subject which even radical ideologies evade, preferring to deal in platitudinous assertions such as indulged in the essay in question: 'a committed work of art . . . must lay bare unambiguously the causal historical and socio-economic network of society in such a way as to enable us to master reality and, in fact, transform it.' All of which is very laudable in the work of art that actually achieves this, but the exhortation does not resolve the fundamental question of the appropriation of any human reality – and especially a cruel one, extracted and presented for the edification of a micro-society. We are speaking here of the very morphology of intellectual base material; of the social evasion that accompanies, deep down, the process of having 'done your bit' for the downtrodden masses; of the unreal nature of any presentation of reality, the psychology of its consumers, the medium of transmission which is at once limited, distortive, an act of fabrication which draws the most committed consumer into a conspiracy of evasion. When the critic says, 'enable us to master reality', we must demand: who are us? Precisely what class? What functions? Could this 'us' by any stretch of imagination be the proletariat?

And here is the clue: it is significant that in arriving at the alienation of the participants – the real, not theoretical, alienation of the players from the played – Ogunbiyi's reader is privileged to know the workings of the mind of the Berlin beggar but not of the ordinary member of the mixed working-class and bourgeois audiences who watched *Opera Wonyosi*. Instead, speculations abound, drawn from, then pushed back into, the background network of an essentially bourgeoisified theory of theatrical responses. But in this tangible, contemporary instance we did learn what effects *Opera Wonyosi* actually had on the audience. We have the concrete information of its effects on a military governor comfortably seated at the opening – to start with, that is. We know of the reaction of a professor's wife, as freely admitted by her afterwards. We know of the effects on the parks and gardens workers and of other low-income workers, such as security officers, who watched the show. We learnt of the reverberations in Dodan Barracks, in military circles, in the National Security Organization. *Opera Wonyosi*, all set to appear in Lagos at the National Theatre, suffered a last-minute cancellation due to reasons which we also know. We, the critics, the producers, the commentators know of the effect on those who participated in the production, not so famous as Lotte Lenya perhaps, but probably more articulate than the beggar along Berlin's Tiergarten.

Any theory of what theatre should or can do, what it can achieve, must be anchored in the sociology of what is actually written, done and experienced. What we are offered in the article under consideration – which we merely use as an example of the increasingly typical – is a criticism rooted in generalized theories of art or, more accurately, in a fragmentary ideology of art, for such an ideology must remain fragmentary unless it is amplified by the dialectics of equal partnership between accumulated theory and the concrete sociology of the artistic event itself. This is how the audience *ought* to feel – ambiguated – says the critic. We know our audiences did not. Well, then, let the genuine dialectic begin!

The search by this particular school of criticism for the 'causal historical and socio-economic network of society' in every work of art is, let it be understood clearly, only a further attempt to protect the hegemony of appropriation by the intellectual critic class *in particular*, and this is especially true when such criticism chooses to ignore the *received* function as manifested in effect. Liberation is one of the functions of theatre, and liberation involves strategies of reducing the status and stature of the power-wielding class in public consciousness, exposing and demystifying its machinery of oppression. Representing Hitler – just to theorize – as an imbecile dripping mucus on his iconographic moustache may not be the social answer to a horrendous aberration, but it is at least more honest and less presumptuous than wishing him away as a mere figment of the socio-economic imagination. The satirist operates with an implicit recognition of the social limitations of his art; his methodology is allied to the social strategy of preparation. The mastering of reality and its transformation requires the liberation of the mind from the superstition of power, which cripples the will, obscures self-apprehension and facilitates surrender to the alienating processes ranged against every form of human productivity. DEFLATING THE BOGEY – this is also socially valid and progressive art: it becomes seriously flawed (a word carelessly employed by our critics) only when it attempts to pander to socio-historical causes by explaining away oppressors in rational (including economic) terms. Bourgeois intellectualism actually prefers the latter, because it wishes to leave the theatre having *understood*, and therefore remaining unchallenged by the need to destroy them. I know that such critical consumers will respond to this with yet more pages on how such and such a 'causated work clarifies and points the way to such destruction', but I must insist on the sociological truth of my observation that, for our critics, either (1) the work is totally deficient in such combative insights – which excuses their lackadaisical withdrawal – or (2) it is filled with heavy insights, after which it serves only as a cause for intellectual satisfaction, settling neatly afterwards into the theoretical lumberyard of sociological inertia. Our leftocracy have so far ignored the Bakalori massacre,[17] but the reason is simple: the playwright has not yet provided them with historico-socio-economic insights into what needs to be done! Art which identifies the enemy in a language that is instantly grasped – the language of satire, for instance – and not merely something available to yet another typewriter to be historically causated, pickled and hung up to dry, may still *not* be proletarian art; it is at least graphic *l'engage* which escapes the bane of leftocratic appropriation and addresses the proletariat *directly*.

Music, essence and class

Consider now the following interjection by our guest scourge of bourgeois values. Roland Barthes is castigating here the degradation of real human beings, real trees, tunnels, mountains and architecture to touristic *signs*, which are couched in the familiar trivializing language of the salesman as it appears in the French *Blue Guide*:

> We find again here this disease of thinking in essences, which is at the bottom of every bourgeois mythology of man.

Here is another:

> We find here again this bourgeois promoting of mountains, this old Alpine myth (since it dates back to the nineteenth century) which Gide rightly associated with Helvetico-Protestant morality and which has always functioned as a hybrid compound of the cult of nature and of puritanism.[18]

As stated earlier, we must give Roland Barthes credit for knowing, discovering and unmasking his own social sensibilities in this direction. The question we now pose is as follows: do African critics, on encountering such categorizing claims, take the trouble to find out the sensibility of the Kilimanjaro goatherd towards his mountains, or do they simply ingest these claims into the language of their own class myths? Now some of us who constantly circle the globe (I am trying to avoid the prejudicial 'globe-trotter') have had the opportunity of visiting these same Alpine natives – Italians, Bavarians, Yugoslavs – and have encountered the peasant stock on its own territory, drunk and danced with them and occasionally wondered whether one had been magically transported among the gorges and ranges of Nigeria's own plateau region. With such a background, one begins to criticize the language of those quotes. It says too much, claims too much. It is rooted in a specific history, a peculiar intellectual development where language has taken over reality as a reaction to another form of productive aberration – the tourist industry – by a specific class at a specific time and in certain specific forms.

In the literary field, there is of course the aesthesiogenic genre of Thomas Mann's *The Magic Mountain*, which would be an emetic even to a moderate hater of the bourgeoisie. Such literary misappropriation of nature, however, and a thousand like it – be these in music, dramatic or graphic forms – cannot contradict the truthful relations of those whose mountains were later appropriated by an élite group for the edification of a mini-society. They cannot be permitted to inhibit our own uncorrupted responses and creative exploitation of the many facets of nature. When the Gikuyu locate their ancestry within the hidden heart of their local mountain, we do not think of Thomas Mann; if we must seek a European affinity – which we are not compelled to do – our 'soul-brother' would probably be the Russian composer Mussorgsky, one of the first composers to use folk music as the basis for a classical work.

It must be emphasized that any work or form of art does lend itself sooner or later to appropriation by a different class from that which produced the original. When Rimsky-Korsakov revised and arranged a work by Mussorgsky as *Night on the Bare Mountain*, the new product was already responding to the sensibilities of a developing class and moved closer to the bourgeois sensibilities of *The Magic Mountain*. That, of course, is another progression (or retrogression) well worth detailed analysis, but not here, for it belongs to the field of music criticism and aesthetics. It is additionally relevant here because Roland Barthes is at his most *embarrassed* when he has to evolve a language of music criticism which evades the clichés and baroque legacies of his society's *langue* of music criticism. He evolves a new music value, the 'grain', whose sum total of innovation appears to lie more in the transference of adjectives to this new value than in the music criticism itself. Mind you, he himself recognized the danger:

> Are we condemned to the adjective? Are we reduced to the dilemma of either the predicable or the ineffable? To ascertain whether there are (verbal) means for talking about music without adjectives, it would be necessary to look at more or less the whole of music criticism. . . . This much, however, can be said: it is not by struggling against the adjective (diverting the adjective you find on the top of your tongue towards some substantive or verbal periphrasis) that one stands a chance of exorcizing music commentary and liberating it from the fatality of predication.[19]

Roland Barthes's essay here is, of course, purely exploratory, but the methodology is clear. We can see that he is struggling against the territory of the ineffable, against a very stubborn product, one whose language is highly arbitrary and less accessible to the authoritarian language of leftocratic criticism. Honesty struggles against music's wilful *métalangue* – 'but isn't the truth of the voice to be hallucinated?' – and compromises, dissolving into clearly embarrassed contortions. At the conclusion of his comparison of the German operatic singer Fischer-Diskau and the Russian Panzera, it would appear that all that Barthes had achieved in this laudable exercise has been already summed up in the American black vocabulary – one has *soul*,[20] the other does not.

Now *soul* is a language of one proletariat that we know, recognize and identify as one of many regional proletariats in need of socio-economic liberation. It is a community that has a very distinct culture, very palpable, almost quantifiable in all its complex structures and their social correlations. I shall not sentimentalize this society, which is at once violent and tender, at once cynical, acquisitive and millennial; I shall content myself with asserting that it exists, that it is part of a much larger society whose capitalist philosophy it shares. This 'other' society also has its own bourgeoisie which to some extent also appropriates the language of the black proletariat; nevertheless, the *signified* of this *parole* – soul – is one which still firmly belongs within this proletariat, not only within the large American continent but in much of the Caribbean, especially Jamaica. Soul has its own mythologies too, and it is highly marketable; none the less it is a summation of music to this very specific socio-polity, and it resists outright appropriation, being woven tightly into the interstices of daily social interaction, in short, into a vocabulary of a socially replete existence.

When Roland Barthes, in his own search for a winnowed value of music, settles on 'grain', he is responding to an apprehension of experience which, he implores, must be rescued from the ineffable. This choice of words is significant, but more informative still is the very explosion, the *cri de cœur* from the paradoxically unmelismatic throat of the social critic. (Picture Lenin's dilemma, if asked to explain why he would sit hour after hour with his Inessa, requesting that she play the same composition over and over again.) Would it really help if we built on Raymond Williams's typology and described music as an analogue of subterranean structures of feeling?

> For structures of feeling can be defined as social experiences in solution, as distinct from other social semantic formations which have been *precipitated* and are more evidently and more immediately available. Not all art, by any means, relates to a contemporary structure of feeling. The effective formations of most actual art relate to already manifest social formations dominant or residual, and it is primarily to emergent formations (though often in the form of modification or disturbance in older forms) that the structure of feeling, *as solution*, relates.[21]

Let us go back again. An analogue? Or perhaps an ellipsis? An ellipsis of subterranean structures of feeling? Music is a clue in the direction of our real battleground; as a language of human aesthetic strivings, but one which reinforces yet resists the language of other forms of artistic production, it leads remorselessly to a value which 'radical' theories of art attempt to deny and even deride. The dictionary meaning of ellipsis is 'a figure of syntax by which a word or words are left out and implied' (Chambers). I favour this expression because the paradox of music is that it exploits the incompletion of *langue* to transmit a language. It is truly a form 'in solution'; even at its most replete, even when the main theme and sub-themes and variations have been explored and brought home with an overwhelming sense of release, the effect of music is that of a linguistic proposition which is still striving towards *total* resolution – hence the failure of criticism to find an appropriate vocabulary, even to narrate the musical experience. The creative vocabulary describes this escapist value, capable only of evocation, as 'essence'. Sometimes reification is a tool for its expression. Poetry also attempts in its own frustrated way to capture the essence of material objects, phenomena, human relationships and feelings. Music, however, since it remains incomplete within man's socially linguistic upbringing, paradoxically projects the existence of this replete, structural reality. Because the obsessed materialists are defeated by the complications of this self-constitutive art which does not pretend to express *everything* but insists that there is *everything* to be expressed, comprehended, embraced and ravaged (Barthes employs the term *jouissance*), they can only take their revenge on the conceptual essentialization of objective reality in other art forms, these being – like the literary – linguistically 'open'. Such critics begin by habit with a foreign social development which gave birth contemporaneously both to those art concepts and to a now reactionary class – the bourgeoisie. The conscious language of that class struggle is then uncritically absorbed by them even through other societies where the language of essential-ization pre-dated the birth of the bourgeoisie in other histories.

Ori, among the Yoruba, is essential conceptualization; so is *ikenga* among the Ibo and *Nommo* among the Dogon. We must return to this subject, and in a different language.

For now we must pause to ask: is this a purely academic problem? Alas, no. It is a serious social productivity problem. When the critics gather together at the Annual Leftocratic Convention[22] in orgies of ideological puritanism, they seem unaware of a process of attrition in the actual productivity of a potential generation of authors. Well, perhaps no literature is better than certain kinds of literature – that is quite possible. I only ask that they understand the negative, sterilizing effect which a misuse of critical notions, a misplacement of their own socio-critical situating, now has on both the quality and the quantity of output among students from their captive audiences in the lecture room. For this also involves some mis-teaching, which fouls up the roots of the neophytes' resources and imprisons their imagination. It is my view that literary infanticide is being committed right now, and by a fanatic minority of leftocrats.

It is one thing to plot the course of European bourgeois Romantic or idealist literature and situate it in its socio-economic context; it is, however, a serious academic lapse to transfer the entirety of that language of criticism to any literature which, while undeniably cognizant of other world literatures, never-theless consciously explores the world-view of its own societies. It is an irony that it is those very critics who decry the 'undialectical' nature of much of today's African writing who resolutely refuse to accept the conceptual heritage or even material artefacts and their authentic significations (in history, origin and social intercourse, orature) as valid dialectical quantities for any received theory. On the streets of Havana and other cities of socialist Cuba, the haunting fusion of magic and revolutionary history by Gabriel García Márquez[23] is hawked daily. Throughout Latin America this unique evocation of timelessness even in the midst of revolutionary wars defies all calculations by remaining a favourite of the proletariat. In Nigeria the millipedes of a future literature are no sooner hatched than they are made to begin to count their feet. Naturally, they never walk.

The fictograph as a *langue* of vacuum

It is possible, however, to sympathize with the extremist position of some of the leftocrats when confronted by non-African interpreters of African literature who, to revert to some African terminology, 'carry their offering beyond the door of the mosque', or 'dye their cloth a deeper indigo than that of the bereaved'. For while the problem of African critics, blinkered by partial dialectics, appears to lie in areas of interpretation, certain European critics proceed from the abyss of ignorance on which they must erect a platform. They appear – superficially, at least – to be good structuralists. I shall call the basic unit of their bricolage the 'fictogram'. The critic Gerald Moore, late developer currently knocking at the portals of the Nigerian leftocracy, for instance, takes one look at the following lines –

> I watch my dreams float vaguely through the streets, lie at the bulls' feet.
> Like the guides of my race on the banks of Gambia or Saloum.[24]

– and, from them, constructs this 'fictograph' of an African world-view: 'Senghor, in any case, has expressed unforgettably the classical African view of the dead as the principal force controlling the living, benevolent and watchful'.[25]

Biodun Jeyifo, in his 'Soyinka Demythologized',[26] efficiently strips away the excesses of these 'enthusiasts', even while (needless to say) refusing to compromise on his own radical stance on Wole Soyinka's writings. Indeed, Jeyifo does not stint on the mandatory declamations that my myth-making is illusory, undialectical and bewitched, with a 'vaporous zone of self-subsistence', and so on. Wole Soyinka wishes to announce his intention of continuing to re-create his own myths, unscrupulously, in images – consciously selective – of vapour and matter for his contemporary needs. But more on that theme in another place.

Gerald Moore's recent book, I began to say, continues very much the old game of foisting typologies on to the works of authors, while evading, in one or two remarkable cases, the ideological grounding he proclaims in his preface. Moore agrees, he announces,

> also with the more basic Marxist proposition that a work of art is not and cannot ever be free from the conditioning imposed by history, class and market conditions. . . . We shall judge him [the artist] by what he makes of the conditions of his time and place in the continuum of history, but we shall not ignore those conditions.[27]

Only Gerald Moore can inform us where in his chapter 'Assimilation or Negritude', which deals with the life and work of Léopold Sédar Senghor, he carries out this vibrant declaration of radical intent. Obviously presidents and statesmen are entitled to a different level of criticism from others. It is necessary to point out only two more of Gerald Moore's canards to indicate just what level of illumination is to be obtained from this book. First, the canard against – who else? – Wole Soyinka, of course:

> And yet Soyinka does not reject modern life in the manner of Yeats, Eliot or Pound. He believes that it can only recover its meaning and its soul by a full-hearted espousal of African values or civilizations; an epousal of which

Olunde's death is meant to serve as an image. The political, social, religious and even economic arrangements of Yorubaland offer a system which only needs reinterpretation to act as the blueprint for tomorrow.[28]

Against this it is necessary only to refer to *Season of Anomy*,[29] where a tiny, atypical corner of Mooreland 'Yoruba' is deliberately quarried out to serve as an active agent in an endeavour to mobilize the rest of the country; it being nowhere suggested that this corner become a model, only that it is historically equipped for its agent role. Moore's claim is equivalent to saying that a Basque communist cell, seeking to revolutionize the entirety of Spain, is attempting to transform the Iberian peninsula in the image of the religious Basque province because that cell has the support of the mayor of its host village and his council! The attempted cellular mobilization of the country, whose main targets are workers' communities, is now transformed by Gerald Moore into the author's approval of the very structures that mobilization is trying to overthrow.

Now what *sociology* – for this is at the heart of my inquiry – what sociology of a critic could have led him to attempt such a brazen reversal of literary evidence? As I have already hinted, it is the sociology of a latecomer knocking at the portals of Nigerian leftocracy, and clinging – as is evidenced in the body of much of his criticism – to the hem of the bush-jackets of Femi Osofisan, Jeyifo, Kole Omotosho, and others, indeed, pushing them ahead in order to attribute any proven gaffes to their proven record in recent critical thinking. 'Against the Titans' can now be seen as Moore's presentation of credentials in this band-wagon exercise, when read against his earlier *Seven African Writers*,[30] his first claim to African literary expertise.

Gerald Moore is, of course, too clever to ignore *Season of Anomy*. However, instead of positing his criticism on the arguable nature and strategy of the revolution which the novel places in action, Moore diverts his readers' sights towards the earlier fictograph: 'Soyinka manages to create the impression that there is something deeply and intrinsically Yoruba about the community's arrangements.'[31] The purpose here is to reinforce the earlier *canard*, one in which the novelist is conspiring to restore a Yoruba-Mooreland feudalistic structure to contemporary Nigeria. For a literary critic to ignore the deliberate distancing of a familiar physical terrain in which action is situated through his utilization of a myth from as remote a culture as Asia – which Moore does recognize – is to damn himself as either a singularly inept practitioner of his trade or as a critic with a hidden, quite unliterary motivation. The creation of a different *langage* – an alien myth – interworking with the personages of the action on local grounds is such an obvious literary signification that only an expert would dare miss it. Perhaps Moore would prefer that the action be located in the 'neutral' Iboyoru of Ezekiel Mphahlele's *The Wanderers*.[32]

No reference is made here to other points of criticism in Moore's essay – these could be sustainable, or errors of judgement, or simply matters of opinion. The deliberate introduction of Yoruba acculturation – and specifically its negative baggage (feudalism, capitalist economic arrangements, etc.) – is the malicious invention of a leftocratic achiever, and one for which he fails to provide evidence, naturally, since there is none. Both the preface and essays in my *Myth, Literature and the African World*[33] should have cured Moore of the extravagant delusion that I believe in 'a full-hearted espousal of African values', but it is doubtful if Moore understands any longer the difference between a contestation of 'world-views' and a blanket endorsement of them. Moore's mendacity is only equalled – and to some extent surpassed – by that of Bernth Lindfors,[34] hagiographer extraordinary, who 're-creates' my juvenilia, in the old University College of Ibadan; every page of his essay contains at least one inaccuracy of time and place and a series of absurd attributions. The lucrative business of juvenile hagiography of everything that moves on two feet, from pop stars to syndicated criminals, is of course very much the lifestyle of American letters. It is to be hoped that it never becomes a way of life in Nigeria.

Others with more leisure and stomach for the task will, of course, catalogue the factual misrepresentations of the nature of the society that Gerald Moore on his part attempts to deal with. I shall refer here, finally, to just a typical sweeping generalization which again takes its root in the sociology of this critic – an egotistical emphasis that makes him compulsively imply greater knowledge of African societies than the knowledgeable African:

> This Africa of vast segregated modern cities, mine-dumps, skyscrapers and jazz clubs was as alien and remote to the Nigerian or Senegalese reader of that time as Dallas or Harlem might have been.[35]

'That time' refers to the time of publication of Ezekiel Mphahlele's *Down Second Avenue*,[36] and 'This Africa' to South Africa. I can only speak for the average Nigerian reader of 'that time', and indeed of at least ten or fifteen years before that time. Such a reader was weaned on *Drum* magazine, a South African black journal whose monthly, racy contents portrayed Ezekiel Mphahlele's country in just these images of Gerald Moore's description. But this is only another shutter on black Mooreland, where reality has yielded place to a fictographic memory.

Power, essence, ideal

We must take into account but reject the burden of bourgeois development of other societies, reject the framework of their bourgeois values and conceptualizations, but, in the process, ensure that concepts that are termed bourgeois in societies of their origination correspond also to the values of bourgeois development in our own societies. For this, we do not even need to prove first the existence of a bourgeoisie or coerce social groups into identical class structures of other societies. Efforts in this direction – that is, attempts at direct correlations with classic European models, with their specific history – have been regularly controverted. The existence of classes, however, is a universal reality; what remains permanently contestable is the *universality* of concepts and values attaching to each group. There is more than matter for suspicion when our leftocracy, for instance, takes on the mantle of abuse from European leftist criticism as it automatically attaches to the sheerest idealist suggestiveness in any form of literature. My theory is that it is a guilty reflex, a defence mechanism. The leftocracy feels it is on trial when it detects any trace of idealism in the arts and literature precisely because the hard evidence of revolutionary history is that, while the motive force of social transformation does exist within the realm of socio-economics, power, that manifestation of idealist craving, has proved a durable partner and an uncertain quantity within such transformations. This is a most embarrassing language, one which belongs to the 'mushy' world of psychology, an upsetting factor even within the internal history of revolutionized societies.

Power and music constitute two of the products and strivings of humankind that are least addressed by radical criticism. Like music, power lacks completion and cannot be quantified or reduced to the language of historicism: it stands outside history. It reaches out constantly towards a new repletion, towards an essentiality, a concept of the ideal. This element of the idealist is therefore present in the fanatic radical critic, who becomes a surrogate of authoritarianism, representing a system which is challenged by the one value that knows itself, like music, as incomplete. What is manifested here, to situate it bluntly but succinctly, is a conflict of interests that straddles both the metaphysical and the political. Marxism has created for our leftocracy a system that declares itself complete, controlled and controlling: an immanent reflection of every facet of human history, conduct and striving, an end known in advance and delayed only by the explicable motions of economic production and development.

E. M. Barth identifies the system of thought to which Marxism belongs:

> The absence of systematic constraints gets it full importance in combination with another feature of the systems of thought we are concerned with here – perhaps with the exception of the works of Nietzsche. This is *the claim to systematic definitive completeness in principle* in the matters dealt with, i.e. completeness as to what is of *fundamental* importance in [the structure of] *a philosophy of human life and affairs*. With the exception of Nietzsche, the authors of these systems are understood by friend and foe to make *at least* this claim (and are frequently understood to make even wider claims, concerning the inorganic sciences as well). They certainly do not refer to other thinkers for fundamental principles which they themselves do not formulate, except in order to refute them.
>
> This claim to definitive completeness leaves no room for serious revision of any one principle and it leaves no room for the addition of one or more new basic principles. These systems are, as one often says, dogmatically closed.[37]

Adherents of a rigid Marxist position *dare not* believe the evidence of their eyes when, for example, the 'mushy' essentiality of power is made manifest – as was the case with Stalin, contemporaneously (such is the irony of history) with that of an obverse ideology, Nazism. The embrace of convenience of those two colossi, Stalin and Hitler, was more than symbolic. It could not last, however, and it did not. The twists and turns of the interpreters of this monstrosity of a wedding do not concern us here; they need be balanced only by the opportunism of the reactionary world which sought, in this very complex aberration, to ring the death-knell of socialist revolution. For my part, as a writer, myth-maker and critic, I invoke such reminders on a metaphoric level, to reinforce the unresolved question mark that hangs over the dialectics of power for any form of ideology – progressive or reactionary.

When radical criticism claims that idealism reinforces a static, historical, irremediable world-view, I recognize immediately that we have a problem of language. Music, whose nature lends itself to largely idealist striving, is not static; on the contrary, the interiority of its language provokes a constant dialectic with the world of reality – which is action, development, motion. The functioning of music in the language of art is parallel with the functioning of power in the realm of politics and economics. The latter is often vital and deadly, but that is no reason for evasion; certainly neither art nor literature evades it. Indeed, literature attempts to *contain* it, and it is the very methodology of containment which arouses radical criticism to ire: why, it demands, have you ignored my *langue*? One response is this: if the revolutionary socio-economist will at least share the burden of containing and controlling the forces and distribution of production, on behalf of the masses, art will try to contain and control power, metaphoric-ally, again on behalf of the masses. Whether as Alfred Jarry's King Ubu, Rasputin, Shakespeare's Richard III, allegories of terrorizing monsters and captive com-munities, Achebe's Chief Nanga, Sembene's Colonial Factor, my Dr Bero, or even mythical constructs such as Ogun, the writer structures into controllable entities – being careful in most cases to give no utopian answers – these faces of ideality, be they evasively disguised as State, Divinity, the Absolute or History. The challenger is a representative of humanity, and this is the essence of a combative, even revolutionary humanism.

Of course, the above examples not only have been carefully chosen to reflect the expression of this particular genre, but also provide the consumer with other facets of reality, not excluding the socio-economic. The emphasis here is that, even where the ruled are not corporately manifested, power is not so abstract or so reified that it does not implicate, even by the very act of naming it, the disadvantaged existence of the ruled. This point must be made for the benefit yet again of those literal-minded critics for whom whatever is not physically portrayed is presumed thereby to be denied, or not manifested. But let us take yet another example of 'essentialist' relations.

I spoke earlier of a difficulty of language in confronting the materialists' bogey, essence. It manifests itself in areas of seeming absurdity but such as can probably be resolved by strategies of redefinition. For instance, I have come across a materialist claim which states that even love, as an emotion, is a product of the socio-economic relations in human society. Now it so happens that many Africans ridicule the concept love, so here, at least, 'African' values do appear to correspond to a non-bourgeoisified view of human relationships. Such an African viewpoint – one I have heard expressed by both the articulate worker and the 'been-to' student – insists that 'love' is a luxury of welfare societies such as we find in Europe, and this of course is quite possible. But is the African here utilizing the same language as his European counterpart? For one thing, the African worker was actually speaking of 'pairing' – by implication declining to forgo his polygamous privileges. The radical interlocutor from Europe is issuing, by contrast, a critique of the development of 'possessions' and, in that particular context, is debunking the notion of an unchanging essence in human relations.

There are immediate complications on both sides, complications such as cannot be resolved in class typologies. 'Pairing' is still observed – among animals – and no evidence has yet been offered concerning the relation of this to the level or their means of production. There is also polygamy among the animal species. Doves and peacocks have elaborate systems of courtship, and male baboons have been known to fight to the death over any attempt to encroach on their harems. The expression that must apply to these forms of attachment must obviously transcend mere sexual terminology or the mere biological activities of hormones and the rounds of mating-seasons. Some may see the baboon's polygamous herd as capitalist accumulation; but for a rational observer it becomes necessary, on discovering similar conduct in human society, to accept the possibility of some other essence of the relationship of living forms which so demonstrably stands outside economic patterns. Since an analogue of this conduct or relationship exists ahistorically in the species we have identified as peacock, dove or ape, it is sheer perversity to deny that love, fondness or some other emotion resulting in personal attachment (or revulsion) has existed ahistorically in human beings. If there is love, then there is hatred, meanness, generosity, perversity, strength, weakness (and variants thereof), perhaps psychologically rooted instinctual conduct, undifferentiated by later class formations – including the power drive or instinct.

The reification of such abstractions in the personae of deities is a device that serves purposes ranging from ethics to poetics. Such activity is, of course, open to social abuse, opportunism, social inertia born of superstition, and so on. But it can also serve society as a mechanism for combating every one of these very anti-humanistic malformations, including the abnormal development of the last-mentioned instinctual drive – the power lust in group or individual – by endowing the mythical figure with the collective force, with the negative or positive attributes of the total community. Concerning this aspect of social mechanics – which, may I emphasize again, is only *one* of the many functions to which myth has been put – when it is objected that such a method is not scientific, the provoked answer is that the so-called scientific systems of society have yet to find a scientific counter to the abnormal and unpredictable development of the personality cult around a strong leader with unsuspected power drive, one who becomes the embodiment of the ideal, infallible and supreme, an essence and an apotheosis of the secret mythological yearnings of its unsuspecting victims.

For the ramifications of the power drive throughout history – at all stages of socio-economic development, within and affecting various human activities in public and private, in magic and technology, in the arts, education and the civil service, across and within the class units of every form of society – any sentient being who refuses to accept the empirical deductions of his or her own environment may turn for a philosopher's view to Bertrand Russell's *Power*.[38] Russell is not, of course, a fashionable philosopher among African intellectuals: he has neither a German nor a Russian name; moreover, his discourse is strangely lucid, easily comprehensible; and the work referred to here has hardly any footnotes. Although there are pitfalls in his exposition, if we ignore those prescriptions that border on political naïveté, Russell's pursuit of the operations of power through the various levels of society down the ages yields enough matter for a true dialectic with other claimants to the motive force of history. For we cannot rest upon any categories of ideas in which any observable patterns, within societies which have produced those ideas, have not been taken into full dialectical partnership: this would be to perpetuate the habit of excision which obscured the socio-economic reading of history in its own time, enthroning the dictatorship of the mutant in the realm of human ideas. As a strategy for power seizure in a revolution or indeed outside a revolution, or – as has been historically demonstrated – for the purpose of preventing a revolution, this might be pragmatically opportune; but, if we have begged the question in this way, the theory of power as a contributory motive force of history could then be held to have made its point.

In conclusion

Sadists remain sadists whether they are fascists or socialists. The former would rationalize their sadism by means of the arrangement of human beings into the superior, acceptable and inferior or non-beings, upon the last of which group any form of dehumanization is permissible: obviously, you cannot dehumanize non-humans; you can only reduce them to what they are. Sadists whose view of society is progressive, even radical, take the battle to opponents of their conduct very simply by sneering at their 'bourgeois sentimentality'.

I am not involved here with ethical judgements in either case. What I wish to recall is that words do not lose their meanings or – shall we call it? – their *signified* because of any one ideology. Even if we spoke entirely in the language of manual signs, every gesture, curve or slice of fingers, every conjunction of motions in wrists and palm, would still signify a field of values, whatever the colouring through which the user were to subject such a signifier at its moment of application. When we use the expression 'sadist', therefore, we are not insisting on an irreducible condition of humanity even as we prove that such a quality cuts across class, ideology or history. Specific cases of sadism can be accounted for by an individual's history or social conditioning, some economic privation in the midst of others' luxurious existence which warped his or her humanity, and so on. Every explanation merely confirms that there is a certain conduct that is observable in human beings which cannot be termed exactly kindness, consideration, humaneness, etc. On the contrary, the expression codifies one simple observation: that some human beings actually enjoy inflicting pain. 'Sadism', then, is a linguistic convention which is used to signify that predilection of certain human beings to inflicting horrific pains – mental, physical, economic or psychological – on others.

A psychologist, painter, musician, historian, linguist, teacher, social worker, dramatist, novelist, poet or architect may therefore each in their individual way become preoccupied by this isolable human condition which clearly falls into a category of its own, and not merely in a linguistic sense, since it does not belong exclusively to any of the other categories we know: social, ideological, class – even human. Animal psychologists, or even owners of domestic pets, recognize its existence in the animal kingdom. Like other values that are signified by expressions such as anguish, ecstasy, euphoria, violence or tenderness, sadism – or its correlative, suffering – may become a subject for exploration, but it cannot be exclusively exposed within those other categories in which it was first observed.

Picasso's Guernica is one famous illustration of the correspondence of (in this case) pictorial art to psychological values within human experience. Three-dimensional art – the sculpture as demonstrated in Rodin, African traditional masks, Vincent Kofi of Ghana – and even some examples of Russian realist art, such as the works of the graphic artist and illustrator Vladimir Favosky, boost the transmission of this essential value. It is an unpleasant fact for the ultra-Marxist critic that realist sculpture and expressionist woodcuts, at their finest, exhibit the paradox of this same essentialist correspondence.

But I deliberately introduced Picasso's Guernica. The kind of ultra-revolutionary critics who have engaged our attention would, of course, damn Picasso's Guernica just as I damn his infamous daubing on the walls of the Unesco foyer; it is called Leisure, and I consider it one of the most notorious con-tricks of art, an Emperor's Clothes delusion, no less. Where I part company with our imagined critics is (1) in their denial of the essential correspondence of Guernica to the historical, independent categories of terror, courage, fear, anguish, etc., and (2) in what I am sure would be their rapid recourse to the examples of revolutionary art especially in the works of Mexican muralists like Diego Rivera and

Orozco, Russian and Chinese proletarian art, and so forth. The contestation, in short, is this: assuming (for it is difficult, they find, to deny it altogether) that these categories of experience have been successfully isolated and rendered concretely – transmitted, if you like – on this canvas, then it is the responsibility of the artist to point the way towards the avoidance of, the resistance to and the triumph of humanity over the mutilating agents of history. Picasso's *Guernica* would, then, stand condemned for daring to stand outside history or, at least, for laying itself open to essentialist interpretation. It would not matter that the event is located even by its very title in a geographical place and is an outcry against fascism, against the sadism of a particular history. Bourgeois art criticism has damned Picasso's *Guernica* by according it the title of masterpiece in universal *l'engage* which extends it beyond the class struggle – indeed, places it outside the class struggle and mounts it on the podium of universal application. And since it is, irreversibly, a permanent abstraction of human anguish, it becomes an embarrassing testament to a historically provoked essentiality.

It is hardly surprising that Barthes's chapter, 'Diderot, Brecht and Eisenstein' (in *Image–Music–Text*), is a marvel of analytical acrobatics. For how is Barthes to cope with the crafted essentialization of emotions in the meticulous, frame-by-frame compositions of the Russian cinema realist, Eisenstein? Barthes's critical honesty cannot deny it; moreover, he would simply render himself absurd to any reader acquainted with Eisenstein's expressionist techniques. Barthes's task is further complicated by the fact that he has elected to place him alongside Bertolt Brecht, a playwright and dramatic theorist whose stark techniques of presentation and emotional distancing are the very opposite of Eisenstein's. But he has problems even with Brecht's formalism:

> Thus . . . it is pointless to criticize Eisenstein's art (as also that of Brecht) for being 'formalizing' or 'aesthetic': form, aesthetic, rhetoric can be socially responsible if they are handled with deliberation.[39]

The prize passage, however, is to come. *En route*, Barthes concedes that the 'tableau' (a favourite Brechtian device) is 'the presentation of an ideal meaning' – a great problem for a materialist, yet Brecht must not be damned. There is nothing for it but to absorb the stubborn paradoxes of Brecht and Eisenstein by jettisoning the rules and providing the artists with a formal absolution – one rule for Brecht, another for Eisenstein:

> Nevertheless, it is true that in Eisenstein . . . the actor does sometimes adopt expressions of the most pathetic quality, a pathos which can appear to be very little 'distanced'; but distanciation is a properly Brechtian method, vital to Brecht because he represents a tableau for the spectator to criticize; in the other two, the actor does not have to distance: what he has to present is an ideal meaning.[40]

Truth will out, it seems. The correlation of artistic forms and idioms with ideological precepts of any line is full of pitfalls which leave the agent or arbitrator dangerously exposed: the greater the intellective faith of the agent, the worse, ironically, are the perils. Despite all evasions and rationalizations, those penalities of willed adherence to compact systems of ideas, the language of art and creativity continues to pose problems beyond the merely linguistic or semiological. Why deny that a frame of the cinema picture, arrested in time, frozen, rendered ineffable, an extract from history yet an emotion or statement that stands outside that sequential, *returns to reinforce the historic moment from which it is built with a force of that other level of truthfulness – recognition?* The viewer's own history completes the forms, the canvas, the sculpture, the ahistorical testimony of a poetic licence.

The tableau is the myth; it may be progressive or reactionary, but one thing it is not is a bourgeois liberal-romantic convention. The actuality of the historical development of these *langues* of individual art forms spans the whole of human history – including, of course, that of the development of the bourgeoisie. Expressionism may have been appropriated by a dissatisfied group of middle-class artists in Germany, but its inspiration came from an ancient period in Africa whose carvers were not of the 'bourgeoisie'! The task of those who continue to find the myth-tableau unacceptable must be to find a relevant language, pejorative still, since no one expects them to change their allegiances, only to make *meaning*. For our part we shall endeavour to enshrine the essence of their negativity in appropriate mythologies.

They may, however, prefer to address an even more fundamental problem of their own situating, one that I have already engaged and that Roland Barthes, our elected pointer, courageously faces even as he pours intellectual scorn on the bourgeoisie of his society. So far the Nigerian (and indeed most African) leftocrats have shirked this responsibility in self-criticism. They have failed to discriminate, even within their ranks, the self-seekers, the opportunists, the radical chic and the starkly ideological illiterate for whom the company is all and for whom no social responsibility exists outside the social 'identifying-with' at repetitious seminars and coffee-rooms or the staff clubs with their holiday-resort facilities, beyond the public gesture of association with an equally unproductive Left. It is time to ask the rigorous question: what are you really contributing to society while awaiting the revolution?

So let our colleague from the semiological ivory tower of France have the last word. He is a teacher like us, one who has honestly assessed his own situation, his relationship to his students, even down to the adoption of the physical stance of a lecturer among his students! Above all, however, as a demolition agent of bourgeois mythologies, he has paused to examine whether he, Roland Barthes, is not part of a new ideo-mythical *langue* which merely occludes the real possibility of an understanding and transmission of a proletarian culture:

Then begins, however, for these procurators of proletarian meaning, a real headache of a problem since their class situation is not that of the proletariat: they are not producers, a negative situation they share with (student) youth – an equally unproductive class with whom they usually form an alliance of language. It follows that the culture from which they have to disengage the proletarian meaning *brings them back round to themselves and not to the proletariat* [my italics]. How is culture to be *evaluated*? According to its origin? Bourgeois. Its finality? Bourgeois again. According to dialectics? Although bourgeois, this does contain progressive elements; but what, *at this level of discourse*, distinguishes dialectics from compromise? And then again, with what instruments? Historicism, sociologism, positivism, formalism, psycho-analysis? Every one of them bourgeoisified. There are some who finally prefer to give up the problem, to dismiss all 'culture' – a course which entails the destruction of all discourse.[41]

Notes

1 I am well aware that the French-language purist will be greatly disturbed by this assault on French grammar, since the correct expression should be *l'engager*. However, I am attempting here only to convey certain conceptual aids, thought processes or mnemonic cues, and not even the Académie Française can legislate against ungrammatical thinking.

2 Lanrewaju Adepoju, Professor alias Majority, Dan Maraya and Salawa are all popular Nigerian music artistes.

3 See Ess Momoh, 'The Two Faces of Violence', *Sunday Times* (Lagos, Nigeria), 20 July 1980, p. 8.

4 A reference to a government decision to place the importation of rice under licence – rice being in short supply in the country at the time. The decision was, of course, only another ploy for the enrichment of middlemen.

5 As a contrasting, harmless example of exchanges using this language of appropriation, see (arbitrarily selected) T. Vidal, 'Of Rhythm and Metre in Yoruba Songs', seminar paper, Department of Music, University of Ife, 20 November 1980.

6 Roland Barthes, *Mythologies*, trans. Annette Lavers (1970; St Albans: Paladin, 1973).

7 Roland Barthes, *Image–Music–Text*, trans. Stephen Heath (London: Fontana, 1977).

8 Barthes, *Mythologies*, pp. 16, 19.

9 Ibid., p. 61.

10 Ibid., pp. 24–5.

11 Norman Mailer, 'A Fire on the Moon', *Life*, 29 August 1969, pp. 22–41, and 'The Psychology of Astronauts', *Life*, 14 November 1969, pp. 50–63.

12 Yemi Ogunbiyi, '*Opera Wonyosi*: A Study of Soyinka's *Opera Wonyosi*', *Nigeria Magazine*, 138–9 (1979), p. 5. *Opera Wonyosi* (London: Rex Collings, 1981) was performed for the Convocation Ceremonies, University of Ife, December 1978.

13 See University of Ife seminar paper 'Sociology of Literature' (uncredited; probably Department of Sociology or Modern Languages, pp. 8–10, for cautionary words to the critic on the subject.

14 Ogunbiyi, op. cit., p. 9.

15 At the other end of the ideological spectrum, see Ali Mazrui, 'Chaka and Amin: The Warrior Tradition in African History', paper delivered at a conference on 'Africa and the Humanities' in Bellagio, Italy (197?).
Whereas Ogunbiyi proposes a socio-economic understanding of an actively destroying social deformity, Mazrui blends it with myth-historic patterns. Both methods of distortion, unlike satire, plead a panacea of intellectual *understanding*, a soporific to the consumer, and a flattering of the type. Given the right socio-economic development and an eradication of the last vestiges of neo-colonialism, all forms of Aminism will vanish from the face of Africa! Empathy with those who experience the *actuality* is crude, unscientific response. I suggest that we ask the opinion of the vanishing breed of Ugandan intelligentsia, to see if they share this luxury of intellectual distancing!

16 Ogunbiyi, op. cit., p. 6.

17 The 2 a.m. massacre (1980) of peasants at Bakalori village in Sokoto State by the armed Mobile Police Unit. These peasants had earlier occupied the offices of a dam construction firm, demanding compensation for their expropriated farms. A policeman was killed in the attempt to dislodge them. That night a squad of the Mobile Police Unit was sent in. They descended on the sleeping village, firing into the thatched dwellings indiscriminately, mowing down farmers, their wives and children as they ran. A hundred and fifty were counted dead, by name. The President of Nigeria, in whose home state this atrocity took place, did not even set up an inquiry. The intellectuals, Left and Right, were content to let it pass.

18 Barthes, *Mythologies*, pp. 75, 74.

19 Barthes, *Image–Music–Text*, p. 180.

20 One of the definitions of soul is as follows: 'the heritage that is black – black authenticity, feeling for one's roots as demonstrated in black music and literature' (Clarence Major, *Dictionary of Afro-American Slang* (1980)). It is a very thin definition, but one that serves as a reminder of the origination of 'soul'. For, like all culture-originated metaphors, 'soul' is now employed to capture the 'ineffable' values of experiencing in other cultures, most significantly in music. Inevitably, categorization tends to be subjective. Mine includes, among others, the music of Amalia Rodriguez (*fado*, Portugal), Russian folk music, a somewhat smaller proportion of Irish folk music, Fatima (Senegal), Brahms's German Requiem (unlike Verdi, Fauré), Edith Piaf (France), Manitas de Plata (flamenco guitar, Spain), a vast number of Egba and Ekiti dirges, Nelly Uchendu (Nigeria) (when she is not singing pop) and the majority of the blues greats, of whom Billie Holliday, Bessie Smith and Ella Fitzgerald remain without equal till today. For all these I would also employ, interchangeably with 'soul', Barthes's most felicitous expression, 'grain'.

21 Raymond Williams, *Marxism and Literature* (London and New York: Oxford University Press, 1977), pp. 133–4. (See chapter 7.)

22 An Annual (Critics') Conference with 'Radical Perspectives', usually held at the University of Ibadan and attended by academics from outside the country. It has been running since the mid-1970s.

23 Gabriel García Márquez, *One Hundred Years of Solitude*, trans. Gregory Rabasa (New York: Avon, 1972).

24 Gerald Moore, *Twelve African Writers* (London: Hutchinson, 1980), p. 28.

25 Ibid., p. 27; my emphasis.

26 Biodun Jeyifo, 'Soyinka Demythologized: Notes on a Materialist Reading of *A Dance of the Forests*', monograph, University of Ife Seminars (1977).

27 Moore, op. cit., p. 12.

28 Ibid., p. 226.

29 Wole Soyinka, *Season of Anomy* (London: Rex Collings, 1978).

30 Gerald Moore, 'Against the Titans', West Africa (1977 or 1978), and Seven African Writers (Harmondsworth: Penguin, 1962).
31 Moore, Twelve African Writers, p. 229.
32 Ezekiel Mphahlele, The Wanderers (New York: Macmillan, 1971).
33 Wole Soyinka, Myth, Literature and the African World (Cambridge: Cambridge University Press, 1976).
34 Bernth Lindfors, 'The Early Writings of Wole Soyinka', in James Gibbs (ed.), Critical Perspectives on Wole Soyinka (Washington, DC: Three Continents Press, 1980), pp. 19–44.
35 Moore, Twelve African Writers, p. 41.
36 Ezekiel Mphahlele, Down Second Avenue (London: Faber, 1971).
37 E. M. Barth, Perspectives on Analytic Philosophy (Amsterdam, NY: North-Holland, 1979), pp. 41–2.
38 Bertrand Russell, Power (London: Allen & Unwin, 1962).
39 Barthes, Image–Music–Text, p. 74.
40 Ibid.
41 Ibid., pp. 210–11.

2 James A. Snead

Repetition as a figure of black culture

The scope of repetition in culture

> The world, as force, may not be thought of as unlimited, for it *cannot* be so
> thought of; we forbid ourselves the concept of an infinite force as incom-
> patible with the concept 'force'. Thus – the world also lacks the capacity for
> eternal novelty.   (Nietzsche, *The Will to Power*)

After all, people have by now had to make peace with the idea that the world is
not inexhaustible in its combinations, nor life in its various guises. How we have
come to terms with the discrepancy between our personal growth – the very
model of linear development – and the physical plane upon which life unfolds,
characterized by general recursiveness and repetition: this must be the concern
of culture. 'Coming-to-terms' may mean denial or acceptance, repression or
highlighting, but in any case *transformation* is culture's response to its own
apprehension of repetition.

Apart from revealing or secreting the repetitions of material existence, a third
response is possible: to own that repetition has occurred, but that, given a
'quality of difference' compared to what has gone before, it has become not a
'repetition' but rather a 'progression', if positive, or a 'regression', if negative.
This third response implies that one finds a scale of tendencies from culture to
culture. In any case, let us remember that, whenever we encounter repetition in
cultural forms, we are indeed not viewing 'the same thing' but its transformation,
not just a formal ploy but often the willed grafting onto culture of an essentially

philosophical insight about the shape of time and history. But, even if not in intentional emulation of natural or material cyclicality, repetition would need to manifest itself. Culture as a reservoir of inexhaustible novelty is unthinkable. Therefore, repetition, first of all, would inevitably have to creep into the dimension of culture just as into that of language and signification because of the finite supply of elementary units and the need for recognizability. One may readily classify cultural forms according to whether they tend to admit or cover up the repeating constituents within them.

The important thing about culture is that it should not be dead. Or, if dead, then its transformations must continue to live on in the present. Culture must be both immanent and historical: something there and something to be studied in its present form and in its etiology. Our modern notion of 'culture' only arises early in this century, after a 500-year period of English usage as a noun of process rather than identification, referring rather to the tending of animals or crops than to types of music, literature, art and temperament by which a group of people is aware of and defines itself for others and for itself.[1] But this initial connotation may still be preserved. 'Culture' in its present usage always also means the *culture of culture*: a certain continuance in the nurture of those concepts and experiences that have helped or are helping to lend self-consciousness and awareness to a given group. Culture must not only be immanent now but also give the promise of being *continuously* so. So the second way in which repetition enters the dimension of culture is in the necessity for every culture to maintain a sense of continuity about itself: internal changes notwithstanding, a basic self-identity must not be altered. Strangely enough, however, what recent Western or European culture repeats continuously is precisely the belief that there is *no* repetition in culture but only a difference, defined as progress and growth.

It was Swift who said that 'happiness . . . is a perpetual Possession of being well deceived'.[2] We are not far here from a proper definition of culture. At least a type of 'happiness' accrues through a perpetual repetition of apparent consensus and convention that provide a sense of security, identification and 'rightness'. Yet, however fervently culture nurtures this belief, such a sense of security is also a kind of 'coverage', both in the comforting sense of 'insurance' against accidental and sudden rupturing of a complicated and precious fabric, and in Swift's less favorable sense of a 'cover-up', or a hiding of otherwise unpleasant facts from the senses.[3] Like all insurance, this type of *coverage* does not prevent accidents but promises to be able to provide the means to outlive them. Furthermore, this insurance takes full actuarial account of the *most* and *least* likely points of intrusion or corruption to the self-image of the culture, and covers them accordingly.

For example, most cultures seem quite willing to tolerate and often assimilate certain foreign *games* – such as chess, imported to Europe from the Middle East as early as the First or Second Crusade in the twelfth century, or lawn tennis, developed and patented in England in 1874 from an earlier form of tennis. The fate of foreign *words* in language, however, has been frequently less happy, as witnessed in the *coverage* that European national languages institute against diluting 'invasions of foreign words', exemplified in England by the sixteenth-century 'Cambridge School' (Ascham, Cheke and Wilson), in seventeenth-century France by the purism of Boileau and the Académie Française (a linguistic xenophobia which has by no means yet run its course) and by the recurrent attempts to expel foreignisms from the German language beginning with Leibnitz in the seventeenth and Herder in the eighteenth century (most recently seen in the less innocuous censorships of the National Socialists in the current century).[4]

Finally, as in all insurance, you pay a regular premium for *coverage*: culture has a price. Might Swift's phrase 'Flaws and Imperfections of Nature' not also include the daunting knowledge that the apparently linear upward-striving course of human endeavor exists within nature's ineluctable circularity, and that birth and life end up in death and decay?[5]

Cultures, then, are virtually all varieties of 'long-term' *coverage*, against both external and internal threats – self-dissolution, loss of identity; or repression, assimilation, attachment (in the sense of legal 'seizure'); or attack from neighboring or foreign cultures – with all the positive and negative connotations of the 'cover-ups' thus produced. In this, black culture is no exception. Cultures differ among one another primarily in the tenacity with which the 'cover-up' is maintained and the spacing and regularity of the intervals at which they cease to cover up, granting leeway to those ruptures in the illusion of growth which most often occur in the *déjà-vus* of exact repetition.

In certain cases, culture, in projecting an image for *others*, claims a radical difference from *others*, often further defined qualitatively as *superiority*. Already in this insistence on uniqueness and 'higher' development we sense a linear, anthropomorphic drive. For centuries (and especially within the last three) Europe has found itself in hot contest internally over this very issue. Culture has been territorialized – and, with it, groups of its diverse adherents. Cultural wars have become territorial wars have become cultural wars again, and indeed into this maelstrom have been sucked concepts of 'race', 'virtue' and 'nation', never to re-emerge.[6] What startles is not so much the content of these cross-cultural feuds as the vehemence and aggression with which groups of people wrangle over where one *coverage* ends and another begins. The incipient desire to define 'race' and 'culture' in the same breath as 'identity' and 'nationality' finally coincides with the great upheavals of the seventeenth and eighteenth centuries in Europe – among them, the overturning of the feudal monarchies of central Europe and the discovery and subjugation of black and brown masses across the seas. The word 'culture' now gains two fateful senses: 'that with which one whole group aggressively defines its superiority *vis-à-vis* another'; and a finer one, 'that held at a level above the group or mass, for the benefit of the culture as a whole, by the conscious few (i.e. the distinction between *haute* and *basse culture*)'.[7] At the same time as Europeans were defining themselves over against other European nations and even some of them against members of their own nations, they were also busy defining 'European culture' as separate from 'African culture', the ultimate otherness, the final *mass*. Only having now reached this stage can we make any sense whatever of the notion of 'black culture' and what it might oppose.[8]

'Black culture' is a concept first created by Europeans and defined in opposition to 'European culture'. Hegel, for example, saw 'black culture' as the lowest stage of that laudable self-reflection and development shown by European culture, whose natural outcome must be the state or nationhood. In his by no means untypical nineteenth-century view, Hegel said that black culture simply *did not exist* in the same sense as European culture did. Black culture (as one of several non-Western cultures) had no self-expression (i.e. no writing); there was no black *Volksgeist*, as in Europe, and not even particular tribes or groupings of Africans seemed in the least concerned to define themselves on the basis of any particular *Volksgeist*. Hegel (like most of Europe) was confused by the African: where did blacks fit into 'the course of *world history*?':[9]

> In this main portion of Africa there can really be no history. There is a succession of *accidents and surprises*.
>
> There is *no goal*, no state there that one can follow, no subjectivity, but only a series of subjects who destroy each other. There has as yet been little comment upon *how strange a form of self-consciousness* this represents.

These remarks give a rather fascinating definition of European culture (at least as Hegel introduces his countrymen in his 'we') by inversion:

> We must forget all categories that lay at the bottom of our spiritual life and its subsumption under these forms; the difficulty [in such forgetting when examining Africa] lies in the fact that we repeatedly must bring along that which we have already imagined.

Because Hegel gives the first and still most penetratingly systematic definition by a European of the 'African character' (and, consequently, of black culture), albeit in a severely negative tone, it is worth quoting him at length:

> In general it must be said that [African] consciousness has *not yet* reached the contemplation of a fixed objective, an objectivity. The fixed objectivity is called God, the Eternal, Justice, Nature, natural things. . . . The Africans, however, have *not yet* reached this *recognition of the General*. . . . What we name Religion, the State, that which exists *in and for itself* – in other words, all that is *valid* – all this is not yet at hand. . . . Thus we find nothing other than man in his immediacy: that is man in Africa. As soon as Man as Man appears, he stands in

opposition to Nature; only in this way does he become Man. . . . The Negro represents the Natural Man in all his *wildness and indocility*: if we wish to grasp him, then we must drop all European conceptions.

What we actually understand by 'Africa' is that which is without history and resolution, which is still fully caught up in the natural spirit, and which here must be mentioned as being on the threshold of world history.

Hegel's African has an absolute alterity to the European. This fact conveniently enables us to re-read Hegel's criticism as an insightful classification and taxonomy of the dominant tendencies of both cultures. The written text of Hegel is a century and a half old, but its truth still prevails, with regard to the tendencies, in the present-day forms to be discussed later, of the cultures that Hegel describes.

What are the main characteristics that Hegel finds to distinguish black culture from European culture? Interestingly, Hegel begins by implying that black culture is resilient because reticent, or by nature of its very backwardness untouchable: it is totally *other* and incomprehensible to the European, whereas other cultures, such as the native American, have combated the European and have lost:

> the subjection of the land has meant its downfall. . . . as far as tribes of men are concerned, there are few of the descendants of the first Americans left, since close to seven million men have been wiped out . . . the entire [native] American world has gone under and been suppressed by the Europeans. . . . They are perishing, so that one sees that they do not have the strength to merge with the North Americans in the Free States. *Such peoples of weak culture lose themselves more and more in contact with peoples of higher culture and more intensive cultural training.*[10]

Noteworthy here is the persistent connection of physical and territorial suppression, attachment and extermination with cultural inadequacy.

Hegel's definition of black culture is simply negative: ever-developing European culture is the prototype for the fulfillment of culture in the future; black culture is the antitype, ever on the threshold. Black culture, caught in 'historylessness' (*Geschichtslosigkeit*), is none the less shielded from attack or assimilation precisely by its aboriginal intangibility (though particular blacks themselves may not be so protected). According to Hegel, the African, radical in his effect upon the European, is a 'strange form of self-consciousness' unfixed in orientation towards transcendent goals and terrifyingly close to the cycles and rhythms of nature. The African, first, overturns all European categories of logic. Second, he has no idea of history or progress, but instead allows 'accidents and surprises' to take hold of his fate. He is also not aware of being at a lower stage of development and perhaps even has no idea of what development is. Finally, he is 'immediate' and intimately tied to nature with all its cyclical, non-progressive data. Having no self-consciousness, he is 'immediate' – i.e. *always there* – in any given moment. Here we can see that, being there, the African is also *always already there*, or perhaps *always there before*, whereas the European is *headed there* or, better, *not yet there*.

Hegel was almost entirely correct in his reading of black culture, but what he could not have guessed was that in his very criticism of it he had almost perfectly described the 'there' to which European culture was 'headed'. Like all models that insist on discrete otherness, Hegel's definition implicitly constituted elements of black culture that have only in this century become manifest. Only after Freud, Nietzsche, comparative and structural anthropology and the study of comparative religion could the frantic but ultimately futile coverings of repetition by European culture be seen as dispensable, albeit in limited instances of 'uncovering'. Moreover, the very aspects of black culture which had seemed to define its nonexistence for the phenomenologist Hegel may now be valued as positive terms, given a revised metaphysics of rupture and opening.[11]

The types of repetition: their cultural manifestations

They are after themselves. They call it destiny. Progress. We call it Haints. Haints of their victims rising from the soil of Africa, South America, Asia . . .

(Ishmael Reed, Mumbo Jumbo)

Hegel as a prophet of historical development was notorious but not unique. We may accept that his assumptions have long been and still are shared, particularly the view that culture in history occurs only when a group arrives at a state of self-consciousness sufficient to propel it to 'their destination of becoming a state':

formal culture on every level of intellectual development can and must emerge, prosper and arrive at a point of high flowering when it forms itself into a state and in this basic form of civilization proceeds to abstract universal reflection and necessarily to universal laws and forms.[12]

The world 'state' (*Staat*) is to be defined not as a strict political entity but as any coherent group whose culture progresses from the level of immediacy to self-awareness.

How, then, do European culture and black culture differ in their treatment of the inevitability of repetition, either in annual cycles or in artistic forms? The truly self-conscious culture resists all non-progressive views; it *develops*. Hegel admits the category of change, and even the fact of cyclical repetition in nature, but prefers not to look at it or, if at all, then not from a negative 'oriental' but from a positive 'occidental' standpoint. In such a view, Hegel states:

Whatever development [Bildung] takes place becomes material upon which the Spirit elevates itself to a new level of development, proclaiming its powers in all the directions of its plenitude.[13]

Hence emerges the yet prevailing 'third option' mentioned above as a response to repetition: the notion of progress within cycle, 'differentiation' within repetition.

So the first category where European culture separates itself from 'oriental' and 'African' cultures is in its treatment of physical and natural cycles. This separation into 'occidental' and 'oriental' must seem amusing to anyone familiar with – among other Western texts – Book XV of Ovid's *Metamorphoses*, where the 'pessimistic' and 'oriental' viewpoint appears in the lips of an 'occidental' predecessor of Hegel, Pythagoras:

> Nothing is constant in the whole world. Everything is in a state of flux, and comes into being as a transient appearance . . . don't you see the year passing through a succession of four seasons? . . . In the same way our own bodies are always ceaselessly changing. . . . Time, the devourer, and all the jealous years that pass, destroy all things, and, nibbling them away, consume them gradually in a lingering death. . . . Nor does anything retain its appearance permanently. Ever-inventive nature continually produces one shape from another. . . . Though this thing may pass into that, and that into this, yet the sum of things remains unchanged.[14]

The truth is that cyclical views of history are not 'oriental', but were widespread in Europe well before the inception of historicism, which began not with Hegel but long prior to the nineteenth century (and here one might mention as Hegel's precursors Bacon or Descartes in the Enlightenment, the progressive *consummatio* in the eschatology of Joachim of Floris, the Thomist orientation towards teleology, or even go back to the 'final' triumph of the Heavenly City of St Augustine of Hippo). The debate in Western culture over the question of the shape of history, for most of its course, has been pretty evenly waged, with the advantage perhaps initially even somewhat on the side of the cyclical view. Only with the coming of scientific progressivism (as predicted and formulated by Bacon in *The Advancement of Learning* in 1605) was the linear model able to attain pre-eminence, and then not for some 200 years.[15] The now suppressed (but still to be found) recognition of cycles in European culture has always resembled the beliefs that underlie the religious conceptions of black culture, observing periodic regeneration of biological and agricultural systems.[16]

Black culture highlights the observance of such repetition, often in homage to an original generative instance or act. Cosmogony, the origins and stability of things, hence prevails because it recurs, not because the world continues to develop from the archetypal moment. Periodic ceremonies are ways in which black culture comes to terms with its perception of repetition, precisely by highlighting that perception. Dance often accompanies those ritualistic occasions when a seasonal return is celebrated and the 'rounds' of the dance (as of the 'Ring Shout' or 'Circle Dance') recapitulate the 'roundings' of natural time: Christmas, New Year, funerals, harvest-time.[17] Weddings especially are a re-enactment of the initial act of coupling that created mankind and are therefore particularly well suited as recognitions of recurrence. Conscious cultural observance of natural repetition no longer characterizes European culture. The German wedding festival, for example, the Hochzeit, is today fully divested of its original ties to the repeating New Year's festival Hochgezît, and the sense of an individual marriage as a small-scale image of a larger renewal and repetition is now gone.[18] Outside of the seasonal markings of farmers' almanacs, the sort of precise celebration of time's passage and return that we see in Spenser's Shepheards Calender or in the cyclical mystery plays has been out of general favor in recent times (or simply consigned to the realm of the demonic as in the Mephistophelean 'I've already buried heaps of them! / And always new blood, fresh blood, circulates again. / So it goes on . . .'[19]).

Yet the year does still go around: how does European culture deal with perceived cycles? Recurrent national and sacred holidays are still marked, but with every sense of a progression having taken place between them. The 'New Year's Resolution' and its frequent unfulfillment precisely recalls the attempt and failure to impose a character of progression and improvement onto an often non-progressing temporal movement. Successive public Christmas celebrations and ornamental displays vie to show increase in size, splendor or brightness from previous ones (although, significantly, the realm of sacred ritual, while immediately coexisting with the commercial culture, still works to bar any inexact reptition of religious liturgy, such as in the Nativity service). Other contemporary cycles, such as the four-year intervals of the Olympic Games and presidential elections, fervently need to justify their obvious recurrence by some standard of material improvement or progress: a new or larger Olympic site or new Olympic records; a new or better political party or personality.

In European culture, financial and production cycles have largely supplanted the conscious sort of natural return in black culture. The financial year is the perfect example of this Hegelian subsumption of development within stasis. For repetition must be exact in all financial accounting, given that, globally, capital ultimately circulates within closed tautological systems (i.e. decrease in an asset is either an increase in another asset or a decrease in a liability, both within a corporate firm and in its relations with other firms). The 'annual report' of a business concern, appearing cyclically in yearly or interim rhythm (always on the same 'balance-sheet date'), contains ever the same kinds of symbols about the concern's health or decrepitude. It is only the properties of difference between year$_2$ and year$_1$ (as quantified by numerical changes in the symbols – say, in the cash-flow matrix) which determine how the essentially exact repetitions are to be evaluated and translated into a vocabulary of growth and development. Capital hence will not only necessarily circulate but must consequently also accumulate or diminish, depending on the state of the firm. Economics and business, in their term 'cyclicality', admit the existence and even the necessity of repetition of decline but continually overlay this rupture in the illusion of continuous growth with a rhetoric of 'incremental' or 'staged' development, which asserts that the repetition of decline in a cycle may occur, but occurs only within an overall upward or spiral tendency.[20]

The discourse used of capital in European economic parlance reveals a more general insight about how this culture differs from black culture in its handling of repetition. In black culture, repetition means that the thing *circulates* (exactly in the manner of any flow, including capital flows) there in an equilibrium. In European culture, repetition must be seen to be not just circulation and flow but accumulation and growth. In black culture, the thing (the ritual, the dance, the beat) is 'there for you to pick it up when you come back to get it'. If there is a goal (*Zweck*) in such a culture, it is always deferred; it continually 'cuts' back to the start, in the musical meaning of 'cut' as an abrupt, seemingly unmotivated break (an accidental *da capo*) with a series already in progress and a willed return to a prior series.[21]

A culture based on the idea of the 'cut' will always suffer in a society whose dominant idea is material progress – but 'cuts' possess their charm! In European culture, the 'goal' is always clear: that which always is being worked towards. The goal is thus that which is reached only when culture 'plays out' its history. Such a culture is never 'immediate' but 'mediated' and separated from the present tense by its own future-orientation. Moreover, European culture does not allow 'a succession of accidents and surprises' but instead maintains the illusions of progression and control at all costs. Black culture, in the 'cut', builds 'accidents' into its *coverage*, almost as if to control their unpredictability. Itself a kind of cultural *coverage*, this magic of the 'cut' attempts to confront accident and rupture not by covering them over but by making room for them inside the system itself.[22]

In one unexpected sphere of European consciousness, however, such an orientation towards the 'cut' has survived: on the level of that psychological phenomenon which Freud fully details as the eruption of seemingly unwilled repetitions of the past into the individual's present life – *Wiederholungszwang* or *repetition compulsion*. On the individual psychic level, cultural prohibitions lose their validity. Hence in repetition compulsion, as Freud describes it, repetition – an idiosyncratic and immediate action – has replaced memory, the 'normal' access to the past. Instead of a dialogue about a history already past, one has a restaging of the past. Instead of relating what happened in his or her history (Hegel's category of objectivity), the patient re-enacts it with all the precision of ritual.[23] This obsessive acting-out of the repressed past conflict brings the patient back to the original scene of drama. Repetition compulsion is an example of a 'cut ' or 'seemingly fortuitous' (but actually motivated) repetition that appears in explicit contradiction to societal constraints and standards of behavior. Society would censure the act of unwilled repetition as much as or even more than the original trespass: both are against custom (*Sitte*), or un-moral (*unsittlich*), but the lack of will in repetition compulsion makes it also uncanny (*unheimlich*). Jacques

Lacan's fruitful idea of the *tuché* – the kind of repetition 'that occurs *as if by chance*' – seems to complete the identification here of repetition compulsion as one further aspect of non-progressive culture to have been identified within the limits of the European individual consciousness.[24] By virtue of its accidence (or of its accidental way of showing through), the cycle of desire and repression that underlies repetition compulsion belongs together with the notion of the 'cut'.

Repetition in black culture finds its most characteristic shape in performance: rhythm in music, dance and language.[25] Whether or not one upholds the poet-politician-philosopher Léopold Senghor's attempts to fix the nature of black culture in a concept of *négritude*, it is true that he has well described the role that rhythm plays in it: 'The organizing force which makes the black style is rhythm. It is the most perceptible and least material thing.'[26] Where material is absent, dialectics is groundless. Repetitive words and rhythms have long been recognized as a focal constituent of African music and its American descendants – slave-songs, blues, spirituals and jazz.[27] African music normally emphasizes dynamic rhythm, organizing melody within juxtaposed lines of beats grouped into differing meters. The fact that repetition in some senses is the principle of organization shows the desire to rely upon 'the thing that is there to pick up'. Progress in the sense of 'avoidance of repetition' would at once sabotage such an effort. Without an organizing principle of repetition, true improvisation would be impossible, since an improviser relies upon the ongoing recurrence of the beat.

Not only improvisation but also the characteristic 'call and response' element in black culture (which already, in eliciting the general participation of the group at random, spontaneous 'cuts', disallows any possibility of an *haute culture*) requires an assurance of repetition:

> While certain rhythms may establish a background beat, in almost all African music there is a dominant point of repetition developed from a dominant conversation with a clearly defined alternation, a swinging back and forth from solo to chorus or from solo to an emphatic instrumental reply.[28]

That the beat is there to pick up does not mean that it must have been metronomic, but merely that it must have been at one point begun and that it must be at any point 'social' – i.e. amenable to restarting, interruption or entry by a second or third player or to response by an additional musician. The typical polymetry of black music means that there are at least two, and usually more, rhythms going on alongside the listener's own beat. The listener's beat is a kind of *Erwartungshorizont* (to use a term taken from a quite different area) or 'horizon of expectations', whereby he or she knows where the constant beat must fall in order properly to make sense of the gaps that the other interacting drummers have let fall.[29] Because one rhythm always defines another in black music, and beat is an entity of relation, any 'self-consciousness' or 'achievement' in the sense of an individual participant working towards his or her own rhythmic or tonal climax 'above the mass' would have disastrous results.

While repetition in black music is almost proverbial, what has not often been recognized in black music is the prominence of the 'cut'. The 'cut' overtly insists on the repetitive nature of the music, by abruptly skipping it back to another beginning which we have already heard. Moreover, the greater the insistence on the pure beauty and value of repetition, the greater the awareness must also be that repetition takes place not on a level of musical development or progression, but on the purest tonal and timbric level.

James Brown is an example of a brilliant American practitioner of the 'cut' whose skill is readily admired by African as well as American musicians.[30] The format of the Brown 'cut' and repetition is similar to that of African drumming: after the band has been 'cookin' ' in a given key and tempo, a cue, either verbal ('Get down' or 'Mayfield' – the sax player's name – or 'Watch it now') or musical (a brief series of rapid, percussive drum and horn accents), then directs the music to a new level where it stays with more 'cookin' ' or perhaps a solo – until a repetition of cues then 'cuts' back to the primary tempo. The essential pattern, then, in the typical Brown sequence is recurrent: 'ABA' or 'ABCBA' or 'ABC(B)A' with each new pattern set off (i.e. introduced and interrupted) by the random, brief hiatus of the 'cut'.[31] The ensuing rupture does not cause dissolution of the rhythm; quite to the contrary, it strengthens it, given that it is already incorporated into the format of that rhythm.

In jazz improvisation, the 'cut' – besides uses similar to Brown's – is the unexpectedness with which the soloist will depart from the 'head' or theme and from its normal harmonic sequence or the drummer from the tune's accepted and familiar primary beat. One of the most perfect exemplars of this kind of improvisation is John Coltrane, whose mastery of melody and rhythm was so complete that he and Elvin Jones, his drummer, often traded roles, Coltrane making rhythmic as well as melodic statements and 'cutting' away from the initial mode of the playing.[32]

Black music sets up expectations and disturbs them at irregular intervals: that it will do this, however, is itself an expectation. This peculiarity of black music – that it draws attention to its own repetitions – extends to the way it does not hide the fact that these repetitions take place on the level of sound only. The extension of 'free jazz', starting in the 1960s, into the technical practice of using the 'material' qualities of sound – on the horns, for instance, using overtones, harmonics and subtones – became almost mandatory for the serious jazz musician and paralleled a similar movement on the part of European musicians branching out of the classical tradition. But black music has always tended to imitate the human voice, and the tendency to 'stretch' the limits of the instrument may have been already there since the wail of the first blues guitar, the whisper of the first muted jazz trumpet or the growl of the first jazz trombonist.

The black church must be placed at the center of the manifestations of repetition in black culture, at the junction of music and language. Various rhetorics come into play here: the spoken black sermon employs a wide variety of strategies, such as particularly *epanalepsis* ('because His power brings you power, and your Lord is still the Lord') or *epistrophe* ('give your life to the Lord; give your faith to the Lord; raise your hands to the Lord'). Emphatic repetition most often takes the form of *anaphora*, where the repetition comes at the beginning of the clause (instead of at the beginning and at the end in the first example above, or at the end in the second case). Such a usage of repetition is not limited to the black church, however, and may even be derived in part from the uses of repetition in the key church text, the Bible, as in the following anaphora from Psalms: 'The Lord remaineth a King forever. The Lord shall give strength unto his people. The Lord shall give his people the blessing of peace' (29:10–11).

Both preacher and congregation employ the 'cut'. The preacher 'cuts' his own speaking in interrupting himself with a phrase such as 'praise God' (whose weight here cannot be at all termed denotative or imperative but purely sensual and rhythmic – an underlying 'social' beat provided for the congregation). The listeners, in responding to the preacher's calls at random intervals, produce each time it 'cuts' a slight shift in the texture of the performance. At various intervals a musical instrument such as the organ and often spontaneous dancing accompany the speaker's repetition of the 'cut'. When the stage of highest intensity comes, gravel-voiced 'speaking in tongues' or the 'testifying', usually delivered at a single pitch, gives credence to the hypothesis, that, all along, the very texture of the sound and nature of the rhythm – but not the explicit meaning – in the spoken words have been at issue.

Repetition in black literature is too large a subject to be covered here, but one may say briefly that it has learned from these 'musical' prototypes in the sense that repetition of words and phrases, rather than being overlooked, is exploited as a structural and rhythmic principle. The sermon on the 'Blackness of Blackness' which occurs early in Ralph Ellison's *Invisible Man* lifts the sermonic and musical repetitions (Ellison says he modeled this sequence on his knowledge of repetition in jazz music) directly into view in a literary text – and not just in the repetitions of its title.[33] The *ad hoc* nature of much black folklore and poetry, as well as its ultimate destination in song, tends to encourage the repeating refrain, as in this paean to the fighter Jack Johnson:

> Jack Johnson, he de champion of de worl'
> Jack Johnson, he de champion of de worl'
> Jack Johnson, he de champion
> Jack Johnson, he de champion
> Jack Johnson, he de champion of de worl'[34]

The 'AABBA' repetitive format of so much black folklore and folk-lyric often finds its way into the black novel (as it does into the blues) in unaltered form. In Jean Toomer's *Cane*, the mixture of 'fiction, songs, and poetry', presented against the theme of black culture in transition, provides a fine opportunity to view some typical (and not so typical) uses of repetition in the black novel. From the poem 'Song of the Son' to the very last page, the repetitive forms of black language and rhetoric are prominent until one notices that gradually the entire plot of the novel itself has all along been tending towards the shape of return – the circle:

> O land and soil, red soil and sweet-gum tree,
> So scant of grass, so profligate of pines
> Now just before an epoch's sun declines
> Thy son, in time, I have returned to thee,
> Thy son, I have in time returned to thee.[35]

Toni Morrison continues this use of repetition, particularly in *Song of Solomon*, with Sugarman's song and the final song of 'Jake the only son of Solomon'. In the latter song, where Morrison describes 'the children, inexhaustible in their willingness to repeat a rhythmic, rhyming action game', and the will of black language to 'perform the round over and over again', she puts into words the essential component of her own written tradition. Leon Forrest (most notably in *There is a Tree more Ancient than Eden*) and Ishmael Reed are able to tap a long series of predecessors when they include folk-poems and folklore in their narratives, whose non-progressive form they need not feel constrained to justify.

But particularly in the work of Reed (mainly *Mumbo Jumbo*, but also quite noticeably in *The Free-Lance Pallbearers* and *Flight to Canada*) the kinds of repetition we have seen to have been derived from spoken discourse become only an emblem for much wider strategies of circulation and 'cutting' in black writing and a model, or supplemental meter, for their future employment. The explicitly parodistic thrust of the title *Mumbo Jumbo* first of all rejects the need for making a definitive statement about the 'black situation in America' and already implies, as all parody does, a comparison with, as well as regeneration of, what has come before and the return of a pre-logical past where, instead of words denoting sense, there was 'mumbo jumbo'. Jes Grew, the main 'force' in the novel, besides being disembodied rhythm ('this bongo drumming called Jes Grew') or Senghor's 'la chose la plus sensible et la moins matérielle', is ironically the essence of anti-growth, the avatar of a time 'before this century is out' when, Reed predicts:

> men will turn once more to mystery, to wonderment; they will explore the vast reaches of space within instead of more measuring more 'progress' more of this and more of that.[36]

Jes Grew epidemics appear and reappear *as if by accident*: 'So Jes Grew is seeking its words. Its text. For what good is a liturgy without a text?'[37] But there is no text to be found (besides Jes Grew's 'rhythmic vocabulary larger than French or English or Spanish'), for the 'text' is in fact the compulsion of Jes Grew to recur again and again – the 'trace' of one such appearance is Mumbo Jumbo, the novel, but at the end of it we are left again with the text of the quest, which is the repetition of the seeking.

Reed elides the 'cut' of black culture with the 'cutting' used in cinema. Self-consciously filmable, Mumbo Jumbo ends with a 'freeze frame' not only under-scoring its filmic nature, but also itself an example of a common cueing device for cinematic 'cuts'. Reed, also, in the manner of the jazz soloist, 'cuts' frequently between the various subtexts in his novel (headlines, photographs, handwritten letters, italicized writing, advertisements) and the text of his main narrative. The linear narrative of the detective story and the feature film (opening scenes, title, credits, story, final freeze frame) also structures Mumbo Jumbo, but there is no progressive enterprise going on here, despite such evidence to the contrary. The central point remains clear right to Reed's very last words: 'the 20s were back again. . . . Time is a pendulum. Not a river. More akin to what goes around comes around.'[38] The film is in a loop.

The return of repetition

> Repetition is reality and it is the seriousness of life. He who wills repetition is matured in seriousness. . . . Repetition is the new category which has to be brought to light.
>
> (Kierkegaard, Repetition)

In almost conscious opposition to Hegel's idea of 'progressive' culture, Euro-pean music and literature, perhaps realizing the limitations of innovation, have recently learned to 'foreground' their already present repetitions, 'cuts' and cyclical insights. As European music uses rhythm mainly as an aid in the construction of a sense of progression to a harmonic cadence, the repetition has been suppressed in favor of the fulfillment of the goal of harmonic resolution.[39] Despite the clear presence of consistent beat or rhythm in the common classical forms of the ostinato or the figured bass or any other continuo instrument, rhythm was scarcely a goal in itself and repetition seldom pleasurable or beautiful by itself.

Although the key role of 'recapitulation' in the 'ABA' or 'AABBAA' sonata form (often within a movement itself, as in the so frequently ignored 'second repeats' in Beethoven's major works) is undisputed in theory, in live performance these repetitions often are left out to avoid the undesirability of having 'to be told the same thing twice'. Repeating the exposition, as important as it no doubt is for the 'classical style', is subsumed within and fulfilled by the general category called 'development'. By the time the music does return to the home tonic, in the final recapitulation, the sense is clearly one of repetition with a difference. The momentum has elevated the initial material to a new level rather than merely re-presenting it unchanged.[40] Even though the works of Wagner and his followers represent a break from this traditional formal model of development derived from the sonata form, the Wagnerian leitmotiv, for instance, is anything but a celebration of repetition in music. In the *Ring*, Wagner's consummate vehicle for the leitmotivic style of composition, the recurrent musical phrases are in fact a Hegelian progression or extended accumulation and accretion to an ultimate goal or expression that begins somewhere during the early part of the *Götterdämmerung*, or even starting late in *Siegfried*; the leitmotivs are invested in installments throughout *Das Rheingold* and *Die Walküre* and are then repaid with interest by the end of the *Götterdämmerung*.

In the pre-serial era, only Stravinsky took the already present expectations of concealed repetition in the classical tradition and uncovered them by highlighting them. In *Petrushka* (1911) and *Le Sacre du printemps* (1913) particularly, the use of the 'cut' and the unconcealed repetition is striking. In the First Tableau of *Petrushka*, an abbreviated fanfare and tattoo from snare drum and tambourine set off the first section (rehearsal numbers 1–29) – itself in ABACABA form – from the magic trick (30–2), which is the new, much slower tempo after the 'cut'. The magic trick concludes with a harp glissando and a brief unaccompanied piccolo figure – the next 'cut' – leading to the famous 'Danse russe' (33–46), overtly repetitive in its ABABA form, which then ends in a snare-drum 'cut' (here, in 47, as well as elsewhere – at 62, 69 and 82). In *Le Sacre du printemps* exact repetition within and across sections exceeds anything that had come before it. Moreover, Stravinsky has developed his use of the 'cut', varying the cue-giving instrument.[41] Interestingly, both Stravinsky compositions resemble black musical forms not just in their relentless 'foregrounding' of rhythmic elements and their use of the 'cut' but also in being primarily designed for use in conjunction with dancers.[42]

In European literature, the recovery of repetition in this century is even more striking. Blatant repetitions of the folkloric, traditional or mnemonic sort that had characterized European oral poetry, medieval sagas and other forms of narrative right into late sixteenth-century baroque literature began to be transformed into the pretense of an external reality being depicted, culminating in *literary realism* in the late nineteenth century. The picaresque 'cuts' found in the segmented narratives of *Lazarillo de Tormes* (1554) or even *Don Quixote* (1605) – where a quite literal 'cut' breaks off the manuscript before chapter 9 – were soon becoming a thing of the past, aside from the rare extravagance of Sterne, whose *Tristram Shandy* (1760–7) was an outstanding exception. In a sense, all representational conventions such as literary realism suppress repetition and verbal rhythm in the telling in favor of the illusion of narrative verisimilitude. Thus they would portray an outside world, exhaustible in its manifestations, by the supposedly inexhaustible and ever-renewable resource of writing – hence evading the need for 'repeated descriptions' of that world.

Until recently – particularly before the Dadaists, and their 'cutting' practices; or the cinema-inspired 'montagists', Joyce, Faulkner, Woolf, Yeats and Eliot – this practice had been dominant. Now its dominance has begun to ebb somewhat. With Joyce, most of all, we have realized that the incessant repetition of particular words (such as 'pin' or 'hat' in the early Bloom chapters of Ulysses) are not descriptions of objects seen repeatedly in the external environment and then described, but intentional repetitions of words scattered here and there in a text by its author as if by accident.

Narrative repetition tends to defuse the belief that any other meaning resides in a repeated signifier than the fact that it is being repeated.[43] Among European or American dramatists, Tom Stoppard, in Travesties, comes closest to understanding this insight. This play (in which Joyce plays a major role, along with Tristan Tzara and Lenin) not only refuses to cover up its repetitions but makes clear that there must be a definite 'cut' between them. The 'cut' is explained in the stage directions as a manifestation of the unreliable memory of the main character, Henry Carr:

> One result is that the story (like a toy train perhaps) occasionally jumps the rails and has to be restarted at the point where it goes wild. . . . This scene has several of these 'time slips', indicated by the repetitions of the exchange between BENNETT and CARR about the 'newspapers and telegrams'. . . . It may be desirable to mark these moments more heavily by using an extraneous sound or a light effect, or both. The sound of a cuckoo-clock, artificially amplified, would be appropriate since it alludes to time and to Switzerland.[44]

Underlying this notion of 'time' is not just Freud's idea that repetition is a remedy for the failure of memory, but the related and necessary acceptance of rupture: in the smooth forward progress of the play; in the insistently forward motion of 'time' on those occasions when history 'jumps the rails and has to be restarted at the point where it goes wild'.

The cuckoo-clock in Travesties (borrowed from the 'Nausicaa' chapter of Ulysses, where it has a slightly different function) is the perfect signal for 'cuts', being itself an emblem of time. When in Act I Tzara repeats the word 'DADA' thirty-four times in response to Carr's homily 'It is the duty of the artist to beautify existence', one begins to think that the word's meaning in the context, or even its etymology (interesting as it might be for 'DADA'), are beside the point. A previous 'cut' has made the point more clearly. Tzara (well known in real life for his 'cut-ups', or poems stuck together at random), while trying to seduce Gwendolen, cuts up and tosses the words of Shakespeare's eighteenth sonnet (which she has been reciting) into a hat, shakes them up, and pulls the words one by one out of the hat. Instead of the expected random version of the original, a quite lewd poem, using the same words as the former sonnet, emerges:

Darling, shake thou thy gold buds
the untrimmed but short fair shade
shines –
see, this lovely hot possession growest
so long
by nature's course –
so . . . long – heaven!
and declines,
summer changing, more temperate complexion. . . .[45]

What is the point of Stoppard's 'travesty' of Shakespeare? The cutting of the sonnet should have produced only 'mumbo jumbo', or at best 'clever nonsense', as Carr had called Tzara's prior recitation of the word 'DADA'. But the emergence of the 'new' poem is the emergence of the real: instead of poetry, lechery is Tzara's concern. The true message of the sonnet is not transcendent (about beauty) but immediate, in that it consists of words on paper that can be cut, but which signify only in the context of speaking, not by virtue of being masterfully arranged. Language – even Shakespeare's – here is shown to be, on the most obvious level, exactly what is there, not what is elsewhere: it is of desire, not of meaning.

The outstanding fact of late twentieth-century European culture is its ongoing reconciliation with black culture. The mystery may be that it took so long to discern the elements of black culture already there in latent form, and to realize that the separation between the cultures was perhaps all along not one of nature, but one of force.

Notes

1 Raymond Williams, who calls the word 'culture' 'one of the two or three most complicated words in the English language', gives a thorough survey of the usage of the word in Keywords (London and Glasgow: Fontana, 1976), pp. 76–82.

2 Jonathan Swift, A Tale of a Tub, and Other Satires (1704; London: Dent, 1975), p. 108.

3 Throughout A Tale of a Tub, Swift (like Carlyle after him) employs images of undress and disrobing to denote death and pathology, while equating dress with the power of culture and language.

4 For the English examples, see Simeon Potter, Our Language (Harmondsworth: Penguin, 1976), pp. 59–61, 117–21. For the German attempts to expel foreign – especially French – words, see Robert Reinhold Ergang, Herder and the Foundations of German Nationalism (New York: Columbia University Press, 1931; repr. Octagon, 1966), pp. 131–2, 142–3, 163.

5 Contrast the Lenten admonition for the administering of ashes on Ash Wednesday, a statement of life as inevitable decay – 'Memento, o homo, quod cines es, et in cinerem rivertaris' ('Remember, O man, that dust thou art and to dust thou shalt return') – with Pascal's use (in Fragment d'un traité du vide) of metaphors of human growth when speaking of the development of culture: 'not only each man advances in the sciences day by day, but . . . all men, together make continual progress in them as the universe grows older.' Quoted in The Encyclopedia of Philosophy (New York: Macmillan, 1967), p. 484.

6 Ergang, op. cit., p. 7. See also Leo Weinstein, *Hippolyte Taine* (New York: Twayne, 1972), pp. 81–2.

7 That this separation between 'culture' and 'mass' is a 'central concept of German fascist ideology' and directly leads to the identification of the 'élite' army with the forces of national culture (and, conversely, the transformation of culture into a weapon) is most convincingly shown in Klaus Theweleit, *Männerphantasien 2: Männerkörper – zur Psychoanalyse des weissen Terrors* (Hamburg: Rowohlt, 1980), pp. 47–64, in the chapter 'Masse und Kultur – Der "hochstehende Einzelne" ', and pp. 64–74, 'Kultur und Heer'. Goering is quoted as saying during the Nuremberg trials: 'The Americans simply are not cultured enough to understand the German point of view', in ibid., p. 47.

8 I have chosen for the purposes of this essay to discuss 'European culture' in contrast to 'black culture' meaning the culture of both Africans and Afro-Americans, as the only usefully identifiable entities. I have refrained from any mention of 'American culture', agreeing on the whole with Ralph Ellison when he states 'I recognize no American culture which is not the partial creation of black people', and confident in the assertion that the terms 'European' and 'black' effectively exhaust the major manifestations of culture in contemporary America. See John Hersey (ed.), *Ralph Ellison: A Collection of Critical Essays* (Englewood Cliffs, NJ: Prentice-Hall, 1974), p. 44.

9 Hegel's quote and those below it are from G. W. F. Hegel, *Die Vernunft in der Geschichte*, 5th rev. edn (Hamburg: Felix Meiner, 1955), pp. 216–18; translation and italics are mine.

10 Ibid., pp. 200–1; translation and italics are mine.

11 I use the word 'revised' advisedly here, since the proponents of the 'new openness' never cease to point to historical benefactors going as far back as Plato. My tendency is to pick out Nietzsche as the principal 'revisionist', but the key role of 'rupture' in Freud, Heidegger and Husserl compels their mention here. For Jacques Derrida's views on Nietzsche, for instance, see *Spurs: Nietzsche's Styles*, trans. Barbara Hariow (Chicago, Ill.: University of Chicago Press, 1979); French title *Éperons: Les styles de Nietzsche* (Venice: Corbo e Fiori, 1976). For the idea of 'opening', see Derrida, *Of Grammatology*, trans. Gayatri Chakravorty Spivak (Baltimore, Md: Johns Hopkins University Press, 1977), 'The Hinge' ('La Brisure'), pp. 65–73; French title *De la grammatologie* (Paris: Minuit, 1967). See also Spivak's preface, pp. xxi–xxxviii, for a good introductory summary of the Derridian–Nietzschean critique of 'the metaphysics of presence'. See also Geoffrey Hartman's well-known essay 'The Voice of the Shuttle: Language from the Point of View of Literature', in *Beyond Formalism* (New Haven, Conn.: Yale University Press, 1970), pp. 337–55, and his more recent *Saving the Text: Literature, Derrida, Philosophy* (Baltimore, Md: Johns Hopkins University Press, 1981).

12 Hegel, op. cit., pp. 163, 173; translation is mine.

13 Ibid., pp. 35–6.

14 Ovid, *The Metamorphoses*, trans. Mary M. Innes (Harmondsworth: Penguin, 1970), pp. 339–41, ll. 148–271. Pythagorean ideas on recurrence derive both from a belief in metempsychosis (transmigration of souls – see Plato's *Phaedrus*, 248e–249d) and from Pythagoras' likely belief in a periodic historical cycle (Great Year) of 9000 years or more, which involved an exact repetition in each phase. See J. A. Philip, *Pythagoras and Early Pythagoreanism* (Toronto: University of Toronto Press, 1966), p. 75.

15 The area of philosophy dealing with such issues – the philosophy of history – has been recently (approximately since Croce and Toynbee) rather neglected. The view of Hegel or Augustine on one side, being roughly opposed in their historical concept to Nietzsche or Vico on the other, may be said approximately to delimit the poles of Western discourse on the subject, although the opposition is more fluid than a simple counterposition. For fuller discussion of this broad and highly complex issue, consult: on Bacon, Benjamin Farrington, *Francis Bacon: Philosopher of Industrial Science* (London:

Macmillan, 1973); on the general topic of the philosophy of history, Sir Isaiah Berlin, *Vico and Herder: Two Studies in the History of Ideas* (London: Hogarth Press, 1976), Manfred Buhr, *Zur Geschichte der klassischen bürgerlichen Philosophie: Bacon, Kant, Fichte, Schelling, Hegel* (Leipzig: Phillip Reclam, 1972), Kenneth Burke, *Permanence and Change: An Anatomy of Purpose*, 2nd rev. edn, Library of Liberal Arts (Indianapolis: Bobbs-Merrill, 1965), Karl Löwith, *Meaning in History* (Chicago, Ill.: University of Chicago Press, 1949), and G. A. Wells, *Herder and After: A Study in the Development of Sociology* ('S-Gravenhage: Mouton, 1959). For a recent attempt, see Peter Munz, *The Shapes of Time: A New Look at the Philosophy of History* (Middletown, Conn.: Wesleyan University Press, 1977). See also Sacvan Bercovitch, *Puritan Origins of the American Self* (New Haven, Conn.: Yale University Press, 1975), on the idea of progress and growth in English and American thought in the seventeenth century.

16 See Mircea Eliade, *The Myth of the Eternal Return, or, Cosmos and History*, trans. Willard R. Trask (Princeton, NJ: Princeton University Press, 1974), in the chapters 'Archetypes and Repetition' and 'The Regeneration of Time', pp. 3–92; French title, *Le Mythe de l'éternel retour: archétypes et répétition* (Paris: Gallimard, 1949). See also Eliade, *Patterns in Comparative Religion*, trans. Rosemary Sheed (Cleveland, Ohio: World, Meridian Books, 1963); French title, *Traité d'histoire des religions* (Paris: Gallimard, 1949). Indeed, it may be that black culture in its initial stages is rarely found outside such ritualistic employment, and that 'African Art in Motion' (to use Robert F. Thompson's phrase) is closely linked to those cyclical events that speak of the return and reproduction of a previous event, in which there can be no question of 'progress'.

17 Robert F. Thompson, in 'An Aesthetic of the Cool', *African Forum*, 2, 2 (Fall 1966), p. 85, refers to African religions as 'danced faiths'. See also Eileen Southern (ed.), *Readings in Black American Music* (New York: Norton, 1971), pp. 41–7, for James Eights's description of the yearly 'Pinckster' slave celebrations that originated in the Middle Colonies of early America, and pp. 50–1 for Latrobe's description of festival dances of African origin in New Orleans. For a precise listing of particular dances used in conjunction with particular annual festivals, see Leonore Emery, *Black Dance in the United States, from 1619 to 1970*, University of Southern California, Ph D (Ann Arbor, Mich.: University Microfilms, 1971), the section 'Special Occasion Dances', pp. 50–102.

18 Eliade, *The Myth of the Eternal Return*, p. 26. Keith Thomas, *Religion and the Decline of Magic* (New York: Scribner, 1971), explains this transition in perhaps more unconventional terms.

19 Johann Wolfgang von Goethe, *Faust, Part One*, trans. Louis MacNeice (Oxford: Oxford University Press, 1952), p. 49; Goethe, *Faust*, kommentiert von Erich Trunz (München: Beck, 1972), p. 48, 11. 1371–3: 'Wie viele hab' ich schon begraben! / Und immer zirkuliert ein neues, frisches Blut. / So geht es fort. . .'

20 See Paul M. Sweezy, *The Theory of Capitalist Development* (Oxford: Oxford University Press, 1942), for a fuller – and for Marx's – analysis of this need for upward growth. Max Weber, *The Protestant Ethic and the Spirit of Capitalism* (New York: Scribner, 1958), chs 2 and 5, illustrates the psychological ramifications of this need for growth.

21 The 'cut' is most often signaled by a master drummer, as in the description of the Dagomba 'Atwimewu' drum in John Miller Chernoff, *African Rhythm and African Sensibility: Aesthetics and Social Action in African Musical Idioms* (Chicago, Ill.: University of Chicago Press, 1979), pp. 43–67. See also the cinematic definition of 'cutting, editing, or montage, which changes the picture all at once from one view to another', in Ralph Stephenson and J. R. Debrix, *The Cinema as Art* (Harmondsworth: Penguin, 1965), p. 238.

22 Examples of such systematization of accident are found in all cultures where oracles play a strong role. Two examples are the *sortes Virgilianae* in early European history, or the randomized systematology of the *I Ching*, or 'Book of Changes', in China, which uses random entry into a fixed, stable system.

23 Sigmund Freud, 'Erinnern, Wiederholen, und Durcharbeiten' (1914), in *Studienausgabe*, ed. A. Mitscherlich, A. Richards, J. Strachey, 11 vols (Frankfurt a.M.: S. Fischer, 1969–), *Ergänzungsband: Schriften zur Behandlungstechnik*, pp. 210–11. The definitive statement on *Wiederholungszwang*, insofar as Freud was capable of making such statements, is to be found in 'Jenseits des Lustprinzips' (1920), *Studienausgabe*, vol. 3, pp. 228–9. For the interesting and related phenomenon of *déjà raconté*, see Freud, 'Über fausse reconnaissance [déjà raconté] während der psychoanalytischen Arbeit' (1914), *Studienausgabe*, *Ergänzungsband*, pp. 233–8.

24 Jacques Lacan, *The Four Fundamental Concepts of Psychoanalysis*, trans. Alan Sheridan (London: Hogarth, 1977), p. 54; French title, *Les Quatre Concepts fondamenteaux de la psychanalyse: Le Séminaire, Livre XI* (Paris: Seuil, 1973).

25 Chernoff, op. cit., p. 55: 'In African music, the chorus or response is a rhythmic phrase which recurs regularly; the rhythms of a lead singer or musician vary and are cast against the steady repetition of the response. . . . We [in the West] are not yet prepared to understand how people can find beauty in repetition.' Chernoff puts it well in another passage: 'The most important issues of improvisation, in most African musical idioms, are matters of repetition and change' (p. 111).

26 Quoted in ibid., p. 23: 'Cette force ordinatrice qui fait le style nègre est le rythme. C'est la chose la plus sensible et la moins matérielle.'

27 See ibid., p. 29, on the continuity of African rhythmic forms in America. Also see Ruth Finnegan, *Oral Literature in Africa* (Oxford: Clarendon, 1976), and Southern (ed.), op. cit., *passim*. Also of interest in this regard is Janheinz Jahn, *A History of Neo-African Literature: Writing in Two Continents*, trans. Oliver Coburn and Ursula Lehrburger (London: Faber, 1968); German title, *Geschichte der neoafrikanischen Literatur* (Düsseldorf and Cologne: Eugen Diederichs Verlag, 1966).

28 Chernoff, op. cit., p. 55. Although the beat need not have been begun and kept from a conductor's initial count (because it may have in the interim 'cut' or changed to another meter), it must be there at every point to 'pick up' or to 'follow'.

29 The term as I use it derives from the work of H. R. Jauss, as in the article 'Literatur als Provokation der Literatur-Wissenschaft', contained in the collection *Literaturgeschichte als Provokation* (Frankfurt a.M.: Suhrkamp, 1970).

30 Chernoff, op. cit., p. 55.

31 Thompson, in his *African Art in Motion: Icon and Act in the Collection of Katherine Coryton White* (Los Angeles, Calif.: University of California Press, 1974), pp. 10–13, takes Hegel's term *Aufheben*, meaning 'a simultaneous suspension and preservation', and uses it of the African 'cut' in the concept of 'Afrikanische [sic] Aufheben'. Thompson's term must be mentioned here as a good approximation of the nature of the 'cut', in which every previous pattern that had first been 'cut' away from still exists in suspended form until it is 'cut' back to.

32 See Bill Cole, *John Coltrane* (New York: Macmillan, 1976), pp. 72–3 and *passim*.

33 See Ellison's interview with John Hersey in Hersey (ed.), op. cit., pp. 2–3, 11.

34 Lawrence W. Levin, *Black Culture and Black Consciousness: Afro-American Folk Thought from Slavery to Freedom* (New York: Oxford University Press, 1977), p. 432.

35 Jean Toomer, *Cane* (New York: Boni & Liveright, 1923), p. 21. For the circular form of the novel, see Brian J. Benson and Mabel M. Dillard, *Jean Toomer* (New York: Twayne, 1980), pp. 82–6. See also Addison Gayle, *The Way of the New World: The Black Novel in America* (Garden City, NY: Doubleday, 1975), p. 98.

36 Ishmael Reed, *Mumbo Jumbo* (New York: Bantam, 1972), pp. 247, 28.

37 Ibid., prologue, p. 5.

38 Ibid., p. 249.

39 Schenker's analyses present the extreme pole of the view that linear, descending cadential resolution is the aim of every tonal work. For discussion of this idea, see Maury Yeston (ed.), *Readings in Schenker Analysis and other Approaches* (New Haven, Conn.: Yale University Press, 1977).

40 For two splendid analyses of the role and consequence of repetition in the sonata, see Donald F. Tovey, *Essays in Musical Analysis*, vol. 1: *Symphonies* (London: Oxford University Press, 1978), pp. 10–14; Charles Rosen, *The Classical Style: Haydn, Mozart, Beethoven* (London: Faber, 1977), pp. 30–4. Also see W. H. Hadow, *Sonata Form* (London: Novello, n.d.).

41 A fairly complete catalog of 'cuts' in *Sacre* follows, with the instruments involved and practice numbers in brackets: violin (12); timpani and brass drum (37); clarinet and piccolo (48); piccolo and flute (54); viola, cello, double bass, tuba, trumpet (57); bass drum (72); clarinet and violin (93); cornet and viola (100), addition of tuba, bassoons, timpani and bass drum (103–18); bass clarinet (141); piccolo, flute and timpani (201).

42 Chernoff, op. cit., pp. 65–7, speaks very well on the essential inseparability of drumming and the dance. He quotes one African drummer (p. 101) as saying 'every drumming has got its dance'.

43 For a brief and fascinating philosophical speculation on one kind of narrative repetition, see Jacques Derrida, 'Ellipsis', in *Writing and Difference*, trans. Alan Bass (Chicago, Ill.: University of Chicago Press, 1978), pp. 294–300; French title, *L'Écriture et la différence* (Paris: Seuil, 1967). See also Daniel Giovannangeli, *Écriture et répétition: approche de Derrida* (Paris: Union Générale d'Éditions, 1979), for the effects upon the signifier/signified relationship of repetition.

44 Tom Stoppard, *Travesties* (New York: Grove, 1975), p. 27, Act I.

45 Ibid., pp. 53–4.

3   Jay Edwards

Structural analysis of the Afro-American trickster tale

Introduction

The purpose of structural analysis is often unappreciated, even by those who could find the greatest benefit in this method.[1] It is clear, I believe, that those of us who see structural analysis as the key which unlocks the central meanings of all shared, complex forms of human culture have not yet succeeded in communicating the critically important role of this method to the majority of students of culture. It is often surprisingly difficult to convince the folklorist, the cultural materialist, the art historian or the architect that the traditional forms of African-based folk and vernacular culture are highly intricate, multi-dimensional systems of communication, worthy of first-rate scholarly attention. Whether the widespread academic preference for drawing simple pictures of complex things springs from a crypto-ethnocentrism on the part of some who view superficially uncomplicated forms of folk culture from the perspective of the supposed 'superiority' of hyper-specialized Western cultural forms, or whether it stems primarily from the demands placed on scholars repeatedly and publicly to display elements of empirical truth in simple and palatable form, I cannot say.

An essential role of structuralism is to provide scholars of world culture with a bulwark against the temptation to gloss over and thereby diminish the significance of the cultural achievements of people who have lived in a world of relative material simplicity coupled with a rich mental and social life. If it is to accomplish this aim, structuralist scholarship must be judged by clearly established canons. A keystone among these principles is the rule of ethnographic adequacy. This principle holds that no description of a cultural system is adequate unless it provides investigators with an understanding such that they could produce culturally appropriate behavior given the same context-specific information available to the native. This principle holds ethnographers to a level of professionalism seldom actually attained in ethnology, though more closely approximated in linguistics. Its implication is that students of culture must totally deconstruct the cultural institution under investigation. Their goal must be to reveal all of its levels of rule-governed structure and all of its component parts, as well as its major extra-systemic connections and functions.

As anthropologists, folklorists and linguists, we deal repeatedly with patterns of culture which are realized as many individually distinct forms but which are united through shared systems of cultural cognitive organization. The structure of any such system of communication, whether family relationships, vernacular dwellings, sentences of a dialect or folktales, is hierarchical and complex. Numerous studies have pointed to the fact that the structures of such a system are roughly analogous to the structures of sentences. These structures are composed of a hierarchy of constituent parts. Each level plays its own special role in the make-up of the entire shared cognitive structure. Unless investigators are willing to go to the trouble of unveiling all the various levels and their interrelationships, they will be unable to account for the system in the totality of its formal and functional dimensions. Sooner or later questions raised by the elements they leave unanalyzed will return to plague them.

Sets of interrelated constituent parts operating at different levels of the structural hierarchy carry different forms of meaning. They also carry semantic, logical and syntactic components simultaneously. Such systems demand to be unpacked and explained. They carry inherent meanings that range from cultural universals at the higher levels of abstraction, to context-specific communications at the surface levels. Some configurations within these structures provide the native interpreter (myth-maker, poet, architect) with natural vehicles for the development of metaphoric messages and images. Unless investigators have fully and correctly identified the configurations of structure, they will be unable to account for the productivity of the system in terms of the poetics of its cultural context.

All of this requires that the investigator develop what Lévi-Strauss refers to as a mechanical model of the cognitive system. A major component of this model is an analytical vocabulary sufficiently detailed that it can provide a complete and unambiguous discussion of the several constituents of the model and their operations. Unless investigators fit their technical terminology to the level of complexity of their system, they run the risk of confounding their readers and themselves as well, through ambiguity. For example, as I have tried to show elsewhere, the use by pioneering investigators of the technical terms 'function', 'motifeme' and 'mytheme', to refer to constituents operating simultaneously at different levels in the structural hierarchy, has had the effect of masking certain aspects of the organization of the folktale and myth.[2] The ultimate result, I believe, has been to retard the development of fully adequate structural models of oral narrative. The principle I have adopted in previous research on the folktale is that, if through comparative study there is reason to believe that a level or pattern of structure is consistently represented in the texts of a genre, then that level or pattern must be formally inserted into a structural model of the genre, and its role explored. It is even better, heuristically at least, to insert potential components not completely understood or analyzed than it is to omit them entirely. If analysis of apparently simple folktales reveals the regular occurrence of complex structural components, then how can we avoid naming and discussing them? The critic's call for simpler structural models must then arise out of a new comparative analysis of the same genre, demonstrating the superfluous nature of components of the previous model, or it must represent an unwillingness to do the work involved in understanding the inherent complexities of the system. For my part, omit nothing inherent, and then let Occam's razor govern.

The purpose of this paper is twofold. I shall begin by exploring briefly a few of the more significant recent contributions to the development of structural models for the African-based folktale. I shall proceed on the assumption that readers are generally familiar with the contributions of Vladimir Propp, Alan Dundes and Claude Lévi-Strauss.[3] Only recent contributions stemming from the work of these pioneers will be reviewed. It matters little that most of the contributions I shall touch on have been made in the study of African, rather than Afro-American, folklore. Both traditions share similar narrative structures. The Afro-American tales we have dealt with have many analogues in West African oral literature.

The second part of the paper will be devoted to what I feel are several of the more interesting open questions in the development of a fully adequate structural model of the folktale. I shall explore, if only briefly, the basic components of a structural model of the folktale, the role of semantics in that model, the place of transformational rules, and the problem of culture-specific metaphoric formulations of structural elements.

Recent contributions

Hermeneutics

A recent major study on the West African trickster well illustrates the problems involved in analysis of African (or any) oral literature by even well-read and well-intentioned scholars who undertake comparative analyses without the benefit of structuralist methodology. Robert D. Pelton, a Catholic priest, focuses on the major trickster figures of the Asante, Fon, Yoruba and Dogon in his recent book, *The Trickster in West Africa: A Study of Mythic Irony and Sacred Delight* (1980).[4]

Although Pelton also finds value in the symbolic anthropology of Mary

Douglas and Victor Turner, he simply does not consider the majority of published structural interpretations of African oral literature. Indeed, he specifically rejects any form of comparison based on structural models. In considering
the value of various approaches in analyzing Asante Anansi tales, he states:

> the story of Ananse and Hate-to-be-contradicted shows that neither motif-
> analysis nor a purely descriptive morphology will disclose the deepest
> meanings of Ananse and other tricksters . . . the very range of the oppositions
> in this story gives it a depth that a listing of motifs and submotifs cannot
> exhaust.[5]

It is apparent that Pelton is operating under the assumption that the most that
structural analysis has to offer is a relatively shallow description of the principal
syntagmatic elements of the tale, one which would reveal little that the interested
reader could not uncover without resorting to formal analysis. Pelton provides
no alternative to structuralism, and therefore neglects detailed comparisons in
his exposition of the trickster. What, then, defines the trickster character and the
trickster-tale genre? What exactly is shared between the tales of a genre or a
culture? Why does each culture select its favorites from among the total
repertoire of tale types, and what messages does it abstract from the various tale
types it finds most productive? These questions are left unanswered by Pelton.
Because his comparison is not based on structures, the emphasis is shifted from
degrees of sharing among the tales to what is unique about them. Since each plot
is ultimately unique, the only thing that unites them is the ludic unpredictability
of the trickster character himself. The reader is provided an imaginative but
rather amorphous interpretation of the role of the trickster in the life of West
African peoples. That interpretation is rather like a list of possible functions (i.e.
boundary testing and maintenance, liminality, a force for change), which are
variously emphasized by the trickster in the different tales.

Syntagmatic analysis: French neo-Proppians

Following the lead of Vladimir Propp and Alan Dundes, two French scholars
have contributed to our understanding of the syntagmatic structure of the
folktale. In 1970 Claude Bremond published an article on the French folktale in
which he suggested two important modifications of Propp's original syntagmatic
schema. Instead of giving Propp's 'functions', or elemental units of plot, equal
weight within the narrative, Bremond suggests that functions are grouped into
triads which he calls 'elemental sequences'. The first function of each sequence
states a potential, such as Lack or Task to Accomplish; the second describes
the process of actualizing the potentiality, for instance, Plan or Deceit; and the
third function announces the accomplishment of the original aim or its
failure, i.e. Success, Lack Liquidated or Failure. Elemental sequences are inter-
twined or chained together in various ways in folktale narratives to produce

plot complexity. Bremond notes that the same event may perform multiple functions from the perspective of either a single actor or each of two different actors.[6]

Bremond's second modification of the Propp/Dundes theory of syntagmatic analysis is that all plot sequences move in a continuous cycle from a state of deficiency through a state of improvement to a satisfactory state, and through a procedure of degradation back to a state of deficiency once again. Action generally begins at either a satisfactory state or a state of deficiency. Thus a single triad of motifemes describes movement either out of a state of deficiency, or into such a state. The European Märchen-type tale generally terminates in a satisfactory state for the hero. The tripartite elemental sequence may be complicated by the insertion of one or more secondary sequences, such as tasks, tests and contests which are embedded into the main plot. Bremond then goes on to classify various sequences of motifemes identified in the French folktale.

In a series of articles, Denise Paulme further develops the theory of the syntagmatic structure of the African folktale.[7] More relevant to our immediate subject is Paulme's article on the 'Morphologie du conte africain'.[8] She begins by pointing out that syntagmatic theory, as developed by Propp, did not go very far towards analyzing the differences between tales. Her aim, like that of Bremond, is to develop a classification of folktales based on differences between their syntagmatic structures. Paulme follows Bremond in assuming that each tale is composed of one or more elemental sequences of motifemes, which she describes as propositions involving the substitution of a predicate by its opposite (Lack/Lack Liquidated, etc.). Narrations are made up of sequences of functions, held together by cause and effect.

Plots differ from one another in two ways. In simple plots, branching is possible, so that a sequence that begins with a single goal may end in different ways. The creative narrator is free to select from among various possibilities at certain points in the narrative. In addition, complex plots may be composed by the simultaneous intertwining of two or more simple plots. Paulme follows Bremond in assuming that all elemental sequences involve some combination of ascending or descending actions, each terminating in a fixed state of Lack or Success (see Figure 3.1). Most African narratives involve progress from Lack to its negation, but some involve the reverse process, in which a stable situation is disrupted, ending in punishment or death due to a fault of the actor.

Paulme describes three forms of simple plot (Ascending, Descending and Cyclical), and four complex plots (the Spiral, the Mirror, the Hourglass and the Complex type). The Spiral type is one which cycles through several sequences of Lack/Lack Liquidated, but in which each successive state of equilibrium has been raised to a new level, the final state not being the equal of the initial state. Paulme's Mirror plot is identical in form to the Foolish Imitation or Sorcerer's Apprentice type, which elsewhere I have labeled Class II.[9] The Hourglass plot is one in which there is an ascending progression on the part of the hero, coupled

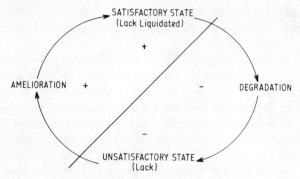

Figure 3.1   The cycle of narrative action in the folktale
Source: After Denise Paulme, 'Morphologie du conte africain', Cahiers d'études
africaines, 12 (1972)

with a simultaneous descending movement on the part of the anti-hero, the two
having exchanged positions by the end of the narration. The Complex type is
what I refer to as Compound. It is composed through the chaining together of
otherwise well-formed simple tales to produce more complex and lengthy
forms. Paulme illustrates several variants of each of these types and points out
that other forms of plot construction are possible in African folktales.

While the analyses of Bremond and Paulme represent advances over simple
syntagmatic analyses of African folktales, such as those of Dundes and Haring,[10]
they still leave open questions. Neither description deals with the important
problem of the nature of the semantic basis of the tale sequence. Paulme states
that the modification of the initial state involves a logical operation supported by
semantic content. She does not continue this line of reasoning further, and the
reader is left to assume that the semantic component is of a surface nature and
unique to each tale.

Neither author comes to grips with the question of a possible rule-governed
syntax for the kernel tale. Neither discusses whether the tale type or sub-genre is
best viewed analytically from the perspective of a single character role (hero,
trickster) or from some more inclusive perspective. If one actor is taken as basic
for analytical purposes, what principle are we to adopt to determine which of the
characters is the most basic?

An additional open question concerns the nature of the basic motifemic
element at the deepest (most abstract) level of its realization within the kernel
tale. Bremond apparently assumes that the three motifemic elements of the
elemental sequence are of equal structural weight within the kernel tale. Paulme,
in describing the modification of the initial state by the substitution of an
opposite predicate, appears to assume that the various motifemes (i.e.
Lack, Encounter, Trick, Triumphant Test, Lack Liquidated, etc.) are distributed
between two sets of super-motifemic constituents: Degradation/Lack, and

Amelioration/Equilibrium. In both cases the semantic content of these constituents is assumed to be minimal or nonexistent.

Recently the Israeli folklorist, Heda Jason, has suggested an interesting modification of the syntagmatic theory. Borrowing from Bremond, Jason suggests that every narrative is composed of a series of tripartite moves. Each move has three functions – A, stimulus; B, response; and C, result (compensation) – and consists of interaction between only two roles: hero and donor. Her theory is generative in its basic form, because each tale represents an expansion of a single move. Expansions introduce multiple layers in which moves are embedded into one another and in which named characters may play different roles. Another component of narrative is called 'connectives'. These provide information or transfers of state, time or place. There is much merit in Jason's approach, although Bremond objects to her removal of the semantic concepts of reward and punishment (Improvement, Deterioration) from the structural component.[11]

Syntagmatic analysis: American neo-Proppians

To my knowledge, few authors have attempted to come to grips with the questions just raised. Perhaps the approach that promises the most productive answers is that of generative-transformational grammar (GT). This approach was first suggested as appropriate to folktale analysis by Robert A. Georges in his 1970 article on 'Structure in Folktales'.[12] His description of the role of GT theory in folklore narrative analysis remains perhaps the clearest yet published. Georges's main criticism of earlier syntagmatic studies is that they fail to account for dynamic operations, rather than just states, in narrative structures. GT analyses begin at the highest level of abstraction in the narrative structure and generate the various types of tales through sets of rules or constraints on elaboration. The product of the generative process within the deep structure is kernel narratives: strings of basic motifemes. Through the application of transformational rules, these are elaborated into more complex tale forms.

Similar approaches have been suggested for the analysis of African folktales by George Horner and by Oja Arewa and G. M. Shreve.[13] All three generative models resemble one another in that their view of the deep structure is essentially syntagmatic. The deep structure of the folktale consists of strings of constituents at each level within the structure. To their credit, these models articulate the various structural levels in a generative hierarchy.

In Georges's model, semantic content is introduced into the deep structure at the fourth (lowest) level of development. Here motifemic slots, such as Lack, are given semantic content ('There was no water'). All superior levels consist of pure structural pattern only:

1 Move/Countermove
2 Initial motifemic cluster/Final motifemic cluster

3 Lack, Task, Interdiction + Violation/Deception + Consequence, Task Accomplished, Lack Liquidated

4 There was no water + (etc.)

As in other syntagmatic models, the nature of the logical relations between structural constituents in the deep structure is assumed to be no more complex than mere opposition.

A syntagmatic-paradigmatic-generative approach: the LSU school

In 1978 I published a monograph in which I attempted to combine the benefits of the paradigmatic approach originated by Claude Lévi-Strauss with the syntagmatic approach of Propp and Dundes, and the generative-transformational approach of Noam Chomsky.[14] Like Georges, I viewed the folktale as being composed of a hierarchical series of oppositions in which the constituents of the more abstract levels are repeatedly segmented to generate the output of the next, more concrete levels (see Figure 3.2). This theory of folktale structure was, however, distinct from the theories of both the French and the American neo-Proppians.

I assumed, first, that the complete, well-formed folktale is composed of five basic components. The first two (formulaic opening and atemporal introduction) and the last two (concluding element and formulaic closing) play no role in the narrative structure of the tale, but they are regularly included in folktale narratives in order better to fit them into the social context. Etiological conclusions, for instance, lie outside the main structure of the narrative, but function as literary devices which are often considered to play an important didactic role by the tale-tellers and their audience. Only the third component, the narrative body, contains complex hierarchical structure.

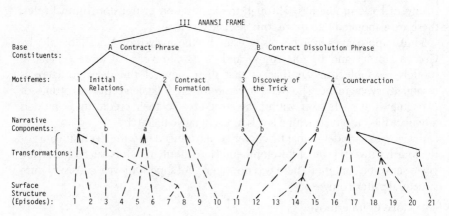

Figure 3.2 Generalized Anansi story structure

Second, my structural model evolved out of a general semiotic and anthropological theory of the folktale as a universal cultural institution. Following Lévi-Strauss, I reasoned that the tale functions as an oral literary device for exploring the logical consequences which flow from the conjunction of two or more pairs of sememic contrasts.[15] Because cognitively established binary oppositions (such as Life/Death, Male/Female, and Consanguinal Kin/Affinal Kin) cannot be easily resolved, the folktale provides a method of interrelating and mediating them. It performs its function by setting out an array of possibilities in narrative form for the appreciation of children and others. Folktales often deal with basic moral-philosophical dilemmas and the cultural norms for handling them. As T. D. Beidelman recently stated, trickster-based 'anomalies serve didactically to stimulate . . . moral imagination so as to understand existential dilemmas which involve choice in conduct and ends'.[16]

Since most normative postulates are semantically complex, the folktale must necessarily deal with more than one set of oppositions if it is to perform its function. These oppositions are conjoined and dramatized through the actions of actors and mediators. The various positive and negative states (Lack/Lack Liquidated, Social Harmony/Social Disharmony) are conjoined by pairs into sets until all possible combinations have been realized or until the mediation process is complete. In paradigmatic perspective, then, the folktale should be viewed as a kind of table of permutations through which the possible combinations of positive and negative states of paired superstructural ideas are interrelated and arrayed linearly. The most basic folktale structure consists of a frame composed of four cells, with each cell representing a unique combination of semantic valence states $(+ -, - -, - +, + +)$.

All of this implies that, somewhere in its most abstract levels of structure, the folktale is not just semantic but polysememic. It pulls together semantically unrelated sets of ideas, reduces them to elemental semantic forms which I call 'superstructural ideas' and distributes them by pairs as a framework for plot action. This implies that the deep structure is not best viewed as being composed of a linear or syntagmatic sequence of constituents. It is, rather, a paradigmatic complex in which superstructural ideas are associated with one another in different combinations. Such a complex is conveniently modeled as a set of cells arrayed as in a componential analysis (see Figure 3.3).

A third distinction between the LSU (Louisiana State University) theory of the folktale and those of the neo-syntagmatic theorists concerns the nature of syntactic relations within the deep structure of the tale. It is my view that there is a logically complex relationship between the various slots, or semantically loaded constituents (motifemes), in the deep structure. The model which best accounts for the facts is analogous to the one developed by Claude Lévi-Strauss in his famous paper on myth analysis.[17] This formula has been analyzed by Pierre and Elli Köngäs Maranda[18] and by Sunday Anozie,[19] and it has been shown to have very wide applicability in human oral literature.

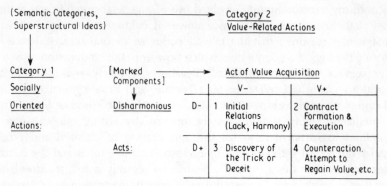

Figure 3.3   Trickster tale base paradigm
Note: Cells 1–4 = Motifemes

In Lévi-Strauss's model, as it applies to the most elemental level of tale structure, only two character roles are found. At the highest level of abstraction, action always occurs only between two roles, though either may be realized by more than one character at the surface level (twins, for instance). The roles are distinguished from each other structurally. One character (or 'term'), called Role A, is always univocal. This role carries but a single relationship to a specified superstructural idea, usually lack of something of Value (V−) or lack of Social cohesion or contract (S−). The second role, Role B, is ambiguous or bivocal with respect to the same superstructural idea. The role is characterized by first one relationship, say S+, and then its opposite, S−. This role is normally assumed by the trickster or mediator.

The kernel tale is segmented into four basic deep-structural constituents called motifemes. In the first, Role A suffers Lack, Task, Social Separation, etc. In the second, Role B offers to Liquidate the Lack, or reverse the condition, etc. In the third slot, Role B reverses his intention or violates his contract (by stealing the Value, for instance). In the fourth slot of the Lévi-Strauss frame, a moral is presented, for instance: 'The function of (promised) Value is to subvert Dupes by tempting them to place their trust in Tricksters.' This last element or motifeme is generally implied but unstated in the tale narrative. In place of a stated moral, the fourth slot may be represented in character action by the initiation of counter-action or the beginning of a new kernel plot. Thus, although only three necessary narrative constituents occur in the deep-structural models of both Lévi-Strauss and Bremond, the syntax or logic of the relationships between them is quite different. The syntagmatic models are all based on the changing relationships of a single character role (undergoing degradation to Lack, for instance), while the paradigmatic model of Lévi-Strauss centers on the inter-relationships between the two character roles. Many folklorists have noted that action in oral narrative is generally divided into units in which only two roles are involved at one time. The Lévi-Strauss model accounts neatly for this observation.

The paradigmatic model of the deep structure of the folktale (kernel) is substantially more complex than any syntagmatic model. Not only are two character roles and the relations between them inherent to this model, but so are two sets of elemental semantic concepts or superstructural ideas. The significance of this observation is great, but apparently little appreciated by those who study folktales from either the hermeneutic or the neo-Proppian positions. I will suggest only one example of its implications. It is generally assumed that the character who plays the trickster in African and Afro-American tales assumes his unique and powerful role by virtue of his crossing and violating boundaries. He gives, or he takes away, by trickery or guile. In most Afro-American tales he is a power broker. It is he who has the power to deceive, for either his own benefit or that of others. In other words, he plays Role B in Lévi-Strauss's model. It should be noted, however, that the trickster can and does assume the other role, Role A. An example common to both African and Afro-American cultures is found in the tale of 'The Gift of Flight'.

Anansi, Tortoise, etc., wishes to go to a feast being given by the Sky King, Sky God, etc., but he cannot fly. He wishes for the power of flight. The birds take pity on him and give him feathers, or, alternatively, they carry him to the feast. Once there, Trickster disgraces himself through his gluttony or, worse, through some (embedded) trickery which he employs to obtain all of the food. This, naturally, sours the opinion of the birds towards him. On the way back home they remove his feathers, or drop him, or they abandon him in the Sky God's palace. Falling to earth, he survives in various ways, but seldom unscathed. The variety of the natures of his landings has stimulated numerous concluding etiological explanations in the different versions of this tale. The important thing is that in this (and other Anansi-type tales) Trickster also assumes the role of the Dupe, while the birds have become the power broker, Role B. The significance of these role reversals has not been discussed by students of the trickster to my knowledge. It is of interest that such trickster role reversals are exceptionally common in certain cultures – for instance, among the Coyote trickster tales of the Navahos and other American Indian groups. The preference for different kinds of trickster roles among different cultures raises interesting questions about the function of the trickster, and whether any universal definition of the trickster is possible.

The model of the folktale originally described in my The Afro-American Trickster Tale did not include a complete grammatical description. The phrase-structure rules for the development of kernel tales were not formalized. The role of the transformational component was only hurridly sketched in, and the manner in which the surface level (incidents) was to be mapped into the various structural slots (called motifemes and narrative components) was omitted. Finally, the way in which the Lévi-Straussian syntactic model was to be incorporated into the phrase-structure rules was not specified with sufficient clarity, raising questions from several reviewers.[20] On the other hand, rather careful consideration was given to the role of the structure of the tale in the social life of Afro-American people.

From the perspective of this model, two aspects of the Afro-American trickster tale quickly became clear. Though these tales were of several different types, one principal type (called Class I) predominated in almost every collection. I argued that the significance of this type lay in the special role it played in the daily lives of Afro-Americans. It provided a cultural cognitive model which enabled them to reflect on the moral dilemmas imposed upon them under conditions of servitude and economic bondage. The structure of this tale type embodied a syllogism or metaphor which captured a central ethical dilemma of Afro-American life. The syllogism could be read something like this: 'Dupe's Trust is to Dupe's Loss, as Trickster's (asocial) cunning Plan is to Trickster's Acquisition of Value'. In other words, 'Trickster strategies involve the maximization of short-term (economic) gain at the expense of long-term social cohesion.' Though neither trickery nor trust is clearly favored in the folktale cycles (the trickster loses as well as wins), the problem of which strategy to adopt was one which constantly cropped up in the lives of people forcibly prevented from developing cooperative social contracts for their own long-range self-improvement. The favoring of a specific structural type can be accounted for only by the clarifying ethical vision it provided in the context of recurring moral and philosophical problems. It is no accident that the climax of the trickster tale is characterized by a double twist which occurs in the instant that the Dupe realizes not only that he has lost his Value, but that Trickster's friendship was false and motivated only by greed. Unlike the majority of European folktales, Afro-American tales invariably terminate in a condition of disharmony between the two principal actors caused by the violation of an agreement and an unreciprocated exchange of value. These characteristics, clearly represented in the structural model at the motifemic level, are not characteristics that predominate in many tale-telling traditions. Had Africans migrated voluntarily into the New World, and had they found social and economic equality here, the pattern of tale types selected into their repertoire would probably have been substantially different.

Generative-transformational analysis of a folktale

With this all-too-brief background, I shall now illustrate my remarks by presenting a structural analysis of the deep structure of a single Afro-American trickster tale. If structural analysis is to be worth the rather considerable effort expended in close reading and formal coding of numerous examples of a genre, it must provide significant benefits. One of those benefits is that it should establish for each tale a set of specific and ordered elements which provide the basis of any point-by-point comparison with other tales. It is only through a systematic comparison of all of the principal levels embodied in a corpus of tales that genres and sub-genres may be defined. The comparison of structures establishes precisely those features that the tales have in common and the manner in which they differ.

A side-benefit of the structural approach is that it often uncovers covert organizational similarities shared between forms that at first view would be assigned to different classes or types. It is not uncommon for shared unity of structure to be masked by surface differences so dramatic that they belie any degree of obvious similarity between the different forms. Yet the unity between them may be strong. This truism is particularly well illustrated in the case of comparative folktale study.

One technical point should be mentioned before I begin my sample analysis. In some of my models I have found it convenient for coding purposes to group together certain classes of actions which the syntagmatic theorists prefer to distinguish. I refer specifically to the concepts 'Degradation' and 'Amelioration'. These concepts often do not fit comfortably into a binary coding system such as that required for a GT analysis. In the interpretation of narrative action it is sometimes difficult to know just when Degradation has occurred, except in reference to some final act of Lack. In our opinion, these concepts are so closely tied to their resultant conditions of state (i.e. Degradation to Lack, and Amelioration to Lack Liquidated, etc.) that at the deepest levels of folktale structure they may be conveniently encoded with the same symbols (for example, V+ for Value-oriented actions and V+ for Value acquisition). It is in this way that they are encoded at the motifemic level.

Folktale: 'Dupe Tiger as Riding Horse'

As an example of this method, I shall analyze a relatively simple tale. It is one of the most popular of all themes in the Afro-American tradition, being found in the French and British West Indies, in the Brer Rabbit tales of the southeastern United States, and in the Creole French of Louisiana. This tale is transcribed from a modified Jamaican Creole.

 I Here is the tale of Bra Nansi's old riding horse.

 II a Tiger and Anansi were fond of the same girls,

 II b but Tiger was not as cunning as Anansi.

 III 1 Tiger was very handsome and he used to visit the two girls every week.

  2 Nansi noticed how the two girls were becoming sweet on Tiger.

  3 One day Anansi went to the girls' house and said, 'Girls, I'll show you that Tiger is only my father's old riding horse.'

  4 'How is that?' they said.

  5 'Next time I come to call on you, you will see,' he said.

6 The next Sunday Tiger visited the girls; they told him what Anansi had said.

7 Tiger flew into a rage and went running in search of Anansi.

8 Tiger arrived at Anansi's house and knocked on the door. He was plenty vexed.

9 Anansi called in a very weak voice, 'Yeeeas, whooo there?'

10 Tiger demanded to be let in.

11 Anansi, lying in bed, told him to enter.

12 Anansi said he would like to offer Tiger tea, but he was feeling so poorly right now he couldn't rise.

13 Tiger asked why Anansi had told the girls that he was only Anansi's father's old riding horse.

14 Tiger told Anansi that he wanted him to come and tell the girls that what he had said was untrue.

15 Anansi said, 'I never said it, and I would come, but I can't walk at all.'

16 'I'll tell you what,' said Tiger. 'If I carry you on my back, will you come?'

17 'Well, if you insist, I will do it!' said Anansi.

18 Anansi climbed on Tiger's back, but acted as if he was too weak and would fall off.

19 'You'll have to get my saddle,' said Anansi.

20 'OK, I'll do anything, just so you come,' said Tiger.

21 Next, Anansi had Tiger get the bridle.

22 'What you going to do with that?' asked Tiger.

23 'That's so if I start to fall, I can catch up,' replied Anansi.

24 Tiger started to go, but after a few steps Anansi fell off.

25 'I can't stay on your back without those little things called spurs,' cried Anansi.

26 'OK, OK, I don't care what you do, let's get on with it,' said Tiger.

27 As they were riding towards the girls' house, they went through a wood.

28 'Hold up here, one minute,' said Anansi, 'I need to cut a whip so I can let you know when to go slower.'

29 Tiger agreed, and finally they got near to the girls' yard.

30 No sooner were they at the girls' yard than Anansi began whipping Tiger with his whip, and juked him hard with his spurs.

31 Tiger let out a yell, and began to run as fast as he could.

32 Anansi waved to the girls, then jumped off Tiger's back and climbed up onto the veranda.

33 'You see, Tiger is not only my father's old riding horse, but for me also.'

34 And Tiger was so ashamed, he ran into the woods and didn't return.

IV (Omitted)

V Jack Mandora, me no choose none.

Before beginning my analysis at the deepest level of tale structure, the phrase-structure rules, it is first necessary to distinguish between a Narrative and a Tale.[21] As a working definition, Narrative is a story, told orally, which includes at least one well-formed Kernel Tale together with other optional material. That material, as described earlier, includes introductory and concluding elements, many of which have traditional form in individual tale-telling communities. Thus a Tale is completely structural, while a Narrative contains additional material, not structurally relevant.

Rule 1: Narrative → (GNE) I + II + III + IV + V

This rule reads: Narrative is composed of Gross Narrative Elements I (formulaic opening), II (atemporal introduction), III (Tale), IV (concluding element) and V (formulaic closing). Only Gross Narrative Element III, the Tale, contains deep structure. Only III is characterized by structural closure, and by a limited number of functional elements. Closure refers to the fact that tales of each type move through a set number of reciprocally positive and negative states to a definite resolution, the characteristics of which are in part predictable from a knowledge of the structure (see Figures 3.3 and 3.4).

Rule 2: GNE III → Tale (K) 1 + Tale (K) 2 . . . + Tale (K) n

Each complete Tale is composed of a series of Kernel Tales, including no less than one well-formed Kernel Tale with all essential components.

Rule 3: Tale (K) → Contract (Formation) Phrase + Contract Dissolution Phrase

The Kernel Tale is subdivided into two principal components, i.e. the Contract Formation Phrase and the Contract Dissolution Phrase. These terms apply to Class I trickster tales, but not to all folktales. The more general terms employed by Georges are 'Move' and 'Countermove'.

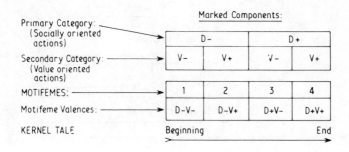

Figure 3.4   Valences of the motifemes

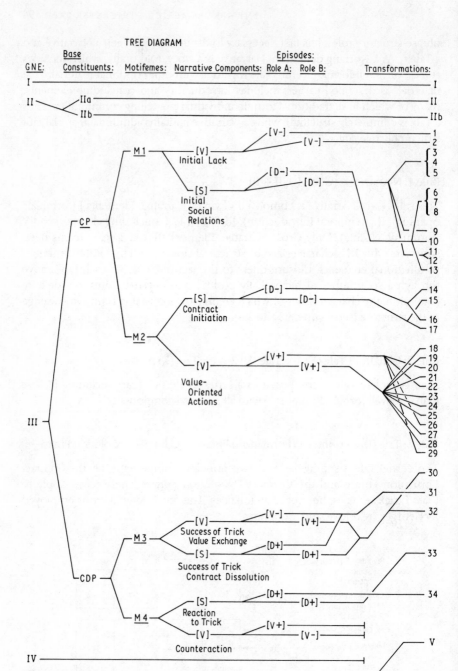

Figure 3.5 Dupe Tiger as Riding Horse

Surface Structure: Narrative

IIa: _____
T: Tiger
A: Anansi
G: Girls

I   Here is the tale of A (father's) Old Riding Horse.

IIa T and A were fond of the same G.

IIb but T was not as cunning as A.

1   T was very handsome. T visits G every week.
2   A notices how G are sweet on T.
{ 3   A goes to G's house. A says he will show G how T is A's father's old riding horse.
  4   'How is that?' G asks.
  5   'Next time I come, I will show you', A replies.

{ 6   Next Sunday T visits G. G tells him what A said.
  7   T flies into rage. T runs to find A.
  8   T arrives at A's house and knocks. T is vexed.

9   A replies in a weak voice, 'Who is there?'
10 T demands to be let in.
11 A is in bed. A tells T to enter.
12 A says he would offer T tea, but he is too weak.
13 T asks why A told G that T was A's father's old riding horse.

14 T tells A that he wants A to return with him to G and retract the lie.
15 A says he didn't say it. A would come but he can't walk.

16 T tells A that he will carry him on his back.
17 A accepts (the contract).

18 A gets on T's back, but is too weak to ride.
19 A tells T to get his saddle.
20 T agrees.
21 A tells T to get his bridle.
22 T asks why?
23 A replies it will keep him from falling off.
24 T begins to carry A, but A falls off.
25 A asks T to get his spurs.
26 T agrees.
27 A on T's back, ride through some woods.
28 A asks T to stop so he can cut a whip 'to let T know when to go slower'.
29 T agrees. A and T approach G's yard.

30 A begins whipping T. A spurs T.

31 T yells and runs as fast as he can.

32 A waves to G. A jumps off T's back and goes to G.

33 'You see, T is my old father's riding horse, and mine also', says A.

34 T is ashamed. T runs into woods and does not return.

V   Jack Mandora, me no choose none.

Rule 4: Contract (Formation) Phrase → [M1] + [M2]

The initial portion of the Tale is bifurcated into two Motifemes. Motifemes are the heart of the complex structure of the Tale. Each well-formed Kernel Tale consists of four Motifemes (Figure 3.4). Two character Roles and their functions are defined in semantic form within the Motifemes. The actions in the first two Motifemes are both characterized by Social harmony (S+), here symbolized as negative Disharmony (D−). Those in the Contract Dissolution Phrase are both characterized by a lack of Social harmony (S− or D+). It is in the Motifemes that the two Superstructural Ideas are combined in binary form and apportioned among the character Roles. In the case of the trickster tales, the principal dominant Superstructural Ideas are Social harmony (D−) and its negation, and Value (V+), with its negation, Lack (V−). Other Superstructural Ideas − Power, for instance − may also be present in these tales and may dominate the Motifemic level of other tale classes.

Rules 5.1–5.4: Motifeme(s) 1–4 → NC(V) + NC(S)

Rule 5.1 reads: Motifeme 1 is segmented into two Narrative Components, a Value component and a Social component. Rules 5.2 to 5.4 read similarly. There is, however, one significant distinction between Motifemes 1 and 3 on one hand, and Motifemes 2 and 4 on the other. This involves the direction of branching. In the first and third Motifemes, the Value component is branched to the right (i.e. placed in first position). In the second and fourth Motifemes, the reverse is true (i.e. the Social component is branched to the right; see Figure 3.5). This generalization stems from the observation that most Afro-American trickster tales follow this order. In the fewer number of cases in which the order of the Narrative Components is reversed beneath a Motifeme node, a transformational rule must be written to account for the ordering preference of the narrator. The NC(V) or Value-determining Narrative Component defines the valences or qualities of Value-oriented action under its appropriate node, and the NC(S) defines the valences of the Social relations in that Motifeme. The combinations of positive and negative valences are different for each Motifeme.

Rules 6.1–6.4: NC(V) → VE R(a) + VE R(b)

The Value-specifying Narrative Component for Motifeme 1 is further segmented into a Value-specifying Episode for Role A and one for Role B. The form of Rule 6 is identical for each of the eight Narrative Components. Only the semantic content differs for each of the Motifemes. For NC(V)1, for instance, that rule is:

Rule 6.1: NC(V)1 → [(a)V−] + [(b)V−]

This may be read 'Dupe (Role A) suffers Lack of Value' and 'Trickster (Role B) suffers Lack of Value'. Note that the Value or element lacked by Role A is often not the same as that sought by Role B.

Rules 7.1–7.4: NC(S) → SE R(a) + SE R(b)

This rule is similar to Rule 6 in that it apportions the Social-relation valences among the two roles, A and B.

Rule 7.1: NC(S)1 → [(a)D−] + [(b)D−]

This is read: 'Dupe's relationship to Trickster is positive, or, at least, not sufficiently negative for a contract not to be acceptable. The same is true for the Trickster.'

Both Rules 6 and 7 are repetitive in form and apply to all eight Narrative Components. However, because the semantic content, or the combinations of V and S values, differs for each Motifeme, all rules must be written in a complete description.

Rule 8 is analogous to Rule 4. It divides the Contract Dissolution Phrase of the Kernel Tale into Motifemes 3 and 4. Rules 5.3, 6.3 and 7.3 then apply to Motifeme 3, and Rules 5.4, etc., to Motifeme 4, resulting in a string of sixteen Episodes which define the Kernel Tale. Those values are listed in their most common order, under the subtitle 'Episodes' in Figure 3.5, which provides a tree diagram of the tale, 'Dupe Tiger as Riding Horse'. Note that several kinds of trans-formations may be applied to the output of the structural Episodes. They may be further branched into two or more Component Episodes, realized as surface-level sentences in the tale. They may also be reordered with respect to one another, and they may be deleted. In simple tales consisting of only one Kernel Tale, such as the one illustrated here, deletion of episodes under Motifeme 4 is common, as counteraction is limited or nonexistent. In more complex tales, such as those analyzed in *The Afro-American Trickster Tale*, counteraction is common in the Principal Kernel Tale, so deletion is less common. In actual narration, there is considerable freedom in the ordering of the Value and Social-contract Episodes within any single Narrative Component. There is less freedom to reorder surface-level episodes between Motifemes.

The phrase-structure rules 1–8 account for the generation of all deep-structural nodes in the Class I Afro-American trickster tale. In other words, the Class I kernel trickster tale is defined by these rules. Note that this is the simplest possible form of the Tale. Kernel Tales and portions of Kernel Tales are synthesized in various ways to produce more complex forms, which are by far more common than simple tales.

Three more elaborate forms of Tale may be described. A Complex Tale is one in which one or more subordinate Kernel Tales are embedded into the Primary

Kernel Tale. If the Kernel Tales are of the identical type to the Primary Kernel Tale, we call it a Type 1 Complex Tale. If subordinate Kernels with different deep-structure patterns are embedded, it is a Type 2 Complex Tale. Compound Tales are tales in which two or more Primary Kernel Tales are chained together, all of which share a single set of introductory and concluding Gross Narrative Elements. Most tales are of the Complex or Compound types. Experienced raconteurs eschew simple tales in most cases.

Concluding discussion

It should now be apparent from this discussion that the identification of polysememic motifemes is the key to the structural analysis of any tale class. The sequence of semantic values in the four motifemes of the kernel tale defines the classes of action which may occur in subordinate nodes. This sequence establishes the gross order of actions which characterize each class of tales.

In the next lower level, that of narrative components, the sequence of actions is further defined. It is here that an additional level of content is added to the structure of the tale. This allows us to define a syntagmatic array of eight sequential elements of the Class I tale. These are:

M 1 V: 1 Initial statement of Lack
M 1 S: 2 Initial Social relations (meeting)
M 2 S: 3 Contract formation between Roles A and B
M 2 V: 4 Value-oriented actions on the parts of one or both roles
M 3 V: 5 Success (or failure) of the trick: exchange of Value between the roles
M 3 S: 6 Success (or failure) of the trick: contract dissolution
M 4 S: 7 Emotional reaction to the trick (common but optional)
M 4 V: 8 Value-oriented counteraction (optional)

The sequence of narrative components defines the structurally significant categories of action within the Class I kernel tale. The part that the two character roles will play in those action categories is added to the deep structure at the level of (structural) episodes. This is the output of the narrative components. It is here that branching rules must be applied to determine the relative syntagmatic positions of action of each character role within a motifemic slot. Here, too, we see somewhat different sequences of functions, in which the two character roles relate to the Value in slightly different ways. Nevertheless, note that each character goes through a complete cycle of positive and negative valences with respect to the two superstructural ideas, Value and Social cohesion. This is the structural closure mentioned above. It is my belief that closure is inherent and implied in the semantic-motifemic definition of any structurally defined class of tales. Even though all classes of actions may not occur in every tale, they do occur in a sufficient proportion of Class I trickster tales to support this belief.

Finally, I would close by touching on some of the principal characteristics of the three models of folktale deep structure outlined in this paper: the syntagmatic model, the Lévi-Straussian formula and our model which embodies polysemantic motifemes. You will recall that Lévi-Strauss's famous formula

$$F(a)X : F(b)Y :: F(b)X : FY^{a-1}$$

specifies a universal relationship in dramatic narrative between a univocal role (A) and a second role which promises to liquidate A's Lack, and then, in reversal, actually causes Lack for A. That formula is fully consistent with the roles played by the characters in my model.

The major significant differences between the models I have been discussing are these. The syntagmatic models of Propp, Paulme and Bremond begin by defining the actions of a single character role with respect to sequences of functions or motifemes (defined as monosemantic notions). Strings of Proppian functions define basic tales, with different motifeme clusters defining different moves of a tale. An example would be: Lack + Lack Liquidated + Interdiction + Violation + Consequence. What unites the entire sequence is unclear from the syntagmatic position. This simple sequence, characteristic of numerous American Indian tales such as the Star Husband Tale,[22] for example, is conceived of as being composed of two independent structural units. Syntagmatic theorists have not attempted to demonstrate that tale sequences such as this are united by more abstract sets of superstructural ideas. This particular tale is united by the alternating L + LL + L related actions in which the Value is 'being joined in marriage to the stars'. The same tale is united by an exchange of Social contract valences: S− + S+ + S−, representing the acquiring of a (Social) contract and its violation. In our view, the S and V relations are characteristic of the entire tale, not simply portions of it. By selecting monosemantic motifemes such as Lack and Interdiction, the syntagmatic analyst is stating implicitly that only one of the roles of the tale (the girls) has structural predominance. The other role is only implied or given a structurally subordinate role in each specific sequence of motifemes. Tales may be built up of sequences based on different roles, of course.

If the syntagmatic theory gives primacy to single roles, the model of Lévi-Strauss gives primacy to only a single superstructural idea. While it goes beyond the syntagmatic model in illustrating the relations between two roles, it models that relation on the basis of only one superstructural idea at a time. Thus, 'Dupe suffers Lack: Trickster offers to Liquidate Lack :: Trickster then causes Lack : thus, the Function of promised Value is to subvert the Dupe.' Note that nothing is said about Social contract or any other possible superstructural idea. In order to incorporate another such idea into the deep structure of the myth or tale, Lévi-Strauss must propose another parallel model.

What I have tried to show is that an expansion of both of these theories is needed if we are successfully to account for the functioning of the deep structure of the folktale. The folktale is really about the interplay of essential ideas.

Characters have the function of dramatizing the interrelationships between these ideas in actions, and making them concrete. The Lévi-Straussian model, then, interprets approximately one-half of the entire deep structure of the kernel tale at one time. The only fully successful model of the deep structure of the folktale will be one which combines the features of the polysememic paradigm, the sequencing of actions illustrating that paradigm, a definition of the well-formed kernel tale, and acceptable variations of that kernel. Although I have not completed this task here, I hope that I have helped to point the way.

Notes

1 Nowhere is this better illustrated than in the structural analysis of African and Afro-American folktales. Some scholars complain of the over-complexity and 'excessive' use of jargon by those who attempt a major deconstruction of a genre such as the African folktale. Others simply ignore structural analysis as apparently irrelevant. Articles or other works that approach the subject from the standpoint of literary or thematic analysis, and even those that attempt a simple structural analysis of a single level of structure, remain generally immune from such treatment.

2 Jay Edwards, *The Afro-American Trickster Tale: A Structural Analysis*, Monograph 4 (Bloomington, Ind.: Indiana University Folklore Publications Group, 1978), pp. 9–13.

3 See Vladimir Propp, *Morphology of the Folktale* (1928), rev. edn (Austin, Texas, and London: University of Texas Press, 1970); Alan Dundes, *The Morphology of North American Indian Tales* (Helsinki: Folklore Fellows Communications, 1964); Claude Lévi-Strauss, *Structural Anthropology* (New York: Basic Books, 1958) and *The Savage Mind* (1962; Chicago, Ill.: University of Chicago Press, 1966).

4 Robert D. Pelton, *The Trickster in West Africa: A Study of Mythic Irony and Sacred Delight* (Berkeley, Calif.: University of California Press, 1980).

5 Ibid., p. 28.

6 Claude Bremond, 'Morphology of the French Folktale', *Semiotica*, 2, 3 (1970), p. 250.

7 See Denise Paulme, 'The Theme of Successive Exchanges in African Literature', *L'Homme*, 9 (1969), pp. 5–22, and 'Impossible Imitation in African Trickster Tales', in Bernth Lindfors (ed.), *Forms of Folklore in Africa* (Austin, Texas: University of Texas Press, 1977), pp. 64–103.

8 Denise Paulme, 'Morphologie du conte africain', *Cahiers d'études africaines*, 12 (1972), pp. 131–63.

9 Edwards, op. cit., pp. 57–66.

10 See Alan Dundes, 'The Making and Breaking of Friendship as a Structural Frame in African Folktales', in Pierre and Elli Köngäs Maranda (eds), *Structural Analysis of Oral Tradition* (Philadelphia, Pa.: University of Pennsylvania Press, 1971), pp. 171–89; Lee Haring, 'A Characteristic African Folklore Pattern', in Richard Dorson (ed.), *American Folklore* (Garden City, NY: Anchor-Doubleday, 1972), pp. 165–82.

11 See Heda Jason, 'A Model for Narrative Structure in Oral Literature', in Heda Jason and Dimitri Segal (eds), *Patterns in Oral Literature* (Chicago, Ill.: Aldine, 1977), pp. 99–140. See also Claude Bremond, 'The Morphology of the French Fairy Tale: The Ethical Model', in ibid., pp. 49–76.

12 See Robert A. Georges, 'Structure in Folktales', *The Conch*, 2, 2 (1970), pp. 4–17.

13 See George Horner, 'Structural Analysis of Bulu Folktales', *The Conch*, 2, 2 (1970), pp. 18–29; Oja Arewa and G. M. Shreve, *The Genesis of Structures in African Narrative*, Studies in African Semiotics, No. 3 (New York: Conch Magazine, 1975).

14 At the time my monograph was written, I was unaware of the excellent work of Georges, Anozie, Arewa and Shreve. My study was limited exclusively to the Afro-American tale and dealt with a narrower selection of folktale types than the articles of several of the above-mentioned authors. Another contributor to the Louisiana State University school is John Thormeyer, whose MA thesis 'A Structural Analysis of Navaho Coyote Tales' (1980) is available through the LSU library.

15 Edwards, op. cit., pp. 23–6.

16 T. D. Beidelman, 'The Moral Implications of the Kaguru: Some Thoughts on Tricksters', *American Ethnologist*, 9, 1 (1980), p. 32.

17 Lévi-Strauss, *Structural Anthropology*, p. 228.

18 Maranda (eds), op. cit., Introduction, pp. ix–xxxiv.

19 Sunday O. Anozie, 'Structuralism in Poetry and Mythology', *The Conch*, 4, 1 (1972), pp. 1–22.

20 See Roger Renwick and John Vlach, review of *The Afro-American Trickster Tale* in *Folklore Forum*, 12, 1 (1979), pp. 97–9; John Roberts, review of *The Afro-American Trickster Tale* in *Journal of American Folklore*, 94 (1981), pp. 392–3; John Thormeyer and Frank Parker, 'The Structural Analysis of Folktales: A Preliminary Model', paper delivered at the 1981 meeting of the Linguistic Association of the Southwest (Austin, Texas, 24 October 1981).

21 All the major structural components in my model – including slots or nodes, functions, semantic values and character roles – are capitalized for clarity of identification.

22 See Stith Thompson, 'The Star Husband Tale', repr. in Alan Dundes (ed.), *The Study of Folklore* (Englewood Cliffs, NJ: Prentice-Hall, 1965), pp. 414–74.

4   Sunday O. Anozie

Negritude, structuralism, deconstruction

Dans les œuvres poétiques, le linguiste discerne des structures dont l'analogie est frappante avec celles que l'analyse des mythes révèle à l'ethnologue. De son côté, celui-ci ne saurait méconnaître que les mythes ne consistent pas seulement en agencements conceptuels: ce sont aussi des œuvres d'art . . .

With this preface, Lévi-Strauss and Roman Jakobson embarked upon one of the rare interdisciplinary collaborations in recent memory between an ethnologist and a linguist – the dissection of Baudelaire's poem, 'Les Chats'.[1] Since this date and as a result of innovative work in generative grammar[2] and in semiotics,[3] critics especially in the United States and France have begun to show some interest in the structural-linguistic analysis of literary works, particularly poetry.[4] In each case the underlying assumption is twofold. The first is the realization that a poetic work contains a system of ordered variants which can be isolated and represented vertically in the form of superimposed levels such as phonology, phonetic, syntactic, prosodic and semantic. The second is that modern structuralism – especially in the form of its offshoot, generative grammar – provides an adequate theory and method for accounting for such levels and in dealing with the internal coherence of the given work of art.

Some African critics of African literature have objected to this search for internal coherence. Abiola Irele, a Nigerian critic well known for his several defenses of negritude, for example, has argued strongly in favor of a 'sociological imagination' on the part of a critic of African literature, without showing in what essential way(s) this differs from a structuralist imagination.[5] Is it true, for example, that the assertion that man is a structural animal precludes the African?[6] On the contrary, the present writer has argued elsewhere that no adequate sociological theory of African literature, the novel in particular, can be formulated outside a framework of structuralism.[7] More recently, too, I have insisted on the possibility of defining such a structuralist framework within the terms, necessarily more narrow, of the conceptual framework of negritude.[8] Such integration will serve not only to revitalize but also to provide negritude with the one thing it so far lacks – a scientific method of inquiry.

In the present contribution, I wish to add to this argument by submitting that negritude and structuralism have more in common than at first may strike the eye of a casual observer and, consequently, that the search for internal coherence in an African or any other work of art does not necessarily detract from its aesthetic or ideological value as such; if anything, it can enhance appreciation and respect for both.

In the first part of this essay, I shall sketch a brief structural analysis of one of Senghor's shorter poems, 'Le Totem'. I shall then examine, also briefly, a few developments within negritude, especially Senghor's, in relation to the concept of structuralism, especially Lévi-Strauss's. Finally, I shall look at a particular aspect of Senghor's thought from a deconstructive perspective. This movement from practice to theory will, I hope, underline, if not the innate scientific disposition of negritude, at least my belief in its potential to develop into one.

The concept of 'problematic' in poetry

Two remarks must be made from the outset. The first is that the composition of Senghor's 'Le Totem' contains no diachronic problematic. As an isolated event, it has no special recorded 'history' of its own (if it does, this paper is not at any rate interested in that but in the poem itself as a synchronic event) beyond the fact that it is the fourteenth poem in the author's 1945 collection of poems published under the title of *Chants d'ombre*.[9] I use the term 'problematic', in the same way as both Althusser and Lévi-Strauss, to define a particular theoretical system or 'thought structure'.[10] Glucksmann has cogently demonstrated the correlations between the uses of the concept of 'problematic' by Althusser to define the specificities of Marx's theory and by Lévi-Strauss to designate systems of totemic classification in 'primitive cultures'.[11] Thus in refusing to see in Senghor's 'Le Totem' a diachronic problematic, I merely deny that it provides any substantive account of history. Instead the poem's – any poem's – problematic should be sought in the fact that it is first and foremost a synchronic event (in it, as in any language system, history is transfixed, so to speak, into an instant of time), and therefore essentially mythical. According to Lévi-Strauss:

> Mythical thought, that bricoleur, builds structures by bitting together events, or rather the remains of events, while science, 'in operation' simply by virtue of coming into being, creates its means and results in the form of events, thanks to the structures which it is constantly elaborating and which are its hypotheses and theories . . . the scientist creating events (changing the world)

by means of structures, and the 'bricoleur' creating structures by means of events.[12]

Lévi-Strauss's concept of the problematic is therefore in direct relationship to objective knowledge and cosmology in 'primitive' societies where myths are shown to operate from an awareness of oppositions to their satisfactory mediation. Recently too, Senghor has spoken of the problematic of negritude in an attempt to re-evaluate this ideology in the context of a global awareness of developments in the social sciences and the humanities.[13] I shall return to this point later.

The second remark I wish to make is that it is especially not difficult to assign a correct reading to the Senghor poem, 'Le Totem'. A careful attention to the organization of details in the poem coupled with a knowledge of its cultural codes (the African totemic configuration) will certainly enable an alert critic, native or foreign, to read a correct meaning into the poem. Thus, in an explicatory footnote to the poem, Shelton rightly observes:

> This is the actual totem. A totem is the spirit of an animal, usually, considered to have aided a founding ancestor in a critical moment at the beginning or early part of the clan's history, or considered spiritually related to the members of the clan. Among the Wolof (Senghor is Serer, a related group), each clan group has totem animals: Diop, the crown bird; Njai, the lion; Toure, the frog, etc. *The totem in the poem suggests the real self of the poet, as distinct from the artificial, Europeanized surface of the acculturated African.*[14]

I have italicized in the above quotation the sentence that appears to me to contain a crucial interpretation of the Senghor poem. Similarly referring to the frequency in Senghor's poetry of images derived from the vegetable and animal kingdoms, Robert Mercier speaks of

> une influence de la coutume africaine attribuant à chaque individu, comme 'totem', un animal dont il revêt plus ou moins la personnalité. L. S. Senghor fait allusion lui-même à cet usage et à l'interdiction de révéler aux autres ce patronage.

Continuing, he says,

> Mais si le secret doit être gardé par chacun sur son propre totem, les rapprochements métaphoriques, fondés sur la ressemblance de caractères entre un homme et un animal, sont un jeu inoffensif. . . . Ce double sens des échanges entre l'homme et le monde est une constante de l'imagination de L. S. Senghor.[15]

Mercier is content not merely with pointing at 'totem' as a cultural code in Africa, but with showing it as performing a significant metonymic function in Senghor's poetry. Finally, Bâ seeks to integrate the Senghorian concept and use of 'totem'

within the wider philosophical context of African life forces – first enunciated by
Father Tempels and remarkably evident in Jahn's work as part of the criteria of
neo-Africanism:

> In a world where significance is attributed to all forces and with such
> interdependence of action, the wisdom of the ages is implied by the basic
> principle of life forces and simplified by the concrete nature of its expression.
> It is these concrete symbols that the initiate learns to understand. We can now
> better understand why Senghor insists that totemism only seems monstrous.
> Some animal or tree is often identified with a clan through the common
> ancestor whose life is then made known through a totemic or astral myth. This
> tendency toward identification with inferior, that is, nonrational, forces is
> described by Senghor as anthropsychism: the tendency to relate to other
> objects or forces as though they were persons. The purpose of such identi-
> fication with totem is the appropriation of the psychic force associated with
> the particular totem. The ancestor totem constitutes a doubly protective force,
> destined by its very nature and composition to preserve the life principle of
> those under its tutelage.[16]

Thus, from the recognition of 'totem' in the Senghor poem as denotative of
acculturation (Shelton's distinction between real self/surface 'self', Euro-
peanized/African is clear-cut) to that of 'totem' as a cultural code with stylistic
function (Mercier calls it an imaginative 'constant') in Senghor's poem, finally,
to Bâ's assimilation of 'totem' into an ideology based upon 'life forces', it can
be inferred that the semantic component of 'Le Totem' is both normatively
circumscribed and exhaustive; in other terms, that no meaning can be assigned
to this poem, outside the referential framework of 'totem' as a 'thought
structure'. This inference is valid – for reasons I prefer not to elaborate here and
now. Consequently, further attempts at interpretation in this paper can serve
only one useful purpose – to relate the semantic component of the poem to its
syntactic structure, that is to say, define the nature of the poem's problematic.

Syntactic structures in 'Le Totem'

     I   Il me faut le cacher (a) aux plus intimes de mes veines (b)
    II   L'Ancêtre (c) à la peau d'orage sillonnée d'éclairs et de foudre (d)
   III   Mon animal gardien (e), il me faut le cacher (f)
   IV   Que je ne rompe le barrage des scandales (g).
    V   Il est mon sang fidèle (h) qui requérit la fidélité (i)
   VI   Protégeant mon orgueil nu (j) contre
  VII   Moi-même (k) et la superbe des races heureuses (l).

    I must hide him in my innermost veins
    The Ancestor with the stormy skin streaked with thunder and
      lightning

My guardian animal, I must hide him
That I may not burst the dam of scandal.
He is my loyal blood that demands loyalty
Shielding my naked pride against
Myself and the arrogance of the blessed races.[17]

The period at the end of the fourth line divides this seven-line stanza into two distinct units of thought: a quatrain and a tercet. With the exception of the /R/ (in foudre and contre) and the /E/ (in fidélité and cacher), the poem has no end rhymes. (Senghor's poems do not as a rule depend on end rhymes for effect, but on internal rhythm instead.) Here the rhythm is conveyed through the preponderance of consonantal sounds at the beginning of words – /l/, /p/, /s/, /d/, /f/, /g/, /s/, /m/, /R/, /b/ – and of vowel and consonant sounds in the middle.

The quatrain displays, on the surface level of propositions, an elegant structural balance. I have denoted with alphabets the different poetic propositions. The term 'proposition' as employed here does not necessarily mean a 'complete thought' in the sense of a sentence; instead it stands for a phrase structure, the smallest significant unit of meaning (a sememe), as far as this poem is concerned. This said, it is obvious that propositions Ia and IIIf are strictly symmetrical, with this significant difference: that the order in which they appear in the lines is reversed. The effect on the two odd lines of the quatrain is identical to the opening and closing of brackets, viz. [ ], implying the exclusion of the even line IV. Given this phenomenon, one could say that the unity of the quatrain has been 'broken', the fourth line being abruptly and artificially excluded from the rest. What is more significant, too, the verb (rompe) appears precisely in the line where this scandal seemingly occurs, and thereby doubly underlines and reinforces the poet's intention and fear. Mercier (cf. above) has rightly spoken of 'l'interdiction de révéler aux autres ce patronage'. And I have shown that this semantic interpretation cannot be divorced from the very syntactic structure of line IV which expresses the interdiction, the central theme of the quatrain. On the contrary, the sense absolutely inheres in the form of the expression. The unity in Africa between man and his 'totem' which consists in a system of both cognitive and existential relations (if we admit also the negritude ideology of 'life forces') is thus reflected in the poem structurally as a system of grammatical interrelationships within the quatrain.

Apart from being related as the two external lines of a quatrain, line IV and line I are linked by other ties: semantically, veines and barrage, for instance, belong to the same category (they are both containers of fluid); morphologically, veines and scandales are both preceded by identical des and are genitive substantives; finally, both lines end with an identical consonantal inflectional suffix '-s' (veine-s, scandale-s) indicating plurality.

Similarly, the propositions Ib and IId appear to be parenthetically separate, the one from the verb cacher, the other from the noun l'Ancêtre, to which they respectively act as complements. This time, however, the evidence of the 'break' is more phonological than syntactical: the presence of vowels and consonants: /o/, /p/, /l/ (in Ib); /a/, /l/, /p/ (in IId). In fact, not only does this situation now justify our establishing a syntagmatic parallelism between Ib and IId, but the phonemic and morphological index, particularly at the beginning of each proposition, seems to point towards a closer link or identity between, and thus the inseparability of, *cacher* and *l'Ancêtre* (Ia, IIc) as a syntagmatic category. Thus the relationship of IIc to Ia, namely, the logical finite predicate, is the same as that of IIIe to IIIf. This further suggests that the initial 'break' in the natural order and balance (*il me faut le cacher* → *l'Ancêtre*) appears now rectified but in a somewhat odd, that is reversed, manner (*Mon animal gardien* ← *il me faut le cacher*). It is also significant that this artificial disjunction is expressed in the odd lines of the quatrain. In line II this disjunction is partly metonymical (*peau d'orage*) and partly a deliberate search for rhythmic balance (*d'orage/d'éclairs/de foudre*). Finally, in line IV, the same phenomenon becomes, on the part of the poet, consciousness of a taboo, expressed in a deprecatory subjunctive mood (*Que je ne rompe . . .*). Also this line contains the only subjunctive verb in the whole poem which links it as an adverb proposition to Ia and IIIf.

Consciousness of an initial separation followed by a search for the restoration of primitive balance and order constitutes not only the global symmetry but also the meaning of 'Le Totem'. Senghor's stylistic execution of this structural principle in the quatrain is literally scientific.

The structure of propositions in the quatrain is defined by the following logical relations.

Ia	≡ IIIf	Equivalent propositions
Ib	// IId	Parallel propositions
Ia	→ IIc	Finite predicate (broken order)
IIIe	← IIIf	Finite predicate (reverse order)
IIc	= IIIe	Equal propositions
IV	↔ I + III	Subjunctive/Adverb proposition

Strictly within the context of these paradigms, is it possible to define other syntagmatic features which will enable us to relate or map the quatrain to the tercet, at the dual levels of the deep and surface structure? Yes. Such evidence is, to take the most obvious case, provided in the form of a substantive followed by an adjective and preceded by a pronoun in the second odd line of the quatrain and the first odd and even lines of the tercet. The result is his symmetrical pattern, with identical morpheme /mɔ̃/:

Pron.	→	N	→	N
mon		animal		gardien (IIIe)
Pron.	→	N	→	Adj.
mon		sang		fidèle (Vh)
mon		orgueil		nu (VIj)

A disjunctive sequence is found in the second odd line of the tercet –

Pron.	V̱ N	→ N	→ Adj.
Moi-même	superbe	races	heureuses (VII)

– as if the poet wishes to emphasize the uniqueness of this closing line of the tercet, also of the poem, in relation to the rest of the lines. Note that the lexical categories contained in III, V and VI are also present in VII but in varying combinations, and with this morphological difference: that the initial pronominal item changes from the possessive form mon [mɔ̃] to the direct-object form moi [mwa]. (Other obvious relations of a semantic nature exist between veines → sang (I, V); gardien → fidèle (fidélité) → Protégéant (III, V, VI.)

A second evidence, this time less obvious because it relates to the deep-structure level, yields itself when we seek to interpret the above change with reference to other syntactic features of the tercet. Consider that the only logical, i.e. grammatical, link between VI and VII is the preposition contre: it serves to map the only participial proposition in the poem to the two conjoined propositions: contre moi-même and [contre] la superbe des races heureuses. The effect of this conjunction is accentuated only if we admit a disjunction, a break, between VIIk and VIIl similar to that witnessed in IV; that is, if we read VI, taking a breath pause after Moi-même in VII. However, whereas the evidence in IV is inclusive (it has nothing to do with breath pause), the disjunction that occurs in VII must be seen as functionally exclusive: it opposes VIIk to VIIl by juxtaposing them.

What one witnesses here is an intriguing phenomenon of balancing opposites, characteristic of Senghor's art in this poem. Furthermore, this can be illustrated even by isolating from VI and VII lexical entries pertaining to the same category: moi-même/races, orgueil/superbe, heureuses/nu. These pairs constitute a system of binary oppositions which can be represented, both horizontally and vertically, in the form of two intersecting circles (see Figure 4.1). The geometrical figure has at the least the merit of displaying visually the area in which the poet's meaning may be said to be embedded. An existentialist predicament expressed in terms of racial (cf. the tercet) and religious (cf. the quatrain) consciousness thus constitutes the problematic of the poem. Such interpretation will confirm Senghor's, who, drawing upon the philosophy of vital forces, has described the black man's metaphysics as an existential ontology.[18]

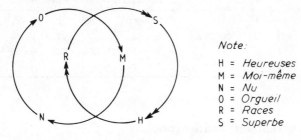

Figure 4.1

Note:

H = Heureuses
M = Moi-même
N = Nu
O = Orgueil
R = Races
S = Superbe

Lines	Quatrain		Lines	Tercet	
I	a	b			
II	c	d	V	h	i
III	e	f	VI	j	
IV		g	VII	k	

Figure 4.2

Let me now briefly summarize the data so far presented in this section. Starting with a division of Senghor's poem 'Le Totem' into two distinct parts, I have tried to reconstitute the unities of the quatrain and of the tercet as well as the relationship between these two parts, by relying almost solely upon the syntactical features, the structure of propositions, in the poem. The poem, as has been seen, contains a striking symmetry of organization, with the tercet seemingly responding to and complementing the quatrain, but clearly exhibiting unique syntagmatic features of its own. The results can be shown graphically, as in Figure 4.2.

Even a schema as simple as this can serve to illustrate the internal mechanism of the poem, the principle of binary oppositions by which it functions and, finally, the attempt at reconciliation, or the restoration of the primary ontological unity. Note that, in explaining how this theme is structurally articulated in line VII, I have taken what may appear to be a slight phonological liberty, in insisting that lines VI and VII be read as if there were a breath pause (caesura) between initial words moi-même and et. Now let me correct this impression by saying that the fact that one recognizes this morphophonemic change or not may not have any major incidence on the analysis, since what really counts in the line in question is the syntagm of juxtaposition.

As a final and more technical evidence of the poet's delicate art of balancing, mention should now be made of the fact that the poem contains a total of fourteen nouns (I regard animal gardien as a substantive unit) numerically distributed as in Figure 4.3. This table permits us to identify a number of relations, identical, inverse or parallel (e.g. 5:4 : : 3:2 or 5:3 : : 4:2; V:IV : : VI:III or III:IV : : VI:V, etc.); it may possibly also constitute a system of permutations.

Lines	M	F		NOUNS			Lines	M	F
I	—	1		M	F		V	1	1
II	3	2	QUATRAIN	5	4		VI	1	—
III	1	—		2	3	TERCET	VII	—	2
IV	1	1		7	7				

Figure 4.3

Totemism, Lévi-Strauss and Senghor

The choice of the poem 'Le Totem' as the subject of analysis is not fortuitous;

in fact, as announced above, the reason can now be explicated. Viewed as an isolated synchronic event, this poem affords as good a starting point as any other for illustrating some of the basic relationships and assumptions of negritude and structuralism. If thus I say that the poem 'Le Totem' stands in relation to Senghorian negritude as 'totemism' does in relation to Lévi-Straussian structuralism, I have merely posed a hypothesis. Such a statement may or may not invite justification or proof. It is not my intention to offer or even attempt any here. Instead I will confine myself in the remaining pages to indicating a line of inquiry which may prove useful in dealing with such a problem.

Senghor's earlier observations about traditional African metaphysics, and his attempts to formulate on the basis of these a theory of African creativity, consitute a major contribution to negritude. Not only do these pronouncements embody important structuralist insights, but, in some respects, they reflect, or at least are reconcilable with, the views expressed by Lévi-Strauss. Take African art, for instance. In Senghor's opinion, all arts in Africa are social, that is, functional in the sense that they are both collective and committed. This view, which is largely shared by several modern scholars,[19] is not much different from that held by Lévi-Strauss. However, when Senghor further asserts that African arts constitute 'techniques of essentialization' for the individual, it is clear that he is endorsing the traditional viewpoint of descriptive anthropologists according to which African art has an exclusive religious determination. Lévi-Strauss differs on this point, since he is more inclined than Senghor to recognize the personality of the artist both as an individual and as a creator. For example, he claims:

> Des travaux récents sur la sculpture africaine montrent que le sculpteur est un artiste, que cet artiste est connu, quelquefois très loin à la ronde, et que le public indigène sait reconnaître le style propre de chaque auteur de masque ou de statue.[20]

Thus, whereas Senghor defends traditional art as an existentialist problematic for the individual, Lévi-Strauss views artistic production as a process of individualization.

Next, Senghor sees African poetry as a form of discourse on the grounds that it rejects the idea of the permanence of art, preferring instead the novelty of what the poet calls 'idées-sentiments' and the dramatic progression of rhythm. On this premise Senghor also condemns the classical Greek and Roman theory of archetypes and mimesis as alien and inapplicable to Africa. The same goes for the art of writing, with regard to which he claims in his 1958 preface to Herbert Pepper's L'Anthologie de la vie africaine as follows: 'l'écriture appauvrit le réel. Elle le cristallise en catégories rigides; elle le fixe quand le propre du réel est d'être vivant, fluide, et sans contours.'[21]

Now, all structuralists of Lévi-Straussian inspiration will agree that poetry is a form of linguistic discourse. Lévi-Strauss himself does not have anything complimentary to say about the art of writing, which he associates with the origin of social cleavages such as the slave, the class and the caste systems – and with the capitalization and totalization of knowledge: 'L'écriture elle-même ne nous paraît associée de façon permanente, dans ses origines, qu'à des sociétés qui sont fondées sur l'exploitation de l'homme par l'homme.'[22] Roland Barthes, in particular, would not hesitate to agree with Senghor that writing impoverishes reality by crystallizing it so as to clarify further the perspective of modern semiology.[23] One need not, however, go into the other negritude view some-what contradictory to Senghor's, according to which Africa is not entirely without her share of the blame for the invention of the art of writing.[24] Instead it is more significant to point out that as early as 1958 Senghor had been aware of the structuralist movement in France. The first reference made by him to Lévi-Strauss is contained in the 1958 preface where the French ethnologist's remarks in favor of 'primitive' people are approvingly quoted. I should add at this point also that the second and apparently the last explicit reference to Lévi-Strauss is contained in Senghor's 1959 essay, 'Éléments constitutifs . . .' This time the context is religion – magic and totemism – and the reference is a negative one:

> Prise dans son sens le plus étroit, la magie peut être définie avec Claude Lévi-Strauss, 'comme un système d'opérations et de croyances qui prétend, à certains actes humains, la même valeur qu'à des causes naturelles.' Prise dans son sens large, la magie est un dogme selon lequel 'le visible est la mani-festation de l'invisible'. On reconnaît là la définition du mysticisme. C'est le sens que je retiendrai.[25]

That Senghor prefers a definition of magic which derives from a marriage of mysticism and surrealism (in the passage in question, for example, he sees Elias Lévi through the eyes of André Breton!) to that deriving from structural anthropology may by itself be instructive, but not a surprise. In fact, this may be seen as part of the general theoretic eclecticism which characterized the development of Senghor's negritude vis-à-vis its treatment of and relationship to other intellectual movements, Marxism, existentialism or structuralism; they served only as expedient reinforcement to the former. What is surprising, then, is the fact that the difference between the two definitions proposed above is indeed more terminological – 'system' and 'dogma', I take it, are inductively synonymous or nearly so – than real. It is thus a matter of the levels of empiricism at which each observer situates himself in relation to the object. For further evidence of this, one need only consider the inductive parallelism established by Lévi-Strauss between science and magic.[26] These are considered as 'two parallel modes of acquiring knowledge', or two systems which require the same sort of mental operations and which differ not so much in kind as in the different 'types of phenomenon' to which they are applied. Hence what Senghor views as mystical about magic, it seems to me, may be nothing but the pure supernatural state of magic considered as a 'life force', its abstract power of symbolization, not the fact that magic may also constitute an integral science whose operations can be rationally explicated and understood.

A delightful awareness of magic in the sense already indicated, which stems partly from his intensely African religious background and partly from the influence of French medieval and modern mystics, poets and philosophers, also underlines Senghor's views on African poetic rhythm and imagery. Let me note in passing that a similar romantic strain runs through much of the anthropological writings of Lévi-Strauss, who besides has claimed Jean-Jacques Rousseau as a major influence. On the subject of poetic image, Senghor argues:

> Il s'agit de la double valeur du mot. Celui-ci peut être perçu comme signe ou comme sens; très souvent, en poésie, comme signe et sens en même temps. Le mot peut avoir la valeur quasi-abstraite d'un signe algébrique.[27]

Clearly, then, Senghor recognizes not only the double quality of denotation and connotation in words but also the relationship between the signifier and the signified, a central point in structural linguistics.[28] One would have wished that Senghor had further developed these technical insinuations in a way that would have been both consistent and beneficial in any methodological considerations within negritude.

As for 'rhythm', Senghor defines it variously as 'the architecture of being', 'the internal dynamism', 'the system of waves', 'the pure expression of the Life-force', and so on. Now, all these are imprecise and, strictly from the point of view of analytic methodology, unreliable definitions. They do not transcend the level of mysticism, nor were they originally intended to, in delineating this particular problematic, Senghor's negritude. But, far from dismaying by their so-called imprecision, such definitions should impress by the structural perspective within which they already appear to be inscribed, namely, that of descriptive exhaustion of the object contemplated – in other terms, the perspective of phenomenology.

Phenomenology, according to Senghor, is nothing but 'la description des faits pour en comprendre les significations. C'est la dialectique vécue de l'objet et du sujet, de l'abstrait et du concret, de la théorie et de la pratique, de l'action et de la mystique.'[29] It is therefore in this dialectical sense that one must interpret Senghor's equation of life forces with super- or surreality as indeed no more than a mystical affirmation of structural relationships within a given system, whether of cosmology such as the African universe in which man, according to the poet-humanist, holds the central place; or ontology, such as the relationship between an individual and his clan totem in traditional Africa. In any case, this interpretation, if upheld, should lead us to reconsider the role and meaning of the term 'life force' in negritude, in such a way as to enable us to appreciate the close resemblance between the use of the term 'life force', in Senghor's phenomenology of religious and cultural perception, and the idea of 'structure', particularly in the reductionist phenomenology of Husserl and Merleau-Ponty.[30] In either case, the concepts are used in a transcendental and subjective manner to invoke a systemic, in the sense of a rational and objective, view of the world. Hence the poet has argued, too, that the perception of 'life forces' is possible only through emotion and intuition – two modes upon which he conferred an epistemological and cognitive role among the blacks.

However, in a recent review of the problematic of negritude, Senghor has again defended his position against his critics by rightly emphasizing that 'emotion' signifies 'intuitive reason'. Although this position is by no means new, Senghor nevertheless ascribes it to what he terms 'the triumph of the new epistemology'. Also, without specifically mentioning the name of Lévi-Strauss as one of the architects of 'the new epistemology', it is clear that Senghor had the ethnologist in mind when he referred to the recent development of the structuralist and functionalist theories in the human sciences, and when he argued:

> La connaissance contemporaine est une confrontation du sujet et de l'objet, dont l'initiative, au demeurant, n'est pas toujours du sujet. C'est une participation, une communion, où le sujet et l'objet sont, chacun et en même temps, regardant et regardé, agent et agi. C'est l'acte d'amour de la raison-œil et de la raison-toucher. Or, c'est ainsi, par les mots de 'participation' et 'communion', que les ethnologues ont toujours défini la connaissance des Nègres.[31]

Senghor's claim, implied above, that the orthodox position of negritude has been vindicated by developments in contemporary knowledge, is characteristic but vague. The question is indeed not whether terms like 'participation' and 'communion' have been employed by past anthropologists[32] to describe the people whose cultures they studied, but whether the properties of the terms have been correctly described and specified and by what methods. A significant development in Senghor's new thinking, as defined in the above, is therefore the implied critique of 'reductionism' which in Husserl's philosophical system argues that all signification attached to the world of phenomena originates from the consciousness, that is, the intentionality, of the contemplating subject, since 'all consciousness is of something'. Also Senghor correctly states the position of modern structuralism, considered as a system of epistemology, when he acknowledges that the 'initiative' (in determining the structure of signification, that is), does not always lie with the subject. In the methodological specification of the laws governing the new 'participation' and 'communion' between subject and object, which Senghor refers to, however, structuralism has progressed, whereas negritude has remained static.

Lévi-Straussian structuralism is a paradigmatic science. Its method consists essentially in erecting conceptual models which mediate between contradictory, or binary, relations.[33] Myths, for example, are considered not only as systems of abstract relations but also as aesthetic objects. The creative act which gives rise to myths, Lévi-Strauss claims,

> is in fact exactly the reverse of that which gives rise to works of art. In the case of works of art, the starting point is a set of one or more objects and one or more events which aesthetic creation unifies by revealing a common structure. Myths travel the same road, but start from the other end. They use a structure to produce what is itself an object consisting of a set of events (for all myths tell a story). Art thus proceeds from a set (object + event) to the discovery of its structure. Myth starts from a structure by means of which it constructs a set (object + event).[34]

Senghor's poem 'Le Totem' provides an eminent illustration of this statement. As a form of myth, it starts from a given structure, namely, the primitive unity within the dualism which is part of the totemic belief; as an art – that is, a conscious exploration in the medium of language – it moves from a series of disjunctions (images, symbols or propositions) towards a search for the principle of their unification. Thus the same system of permutations, which in totemism mediates ideal relations between the two privileged series of nature and culture, are also present at a phenomenological level of perception in Senghor's 'Le Totem'.

The deconstructive connection

Since the above reading of Senghor's 'Le Totem' was first written and published in 1976,[35] so many interesting developments have taken place within literary theory – due in part to the influence of the critical and philosophical writings of Jacques Derrida, and in part to the works of other post-structuralist critics, particularly at Yale – that one cannot honestly claim that one particular theory or reading of a work of art can take precedence over all the others. In this concluding section it is not my intention to review this post-structuralist literature – something that I have attempted elsewhere[36] – nor to present my reasons for believing that the critical movement known as 'deconstruction' has a relevant message for our time and so deserves continued attention.[37] For different reasons I think it will be useful here to isolate and examine briefly, in the light of part of the deconstructional message, one implication for the development of African literary theories of a particular aspect of Senghor's ideas concerning Africa and writing.

In the section 'Totemism, Lévi-Strauss and Senghor' I compared Senghor's views about writing (l'écriture) with Lévi-Strauss's as further evidence of a possible concordance of views between two contemporary intellectual movements – negritude and structuralism. Whereas Lévi-Strauss condemns what he perceives as the negative social, economic and political consequences of the introduction of writing, Senghor is more concerned about writing as a means of segmenting reality (African reality, that is) – in other words, as a triumph of the system of analytical reason over 'reason-by-embrace'. Here is the passage in which Senghor deplores writing:

> C'est la chance de l'Afrique noire d'avoir dédaigné l'écriture, même quand elle ne l'ignorait pas. Et de fait, on peut compter de nombreux alphabets inventés par des Nègres. C'est que l'écriture appauvrit le *réel*. Elle le cristallise en catégories rigides; elle le fixe quand le propre du réel est d'être *vivant*, fluide, et sans contours. Voulant saisir et exprimer la vie Africaine, Herbert Pepper a, lui aussi, dédaigné l'écriture, du moins l'écriture musicale, la plus infidèle.

In the next paragraph, Senghor offers an ontological basis and rationale for his preference for speech:

> C'est qu'en Afrique noire, dans une civilisation non pas 'en deçà' mais 'au-delà' de l'écriture, l'art majeur est celui de la *parole*. La parole y exprime la force vitale, l'*être* du nommant et, en même temps, l'*être* du nommé.[38]

What is a Derridian deconstructionist, for instance, to make of this declaration? That Senghor is simply a colonial prisoner of a much larger Western European world-view whose 'logocentric metaphysics' he has learned, was forced to learn and to share? Or that the African civilization is, because Senghor says so, indeed a civilization located 'beyond' writing? I do not think that the answer to either of these questions need necessarily be affirmative, since one may thereby risk confusing reality with a theoretical bluff, a phenomenological pose, as is often the case with many a programmatic pronouncement within negritude. I have already observed in the above analysis of Senghor's poem the dominant metonymic and metaphoric functions of the totem as poetic image: the first function characterizes the general style and tone of the composition and even informs the internal mechanics of the poem; the other function – a true metaphor of self, an ambivalent self-image – yields quite naturally corresponding images of a break, a disfunction and a search for balance and unity. Now I shall contend here that the same problematic of negritude so well typified in the poem 'Le Totem' also permeates Senghor's pronouncements on writing and speech; in fact, it is such pronouncements as these that can lead one to suspect a certain 'blindness' (in de Man's connotation of the term[39]) in many of Senghor's otherwise 'insightful' thoughts on Africa.

The immediate context of the Senghor statements is his essay, 'Le Langage intégral des négro-africains'. Ostensibly a preface to Herbert Pepper's L'*Anthologie de la vie africaine* (a rather ambitious ethno-musicological book that purports to establish the common musical heritage and language of all black Africa and which Senghor calls 'sans nul doute, une révolution'), Senghor's essay deals with the question of aesthetic holism in Africa or what he calls le *langage intégral*. The qualities he admires in Pepper's book are also revealing. He applauds the author's 'natural predisposition' 'à comprendre l'âme mystique des Négro-africains'; the very title of the anthology 'vise à une saisie totale du réel'; but, above all, 'Herbert Pepper s'est fait "nègre avec le nègre" pour *comprendre* le Nègre, ce qui était la méthode la plus efficace'.[40]

I suspect that Senghor has made a *faux pas* here. By what feat of imagination, or metaphorical slip of the tongue, can one assert that a white person can *understand* what it is to be a black man? All dictates of common sense and reason suggest the contrary to be the case: that only a black man – whether in America, Africa, Europe or elsewhere – can understand what it really is to be a black. The articulation, in writing or speech, of this black existentialist position may be a burden for the few – black creative writers, black artists and black intellectuals who have acquired the necessary protocols and rhetorics of writing and speech. But the actual living, the reality and meaning of the existence of true 'blackness', is not a burden but a gift to the many who do not have these cumbersome credentials, and therefore lack the 'blindness' of their intellectual fellow blacks. It is this same quality of 'blindness', I think, that Derrida associates with Rousseauist ethnocentrism and deplores particularly in Lévi-Strauss's treatment of the Nambikwara Indians, although Derrida connects this with a stunning but cunning defence of the art of writing among the so-called 'innocent' and 'primitive' people.[41] Leaving aside for the moment Senghor's rather defective phenomenological and ontological reasoning about the black world, let us pursue instead his methodology.

Senghor's affective method of reflection, as shown in the last passage quoted, which when translated into the politics of negritude easily amounts to a gospel of the totalization of feelings and opinions in Africa, disregards what Derrida calls *différence* or *différance*. These two terms, in the hermetic terminology of Derrida's philosophical reflections, are difficult to gloss except by invoking other linguistic parallelisms. Derrida has provided, for example, provisional definitions of the two terms as follows:

> We provisionally give the name *differance* to this *sameness* which is not *identical*: by the silent writing of its *a*, it has the desired advantage of referring to differing, both as spacing/temporalizing and as the movement that structures every dissociation. . . . As distinct from difference, differance thus points out the irreducibility of temporalizing. . . . Differance is not simply active (any more than it is a subjective accomplishment); it rather indicates the middle voice, it precedes and sets up the opposition between passivity and activity. With its *a*, differance more properly refers to what in classical language would be called *the origin or production of differences and the differences between differences, the play* (jeu) *of* differences. Its locus and operation will therefore be seen wherever speech appeals to difference.[42]

Good linguistic parallels of Derrida's terms *différance* and *différence* may be found in what Saussure (an especial target, ironically, of Derridian deconstructive attacks) proposed as the two complementary facets of language: *langue* and *parole*;

the one representing, roughly speaking, language as an inert mass or as a subconscious system, the other the articulatory habits and variations which each user of the language consciously operates on the system. If this watered-down version of Derrida's terminologies is accepted, then what Senghor's negritude methodology, based on 'affective presence', circumvents or conceals is, it seems, the existence of *différance* as part of the underlying principles of African cultures and civilizations: it conceals it under an ideological but, in my view, false cloak of cultural monolithism. On the other hand, what it interdicts or resists – this time rather unsuccessfully, since most African intellectuals, particularly in the English-speaking African countries, were reluctant to agree – is the need for *différence* to exist and flourish. In effect, Senghor's affective stance, if interpreted as a system of prescriptive ethics (that is to say, a common *langue*) in Africa, assumes that *sameness* is all that counts, and that dissent, or differing voices (whose principle in this respect is, according to Derrida, *différance*), can for ever be held back, *deferred* or even suppressed.

From this one can see clearly what it is that Senghor is defending in his prefatory note to the *Anthologie*: an intrinsic and univocal solidarity, in social and political purpose and determination, of all departments of aesthetic production and, by inference, all aesthetic criticism and interpretation in Africa. It is not surprising, then, that Senghor's *langage intégral* – which, as I have said, amounts to an affective, totalizing metalanguage for African literary and aesthetic theory – should lead logically, that is to say in a phenomenological sense, in a *magical* sense, to what he terms a *technique intégrale* in African art.

Again deploying a Derridian terminology, I will quite summarily qualify Senghor's *technique intégrale* as an *arch-écriture*, and once more beg the reader's indulgence for a certain haziness in my mind concerning the meaning of this latter term, since it reaches us fully wrapped in the intricate, typically Derridian philosophical package. For example, at the end of the essay 'Nature, culture, écriture: de Lévi-Strauss à Rousseau', Derrida says:

> To recognize writing in speech, that is to say the differance and the absence of speech, is to begin to think the lure. There is no ethics without the presence of the other but also, and consequently, without absence, dissimulation, detour, differance, writing. The arch-writing is the origin of morality as of immorality.[43]

This passage is like a double-edged sword, as is true also of the meaning of Senghor's *langage intégral*. We cannot accept the presence or principle of a common aesthetic language of art in Africa (or, for that matter, of a common literary theory or language) without at the same time denying the presence of and the right for differing individual aesthetic visions to exist. This is a question of basic morality and commonsense logic: if A, then not B; if B, then not A, and so on. Isn't this how politics operates in Africa and elsewhere: tension between the 'ins' and the 'outs'? But it so happens that 'arch-writing' – to translate

Derrida's words literally – is at the same time both 'in' and 'out', both A and B. Simplifying the equation, symbolically, one can state that: $W^0 = (A, -B) + (B, -A) = \emptyset$, where W^0 means writing to degree zero (arch-writing), A means writing, B means speech, and $\emptyset$ stands for a null entity, a zero degree or a melting-pot.

If Derrida's 'arch-writing' can be reduced to a sort of melting-pot or even arbitrarily to what Barthes has called the 'degree zero' – despite the latter's Freudian psychologizing on writing as a self-definitional, intransitive process – then 'arch-writing' incarnates an ambiguity. It is neither 'morality' nor 'immorality', but simultaneously 'immorality' and 'morality': it mediates the tension or opposition between the two terms. Consequently, one can say that Derrida's 'arch-writing' is a trickster concept. In African trickster tales, especially those dealing with the origins of things – the universe, life and death, heaven and earth, etc. – we have proper names that designate the trickster figures, based upon the ambiguous functions and roles they perform in the tales, and upon the ease with which they flout or transcend codes of morality and immorality, overcome their foes and cheat their friends, or surmount obstacles – all by their special gift of words (speech?) and by their cunning tricks (writing?). We call them *Esu* (in Yoruba), *Mbe* (in Ibo); in the New World there also exist various terms for the trickster figure.[44]

Arch-écriture, the old trickster, is also (let us say, the name of) the Nambikwara Indian chief to whose cunnings, wiles or alphabetic sleights of hand – if we should believe Derrida's ironic point – poor Lévi-Strauss ironically succumbs as victim:

> Empirical violence, war in the colloquial sense (. . . ruse and perfidy of the Indian chief playing at the comedy of writing, *apparent* ruse and perfidy of the Indian chief borrowing all his resources from the Occidental intrusion), which Lévi-Strauss always thinks of as an *accident*. An accident occurring, in his view, upon a terrain of innocence, in a 'state of culture' whose *natural* goodness had not yet been degraded.[45]

Accident? Hardly. Perfidy? Maybe. By whichever term we may choose to call it, Senghor's *technique intégrale*, whose implied purpose is to maintain the indivisibility of voice in matters of aesthetic production and perception in Africa, is, as stated before, at the same time a totalizing, emotional, reductionist and therefore misleading concept. Misleading because in an earlier passage Senghor speaks eloquently about the liberating character and force of reality, its refusal to be fixed, categorized and frozen, and its desire to maintain a lively fluidity of existence. If that is what reality indeed is or wants, then I think that is also what the 'history' of ideas in Africa once was, and wishes to remain. Thus the affective technique of reflection, which is the methodology that Senghor recommends, is one that represses objective differences of thought and opinion in Africa, and can only lead to artificial systems of syntagmatic relations such as he sees linking 'le poème à la musique, la musique à la danse, la danse à la sculpture, et celle-ci à la peinture',[46] without any objective mediation. What we need to establish for Africa is not merely the historical processes, or the chronological evolution of aesthetic thoughts and feelings; rather, by utilizing all objective means possible for conducting such an inquiry, we need to locate and re-construct the very paradigmatic base of such thoughts and feelings. But to reconstruct effectively one needs first to deconstruct – especially old myths and metaphysics about, as well as in, Africa.

'C'est la chance de l'Afrique noire d'avoir dédaigné l'écriture,' Senghor's manifesto says. We might never know whether that indeed was good or bad 'luck' for Africa, if we did not also perceive the underlying ruse or blindness – since Senghor was here thinking more about alphabetic writing than about sign or surrogate language, cryptograms, ideograms, 'arch-writings', etc. – when he added, as an afterthought, 'même quand elle ne l'ignorait pas.'

Now consider this different variation on the same theme, taken from another negritude advocate, the Cameroonian Professor Engelbert Mveng:

> la civilisation négro-africaine n'est pas seulement orale; elle est aussi écrite, et son écriture, c'est notre art traditionnel. Les dessins des tissages touareg du désert, des tissages dogon du Mali, des motifs adinkra du Ghana, des poids ashanti et baoulé de Côte-d'Ivoire, des bas-reliefs d'Abomey, du Bénin ou de Foumban, les motifs abbdia du sud-Cameroun, les scènes sculptées des Tchokwé de l'Angola, les symboles des Bakuba du Kassaï, et les graffiti des parchemins populaires d'Éthiopie, tout cela constitue un langage écrit qui raconte l'histoire et la vie quotidienne de nos peuples. Or, ce langage écrit remonte loin, très loin dans le passé: avant la naissance d'écriture en Égypte![47]

This passage is not only a good meditation on the subject of 'writing and difference'.[48] It also points out a central paradox within the philosophy of negritude by showing that Senghor and Mveng, judging by their statements, cannot possibly be in agreement on what meaning or origin to assign to writing (l'écriture), as far as Africa is concerned. But, more important, what Mveng is suggesting in the text above, though from a perspective of historicity, is that in Africa that which we call writing (l'écriture) is nothing but a lived system of signs and symbols, a sort of experiential semiology shared by all. Thus, to look for the principles of an African aesthetic or literary theory, one may well start by understanding the metaphorical languages 'spoken' by all the various signs and symbols that one finds, not in parole, but in traditional African decorative arts, sculptures,[49] graffiti, and so on. It seems appropriate, therefore, to conclude this essay, without further comment, by quoting Derrida's meditation on the same subject:

> one should meditate upon all of the following together: writing as the possibility of the road and of difference, the history of writing and the history

of the road, of the rupture, of the *via rupta*, of the path that is broken, beaten, *fracta*, of the space of reversibility, and of repetition traced by the opening, the divergence from, and the violent spacing, of nature, of the natural, savage, salvage, forest.[50]

Notes

1 Roman Jakobson and Claude Lévi-Strauss, ' "Les Chats" de Baudelaire', *L'Homme*, 2, 1 (1962), pp. 5–21.

2 Noam Chomsky, *Syntactic Structures* (The Hague: Mouton, 1957) and *Aspects of the Theory of Syntax* (Boston, Mass.: MIT Press, 1965).

3 Roland Barthes, 'Éléments de sémiologie', *Communications*, 4 (1964), pp. 91–135; repr. as *Elements of Semiology*, trans. Annette Lavers and Colin Smith (London: Cape, 1967).

4 See, e.g., Samuel R. Levin, *Linguistic Structures in Poetry* (The Hague: Mouton, 1969).

5 Abiola Irele, 'The Criticism of Modern African Literature', in Christopher Heywood (ed.), *Perspectives on African Literature* (New York: Africana, 1968), pp. 9–30.

6 Cf. Roland Barthes, *Essais critiques* (Paris: Seuil, 1964), trans. as *Critical Essays* by Richard Howard (Evanston, Ill.: Northwestern University Press, 1972).

7 Sunday O. Anozie, *Sociologie du roman africain* (Paris: Aubier-Montaigne, 1970) and 'Genetic Structuralism as a Critical Technique', *The Conch*, 3, 1 (1971), pp. 33–44.

8 Sunday O. Anozie, 'Structuralism in East and West Africa', in T. E. Sebeok (ed.), *Structuralism around the World* (The Hague: Mouton, forthcoming).

9 Léopold Sédar Senghor, *Chants d'ombre* (Paris: Seuil, 1945).

10 Louis Althusser and Étienne Balibar, *Reading 'Capital'* (London: New Left Books, 1970); Claude Lévi-Strauss, *The Savage Mind* (Chicago, Ill.: University of Chicago Press, 1966).

11 Miriam Glucksmann, *Structuralist Analysis in Contemporary Social Thought* (London: Routledge & Kegan Paul, 1974).

12 Lévi-Strauss, op. cit., p. 22.

13 L. S. Senghor, 'Problématique de la négritude', *Présence africaine*, 78 (1971), pp. 3–26.

14 Austin J. Shelton, *The African Assertion* (New York: Odyssey Press, 1968), p. 73.

15 Robert Mercier, 'L'Imagination dans la poésie de Léopold Sédar Senghor', *Literature East and West*, 12, 1 (1968), pp. 44–5.

16 Sylvia Washington Bâ, *The Concept of Negritude in the Poetry of Léopold Sédar Senghor* (Princeton, NJ: Princeton University Press, 1973); Placide B. Tempels, *La Philosophie bantoue* (Paris: Présence Africaine, 1949); Janheinz Jahn, *Muntu: L'Homme africain et la culture néo-africaine* (Paris: Seuil, 1958).

17 Translation by Bâ, op. cit., p. 197.

18 L. S. Senghor, *Liberté I: Négritude et humanisme* (Paris: Seuil, 1964), p. 203.

19 W. L. d'Azevedo (ed.), *The Traditional Artist in African Societies* (Bloomington, Ind.: Indiana University Press, 1973).

20 J. Charbonnier, *Entretiens avec Lévi-Strauss* (Paris: Plon, 1961), p. 70; trans. as *Conversations with Claude Lévi-Strauss* by John and Doreen Weightman (London: Cape, 1969).

21 Senghor, *Liberté I*, pp. 238–9.

22 Charbonnier, op. cit., pp. 33, 71.

23 Roland Barthes, *Le Degré zéro de l'écriture* (Paris: Seuil, 1953); trans. as *Writing Degree Zero* by Annette Lavers and Colin Smith (London: Cape, 1967).

24 C. A. Diop, *The African Origin of Civilization*, trans. M. Cook (New York: Lawrence Hill, 1974).

25 Senghor, *Liberté I*, p. 267.

26 Lévi-Strauss, op. cit., p. 12.

27 Senghor, Liberté I, p. 161.
28 Cf., e.g., Ferdinand de Saussure, Cours de linguistique générale (1915: Paris: Payot, 1968); trans. as Course in General Linguistics by Wade Baskin (New York: McGraw-Hill, 1966; London: Fontana, 1974).
29 Senghor, Liberté I, p. 386.
30 Phenomenology developed with Edmund Husserl as a protest against neo-Kantism (strong in German universities at the turn of this century) and empiricism. It was presented as a principle or method of describing things which would give priority of consideration not to any pre-existing conceptual framework but to the intuitive rapport between the subject and the object. For things in their raw state (that is, the world) do not possess a meaning; they do so – that is, become 'phenomena' – only when they are lived, that is, illuminated by an act of consciousness of the subject (the 'transcendental Ego'). It is sometimes referred to as 'a science of essences' (or 'eidetic' science), and one of phenomenology's many concerns is therefore to discover, using its own method of intuitive reasoning, the transcendental structures of the consciousness that is present in every signifying act. Thus the evolution of Husserl's phenomenology can be said to be towards a philosophy of perception and of history. In this respect, Merleau-Ponty was his principal continuator and disciple in France. I can understand any critic who prefers to link Senghor's negritude, in terms of direct influence, with Bergson's descriptive psychology rather than with Merleau-Ponty.
31 Senghor, 'Problématique de la négritude', pp. 13–26.
32 Cf. Lucien Lévy-Bruhl, 'Les Carnets de Lucien Lévy-Bruhl', La Revue philosophique, 7–9 (July–September 1947), pp. 257–81.
33 Sunday O. Anozie, 'Structuralism in Poetry and Mythology', The Conch, 4, 1 (1972), pp. 1–21.
34 Lévi-Strauss, op. cit., pp. 25–6.
35 See Sunday O. Anozie, 'Negritude and Structuralism', in Bernth Lindfors and Ulla Schild (eds), Neo-African Literature and Culture: Essays in Memory of Janheinz Jahn (Wiesbaden: B. Heymana, 1976), pp. 43–56.
36 See Sunday O. Anozie, Structural Models and African Poetics (London: Routledge & Kegan Paul, 1981), esp. chapter 6.
37 The following are useful introductions to the subject: Geoffrey Hartman (ed.), Deconstruction and Criticism, preface by Geoffrey Hartman (New York: Seabury Press, 1979); Christopher Norris, Deconstruction: Theory and Practice (London: Methuen, 1982) (excellent); Jonathan Culler, On Deconstruction (London: Routledge & Kegan Paul, 1982); and Vincent B. Leitch, Deconstructive Criticism (New York: Columbia University Press, 1983). For examples of the possible adaptation of deconstructionist theory in the treatment of particular subjects, see, for instance: Thomas J. J. Altizer, Deconstruction and Theology (New York: Crossroad Press, 1982), and Sunday O. Anozie, Deconstruction and Politics: Language, Criticism, and the Speakerly Text (forthcoming).
38 Senghor, Liberté I, pp. 238–9.
39 See Paul de Man, Blindness and Insight: Essays in the Rhetoric of Contemporary Criticism (New York: Oxford University Press, 1979).
40 Senghor, Liberté I, p. 238.
41 See Jacques Derrida, 'Nature, culture, écriture: de Lévi-Strauss à Rousseau', Cahiers pour l'analyse, 4: Lévi-Strauss dans le 18e siècle (September–October 1966), pp. 1–45. This essay is reproduced in English translation as 'Violence of the Letter', in Jacques Derrida, Of Grammatology, trans. Gayatri Chakravorty Spivak (Baltimore, Md: Johns Hopkins University Press, 1977).
42 Jacques Derrida, Speech and Phenomena (and Other Essays on Husserl's Theory of Signs), trans. David B. Allison (Evanston, Ill.: Northwestern University Press, 1973), pp. 129–30; my emphasis.

43 Derrida, Of Grammatology, pp. 139–40.
44 See, e.g. Henry Louis Gates, Jr, 'The "Blackness of Blackness": A Critique of the Sign and the Signifying Monkey', Critical Inquiry, 9, 4 (June 1983), pp. 685–723. This essay, reproduced in the volume, is the first and most engaging attempt I have so far come across to examine the potential of the trickster figure as the basis for formulating an original black literary theory.
45 Derrida, Of Grammatology, p. 112.
46 Senghor, Liberté I, p. 238.
47 Rev. Engelbert Mveng, 'Négritude et civilisation gréco-romaine', in Colloque sur la négritude (Paris: Présence Africaine, 1972), p. 50.
48 See Jacques Derrida, Writing and Difference, trans. Alan Bass (Chicago, Ill.: University of Chicago Press, 1978).
49 See Anozie, Structural Models and African Poetics, pp. 6 ff.
50 Derrida, Of Grammatology, pp. 107–8.

5

Anthony Appiah

Strictures on structures: the prospects for a structuralist poetics of African fiction

> Jakobson . . . emphasized that the basis for pronouncing judgement over any literary or scientific movement should be the actual performance of production, not the verbal rhetoric of its manifesto. Indeed, it is difficult not to agree with this viewpoint.   (Sunday O. Anozie)[1]

If, like me, you are interested in African literature, and are aware of the great changes on the face of literary studies that structuralism – and now the various post-structuralisms – have produced, you will want to ask what structuralism can do for African fiction. And, since Sunday O. Anozie has pioneered the structuralist criticism of African literature, at least in English, we shall surely want to start with *Structural Models and African Poetics*, which represents his latest extended thoughts. If Anozie does indeed endorse the view he ascribes to Jakobson in the passage which provides my epigraph, he should find our attention welcome.

Sunday Anozie carries in his name the nature of his problem. His Christian name (what name more Christian?) reflects, in its Englishness, his status as a citizen of the lost British Empire; his family name his Ibo heritage.[2] If I were Derrida, I might, perhaps, add that the 'O' which mediates between the names is a zero, an absence, a nothing – the nothing, in fact, which joins Africa and Europe together. But a large part of my difficulty in reading Anozie's book, which sets out to turn this nothing into a something, this absent mediation into a presence, is that everything in my training, my thought and my culture resists the desire, which pervades much of contemporary American culture, to be Derridian; or, more precisely, since Derrida is here only (as they say) a metonym, to engage with the problematic in which Derrida lives and moves and writes his being.

So much I say to begin with, because it seems to me fair. I do not come to a work of contemporary literary theory without presentiments. I anticipate a style of writing, and thought, which mistakes the obscure for the profound; which confuses a reading of philosophy with a philosophical reading; which dispenses, in fact, with the urge for clarity and reason that lies at the root of the philosophical tradition of the country from which so much darkness and unreason now emanates. Occasionally, I am pleasurably surprised, but rarely. In short, I expect little pleasure from such texts.

Yet, even by the standards of a practice for which I have little taste, Anozie's book seems to me to lack merit. It exemplifies the dangers of recent literary theory, not so much because it follows that theory but because it manages to combine a command of the relevant lexical range (i.e. jargon) and syntactical idiosyncrasies (i.e. style) with an almost total failure to grasp its semantics (i.e. claims). I am inclined to think that this failure is not, *au fond*, Anozie's fault; it is certainly not his unique distinction. The terrible failings that lie scattered on the surface of his text lie often, I believe, at the heart of the project with which he wishes to be allied. To argue *that*, however, would be the task of an essay longer than this one; but I believe that an examination of *Structural Models and African Poetics* will lend support to my claim.

Anyone who is even slightly unclear about the role that structuralism, whatever it is, has played in recent literary theory – anyone, that is, who wonders about the directness of the relevance of technical linguistics to literary theory, or about the distinction between *langue* and *parole*, or about the sense in which the nature of the 'signified' is as arbitrary as the nature of the 'signifier' – anyone who wonders about any of these things will find no help in Sunday Anozie's book. Despite the fact that he purports to offer us an introduction to the structure of structuralism, we enter its world in *medias res*. From the very beginning, for example, we are engaged with linguistics; the introduction gives us the outline of Greenberg's classification of African languages, an outline which occupies more than a page, and which imparts the following sort of information:

I   CONGO-KORDOFANIAN
IA   Niger-Congo
IA1 West Atlantic
IA2 Mande
IA3 Voltaic
IA4 Kwa

(I stop here only because the Kwa group includes my father's language; apart from three rivers and an ocean, most people would recognize nothing on this list.) So I hope I may be excused an excursus into the archaeology of structuralism, by way of providing some point of entry to Anozie's threateningly hermetic text.

It is clear to all that the fundamental idea of structuralism was to model our understanding of all 'meaning-bearing' cultural systems on linguistics and, in particular, on the kind of linguistics pioneered by Saussure. It is by no means clear to many, among whom I happily include myself, what this project entails. But a helpful starting place is an account of some of the distinguishing marks of Saussurean linguistics and its methods.

If we ask which theses are most frequently associated with Saussure, we shall, I think, have to mention at least four: the arbitrary nature of the sign; the purely relational, or structural, character of linguistic systems; and the importance of the distinctions between *langue* and *parole*, on the one hand, and synchronic and diachronic perspectives, on the other. In examining these theses one can begin to establish what is distinctive in Saussure's linguistic theory.

The thesis of the arbitrary nature of the sign has two elements which are, I think, worth distinguishing. Saussure conceived of signs as being made up of two components: the *signified* and the *signifier*. The signifier is just the spoken or written word, the word as object, in that special sense in which the word *table*, printed here in italics, and the word 'table', uttered by you as you read this passage out loud, are the same (kind of) thing. The signified, on the other hand, is not, as the term might suggest, the table itself, the physical object, to which I refer when I say 'Let's sit at that table'; it is rather the idea, the mental object, which you have and which you succeed in communicating when you get your message across.[3]

This distinction between signifier and signified, of which so much has been made, is hardly very interesting in itself. If anything could lay claim to being the commonsense view of language in Western culture (a common sense articulated, of course, by philosophers from Port-Royal on), it is the view that words become meaningful because of their association with 'ideas'. But that this notion is commonsensical enough does not mean that it is uncontroversial; indeed, the consensus of opinion among (analytical) philosophers of language for some time now has been that it is mistaken. For there is a strong body of argument which tends to show that the meaning of a term can be different for two people, even if the idea that corresponds to it is the same for each of them; and, conversely, that the possession of different mental items associated with the same word(s) does not guarantee difference of meaning. If this is right, then expressing the same idea is neither necessary nor sufficient for two words to have the same meaning.[4]

Within this theory, and using its terminology, we can, however, say what is involved in the thesis of the arbitrary nature of the sign. Once again, a part of the claim is neither very exciting nor very original: the relationship between the signified and the signifier that make up *any* particular sign is conventional and not natural. *Tisch* would have done just as well as *table* as the word the English speakers associated with the signified idea of a table. But this is not all that Saussure means. He means also that neither the content of the signified idea nor that of the signifying word can be taken for granted as natural either. Neither is, to use a fashionable turn of phrase, 'always, already given'.

Let us try to be clear what this means. In the case of the signified, it is perhaps easy to grasp. What Saussure meant was that the way our ideas (signifieds) partition up reality is itself arbitrary, in the sense of conventional. In the familiar case, different languages partition the visual spectrum in different ways. It is not that there is an idea of greenness, a signified, waiting for the word *green* (or *vert* or *grün*) to come along to signify it; rather, in learning the sign we also learn to classify together, as green, things which in other cultures may be classified in other ways. In the case of the signifier, an analogous situation obtains: it is not a natural fact but a conventional one that, when I mutter *table* in my deep baritone and my mother enunciates it clearly in her elegant soprano, we are taken as having uttered the same word. That this is a consequence of a complex social convention comes out clearly if we consider the way in which certain sounds which are different phonemes in one language (/s/ as in *snake*, /sh/ as in *sugar*, for example, in English) are treated as the same phoneme in other languages (Ga, for example). This fact explains why the Twi-speaking kingdom which is known to its inhabitants as *Asante* is known to English speakers as *Ashanti*. 'The English spelling *Ashantee* is owing to the circumstance that the interpreter of Mr Bowdich (the author of the most important book hitherto written on Asante) was an Akraman', a Ga speaker, who couldn't 'hear' the difference between the two.[5]

Just as the thesis that the sign is in some way made up of a mental and an acoustical or written component is not uncontroversial, so too there are those who doubt the extent to which signifiers and signifieds are as arbitrary as Saussure thought. There are, after all, phonological laws which are alleged to be invariant across languages; and, more important, there is a significant school of opinion, associated most notoriously with Chomskyan psycholinguistics, that claims that ideas, far from being constructed in our socialization, are simply 'triggered' from an innate stock by our exposure to experience in general, and language in particular.[6] If this is so, then the most interesting aspect of the Saussurean thesis – namely its claim that our concepts are determined by our culture – is true only in the rather unexciting sense that, without exposure to other speakers, we might never come to express the ideas that lie hidden in us from birth. I have been insisting that Saussure's views on the nature of the sign are controversial, because it is sometimes important to keep insisting on what may be obvious: Saussure has no especial privilege as a source of truths about language. Actually those aspects of his theory of the sign that I have discussed so far seem to me to be correct in their broad outlines, even if they might need substantial development to cover all cases. But, if literary theory is to gain anything from linguistics (or, for that matter, from philosophy), it cannot be indifferent to the question of the adequacy of the theories of which it makes use. When Anozie tells us that he 'has Saussure to his father', we must surely feel inclined to ask whether this parentage is not more burden than privilege.

My scepticism concerning Saussure's views about the arbitrary nature of the sign is, thus, methodological; but, when I turn to his account of the purely structural nature of linguistic systems, that scepticism becomes substantive. And this, of course, is important; for it is Saussure's contribution of this thesis that makes him a founding father of structuralism.

What does Saussure mean, then, by saying that the system of language is purely structural, that the essential properties of signs are those they have by virtue of their relationships with each other? We can begin by examining the claim in the case of phonology, for here it is at its most plausible. Saussure distinguished between two kinds of relational features of signs: paradigmatic and syntagmatic. In the case of phonology, /b/ and /p/ can replace one another in most words and still produce a sound which is a potential word of English. Replacing /b/ with /l/ in many contexts, however, will not produce such a phonologically acceptable word. Thus *prake* is not a word of current English, but could have been, while *lrake* could not. Facts of this kind, facts about which phonemes can stand in the same phonological environments and which cannot, are what Saussure calls paradigmatic; they have to do with whether or not elements can fit into the same patterns. Syntagmatic relations between phonemes, on the other hand, have to do with the way in which they relate to each other within the patterns: it is a syntagmatic fact that /b/ can occur before /r/; another that /l/ cannot (at least within the same syllable in English).[7]

Now syntagmatic and paradigmatic relations between elements of the phonological system are, in a good sense, purely structural; if we knew all the syntagmatic and paradigmatic facts about the elements, we would understand the structure of the phonological system. And, given the way in which phonemes are classically defined, it might appear that in stating these structural facts we had captured the system's essential features. It is due to the fact that the /sh/ in *sugar* and the /s/ in *snake* sometimes produce different English words when substituted for each other in phonological contexts (*-ake*, for example) that they count as different phonemes of English; relatedly, the fact that the rolled 'r' sound and its unrolled counterpart do not produce different words when substituted for each other in a phonological context permits them to count as the same phoneme of English.

But appearances here are deceptive, and we need to go carefully. Suppose we were to characterize the sound system of English by saying that it consisted of so many elements, the phonemes; that these fell into certain classes (voiced, unvoiced, and so on); and that there were such and such rules for combining them. We should then have stated all the syntagmatic and paradigmatic facts, and thus completely specified the structural essence of English phonology. Could we then say that we had said everything about the sound system of English?

Obviously not. For, in order to tell whether a certain sound uttered by a speaker was phonologically a possible English word, we would need to know more than the structural facts: we would need to know also what sorts of sounds counted as phonemes. You could know all the structural facts about English phonology and fail to recognize an English syllable enunciated clearly before your very ears.

At this point Saussure might reply that saying what the sounds are is the task not of phonology but of phonetics, the study of the physical (acoustic) properties of the linguistic system. But, though this distinciton is worth maintaining, it will not do to defend the claim that phonemes are purely relational entities. For the distinction just drawn between phonology and phonetics is just the difference between the study of the structural relations among the elements of the sound system, on the one hand, and the study of their intrinsic physical properties. If we just labelled the different phonemes with numerals, then many different sound systems could exist, which conformed to the same structural rules, but which differed in that, for example, the phonemes were replaced by the notes of a musical scale. Now Saussure wished to characterize the features of the linguistic system structurally at every level – phonological, syntactic, semantic. At each level, there exists the corresponding possibility of a distinction between syntagmatic and paradigmatic features. Simplifying grossly, we could say, for instance, that the relations between nouns are paradigmatic, in that they can replace each other while still producing grammatical sentences, whereas the relations between nouns and verb-phrases are syntagmatic, since they can be combined together to form grammatical sentences. But, once again, though syntactic structure is important, it cannot be what essentially characterizes a language. If it were, a language in which the words of English were replaced by different words, each of which obeyed the corresponding syntactic rules, would have to be regarded as essentially the same as English; whereas, while it would, of course, have the same syntactic structure as English,[8] it would constitute a different language.[9]

Now it is one thing to deny, as I do, that a language is completely exhausted by its structure – that its structure is its essence – and quite another to deny that structure is the most important of a language's features. Indeed, it seems to me that thinking about a language as a complex, structured system, with syntagmatic and paradigmatic features, is highly instructive. But it also remains important to allow that the elements that enter into these structural relations have interesting features – to allow that there may be interesting facts about a system which are not structural – especially when, later, we come to consider the relevance of Saussure's work to literary theory.

In discussing Saussure's use of the notions of syntagmatic and paradigmatic features of the *langue*, it is useful also to draw attention to an aspect of his theorizing that has proved congenial to literary theory – namely, the way in which he continually stresses the holistic character of his account. If elements of the linguistic system are understood through their syntagmatic and paradigmatic relations, and all these relations constitute their collective essence, then any change in one element in the system will affect the essential character of all the others. Thus (to take an example discussed by Jonathan Culler), for Saussure the fact that the French *fleuve* and *rivière* contrast in that one flows into the sea and the other does not, while the English *river* and *stream* contrast in being bigger and smaller, means that *rivière* and *river* differ in their essential character.[10]

Though the thesis of the dependence of the essence of everything on the character of everything else has a certain appeal for those of a mystical disposition, we need to enquire carefully into the sense in which the ascription of syntactic or semantic characteristics to signs is holistic. Anozie's discussion of structuralism (*SMAP*, pp. 28–30) is replete with quotations from such luminaries as Lalande, Piaget, Boudon and Flamment, which appear to *equate* structuralism with holism, asserting that every structural fact is essential. But it is only generality of theoretical sweep that makes this proposition attractive. *Rivière* and *fleuve* may seem to support Saussure; but let us consider *blue* in (British) English and *blau* in German. Is it really true that because English has the term *vermilion*, for which (let us suppose) there is no precise translation into German, *blue* and *blau* must mean different things, have semantically different essential properties? Is it really so that someone who is unaware of the existence of the word *vermilion* in the paradigmatic series of the English colour terms does not fully know what *blue* means? I am frankly sceptical. The trouble with the view that everything is important is that it can't be true. What is important is important by contrast with what isn't.

It is one thing to say that structural facts matter, and another to say that *every* structural fact matters. Yet the theory of structural holism amounts precisely to the latter claim. Indeed, structural holism, together with the thesis that structural facts constitute the essence of signs, entails that all and only the structural facts matter. This claim seems to me hyperbolic; and I shall later show the manner in which uncertainty about which structural facts are relevant diminishes what is, for me, one of the few really worthwhile passages in Anozie's book: namely, his discussion of Senghor's 'Le Totem'.[11] But I want to describe briskly the last pair of Saussurean distinctions, between *langue* and *parole*, and the synchronic and the diachronic perspectives, before returning to detailed discussion of the book.

Here, as with his account of the arbitrary nature of the sign, Saussure seems to me to be fundamentally correct. For having insisted, as he does, on the distinction between the abstract system of formal rules of phonology, syntax and semantics, on the one hand, and the actual speech of language users, in which those rules are somehow embodied, on the other, it is possible to ask one of the most fundamental questions in the philosophy of language: how is it that we are able to find in the inchoate mass of ordinary utterances, which Saussure called *parole*, that abstract system of rules he called the *langue*? It is because the Chomskyan notions of *performance* and *competence* provide an answer to this question that they are often mentioned in the same breath as the *langue/parole* distinction. Chomsky's claim is that speakers have an implicit grasp of the rules of the abstract system of *langue*, which grasp constitutes *competence*, and guides their actual *performance* in *parole*. Differences between what the *langue* prescribes and the raw stuff of ordinary speech are to be explained in terms of the failure of psychological processes which actually apply the rules. Analogously, we can claim that driving is governed (in Britain) by the rule 'Drive on the left in two-way traffic', while allowing that some people drive on the right when they aren't concentrating.[12] Saussure's distinction allows us to pose the question that Chomsky answers. And even if we do not like Chomsky's answer (what, after all, is the evidence that anyone has an implicit grasp of the rules of a transformational grammar?), we owe to Saussure a clear formulation of the question.

What the *langue/parole* distinction also allows is a clear statement of the Saussurean view of the task of linguistics; for linguistics is the study of the *langue*. Here, too, it seems to me that Saussure's approach has been productive. Though there is some study of *parole*, it is neither so developed nor so interesting as the body of systematic study of *langue* which stretches from Saussure to Chomsky and beyond.

Saussure's insistence on distinguishing synchronic and diachronic issues in linguistics has also proved extremely fruitful, and for a reason which turns out to be crucial when we move to literary theory. If we consider a particular *langue* at some time (and, as Saussure would have been the first to admit, this involves some idealization), then its rules and structures are, at some level, present to the minds of its speakers. It may be that the Chomskyan account of the relation between the rules the linguist discovers and the speaker's performance is too crude; but speakers *do* acknowledge the rules of the grammar, at least to the extent of recognizing, and generally avoiding, the utterance of ungrammatical sentences.[13] On the other hand, if we look at the history of a natural language and see it, through Saussure's eyes, as a series of *langues* succeeding one another, then whatever laws there are – for example, about phonetic shifts – are not (or, at least, do not *need* to be) part of the awareness of any community of speakers. Indeed, it is conceivable that a single speaker's language might undergo a phonetic shift without her noticing it; in fact this often occurs when speakers move between places where different dialects of English are spoken.

If we ask ourselves the reason for this, the answer, I think, is clear. The laws governing the *langue* are complex social facts whose existence is constituted by the participation of speakers in the complex conventions of language.[14] But the laws of phonological shift are not the consequences of conventions; they are, no doubt, in part sociological laws, in part consequences of the biology of our production and perception of sounds. In Saussure's Durkheimian terminology, the *langue* is present to the collective consciousness, but the laws that govern the development of a language are not.

So much by way of introduction to the Saussurean account of language. But, if his linguistics is to provide a model for literary theory, we must still ask how we are to take the analogy between natural languages and literary productions as systems. Structuralists have not given a univocal answer to this question. Saussure himself saw linguistics as but a part of the theory of signs in general, but he took it to be a model for that general theory. If one is to follow him in this, one must suppose that such sign-systems as, for example, dress codes can be analysed as abstract systems, like the *langue*, in which syntagmatic and paradigmatic relations of the elements define a structure of relations. Persons thus minded might even suppose that they could study diachronically the development of dress as a sequence of movements between synchronic dress codes.

It is fundamentally this application of the analogy with natural languages that has engaged Lévi-Strauss; and his account of the language of myth – whose elements include such episodes as the killing of a father by a son – is, in this sense, Saussurean. Lévi-Strauss has taken from Jakobson, whom Anozie cites frequently, the idea that the fundamental structures are defined by binary relations, analogous to the oppositions between vowel and consonant, or voiced and unvoiced phonemes, which constitute the paradigmatic relations of phonology. These fundamental binary oppositions, taken themselves in pairs as the axes which define a two-dimensional plane, determine also the triangular pattern to which Lévi-Strauss so often returns.

Thus, to take an example which is helpfully explicated by Edmund Leach,[15] the triangle (see Figure 5.1) is defined by a horizontal axis representing the polarity culture–nature, and a vertical axis representing what Lévi-Strauss calls 'degree of elaboration'. The Jakobsonian primary-vowel triangle, by comparison, has *a* where this has *raw*, *u* where this has *cooked* and *i* where this has *rotten*; and the horizontal and vertical axes are low–high frequency and compact–diffuse loudness respectively.

Lévi-Strauss's use of the very structures he associates with Jakobsonian phonology is not accidental. He believes that the presence of such structures in our accounts of all languages suggests that the structures themselves are a kind of universal of human thought; and this view is confirmed, for him, by his ability to find them in so many mythologies. Though it is the claim that these structures are universal which makes Lévi-Strauss's anthropology of thought exciting, it is not clear to me that the claim is, in the final analysis, one with very much content. For defining a pair of binary oppositions to constitute the axes for a space containing three elements produces so little structure that it is difficult not to suspect that this 'universal of human thought' is an artefact of his system

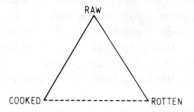

Figure 5.1

of analysis. Nicolas Ruwet writes, in his introduction to Jakobson's *Essais de linguistiques generales*:

> L'hypothèse fondamentale de Jakobson pose que, si l'organisation selon le principe binaire est la plus simple et la plus économique possible pour le savant qui ordonne ses matériaux, elle doit être aussi le principe qui sous-tend les opérations du locuteur et de l'auditeur, puisque celles-ci, du point de vue logique, ne diffèrent pas de celles du savant.[16]

Is it cynical to wonder how good an argument it is, for supposing that a theory about speakers is true, to point out that things would be simpler so – simpler both for the scholar and therefore (dangerous word) for the speaker? Certainly it is not merely cynical to wonder whether the basic features of myths are as universal as the basic phonetic system, which might be supposed to be determined by the biology of the throat, mouth, ear and, of course, brain.

This suspicion is reinforced by the following reflection: given the structures, Lévi-Strauss is able to treat myths as a kind of system of communication. Once we recognize that the tale in which the hunter is trapped by the eagle has a structure which is identical with the story in which the son is killed by the father, it is alleged, we can see that the tale is 'really about' the problematic relation of father and son.[17] The up–down axis of eagle and hunter stands for the higher–lower axis of the relation of kinship; the eagle for the father, the hunter for the son. But, in the case of the natural language, communication occurs when a communicator uses the *langue* to address another speaker. Who is communicating through myth . . . and to whom?

We may begin by asking ourselves who it is that understands the myth. In the case of natural language the hearer understands the message because he or she knows the code of the *langue*. But is it clear – indeed, I am inclined to ask whether Lévi-Strauss cares if it is clear – that those who hear the myth do, in fact, decode its message? And if they do not, then there is, here, a profound disanalogy with the case of natural language. For whereas, as I pointed out earlier, the *langue* is present in the collective consciousness of the linguistic community, the code of the myth is not – is not, that is, if the myth-hearer cannot decode the message of the myth.

I think that Lévi-Strauss's view is that the decoding does occur, but that it is unconscious: this is an interesting thought, for which, if I may speak for myself and the myths of Asante, there does not seem to be much evidence. Of course, it is possible that our myth of origin does address my unconscious and that I am unconscious of the decoded message. All I wish to insist is that the evidence for this, after all, empirical claim is sorely lacking; indeed, it is not clear to me how the decoded message is supposed to manifest itself.

As for the sender of the myth's message, there seems to me no plausible answer to the question who she is.

Lévi-Strauss's way of building on linguistics is not, however, the only way.

There is another way, which would seem to be even more Saussurean. In Saussure's account of the *langue* there is, as in all contemporary linguistics, a sense in which the system has levels. We define the structure of each level by way of the paradigmatic and syntagmatic properties of the elements. Among the rules of any level are syntagmatic rules which tell us how to compose the elements of the next, higher level. The syntactic rules, for example, tell us how to construct the sentences, given the syntactic categories of the morphemes, and the semantics then tells us how to construct the meaning of sentences as a function of their syntactic structures. Now there is an obvious way to continue this process to yet higher levels when we come to analyse texts. We take the semantic structures – the truth conditions, say, of the sentences[18] – as the elements at the next higher level, and look for the structural rules that characterize whole tales, whole novels, whole poems. This is the approach that Roland Barthes, with whom Anozie has studied, has proposed – as when, for example, in 'To Write: An Intransitive Verb?' he says:

> Linguistics suggests ... that we distinguish levels of analysis and that we describe the distinctive elements of each of these levels. ... I feel authorized to work on ... a postulate: the structure of the sentence, the object of linguistics, is found again, homologically, in the structure of works. Discourse is not simply an adding together of sentences; it is itself one great sentence.[19]

The problem with this approach is that, if the project is to work, we need an answer to the fundamental question of whether these codes at the level above the semantics of the *langue* are themselves part of the collective consciousness of the community. Is there any interesting sense in which we all know a set of rules for the construction of each genre of literature?

Interesting here is important. There are, of course, some rules we know; Todorov has studied some of them. Though the current state of the code of the novel is much less determinate than it probably was in the late nineteenth century in England, for example, there are some constraints on sequences of sentences which we all acknowledge as constitutive of the novel as a genre. Furthermore, just as the Saussurean thought suggests, these constraints are defined in terms of the semantic properties of sentences (what they are about) and not in terms of the syntax. But for this fact to be interesting, and interesting to literary theory in particular, we need to suppose that it is the existence of this code that gives the novel its life, and that what is important about any novel can be explicated in terms of its status as a product of that code. Indeed, the truly Saussurean thought is, as I suggested earlier, that all and only the structure of the code matters. I myself am not inclined to make that supposition; but it is an intelligible project to enquire how far we can get by making it. If, however, we agree with Anozie that 'deception – "the disappointment of expectations as to referentiality" – cannot ... work unless there are expectations, the reader's or the consumer's expectations' (*SMAP*, p. 68), then we must surely agree that what is of interest in the deception of the *nouveau roman* arises because it breaks a code and not because it follows it. It is true that the breaking of codes can be a part of a process that leads to new ones – as recalling the uproar at the first performance of Beethoven's First Symphony will remind us – but there is, surely, something to be learned from works that break codes even while they establish new ones, something over and beyond the structure of the new code. Here, it seems to me, the analogy with natural language is, potentially, profoundly misleading. For changes in the *langue* are, on the whole, unintended; while changes in the codes of literary or artistic form may be both intended and understood as intended, and are, indeed, a staple reaction to the 'anxiety of influence'.

In the case of poetry, and particularly of the poetry of the centuries before ours, the straightforward extension of the Saussurean project seems doomed to failure. For though there are rules constitutive of, for example, the sonnet as genre, they do not take the semantics of the sentences of their input. Indeed, the complex of phonological and syntactic factors we need to take into account, along with the semantics, in understanding a sonnet, threatens the whole notion of neatly parcelled levels of analysis. I believe that Anozie is aware of this problem; for he says:

> It is possible to sympathize with Ruwet's view that linguistics plays a modest auxiliary, though indispensable, role in poetic analysis. Such a view is, in fact, demonstrably true, even if we consider nothing else but the nature of poetic images which is supra-segmental. The appeal which such images have, that is, goes beyond the normal constraints of phonology and diction and even prosody. (*SMAP*, p. 131)

There is one problem, so it seems to me, which recurs again and again for structuralist and, indeed, for post-structuralist literary theory, and to which I have returned several times already. If we are to take seriously the claim that there is a code, a *langue*, whose decoding is the project of the reader, then we must suppose that the code exists in the collective consciousness in the same sort of way that the *langues* of natural languages do; the problem is that, for this claim, the evidence is scant. Because literary theorists have also been influenced by Freudian theory, the explanation given to those of us who deny that the codes that literary theory has 'uncovered' do exist in the collective consciousness is to claim that they exist in the collective unconsciousness. This, as I have also said before, is possible; but it needs to be shown. For a breed so given to drawing on a linguistics whose privileged status seems to derive only from the scientism of our culture and its times,[20] literary theorists seem peculiarly resistant to even the most modest form of empiricism. We can acknowledge that all theory is underdetermined by the evidence, that a flourishing undergrowth of theory can subsist on the most meagre evidential terrain, and still require of ourselves that we root our theorizing in the dry earth of experience.

It is against this theoretical background that Anozie's project should be viewed. His task is to say, first, what structuralism is; second, how it relates to certain features that he alleges to exist in 'African thought'; and, third, why we should choose a structuralist approach in our efforts to account for the various semiotic systems of Africa. I have already complained that he hardly succeeds in the first of these tasks, and I shall show, in a moment, why I believe this. But I shall also show the reasons why I reject his attempt at the second task and why, in the light of his contribution to the third task, it would be natural to remain sceptical about the relevance of structuralism to an understanding of African semiotic systems. In detailing the inadequacies of Anozie's approach at each of these levels, we shall be able to refer back to the sketchy account of structuralism I have given earlier; but I shall be trying to support my claim that Anozie's errors are not individual but characteristic, by showing, in those places where I can, how they arise in the very passages from (respected) structuralist authors that he cites.

In chapter 2 of *Structuralist Models and African Poetics*, 'The Structuralist Perspective', Anozie attempts to 'state more positively the nature – to some gratifying – of this experience of encounter with objects conceived of as systems', the encounter being, of course, the structuralist enterprise. And he begins by citing a remark by R. Boudon to the effect that the success of structuralism 'dépend en grand partie de l'objet auquel on l'applique'. With this one is bound to agree. For, according to the view I have suggested, the success of a structuralist analysis will depend on there being, in the domain under study, a system of abstract relations over which one can define something like a syntax and a semantics.

Anozie's gloss on this quotation from Boudon, however, seems to me to misrepresent its content. 'What Boudon means', he tells us, 'is that the structuralist perspective . . . is not totally divorceable from a certain element of subjective intentionality on the part of the analyst' (*SMAP*, p. 22). I have no idea whether this is something Boudon believes, but it is certainly not what he says in the passage cited. And, having made this rather brusque transition from Boudon to Anozie's gloss, the reader is eased, in the next sentence, from the phenomenologist's word *intentionality* to phenomenology: 'Underlying every structuralist enterprise is a certain phenomenological attitude to the world of object-systems'. And it is this move that allows Anozie to state, in the passage I cited earlier, that his task is to examine the nature of the experience of objects 'conceived of as systems'.

From Boudon to these last four words there are but four sentences; and it is in large measure due to the dizzying rate at which Anozie makes such transitions – from a straightforward and sensible remark about structuralism's prospects to the phenomenology of the encounter with objects conceived of as systems – that this book is so hard to follow. Free association – and it is no hyperbole to say that many such passages strike me as having just such a quality – is very interesting in its place, but it is disturbing in what is meant to be a work of theory. The trouble is that, *pace* Anozie, this encounter is not at all characteristic of structuralism. Anyone who thinks of novels as constituting a genre, or of sonnets as constrained by conventions of rhyme and metre, experiences these (literary) objects as systems. It is the distinctively structuralist contribution to the discussion of novels and sonnets, however, to see them as systems of a certain type: systems that can be analysed in terms of structural rules analogous to those of the syntax and semantics (and phonology) of natural languages. Thus, when Anozie proceeds (we are now in the second paragraph of the chapter) to cite Jean Baudrillard, who asks if we can classify 'l'immense végétation des objets' in the way we classify flora and fauna,[21] we still have not reached a distinctively structuralist point of view.

The next few pages discuss a model structural analysis that Anozie proposes of the game of soccer; and by now we are certainly ready for Anozie to display the still-mysterious method. In fact, almost every sentence seems to me to contain a philosophical error or confusion; we end up no further instructed than when we began. The text here does not repay detailed analysis, but it is worth exemplifying the way in which familiar structuralist impedimenta enter into, without illuminating, the account.

The analysis is represented in a 3×3 matrix; the rows are numbered with arabic numerals, the columns with roman ones. Thus every entry can be referred to by a roman numeral followed by an arabic one (or, of course, vice versa). In the course of the discussion, talk of 'binary' couples enters, without fanfare, presumably because of the Jakobsonian tradition. I say 'presumably', because little effort is made to justify the use of this notion. Now I mention all this because some of what Anozie says suggests that, though he is familiar with texts which invoke these binary oppositions, he is not at all clear about their status. He tells us that to 'say that a binary category of description is exhaustive is an important epistemological claim' (SMAP, p. 26). He then goes on, at the beginning of the next paragraph, to

> consider the three rows now together in any form of relationship. Here various possibilities of permutation exist in which direction we may choose to go: (I1, II2), (I2, II3) . . . and so on. . . . These relations need not be expressed in pairs, whether 'ordered' or 'not-ordered' – these terms are used in set theory to indicate elements which form proper constituents of sets or groups. They may also be expressed in groups of three, for example (I1, II2, III3) . . . (SMAP, p. 26)

Now even from a superficial point of view this is not very rewarding reading. (Remember we are trying to understand *soccer*.) Why do binary relations matter if we can write the relations in groups of three? Worse, what does the mere fact that we can write these pieces of formal mumbo jumbo show about anything?[22] And finally, with our confidence already at a low ebb, it is not consoling to find the remark about ' "ordered" pairs', which betrays a fair degree of ignorance of the relevant mathematics.[23]

Now I freely admit that an understanding of the definition of an ordered n-tuple is not something a literary theorist needs to have; but it is not clear to me that it is something he needs to mention either. And the fact that when he *does* mention it – in a form too imprecise to be of any use to anyone who didn't know about it already – he gets it wrong suggests that Anozie ought to agree with me.

This somewhat cavalier, and largely unmotivated, discussion of mathematics is not, I should insist, something that distinguishes Anozie from those whom he admires. Lacan's paper in the now well-known Johns Hopkins symposium volume on *The Structuralist Controversy* contains an almost unbelievably muddled reference to Frege's account of the natural numbers.[24] As I suggested earlier, Anozie here finds himself in good company.

What now follows is one of the many occasions when Anozie's eclectic enthusiasm leads him to endorse a position which appears to be totally out of sympathy with his own. He cites, with apparent approval, some remarks of Richard Macksey's which support Wittgenstein's rather anti-Saussurean reflections on the extent to which many 'language-games' are precisely *not* governed by rigid rules.

I have taken some trouble to show that the whole point of a Saussurean approach is that it engages with the system of *langue* – the (idealized) system of rules underlying the superficial phenomena of *parole*. Someone who happily remarks in passing that all this stuff about rules can be taken too seriously needs, surely, to explain in what sense he is a follower of Saussure.

In succeeding pages, various definitions of *structure* are cited and discussed. It is here, in fact, that the earlier-mentioned equation of structuralism and holism occurs. This is, as I have said, a mistake, and the identification of structuralism with holism is no more successful than the earlier identification with the 'experience of objects as systems'. Neither the comparison between the Romantic contrast of supernatural and commonplace (in Wordsworth and Coleridge), on the one hand, and the contrast of aesthetic (poetic) and scientific, on the other, nor the discussion of existentialism and structuralism which follows that, nor the discussion of structuralism as an introspective science which follows *that*, brings us any nearer to an adequate account of structuralism.

Yet, of course, we find the usual terminology – 'competence/performance', '*structural/structurel*' – along with a little bow in the direction of Marx, Sartre, *et al.* And we find evidence, once more, that Anozie's confusing style is no personal idiosyncrasy. He quotes a certain amount of Fages to the effect that *structurel* is to be reserved for 'concrete forms of organization ... anything that pertains to actual practice ... [and] also every order resulting from "natural" phenomena such as crystals', while *structural* is for 'every order which within human signs produces meaning, for example the opposition red/green in the traffic signal' (*SMAP*, pp. 45–6). But it is hard to see the distinction that is here being sought. The social and economic realities of a region turn out to be *structurel*, whereas we might have expected them to be *structural*, especially in view of Lévi-Strauss's claim, cited later, that 'the term "social structure" has nothing to do with empirical reality but with models that are built up after it. . . . Then the question becomes that of ascertaining what kinds of models deserve the name "structure" ' (*SMAP*, p. 47). Further obscuring the issue is a passage from Pouillon, which ends: 'The term "structural" relates to structures as syntax; on the other hand, "structurel" relates to structure as reality' (*SMAP*, p. 46). As it turns out, Anozie is able to tell us what the relevant distinction is more clearly than anyone he cites: 'the French term *structurel* . . . actually refers to the "objective reality of things", whereas *structural* refers to . . . the "models man has made of them for himself" ' (*SMAP*, p. 47). At last, a useful distinction, one might think – but one whose purpose in the book is uncertain, since this is the last we hear of it.

This discouraging chapter ends with this disconcerting question: 'But if negritude is by its avowed logic and performance a form of humanism, is structuralism necessarily anti-humanist and anti-phenomenological?' (*SMAP*, p. 49).

Anozie's third chapter, 'The Concept of Time in Africa', begins in characteristic style:

> The answer to this question may be sought partly in African linguistic and creative systems, and partly in the African concept and experience of time. The question in other words is: Does there exist in African conceptual systems any reductionist binarism comparable either analogically or effectively, to that which modern structuralists now designate as synchrony and diachrony? (*SMAP*, p. 50)

In an easy bound Anozie has taken us from humanism and phenomenology – 'this question' is the last question of the chapter before – to synchrony and diachrony. And he spends the next page discussing Saussure's conception of semiology – the general science of signs – without saying anything useful about the relations between linguistics and semiology, before passing on to discuss the significance of the contrast between synchronic and diachronic linguistics. He cites a passage from Saussure in which the linguist makes it clear both that he conceives of the structure of *langue* as being situated within the collective consciousness synchronously, and that he conceives of diachronic laws as being about succeeding *termes* which are not so situated. So we have confirmation from the Master, in the very pages of Anozie's book, that Saussure himself conceived of *langue* as a code within the collective consciousness, and that, in consequence, for Saussure, codes do need a collective consciousness in which to function.[25]

But this is all a prelude to a positive answer to the chapter's first question: African conceptual systems *can* reproduce the 'reductionist binarism' of synchrony/diachrony, Anozie believes; and he claims support for this from John Mbiti's *African Religions and Philosophy* (1970). Although what Anozie here says is uncongenial, it is not original. He expounds Mbiti's familiar thesis that 'Africans' distinguish between 'actual' and 'potential' time, and that they (or, perhaps, he and I should say 'we') do not have a conception of the future. Anozie is no doubt drawn to this thesis for a number of reasons: the distinction between '*sasa*' (actual time) and '*zamani*' (potential time) is binary; it is based on the analysis of a piece of linguistic evidence (namely, the forms of Kikamba and Gikuyu verbs); and it allows him to draw a diagram on p. 59.

Unfortunately, Mbiti's thesis simply will not survive examination. Kwame Gyekye, in reviewing Mbiti's book in *Second Order* (*The West African Journal of Philosophy*), has already raised the central objections.[26] But, since the thesis has survived, they bear repeating and developing. In the first place, as Gyekye shows for Twi, the claim that there is no natural way of expressing beliefs about the remote future is simply not true of every African language. As a Twi speaker, I can confidently agree with Gyekye here. But I am also inclined, though with less confidence, to deny that it is true of Kikamba or Gikuyu, certainly on the evidence which Anozie rather uncritically reproduces (*SMAP*, pp. 52 ff.).

Anozie gives a table of forms of the verb for these two languages. It tells us that the 'near future' and 'immediate past' tenses of the verb *to come* in these languages are:

	KIKAMBA	GIKUYU
Near future	Ninguka	Ninguka
Immediate past	Ninauka	Nindoka

He then produces the following argument:

the words expressing the near future and the immediate past appear to be the same except for the transformation of one phoneme from /d/ to /g/ in one, and from /g/ to /au/ in the other. The result is that in these two languages *the future and the past tenses are the same*: 'I will come' = 'I came'. (*SMAP*, p. 54; my italics)

By such an argument, perhaps, Heraclitus proved to himself that everything is One. Only by the most perverse reasoning can it be claimed that someone who shows that A has to be transformed to be identical with B has somehow shown, thereby, that A and B are indistinguishable. Worse follows. Having made an unsubstantiated appeal to a *consensus sapientium* to the effect that 'most students . . . recognize the limited range of expressions for the future tense' in African languages, Anozie then goes on to say that Africans deal with this problem 'by circumlocution'. But if Africans don't have a conception of the remote future, there is no obstacle to talk around: they won't circumlocute, they just won't talk about it at all.

There really is no need to make these mistakes. The words *sasa* and *zamani* are Swahili. As any Swahili dictionary will tell you, *sasa* just means 'now', and *zamani* means either 'period of time' or 'the past' (when it is a noun) and 'some time ago' when it is an adverb, the latter sense having the same ambiguity as English *in* that it often means 'a long time ago' but can mean just 'before now'. Suppose we read *Sasa* as 'The Now' and *Zamani* as 'The Past'? Now the passages cited from Mbiti by Anozie read with less excitement.

> Before events are incorporated into The Past, they have to be realized or actualized within the Now-dimension. When this has taken place, then the events 'move' backwards from The Now to The Past. So The Past is the graveyard of time, the period of termination, the dimension in which everything finds its halting place. (*SMAP*, p. 56)

Two comments are immediately in order. First, this is not very specially African; second, the distinction between present and past is not in any obvious way correlative with that between synchrony and diachrony.

The paragraph in which Anozie introduces us to Mbiti makes painful reading. He mentions Placide Tempels's thesis that 'in Africa ... Being is that which possesses force'. And he points out that this view has been propagated by Janheinz Jahn. What is terrible is that this species of the higher nonsense, invented by a Belgian colonial priest and perpetuated by a German Africanist, should have been accepted by anyone who knows any African conceptual system. I am unclear what 'Being', in this context (and most others), means, but there is no natural way of expressing such a claim in at least one African language, namely, once more, Asante-Twi. If we took *kra* to be vital force, then the claim would be patently false if it meant that everything had *kra*: only living people have them. If we took *sunsum*, then it would still be contentious, since not everything has a *sunsum* either.[27]

Anozie correctly asserts that this notion of 'vital force' is not shared by all African peoples and does not even 'exhaust the worldview of the Baluba' (among whom Tempels preached the gospel). But, this given, it is disturbing to find him accepting Mbiti's generalization instead. Even if it were true, which it is not, it would be quite extraordinary if a claim about 'Africans' could be substantiated by reference to two Kenyan languages and Swahili (from Mbiti) supplemented by Onitsha-Ibo (from Anozie). There are hundreds of African languages with their associated conceptual systems.

Chapter 4 of *Structural Models* is an attempt to connect contemporary European ideas about literature – Proustian 'involuntary memory', Robbe-Grillet's 'deception' – with contemporary African literature. (The examples are actually all West African; in practice, if not in theory, Anozie is less inclined to over-generalization.) The extent to which this attempt is successful is exemplified in Anozie's account of his own study of the (very fine) Nigerian poet Christopher Okigbo, 'whose work', Anozie says in summary, 'is an attempt to recreate the form of time and memory through language, charged with social morality and an awareness of music' (*SMAP*, p. 65). If this sentence had not followed a discussion of Proust (who is mentioned, I suppose, because Anozie has been talking about time), it would not be so clear what is peculiar about this judgement. But in its context one can see at once that Anozie has simply appended a truism about Proust – 'attempt to recreate the form of time and memory' – to a judgement about Okigbo – 'charged with social morality and an awareness of music'.

And here, so it seems to me, we are back to the fundamental problem, the problem to which I referred at the very beginning of this essay, in remarking that Anozie's difficulties arise from his attempt to mediate between Europe and Africa. It is not that a structuralist poetics is inapplicable in Africa because structuralism is European; so far as it is successful in general, it seems to me as applicable to African literary material as to any other. But we should not expect the transfer of a method to a new set of texts to lead to exactly the same results ... indeed, this would surely show that there was something wrong with the method. This should be especially obvious to a structuralist, indeed to anyone who agrees that language 'is a set of culturally transmitted behaviour patterns shared by a group of individuals'.[28] If you believe that a code is an arbitrary construct in the collective consciousness of a community, then it is essentially a social fact, and the code will change from society to society. It is not necessary to show that African literature is fundamentally the same as European literature in order to show that it can be treated with the same tools; this should be as obvious as the correlative observation that African languages do not have to belong to the Indo-European group in order to be given a Saussurean analysis. Nor should we endorse a more sinister line between Anozie's lines: the post-colonial legacy which requires us to show that African literature is worthy of study precisely (but only) because it is fundamentally the same as European literature. It is hard not to suppose that this is part of the problem, when Anozie discusses 'the possibility of conducting an investigation into the use of time in African novels':

> To be of any use at all, such an investigation must have, as its primary purpose, to make more explicit both the nature and the laws governing this internal regulatory dynamic, not to be confused with mere identification of 'seasonal rhythms', as a principle of plot and composition in Africa. No doubt the challenge is great, and so far critics of modern African literature have elected to avoid it. The reason, though unstated, is obvious. For first, the challenge would entail *proving that there does exist*, what Mbiti is now telling us, *a definable African conceptual system, based on time*; second, demonstrating that this system has a regulatory function especially in African novels of traditional determination; and third that such process is repeatable, in other words, that such systematic and conceptual recreation of time is part of the novelist's conscious art and design. (*SMAP*, p. 72; my emphasis)

Why should we need to prove that there is a 'definable African conceptual system based on time'? We can discuss time in the French and German novel without proving that there is a 'definable Franco-German system based on time'. A novel does not have to be about time (as Proust's novel is) for a discussion of time in it to be interesting (as Anozie's third reason implies); nor does the view of time in the novel have to belong to any particular cultural area.

Again and again, Anozie asks the reader to understand Africa by embedding it in European culture – a habit we might perhaps dub 'the Naipaul fallacy'. But what, save a post-colonial inferiority complex, would lead anyone into the assumption that this embedding is either necessary or desirable? It is obvious that, if any reader outside Africa is to come to understand our writers, our literature will need locating. But Anozie seems always to see this placing from the wrong direction. It is because Europe is ignorant of Africa (and not because Africa is ignorant of Europe) that Africa needs explaining to Europeans. African novels do not need justification; they need, as do all novels, analysis, understanding – in short, reading.

In chapter 5, Anozie begins his account of 'Aspects of Senghor's Poetic Theory' with an outline of the Senegalese poet-president's reflections on the linguistics of the (French) word *négritude*. This analysis commences with a distinction between *négrité* and *négritude* and an account of the suffixes -ité and -itude in French. But the core of the exposition is in the development of the claim that the suffixes -ngu and -ngal in the Peul language mark the same distinction. I remain unclear about what the grammar of the Peul language has to do with an African aesthetic-political movement, though Anozie inherits this problem from Senghor. But, if there is any point in explaining negritude through a consideration of an African language, then we don't need all this French linguistic history to start us off. African languages are perfectly all right, whether or not there is a 'morphological parallelism . . . between the French, Latin and some African languages' (*SMAP*, p. 83).

So much, in my view, is amiss in Anozie's grasp of theoretical matters that little is to be gained by a detailed discussion of his own theoretical proposals. He is rather uncertain about structuralism; but even someone as unsympathetic as I am to Derrida's style of thought will find it hard to count Anozie's picture of Derrida (*SMAP*, pp. 224–5) as either fair or helpful. And though I do not think Austin's 'How to do things with words' was perfect, the account of Austin's performative–constative distinction (*SMAP*, pp. 230–1) massacres a perfectly good idea. What are we to say of someone whose reading of Austin leads him to say:

> we can define 'constative' structuralism analytically as that model of structuralist thought, theory or practice which is assertive or declarative in nature, and which, when reduced to the level of a speech act analogue, may be hierarchically equivalent to the sentence: 'I like the red rose.'

Even in context this sentence is simply absurd.

If there is something which saddens me above all else in this book, it is that when Anozie actually settles down to look at a particular poem, Senghor's 'Le Totem', what he says suggests that, unencumbered by his half-digested theoretical baggage, he has much of intelligence to say about literary texts. The poem begins:

> Il me faut le cacher aux plus intimes de mes veines
> L'Ancêtre à la peau d'orage sillonnée d'éclairs et de foudre
> Mon animal gardien, il me faut le cacher
> Que je ne rompe le barrage des scandales.

Anozie points out that the two occurrences of 'il me faut le cacher' 'bracket' the first three lines of this quatrain.

> Given this phenomenon, one could say that the unity of the quatrain has been 'broken', the fourth line being abruptly and artificially excluded from the rest. What is more significant, too, the verb (rompe) appears precisely in the line where this scandal seemingly occurs . . . (SMAP, p. 175; see above, p. 109)

With due allowances for the hyperbolical in his French training ('scandal', surely, overstates the case), I find this observation useful as part of a catalogue of how the poem achieves its effects; and Anozie has other useful comments.[29] Like this one, few of them depend on any great theoretical apparatus; they are insights of the sort we might associate with any intelligent and sensitive practical critic. But as I remarked much earlier, Anozie's uncertainty about which structural facts are of literary interest (an uncertainty which Riffaterre detected in Jakobson's analysis of Blake's 'Infant Sorrow'; see SMAP, pp. 162–4) leads him to make claims about the poem which are of no literary interest; indeed, arguably, of no interest tout court. Let me end with an example which makes it clear that Anozie sees the need to connect structural facts with literary interests, even though he has no clear idea how this is to be done.[30] He says:

> As a final and more technical evidence of the poet's delicate art of balancing, mention should now be made of the fact that the poem contains a total of fourteen nouns (I regard animal gardien as a substantive unit) numerically distributed as in Figure 4.3. This table permits us to identify a number of relations, identical, inverse or parallel (e.g. 5:4 :: 3:2 or 5:3 :: 4:2; V:IV :: VI:III or III:IV :: VI:V, etc.); it may possibly also constitute a system of permutations.

Lines	M	F		NOUNS			Lines	M	F
				M	F				
I	—	1					V	1	1
II	3	2	QUATRAIN	5	4		VI	1	—
III	1	—		2	3	TERCET	VII	—	2
IV	1	1		7	7				

Figure 4.3

(This volume, p. 112; my emphasis.)

We may talk of the 'poet's delicate art of balancing' as we play this numerological game; but that does not guarantee that the numbers have a literary interest. Anozie asks: 'What have we said about Senghor's poem that could not have been said otherwise?' (SMAP, p. 180). Since the question is rhetorical, Anozie presumably agrees that the answer is obvious.

Anozie complains in his introduction that 'structuralism has not yet found a place even in university academic circles . . . in Africa' (SMAP, p. 11), and he seeks to explain why:

> In addition to those [reasons] already implied above, mention must be made of the apathetic attitude of most African academics which, like that of their conservative counterparts in Europe, may best be described as one of downright scepticism vis-à-vis modern structuralism and its objectives. To some structuralism would be no more than one of those esoteric fads or periodic intellectual masturbations of Europe; to others, it might be seen as the prelude to a new bourgeois reactionary and neo-colonialist philosophy.

Anozie's book will certainly not persuade those who have these suspicions. Indeed, if it is read in African university circles, it is likely to have the opposite effect. Those who read it will be confirmed in their 'reactionary' view that literary study is a matter not of the development of theory but of a sensitive understanding of literary texts. Like those 'reactionary' historians who deny that history is a branch of the social sciences, and who resist the sociologist's desire to make a theory, where what is needed is sensitive understanding of a particular texture of historical experience, they will remain faithful to their idiographic calling, resisting the siren's call of the nomothetic. I do not think this will be too bad a thing; not even though I think that theory and practice, in criticism as elsewhere, live fruitfully in friendly tension. As Robert Scholes once wrote, in the course of a defence, please note, of the place of structuralist theory in critical practice: 'In our approach to specific literary texts . . . [structuralism] makes us keenly aware of the communicative aspects of the entire poetic process. But it will not read the poem for us. That we shall always have to do for ourselves.'[31]

Notes

1 Sunday O. Anozie, *Structural Models and African Poetics: Towards a Paradigmatic Theory of Literature* (London: Routledge & Kegan Paul, 1981), p. 134. Further page references to this book will appear in the text prefaced by *SMAP*.

2 It is, perhaps, necessary to point out to readers who are *not* African that the association of an English name with Christianity in Nigeria would be clear; in England, of course, 'Sun-day' might connote paganism. This fact should remind us that words, names among them, need to be interpreted in their cultural contexts.

3 When we need a word for the table, we might as well use the logician's word: *referent*.

4 Cf., for example, Hilary Putnam's 'Is Semantics Possible?', Mind, Language and Reality (Cambridge, Mass.: MIT Press, 1981).

5 The quotation is from J. G. Chrystaller's A Dictionary of the Asante and Fante Language Called Tshi (Chwee, Twi), published in Basle in 1881 for the Evangelical Missionary Society. Twi is one of the Akan languages in Greenberg's Kwa group; see above.

6 Cf. chapter 10 of Jerry Fodor's Representations (Cambridge, Mass.: MIT Press, 1981).

7 The importance of the paradigmatic/syntagmatic dichotomy for literary theory is due to its being thought to be correlative to (or perhaps instantiated at the semantic level by) that of metaphor/metonymy. Anyone who reads the less stylish followers of structuralism will be familiar with the recent reduction of all literary devices to these two.

8 The same syntactic structure, but not the same syntax; for the syntax of a sentence includes a specification of the words it contains.

9 A persistent defender of the view that languages are purely structural could say at this point that the reason this language is different is that we have not specified that it has the same phonological and semantic stucture. But even a language with the same phonological and semantic structure, but with different sounds playing the roles of the phonemes of English, would be a different language – as follows from the fact that it wouldn't sound like English.

10 Jonathan Culler, Saussure (London: Fontana, 1976), pp. 23–4. For what it is worth, this much-discussed case shows considerably less than it is meant to about the significance of structure; after all, some things that are called 'rivers' (the Thames) are not properly called 'rivières'. And this is all you need to say to show that they are different in meaning.

11 Reproduced in this volume in Chapter 4.

12 Anozie tells us that 'Chomsky defines "competence" as the speaker-hearer's knowledge of his language, thereby suggesting the innateness of competence' (SMAP, p. 195). This is a non sequitur. Chomsky holds that much of our competence is innate; but innatists and their opponents can agree on this definition of competence.

13 The relevant level of the mind, when we come to the phonology, is the unconscious; for there is very good psycholinguistic evidence that speakers are unconsciously aware, in a quite detailed way, of the phonology of their language. Cf. Jerry Fodor's The Language of Thought (Brighton, England: Harvester Press, 1976).

14 Cf. David Lewis, Convention (Cambridge, Mass.: Harvard University Press, 1969).

15 Edmund Leach, Lévi-Strauss (New York: Viking Press, 1970), pp. 23–4.

16 Roman Jakobson, Essais de linguistiques générales (Paris: Minuit, 1963), p. 20.

17 This explanation is, be it noted, inconsistent with the view that only structure matters; for the whole point is that the two stories have the same structure. Nevertheless the mythopoets prefer the version about the eagle, which this thesis requires us to regard as identical with it. And why do the mythopoets prefer the eagle story? Precisely because it allows them to conceal the fact that they are thinking about fathers and sons. (The example I have sketched here is very crude; but it does bring out the explanatory force of Lévi-Strauss's claims, at least on one interpretation of them.)

18 This proposal is not meant to be taken very seriously: nobody with any sense or sensibility thinks that truth conditions exhaust the semantic range of any language – least of all the sort of language that characteristically interests literary theory.

19 Roland Barthes, 'To Write: An Intransitive Verb?', in Richard Macksey and Eugenio Donato (eds), The Structuralist Controversy: The Language of Criticism and the Sciences of Man (Baltimore, Md: Johns Hopkins University Press, 1972), p. 136.

20 Cf. Anozie, this volume, p. 106: 'Such integration [of negritude and structuralism] will serve . . . to provide negritude with the one thing it so far lacks – a scientific method of inquiry.'

21 Anozie writes perfectly good English, and studied long in Paris; but his translation here (and, in a few places elsewhere) seems to me less than certain. Baudrillard is not asking the absurd question whether we can classify all objects as flora and fauna (as Anozie's translation would have it); and the talk of *espèces* and *mutations* suggests that the model is not linguistics but natural history.

22 The diagram (Figure 4.1) of the two intertwining circles in Anozie's contribution to this volume prompts the same question; as does Figure 4.2.

23 What Anozie probably has in mind is one standard way of defining an ordered pair <X,Y> as the set whose two members are the set (X) and the set (X,Y). But the only thing that matters about ordered pairs, as opposed to two-membered sets, is that the ordered pair <X,Y> is distinct from the ordered pair <Y,X>; the set (X,Y) and the set (Y,X) are identical. That's why <X,Y> is called 'ordered': the order matters.

24 Macksey and Donato (eds), op. cit., p. 191.

25 When Anozie says, in his gloss on Saussure's extremely clear statement of the difference between synchronic and diachronic linguistics, that 'the term synchrony relates to the *langue* rather than to the *parole* aspect of object-language' (*SMAP*, p. 52), he is in danger of suggesting that diachronic linguistics relates to *parole*. Fortunately he says just the opposite almost immediately; but it seems he has felt the temptation to make an easy connection between the *langue/parole* distinction, on the one hand, and the synchrony/diachrony distinction on the other. The temptation is palpable in this passage, though, as I say, it is finally resisted.

26 See Second Order, 4, 1 (1975).

27 Cf. Kwasi Wiredu, Philosophy and an African Culture (Cambridge: Cambridge University Press, 1980), p. 47. Actually, I think that what Tempels was thinking of is that in African traditional thought-systems, as in traditional thought generally, many things that modern men and women have come to think of as inert are conceived of as personal agencies. This is true. But it is neither distinctively African, nor a feature that Anozie puts to use in his African poetics. This is a pity, since it is important not to confuse images of animated nature in European literature (Wordsworth's 'Prelude', for example) with talk of the natural world as animated (in Senghor's poetry, for instance). In the former, but not the latter, the images are 'metaphorical'.

28 Anozie, citing Greenberg (*SMAP*, p. 4).

29 This analysis is reproduced in Chapter 4 in this volume.

30 I quote the passage in the slightly different form in which it appears in this volume.

31 Robert Scholes, Structuralism and Literature (New Haven, Conn.: Yale University Press, 1974), p. 40.

6   Kimberly W. Benston

I yam what I am:
the topos of un(naming) in
Afro-American literature

I

We must learn to wear our names within all the noise and confusion in which
we find ourselves. They must become our masks and our shields and the
containers of all those values and traditions which we learn and/or imagine as
being the meaning of our familial past.
(Ralph Ellison, 'Hidden Name and Complex Fate')

hang these names, they warp my jaw.   (Mark Twain, 'A Horse's Tale')

Several years ago – so the story goes – Malcolm X was engaged in a heated debate
with a prominent black academic. Sensing that they had reached a moment of
absolute impasse, Malcolm paused briefly, then queried his antagonist: 'Brother
Professor, do you know what they call a black man with a PhD?' 'No. What?'
came the reply, to which Malcolm answered simply: 'Nigger.' The story,
whatever it might suggest about the often internecine dynamics of contemporary
Afro-American culture, subtly proposes a basic interpretation of Afro-American
history and identity. Malcolm swiftly levels distinctions of class, training and
pretension by reminding the professor of a shared origin, returning him to the
debasing ground of Middle Passage and slavery. Indeed, Malcolm calls his rival
'brother' only to dispossess him of his acquired title ('professor') and reductively
christen him with the cursed yet bonding epithet of a nation dispossessed
('nigger'). It is an act of radical unnaming that sees all labels formulated by the
master society ('they') as enslaving fictions, and implies further that no true black
nation, no truly named black self, emerged from reconstructed post-bellum
America.

Malcolm's deconstructed vision of Afro-American history is, of course, neither peculiarly his nor definitive among black artists, intellectuals and citizens. Yet, as the semantic lineage stretching from 'nigger' to 'Colored' to 'Negro' to 'black'/ 'Afro-American' certifies, his cynicism takes account of a central crux of all black self-definitions: how envision and name a people whose very existence was predicated upon expropriation of land, culture, and the binding imperatives and designations of what Ellison terms the 'familial past'. Those who lost their fathers, mothers, priests and gods over the ocean have acquired a painful linguistic marginality. As Malcolm understood, former slaves are not easily turned into self-fashioning revolutionaries, for in what 'language' (Malcolm's primary trope of power) except the master's would that demiurgic act shape them? Language – that fundamental act of organizing the mind's encounter with an experienced world – is propelled by a rhythm of naming: it is the means by which the mind takes possession of the named, at once fixing the named as irreversibly Other and representing it in crystallized isolation from all conditions of externality. Malcolm *Little*, named by the master/father who banished him to his marginal existence, was in some measure the slave his given name signified; a 'so-called Negro', he owned nothing:

As long as you allow them to call you what they wish you don't know who you really are. You can't lay claim to any name, any home, any destiny, that will identify you as something you should be, as someone you should become: a brother among brothers.[1]

For the Afro-American, then, self-creation and reformation of a fragmented familial past are endlessly interwoven: naming is inevitably genealogical revisionism. All of Afro-American literature may be seen as one vast genealogical poem that attempts to restore continuity to the ruptures or discontinuities imposed by the history of black presence in America. At its center – the slave-narrative tradition, which the poet Michael Harper calls the 'sacred texts' of the canon – we find most explicitly the need to resituate or displace the literal master/father by a literal act of unnaming. In the narratives of Frederick Douglass and William Wells Brown, for example, the moment when freedom is finally felt to be irrevocable coincides precisely with a ceremonious exchange of slave surname for an agnomen designating a literally liberated 'self'.[2] Booker T. Washington's discussion of the early development of Afro-American naming explicates cogently the motive behind these highly self-conscious (re)baptisms:

In some way a feeling got among the coloured people that it was far from proper for them to bear the surname of their former owners, and a great many of them took other surnames. This was one of the first signs of freedom. There was a feeling that 'John Hatcher' or 'Hatcher's John' was not the proper title by which to denote a freeman; and so in many cases 'John Hatcher' was changed to 'John S. Lincoln' or 'John S. Sherman', the initial 'S' standing for no name, it being simply a part of what the coloured man proudly called his 'entitles'.[3]

Social and economic freedom – a truly new self – was incomplete if not authenticated by self-designation. The *unnaming* of the immediate past ('Hatcher's John', etc.) was reinforced by the insertion of a mysterious initial, a symbol of the long-unacknowledged, nascent selfhood that had survived and transcended slavery. On the other hand, the association with tropes of American heroism ('Lincoln', 'Sherman', etc.) was also an act of *naming*, a staging of self in relation to a specific context of revolutionary affirmation.

This simultaneous unnaming and naming – affirming at once autonomy and identification in relation to the past – finds its contemporary analogue, as Lloyd Brown suggests,[4] in the Black Muslim movement, whose adherents (like the sometime Malcolm Little) replace their given or 'slave' surnames with a singular 'X'. The Muslim's mysterious variable is a symbol not of something unnamable but of something unknowable – the inaugural African identity that was usurped during Middle Passage. Though more radical in its unnaming of American heritage, the Muslim 'entitle', like its 'freedman' archetype, links the Afro-American to a privileged past and, moreover, functions as a prophetic call to a community-realized *nominatione*: 'Mr Muhammad taught that we would keep this "X" until God himself returned and gave us a Holy Name from His own mouth' (Malcolm X).[5]

The purposefully paradoxical or dialectical nature of the freedman and Muslim appellations extends the 'double-consciousness'[6] inscribed into the race's primary designation, 'African/American'. I want to explore briefly the challenges and opportunities latent in this naming process which several major figures of black writing – and, in particular, Ralph Ellison and Jay Wright – have made manifest. To do so, however, it is necessary to take note of two specifically literary forces which, in addition to the psycho-historical dimension of black selfhood already adumbrated, bear upon the Afro-American poet's acts of naming. First, and most generally, we must keep in mind the roots of the phenomenon termed here 'unnaming', which lie deep within Greek and Hebraic traditions. On the one hand, we need only think of Homer's *Odyssey*, whose hero calls himself 'no name' (or 'no man') whenever he wishes to exercise the shattering power of surprise; and, on the other hand, we may point to the Tetragrammaton (Yahweh), whose King James transcription, 'I Am That I Am', literally translates *namelessness, or that which cannot be named*. Further archaic instances of insistent namelessness could be explored in Hesiod, Pindar and the Hebrew prophetic texts (particularly Ezekiel and Isaiah); in each case, the refusal to be named invokes the power of the Sublime, a transcendent impulse to undo all categories, all metonymies and reifications, and thrust the self beyond received patterns and relationships into a stance of unchallenged authority. In short, in its earliest manifestations the act of unnaming is a means of passing from one mode of representation to another, of breaking the rhetoric and 'plot' of influence, of distinguishing the self from all else – including Eros, nature and community.[7]

The second, and more immediate, influence on the poetics of Afro-American naming is the nineteenth-century *American* artist's concern with labeling as both a structuring and an ethical process. Most especially in the works of Melville, Hawthorne and Emerson we find an unrelieved examination of the relation between consciousness and the objects it seeks to map and appropriate. *Moby-Dick*, for example, may be read as an extended meditation on the metaphysical and normative limitations of the inveterate American urge to delimit experience. Throughout the novel, characters are presented with natural and human texts which, in their overwhelming multiplicity of possible referents, engender a desire to read for singular and final meanings: the painting in the Spouter-Inn with its captivating 'nameless yeast',[8] the mesmerizing doubloon pinned by Ahab to the ship, Queequeg's brands and, finally, Moby-Dick's own accumulated inscriptions (mythical as well as physical) all invite interpretation as a dangerous act of specification. Ahab is, of course, the quest's most persistent and (hence?) tragically failed reader. Perceiving an 'inscrutable' essence behind the whale's being, he attempts to 'strike through the mask' in an obliterating gesture of demystification. To name the ineffable is to kill it: such is the formula of Ahab's pursuit, which proceeds from a linguistic to a violent harpooning, and ends in the inevitable irony of the lying prophet's unnaming by the still-masked object's remystified presence. Rather than subduing and annihilating the whale, Ahab becomes merely another of its self-effacing markings; the object of the quest becomes, finally, its subject – as the novel's title bears witness.

Indeed, the novel's scrupulous hesitancy before final naming is inscribed in the title's doubled and progressively inclusive form: 'Moby-Dick *or*, The Whale' (my emphasis). Ishmael stands over against Ahab precisely in his attentiveness to such enciphered resistance to totalizing names: in Eliot's phrase, he can bear relatively more 'reality' in its mysterious and unspeakable amplitude. Branded, as Marjorie Pryse points out,[9] by his own biblical name, yet also paradoxically larger than its defining implications – isolated by name yet an unnaming voice for all he sees – Ishmael survives because he resists the urge to pin down the metamorphic forms of external being. For him, as for Melville, being's fluidity remains 'ungraspable', if continuously hunted – and thus his singular ability to *tell* his story emerges from his willingness to withhold a total *enumeration* of experience: 'the intense concentration of self in the middle of such a heartless immensity, my God! who can tell it?' Such, too, is the ethic-aesthetic of Melville's own discourse, for, as Ahab constrasts Ishmael with respect to the anger of obsessive naming, so the sub-sub-librarian of the prefatory 'Extracts' – who has 'supplied' a mathematically sublime number of books on whales in a futile comedy of hyper-naming – stands as foil to the author's own awareness that any classification, any figurative 'cetology', is only a partial, expressive delineation (an 'extract').

Hawthorne, too, played upon the need to name and thereby master reality, but he gives this process a decidedly political or social cast. One might say that

Hawthorne suggests the Puritan confrontation with labeling as a mode of cultural control is our self-initiating activity, and so his most difficult and influential novel, *The Scarlet Letter*, emerges from the multiform complexities of a primary 'A'. Hester Prynne's badge is at once the stigma of social exclusion, a device of unnaming alienation, and the imposition of a rigid communal role, a sentence of supposedly immutable naming. To the Puritans who brand Hester, personality is a positivistic datum, an entity entirely determined by requirements of milieu: they are as strictly named as the heroine, their identities as profoundly limited by the prescribed need to adhere rigidly to mutually exclusive conventions. Thus the 'A' becomes in the community a kind of unacknowledged palimpsest for cultural liberation: each reader of Hester's letter sees in it something of his/her own, some trace of an unspeakable mark of difference. Angel, Adulterer, Artist: as named text, Hester becomes all of these, a figure of the New England society's own restless struggle for the unnamed. But Hester herself controls 'A' as an instrument of unnaming: by embracing the ambiguous richness of the letter, she undermines its social function of self-denial and utilizes it instead as a mechanism of self-mystification. The stigma, we are told, 'has given ... *color*' to Hester (my emphasis), the rhetorical structure it had hitherto lacked when enmeshed in the faceless Puritan existence. 'The scarlet letter had endowed her with a new sense,'[10] the narrator tells us – and it is this legacy of understanding and significance, this capacity for independent knowing and being, that Hester intends to pass on to Pearl (both redemptive gem and adornment by inversion, an ornamental *purl*) by 'clothing' her in the initiating language ('A') of her subjectivity. Transforming naming into unnaming, she makes the letter a mirror of culture while saving herself from absorption into the confinements of social stigma. And, as with Ishmael, Hester becomes a model and incentive for a prefatorily inscribed author, a fictionalist who must, as Pryse notes, overcome an initial 'focus on the letter'[11] discovered in the site of convention ('The Custom-House') in order to narrate the tale with 'sense'.

It is just this complex view of naming that animates Emerson's speculations on poetic consciousness, the central *philosophical* ruminations among those affecting Afro-American (as well as 'mainstream' American) tradition. Emerson's Poet virtually creates ('ex-presses') nature by naming it in its multiform 'metamorphosis' ('The Poet').[12] Though the metamorphosis is endless, the Poet's naming of things 'detaches' them from that process, gives them 'boundary' through figured delineation. The Poet is thus envisioned as a Representative Man, a deliverer of the collective's accumulated consciousness: 'language is the archive of history.' Yet the art of first perceiving and then onomastically fixing each 'fact' of nature betrays the underlying desire of 'The Poet' (and all of Emerson, besides): to project the shape of one's own mind against the potentially overwhelming flood of external reality. The true 'freedom' or power of the Poet would tear him loose from all otherness, and take him into a world of his own, restituting him for published representativeness by allowing him the centrifugal tendency of isolation. The Poet's 'true naming', then, is as much an unnaming of relations, of bonds to past language and to other selves, as a fixing of forms for public use. As 'liberating god', he both emancipates us and him from past names and frees him from us: 'O Poet: Thou shalt not know any longer the times, customs, or opinions of men. . . . And thou shalt not be able to rehearse the names of thy friends in thy verse, for an old shame before the holy ideal.'

Any given instance of the Poet's naming, then, enacts an entire dialectical drama: it Adamically brings to life a world of forms while dissolving such forms into the 'whole river of electricity' that is the metamorphosis; or, in other words, it both creates and effaces history. The American encounter of names with what they designate, like the relation of black to mainstream culture, is thus tenuous and charged with ambivalence.[13] The practice of naming in Afro-American literature reflects similar tensions (between self and community, intuition and influence, self-reliance and history) and, as Ellison's and Wright's art exemplify, works manifold variations on the established tropes of 'the calling process'.

II

What's my name!?! What's my name!?!
  (Muhammad Ali, upbraiding a foe who insisted on calling him 'Cassius Clay')

Don't call me out of my name!   (Afro-American street-saying)

Melville, Hawthorne and Emerson all divine an American failure to intuit the 'power of blackness'[14] which might sustain and authorize an effort to overcome the pernicious desire to reduce imaginative energy to suffocating cultural labels. 'Whiteness' in Moby-Dick, in fact, comes to stand for that 'nameless horror' (which is also a horror of the nameless) which both repels and attracts man in his quest for what Ishmael calls a 'comprehensible form' that will 'explain myself'. The Afro-American writer, of course, has struggled with the American insistence on misprising the whitening of experience as a fulfillment of self while assigning all experience of blackness to nameless being. As if proleptically undertaking Malcolm's attack on received names, with its submerged structure of ritual insult, the most effective of these writers have countered the enveloping whiteness of whiteness by what Henry Louis Gates, Jr, has called the 'signifyin(g) sign' of a post-modern (hence rhetorically post-American) 'blackness of blackness'.[15]

To embrace the authority of this dialectical blackness, to orchestrate what Michael Cooke has termed a black 'litany of subdenomination',[16] is in itself a gesture of ambivalent defiance against the white impulse to define itself by both designating and repudiating the 'other'. Allotting black people the brand of 'nigger' indicates a desire to void the possibility of meaning within the 'black-ened' shell of selfhood, thereby reducing substance to the repetitive echo of a catachresis. 'Nigger' is a mechanism of control by contraction; it subsumes the complexities of human experience into a tractable sign while manifesting an essential inability to *see* (to grasp, to apprehend) the signified. If Toomer's white characters speak perplexedly of 'nigger' as a quality (as in 'Blood-Burning Moon'), their translation of slur into modality is only the obverse of an original reification by slander. 'Nigger', as the white name for the blackness of blackness, is a name for difference which serves the ideological function of imbuing 'whiteness' with a 'sense' it primordially lacks.

Black writers have responded to the trope of 'nigger' in various ways, not least of which has been a concentrated investigation of its unnaming violence. Eldridge Cleaver's reaction to discovering an 'Eldridge [who] no longer exists' in the metaphysical isolation of prison was to make for himself an antithetical scapegoat whose rejection would somehow yield his authentic self. 'I tried to repudiate The Ogre,' he tells us in *Soul on Ice*,[17] creating an unnaming, distancing category for a symbolic enemy we only later learn is 'the white woman'. Marked as other, his vengeance was a counter-marking, both literal (rape) and figurative. Thoroughly alienated, he pursued the censure implicit in 'nigger', forcing society to cede him identity through negative affirmation.[18] Like Hester, he endows stigma with authority by purifying and redirecting its destructive force.

Cleaver's insistence on transforming unnaming from victimization to outsider's revenge reflects the influence of his major literary mentor, Richard Wright, whose *Black Boy* contains the literature's most poignant study of black namelessness. The story of Wright's grandfather is a classic recitation of the loss of self through linguistic poverty:

> In the process of being discharged from the Union Army, he had gone to a white officer to seek help in filling out his papers. In filling out the papers, the white officer misspelled Grandpa's name, making him Richard Vinson instead of Richard Wilson. It was possible that Grandpa's southern accent and his illiteracy made him mispronounce his own name. . . . Anyway, Grandpa did not discover that he had been discharged in the name of Richard Vinson until years later; and when he applied to the War Department for a pension, no trace could be found of his ever having served in the Union Army under the name of Richard Wilson.[19]

As if caught in a cycle of Kafkaesque absurdity, Richard's grandfather's life becomes an endless effort to establish his name as an official element in institutional history. He thus becomes a negative exemplum of Richard's own present activity, the *failed* autobiographer whose want of recognized 'records' effaces the self-historian's private mass of data:

> he would name persons long dead, citing their ages and descriptions, reconstructing battles in which he had fought, naming towns, rivers, creeks, roads, cities, villages, citing the names and numbers of regiments and companies . . . and send it all to the War Department.

Wright's grandfather, having lost his name even as 'trace' to the archives of a bloody past, can achieve no authentic public identity, even as he acts as national historian, a kind of displaced *griot*; concomitantly, his private narrative voice is rendered ineffective (he must 'dictate' his accounts to others and, in turn, be read each time the government's unchanging, de-'constructing' reply) or utterly still ('we ate in silence; there was never any talk at our table'). In turn, *Richard's* account of his grandfather's failure is both an elegy and a rebuke, its very literariness (the allusion to Kafka is Wright's) taking wry measure of the distance between the author of *Black Boy* and another of his illiterate male progenitors.[20]

In his youth, Richard too had sought to unveil the mystery of his name, meeting with similarly uncommunicative authority:

'Mama, where did Father get his name?'
'From his father.'
'And where did the father of my father get his name?'
'Like Granny got hers. From a white man.'
'Do they know who he is?'
'I don't know.'
'Why don't they find out?'
'For what?' my mother demanded harshly. . . .
'Then what am I?'
'They'll call you a colored man when you grow up,' she said. Then she turned to me and smiled mockingly and asked: 'Do you mind, Mr Wright?'

The young (black) boy presses his mother for a genealogical logic of designation and thereby discovers the inevitable legacy of naming as an inaugural mark of enslavement. The inherited name emerges at the crossing of possession and unknowing – and the mother (for assuredly complex reasons, those of love and fear more than annoyance) serves as blocking agent against any effort by the son to dis-close and potentially undo this initial (dis)figuring of 'familial past' (like the grandfather, Richard seeks to *reopen* the history of his 'entitlement'). Sensing the antiphonal and bitter tension between the unnaming 'colored' (which carries here the force of 'nigger') and the sardonic 'Mr Wright', Richard finds himself continually at the edge of a world that compels allegiance to social structures which would reduce him to his grandfather's abject status. As if he can 'know who he is' only by insisting on alienation, the boy who not once but twice could not *pronounce* his name in school (recapitulating the grandfather's tragic flaw) must leave the realm that gave him birth in order to 'learn who I was, what I might be'. Providing, in contrast to Grandpa, a successful record of self, his achievement seems contingent on leaving behind all that sought to fix upon him the names of his native landscape. Yet he remains inescapably tied to the violence of an original naming, the unfathomable blackness of blackness: 'Deep down I knew I could never really leave the South . . . [perhaps] light could emerge even out of the blackest of the southern night.'

The blackness of blackness is, of course, Ralph Ellison's antic-deconstructive riff off Melville's meditation on whiteness, and as such it signals, like Wright's sub- and intertextual struggle with his grandfather, a concern with the intricate genealogical imperatives of any Afro-American naming. Ellison, in fact, locates the 'fascination with naming' at the heart of Afro-American experience. 'Our names, being the gift of others, must be made our own,' he declares.[21] But he too recognizes the historical forces that shape the Afro-American ambivalence toward inherited vestiges of the Anglo-American 'familial past':

> When we are reminded so constantly that we bear, as Negroes, names originally possessed by those who owned our enslaved grandparents, we are apt to be more than ordinarily concerned with the veiled and mysterious events, the fusions of blood, the furtive couplings ... through which our names were handed down to us.

Ralph Waldo Ellison's own name, of course, engendered painful intimacy with the 'burdens' and 'mysteries' inherent in one's baptism. Ellison's father, as his son came to realize after many years of discomfort, understood the 'suggestive powers of names and of the magic involved in naming'; indeed, he 'admired this remote Mr Emerson ... so much that he named his second son after him'. Ellison tells us that, having struggled against the 'trouble' caused him by social rituals of self-declaration, he followed Emerson's call for 'self-reliance' and ironically contracted his middle name, *à la* Washington's freedman, to the singular letter, 'W'. This minor gesture of unnaming was Ellison's private act of naming – and its essentially ceremonial and symbolic nature, its turning from both literal and literary ('remote') paternities, could not utterly liberate him from the impinging 'fusions of blood': 'I could suppress the name of my namesake out of respect for the achievements of its original bearer but I cannot escape the obligation to achieve some of the things he asked of the American writer,' Ellison asserts with notable elliptical avoidance, the 'namesake's' name remaining carefully 'suppressed'. And, indeed, Ellison's masterwork, *Invisible Man*, displays an attitude toward naming remarkably close to that of his namesake's heroic Poet – just as his private dialogue with an inherited appellation continued with all the energy of its original dialectical ambivalence: 'I shall never really master [my name].'

The Invisible Man is, of course, black literature's most memorable cipher of the nameless – yet the ambiguities he learns to confront in 'being' at once a subjective absence and total self-presence (invisible/man)[22] arise from the comedy of his vain desire to achieve an empowering name. At every turn in his story he seeks identity in the institutional histories offered by culture: 'If you become a good farmer, a chef, a preacher, a doctor, singer, mechanic ... you are my fate,'[23] intones Norton in a litany of subversive naming. Norton's Emersonian-Washingtonian portfolio of opportunity is an only apparently designating mechanism that actually negatively unnames the hero by limiting his roles to stereotypical forms of 'colored' achievement, roles that are in any case subsumed into the namer's self-voicing *fatum*. Still, the hero's tale evolves from his very inability to decipher such depotentiating naming; seeking notability as a stamp of incorporation by authority, he becomes the instrument of a long series of authoritarian namers who ironically note him for a most Afro-American form of quest romance: 'Keep This Nigger-Boy Running' (p. 33). The businessmen of the Battle Royal, Norton, Bledsoe, the unionists at Liberty Paints and, most pointedly, 'Brother' Jack offer him versions of the 'patterned' selfhood he craves, always at the price of voice and title: he is the 'Sambo' who 'automatically . . . repeats' an unnamed prototype's 'words' at the Smoker (pp. 30–1); he is the naïvely shocked 'nigger' ('He called me *that* . . .') whose tinny 'speechmaking' is mocked and ingloriously exiled by Bledsoe (pp. 137 ff.); he is the silent 'criminal' who 'no longer knew my own name' after the factory blast (pp. 234–5); and, finally, he is the 'new Booker T. Washington' of the Brotherhood (the graduation speech's undesignated author now taking official hold over the hero's 'identity'), the 'disciplined voice' of a dehumanizing ideology whose words 'possessed me' (p. 346). So long as he seeks a name as prescribed social role, the hero discovers only the limitation of exogenous delimitation; he is the narrated, not the narrator: 'they believe that to call a thing by name is to make it so. And yet I am what they think I am' (p. 370).

And yet the tale is superbly, triumphantly, the effect of his voice – an effect for which his failed quest to be culturally distinguished supplies various potential causes. For, even as the hero is jostled from one unsubstantiating name to another, he wanders in a landscape organized as a kind of onomastic classroom. One thinks immediately of the comparative tensions between 'Bledsoe's' hint of spiritual vampirism and 'Trueblood's' assertion of tragically affirmed lineage, between the scatological betrayal of 'Wrestrum' and the protective mysteriousness of 'Tarp', between the illusory humility of 'Hambro' and the deathly loyalty of 'Tod Clifton'.[24] The easy symbolism of a 'Bledsoe' or 'Trueblood', however, is often complicated by more subtle challenges to semantic decoding. Jack, the Brotherhood villain, is called 'The Bear' – but the hero, Jack's main antagonist, is also assigned this epithet. Similarly, Jack and the insidious Bledsoe are both termed a trickster 'rabbit', a title they must share with the exemplary figure of Petee Wheatstraw. Even Barbee's opprobrious surname (the alienating *barbar*, a would-be *bard*, who inhibits – *bars* – *be*-ing), like his blindness, is mitigated or problematized by his given name, 'Homer A.', suggesting finally that, as with Hester Prynne, we must return unprejudiced to examine the character's active enactment of naming, to the unembellished *tabula rasa* of 'A'.

The hero, then, must become a careful interpreter of the world's alluring signs if he is not to become their victum. Two principal types of achieved black selfhood, one 'historical' yet also metaphorical, one symbolic yet also sociopolitical, erupt from beneath the hero's quest and provide him with succinctly contrasting strategies within the novel's mosaic of namings. On one side lies

Rinehart, the enigmatic key to a perception of invisibility. Against him stands Frederick Douglass, touchstone of responsible vision. Rinehart, who encapsulates all available terms as the 'Word' (p. 476), embodies the most radical possibilities of unnaming as a philosophy of being: a faceless trickster, his introduction into the text coincides with the hero's intuition that there never was a 'proper name' to be sought in institutional patterns. Performing a plethora of social functions – numbers-runner, preacher, lover, etc. – the elusive rogue becomes 'one' only with the metamorphic flow which he, like Emerson's Poet, sees as the essence of experience. His strategy proceeds from an improvisational refusal of final form which allows him to hustle beneath a 'history' that reduces human faces to metonymic catalogues of 'so many names' (p. 497). Unlike the namers of fixed cultural 'fates', Rinehart finds freedom in the inherent indeterminacy of the world's enabling terms, 'operating', so to speak, in the *mise-en-abyme* of meaning's 'fluidity of forms' (p. 480). 'Rinehart is real' (p. 487), yet the hero senses he is no ordinary 'character' like Jack or Norton; he is a non-traditional figure, alogical and unamenable to definite interpretation. In his meaning one thing, the power to mean another is implicated:

He was a broad man, a man of parts who got around. Rinehart the rounder. . . . His world was possibility and he knew it. He was years ahead of me and I was a fool. I must have been crazy and blind. The world in which we lived was without boundaries. A vast seething, hot world of fluidity . . . (p. 487)

As Poet of this nether activity, Rinehart is the namer whose limitless designations disrupt or unname the function of social labeling: 'Still, could he be all of them: Rine the runner and Rine the gambler and Rine the briber and Rine the lover and Rinehart the Reverend?'

Beyond culture, 'Rinehart' is, ultimately, a mode of being and, most specifically, a violence to the restrictive designations of cultural nomenclature. His world is plastically conceived; in turn, he deflects any definition of him even as he provokes one into the frustrating process of description. He embodies what Ellison elsewhere calls the liberating 'joke' of the trickster[25] which exposes the world's duplicity, its lack of correspondence to a simple referent, its ability to name two things at once which amounts to an inability to name any one thing conclusively. His 'trick' of constant normative reversals is the very dialectic of unnaming: at once a provider and pimp, dream-merchant and hipster, schemer and improviser, Rinehart seems omnipresent yet is never actually seen – the very other of the Invisible Man for whom he is 'mistaken' ('But that's not my name'; p. 480). With 'Rinehart' we experience the immediacy of history as event, as beginning ('you could actually make yourself anew'; p. 488). His roles take us into the subterranean realm characterized by the manifold of proximate things and breaks down the representational surface to an elemental moment of inaugural naming: 'Could this be the way the world appeared to Rinehart? All the dark-glass boys? "For we see through a glass darkly but then – but then – " I couldn't remember the rest' (p. 480).

In the flush of excitement at experiencing the heedless freedom of Rinehartian namelessness, the hero 'forgets' the riddle's answer of a human face. Rinehart's heroism founders on its very dialectical agility: what it gains in energy it loses in affiliation, for the pure self can have no social existence whatever. A place of no names or limits, a place without motif or structure, can only become a nightmare world of utter formlessness. As he wears the Rinehart mask, the hero feels a 'nameless despair' (p. 485) alongside the exhilaration of uncertainty's openness; and so 'having caught a brief glimpse of the possibilities posed by Rinehart's multiple personalities [he] turned away' (p. 488). Thus, while celebrating Rinehart as an Emersonian Orphic Poet who creates a world of 'infinite possibilities', Ellison also incorporates into his figure the central Melvillean critique of Emersonian fluidity, the distaste for the social parasite who benefits from, yet undermines, cultural forms. 'This confidencing sonofabitch' (p. 477)[26] is finally identified with the 'cynicism' that de-faces communal reality (p. 493). The simple oppositions of 'Rine/Hart', an absence negating or ironizing a presence, awaken the hero to an improvisational freedom but offer no stable theme off which a coherent identity could be riffed. For this, he must turn from the comic apocalypse of the nameless trickster to the tragicomic humanity of those who act with and within the name.

Where the 'magic' of self-effacing metamorphosis is 'glimpsed' through Rinehart (p. 474), the 'magic' of self-creating transformation is first seen by the hero in contemplating Frederick Douglass's portrait, a gift from Tarp which invokes his nameless grandfather's as yet unwanted presence.

> Douglass came north to escape and find work in the shipyards; a big fellow in a sailor's suit who, like me, had taken another name. What had his true name been? Whatever it was, it was as *Douglass* that be became himself, defined himself. And not as a boatwright as he'd expected, but as an orator. (p. 372)

In search of self, Douglass, like the hero, had traversed a series of conventional roles (not unlike those offered by Norton); yet he 'became himself' in an entirely unconventional and unexpected mode. Though it was as a master-named tradesman that he had come 'north' (the hero's trope for freedom's namelessness),[27] it was not as this figure that he embodied his liberation. Beyond the now unnamed delineations of prescriptive roles ('Whatever it was . . .'), Douglass, like Hester, appropriates the force of 'definition' and applies it to the imperatives of self-conception. The act of naming, which had originally been a brand of enslavement, becomes a means for arriving at a nexus of private and public intention. Wielding figuration as functional aspiration, Douglass becomes a model of the freedman as self-named, the name helping the self achieve self-awareness, vocation and, finally, voice. Moreover, Douglass seems to exemplify the heroic modulation of form and chaos, convention and invention, which the hero's college literature teacher, that liminal mental adventurer, *Wood-ridge*, had termed 'creating the *uncreated features of his face*' (p. 346). Embracing 'the unexpected transformations' of black American life (p. 373), Douglass creates one of his people's most extraordinary faces by making his new name an instrument, not a prescription, of cultural process.

Thus we may align Douglass, in his realization that there is 'no scapegoat but the self',[28] with the novel's more obvious figure of proper naming, 'Trueblood'. Like Douglass, Trueblood enacts the drama of self-authenticating definition. Marked both physically ('the man had a scar on his right cheek'; p. 50)[29] and culturally ('now his name was never mentioned above a whisper'; p. 46), Trueblood, like Douglass (with whom he is linked by the recognition of a 'magic in spoken words'),[30] 'became himself' by undertaking the complex transactions of unmarked individuality and defined social being:

> Finally one night, way early in the mornin' . . . I sings me some blues that night ain't never been sang before, and while I'm singin' them blues I makes up my mind that I ain't nobody but myself and ain't nothin' I can do but let whatever is gonna happen, happen. I made up my mind that I was goin' back home and face Kate; yeah, and face Matty Lou too. (pp. 65–6)

The deliberate echo of God's unnaming self-naming ('I Am That I Am') places Trueblood beyond all social patterning; yet, by means of rhetorical apposition ('I makes up my mind . . . I made up my mind'), the *telos* of any 'self-reliant' selfhood is located in the difficult responsibilities toward community, the face-to-face confrontations, that Rinehart merely exploited. Trueblood's very name corrects both the deceitful leeching of 'Bledsoe' and the amoral polarity of 'Rinehart' by reminding us that to be true to oneself is to be true to one's blood, to the inescapable legacies borne by our namesakes.

Despite his conventional predisposition, the Invisible Man sees something of himself in Trueblood's remarkable tale ('I had kept my attention riveted upon his intense *face*'; p. 67; my emphasis); so, too, Douglass's portrait ('like me') and Rinehart's story ('Ain't you Rine the runner?'; p. 480) seem to be mirrors of the hero's own image. And yet they are only hypothetical names or versions of the self, not the 'real thing'. 'Say, you ain't Rinehart, man. . . . *What's your story?*' asks one of the trickster Poppa-stopper's foxes (p. 472; my emphasis), and the novel is the most cogent answer 'possible'. What face, it asks, will the hero choose 'in the scheme of things' (p. 482); what name will be true to this 'blood'?

Writing himself into being while in underground isolation, the hero recognizes the dangers of accepting, Ahab-like, the name for the thing. Just as he names, so may he be named, caught in the rivalry of names. This is a lesson learned, we must remember, not only through the philosophic apposition of variously named characters but through the immediate experience of being un-named by culture's 'trustees', a usurpation of function and destiny not redressed until the hero burns the paper bearing the marks of their authority. 'I have been called one thing and then another,' he laments, 'while no one really wished to hear what I called myself' (p. 560).

What the hero discovers, then, is that names *per se* are neither good nor bad; they are volatile and therefore open to abuse as well as creative manipulation. Rine, the runner, gambler, briber, etc., clearly means different things to different people and is susceptible to apparently conflicting definitions. He is no more a model to the hero than any of the more simply labeled characters, for, as the paratactic accumulation of his epithets indicates, he is a 'man of parts' and can be no more than the sum of appellations that are applied to him. On the other hand, to 'define' oneself as 'Douglass' implies process but also closure. While understanding the urge to fashion for oneself a name and a corresponding value or activity, the hero knows that these are fictions, that no particular name can satisfy the *inner energy* of the questing self. Hence he frames his story with 'Prologue' and 'Epilogue', highly sententious essays which exercise a subtle will-to-power over the main (narrative) text. Here, the controlling voice 'extracts' itself from the war of fictions and labels while compelling a set of quite particular interpretations of those named entities that populate the text. Though we are given a rich assemblage of experiences and epiphanies, the artist-hero refuses to name the totality of those moments – himself ('My past experiences were me; they defined me'; p. 496). And so, in a novel that is very much about the responsibilities to roots, to the past of oneself and of one's blood, the 'final' moment balances on the perception that delimitation also limits, while perma-nent namelessness 'borders' on irresponsibility. Having thrown a harpoon at his multi-named being in the 'compulsion to put invisibility down in black and white' (pp. 13–14), the hero still 'faces' not his newly delineated features but, rather, the impossibility of naming or arresting meaning, of attaching certainty to experience in order to make an ultimate sign of identity.

Emphatically *unnamed*, the hero places himself beyond representation, outside the archival language of history, denying the applicability of words' tropical function to his *yet-unfolding* experience. His remark that 'a hibernation is a covert preparation for a more overt action' (p. 13) suggests that the sublime isolation and deliberate distancing from the reader's logos effected by self-unnaming may be temporary strategies preludial to the assumption of an explicit identity.[31] After all, as his venerable (and similarly unnamed) grandfather often told him, 'You start Saul, and end up Paul' (p. 372). Yet the force of the hero's unwillingness to be named, like the unnaming zeal of Emerson's Poet, signals a refusal of such finality, of 'ending up' the self. It proffers, instead, the hope of endless renewal without denying the security of completion, and dreams of the hypostatic experience that simultaneously names and unnames itself: 'I yam what I am!' (p. 260).

III

There is nothing that there is not; whatever we have a name for, that is.

(Yoruba proverb)

Under the recorded names were other names, just as 'Macon Dead', recorded for all time in some dusty file, hid from view the real names of people, places and things. Names that had meaning. No wonder Pilate put hers in her ear. When you know your name, you should hang on to it, for unless it is noted down and remembered, it will die when you do.

(Toni Morrison, *Song of Solomon*)

The concern with naming in Afro-American literature reaches a new intensity with the rise of 'black consciousness' in the 1960s. Often, in their search for a purified black selfhood, contemporary black poets enunciate one side or the other of Ellison's balanced structure of naming/unnaming. Thus, for example, Amiri Baraka furiously unnames all not validated by present vision, including the specific outline of his own personality: 'LeRoi Jones' becomes 'Imamu', then 'Amiri Baraka'. In his search for a 'post-Western' art and life, Baraka wields language as a curse; he entraps his enemies in the bonds of magical exorcism, engaging them in the perpetual conflict of 'the dozens' through accentuated repetition of the hated names:

> Ford and Rockefeller, Ford and Rockefeller
> Truth be stompin
> Ford and Rockefeller, Ford and Rockefeller
> Truth be boomin
> Ford and Rockefeller, Ford and Rockefeller
> Truth be crackin
> The crackers.   ('Pressure to Grow', performed version)

In his work, names are ruthlessly turned over, explained and condemned, as a means of rejecting the enemy, of *making him pay* in the manner of ancient magicians and satirists.[32] In contrast to Baraka's shattering of nomination – a strategy betraying an aversion to traditional voices (black as well as white) – is Michael Harper's development of the Afro-American praise poem, a vehicle for preserving and extending the spiritual legacy of his forebears (literary, cultural and familial) by repeating and interpreting their 'good names'. In 'Alice', for example, the titular heroine (the poet Alice Walker) weaves a lineage of strong black women (encompassing Zora Neale Hurston and Harper's grandmother) and binds Harper to it by 'writing / your name in theirs, and in mine'. Harper, in turn, completes the familial rite by calling his heroine to himself: 'And for this I say your name: Alice'. Collectively, Harper's praise poems perform a magic not of affliction but of revival; his voice joins its ancestral source by genealogical archeology, a reconstruction of 'The Book of Names':

> By habit
> cultivate your name;
> the dead spoken
> remembered habitual.

No black poet, however, has so integrated his poetic vision with the naming process as has Jay Wright. Neither an unnaming revolutionary nor a naming archivist, Wright seeks a 'rhythm of self' in sanctified acts of naming, summoning his whole being to the possibility of such activity in its simplest forms. For Wright, the motions of encountering, perceiving and essentializing the objects of the self are unified in the 'rhythms' of naming – the named is always present to consciousness as an aura of the name:

> It is always right
> to name the place you move in,
> to name . . . these people now.
> Wherever you are,
> they come upon you like an image. . .   ('The Master of Names')

The core of Wright's 'self', the theme of its efforts to become a 'master of names', is love. 'Love', for Wright as for his chief European and African exemplars (one thinks of Dante, on one hand, of Soyinka, on the other), means the desire to align the self with a universal order, the urge to bring the encountered 'outer' (be it persons, place or poem) in essential form back to the corrected focus of consciousness. It is an acquisitive as well as a reverent power, having its metaphysical grounding in being's thirst for more being: in being's desire to turn the 'outer' into the humanly *ours*, and so to increase. And yet, it seems, we must await and then suffer the other's gift of naming:

> I have learned that you move,
> and change, and come again
> to enchant my eyes with another form.
> . . . you crash and carve
> your name into my soul.   ('Sources (4)')

The atmosphere of the loving self, then, is that of a lacking, and of an appropriate striving to acquire the absent. From this interior situation emerge the ideals and objects which the Wrightian self places before it: the moral and aesthetic standards of self-purification; the humble experience of multiple traditions (Dogon, Ndembu, Yoruba, Nuer, Augustinian, troubadour and Afro-American – to name only the most important); the diurnal pulses of a Mexican or Mississippian hamlet. Such objects are examples of what might fill lacking, unrealized being. But they are more than that: as such, the 'outer' would be like fantasies of physical joy cast by lust onto some inner screen. The distinction of these objects is that they require increase of discipline, refinement of casual self, radical improvement and reorientation of the 'heart'. And in Wright's universe the *tertium quid* unifying all act and desire, all volition and achievement, is the 'Nommo' or creative Word that begins all beginnings, the primal Name that retains the pure motion of experience as its 'Central Source'.

Carefully, painfully travelling toward his native Source, Wright traces in his poems chapters of a specific autobiographical journey – childhood in Albuquerque; exile and education in Harlem; discovery in Mexico – yet autobiography is only one of the elements of his sustained conversation with ancestral origins. To know your name, Wright feels, implies knowing your genealogy; self-definition is more generous, less aggressive, when it comes from a sense of continuity. The major portions of *Dimensions of History* and *Soothsayers and Omens* make a return to what Wright ('tracing' steps from Dogon cosmology) calls 'the first words'; yet the 'I' of the autobiography does not display itself as a force which drives into history so much as a poetic intelligence, a receptacle into which history flows in order to be carried by the vector of the poem into the present. Autobiography is an access to a new understanding of self, at a time when, to use Corbière's words, identity has become 'un mélange adultère de tout'. In other words, what interests Wright in constructing his trans-cultural genealogical myth is the interplay between the human as an element in history and the human as a moment of history.

> A star ascending reaches its
> own domain, its own rest.
> But here we balance in the moon fall,
> and chart the absence in a curve,
> upon a clock,
> the solitary body where the world ends.
> Composed,
> we name the caves from which we rise.   ('What Is True')

Wright builds his poems by insertions of histories, quotations and ritual formulas, which register on us as shards of actuality erupting within an imaginative environment. These fragments of objective data obliterate distance in time and place (birds of the Niger flutter above meticulously clad Brazilian women; a pronouncement by the Afro-American orator Martin Delany interrupts dreams induced by the *Egyptian Book of the Dead*) and emphasize the openness of the pilgrimage. The measured, hypnotic naming of the actual creates its own unity. Superbly exploiting a range of textures from oral traditions to experimental modes of modern written verse, Wright expends much effort to image what is insistently present, not meanings or interpretations, but events, things and actions – a village ritual keenly observed in its intricate solemnity

('The Eye of God: the Soul's First Vision'); the wild enchantment of Guadalajara ('Homecoming'); the sudden illuminations of an evening on horseback in a familiar landscape ('Night Ride'). Yet this is not the romantic 'nostalgia for the object' that, as Paul de Man observes, interferes with the mind's passage past the named particularities of nature to the realm of revelation.[33] Invoking the Dogon symbology of Ogotemmêli,[34] Wright endows the Nommo – the vital logos encompassing body, fire, air, land and water – with a crucial unitary principle: it alone binds concrete objectification and imaginative vision. Nommo effects conception and then calls forth birth; if there were no such magic principle, all forces would be frozen, there would be no procreation, no change, no life. Animated by the Nommo, the poet not only names things; he *produces* them. For him, naming is an incantation, a creative direction of the life force. Wright begins, however, without established lineage, hence without Nommo:

> My dead go rootless,
> without names
> without altar-pots. ('The Dead')

Yet as he calls his ancestors together, 'hardly able to speak the names', he rhythmically dissolves into the 'eye of Death', and emerges at the point of a new baptism:

> this soul [is led] . . .
> into the rhythm of emptiness and return,
> into the self
> moving against itself,
> into the self
> the word, and the first design.
> Now,
> I designate myself your child,
> nani I can name.[35]

This is the crucible Wright submits to again and again, each time experiencing through sacrifice and learning the rebirth that comes only when his *name* is recognized and pronounced. This psychic or visionary *askesis* is, in Wright's experience, an initiation into poetry, into the power of magic breath: to be named is to be called to the Word.[36] In this manner, Wright becomes a shaman, a 'technician of the sacred' as Eliade would say, and accordingly he creates his own linguistic circumstances, unencumbered by any anxieties of marginality. His voices include those of seer, traveler, healer and *griot*, and he forges a language that allows his people to consecrate the love found at the 'centered eye', the Source:

I call my Maitresse
Erzulie Freda Dahomin,
Venus of Dahomey,
Bride of the Loas.
I pierce her heart,
Lay of the Seven Sorrows.
I stand to the music
of my great, grate,
grateful, grating heart,
perfect rhythm of a heart
that never changes.   ('Tamborito')

A 'master of names', Wright's shamanistic voice keeps the ancestral names alive and resonant. His enumeration of 'outer' facts re-calls the words of the tribe – they echo each other in endless re-petition. 'Father,' he intones in 'The Third Word', 'at your side / each name and figure / being born again, / I hear . . . the movement of Nommo.' Yet it is neither the gods nor the fathers that 'designate' his own rebirth: 'nanī I can name.' Healing the tragic *aporia* of African/American 'entitles', the dizzying swing between naming and unnaming, Wright takes responsibility for the rhythms of self by reconciling them with the intolerable music of his familial past:

My tongue is coral,
my lips are emerald.
Feather flame, lucid *guacamaya*,
accept the service of your humble shield.
I write beside your emblem
my father's name,
my mother's name,
your name and mine.
Temple stone, the god endures
such service as you give.
So has the book been written.
So has your heart become perfect.   ('Son')

Notes

1 *Malcolm X on Afro-American History* (New York: Merit Publishers, 1967), p. 14.
2 Douglass gives up 'Bailey' and, after several changes during his escape, settles on a name from the romance epic 'Lady of the Lake' (see *Narrative of the Life of Frederick Douglass* (New York: Signet, 1968), p. 114). William Higgins takes the name Wells Brown after a 'Quaker friend' who had befriended him in the last stages of his run to freedom (see 'Narrative of William Wells Brown', in *Puttin' on Ole Massa*, ed. Gilbert Osofsky (New York: Harper & Row, 1969), p. 221).
3 Booker T. Washington, *Up From Slavery: An Autobiography* (New York, 1910), pp. 37–8.

 4 Lloyd Brown, 'Black Entitles', *Studies in Black Literature*, 1 (1970), pp. 16 ff.
 5 *The Autobiography of Malcolm X* (New York: Grove Press, 1965), p. 199. This notion has an interesting parallel (and perhaps a source) in the cabbalistic doctrine that the two halves of the divine name – the WH and YH of the Tetragrammaton – are separated in the time of exile and will be united forever in the messianic age, thus representing the divine unity. See Gershom Scholem, *Major Trends in Jewish Mysticism*, 3rd rev. edn (New York: Schocken Books, 1971), pp. 47 ff.
 6 This term, as it is (widely) used in Afro-American studies, is taken from W. E. B. DuBois's famous discussion of black psychology in *The Souls of Black Folk* (1903). 'Double-consciousness' was, of course, a favorite expression of Emerson's, and DuBois's usage is not coincidental. DuBois no doubt learned of 'double-consciousness' as a general philosophical coinage from his quasi-Emersonian mentor at Harvard, William James.
 7 By contrast, the Christian and Roman traditions – in which, respectively, coherent ideology and Virgilian *gravitas* are predominant – employ namelessness primarily as a sign of exclusion, bad reputation, or some other form of limitation.
 8 All quotations from *Moby-Dick* are from the edition of Harrison Hayford and Hershel Parker (New York: W. W. Norton, 1967).
 9 Marjorie Pryse, *The Mark and the Knowledge* (Miami, Fla.: Ohio State University Press (for the University of Miami), 1979), pp. 54–5.
10 All quotations from *The Scarlet Letter* are from the Centenary Edition (Columbus, Ohio: Ohio State University Press, 1962).
11 Pryse, op. cit., p. 15.
12 All quotations from Emerson are from his essay 'The Poet', *Works*, vol. 3 (Boston, Mass., and New York: Houghton Mifflin, 1933), pp. 309–20.
13 The kinds of lessons and contrasts afforded by Emerson, Hawthorne and Melville persist in twentieth-century American literature. Wallace Stevens, in dozens of poems, deepens Emerson's urge toward self-reliant unnaming. In 'The Man with the Blue Guitar', for example, he adjures himself:

> But do not use the rotted names. . . .
>   Nothing must stand
> Between you and the shapes you take
> When the crust of shape has been destroyed;

and in 'The Auroras of Autumn' he again declares (if less successfully):

> This is nothing until in a single man contained,
> Nothing until this named thing nameless is
> And is destroyed.

Faulkner, on the other hand, while suspicious of the 'good name' of social reputation, tends to champion acceptance and 'purification' of one's name as a means of mastering, *à la* Hester Prynne, the sign and returning it to its object status. That is why, for example, Mrs Wallstreet Panic Snopes does not want her husband to change his name, no matter how much she hates 'them goddam Snopes'. As V. K. Ratliff explains, 'She don't want to change it [the name]. She jest wants to live it down. She aint trying to drag him by the hair out of Snopes, to escape from Snopes. She's got to purify Snopes itself' (*The Town*).
14 Harry Levin, *The Power of Blackness: Hawthorne, Poe, Melville* (New York: Knopf, 1958).
15 Henry Louis Gates, Jr, 'The Blackness of Blackness: A Critique of the Sign and the Signifying Monkey', in *Figures in Black* (New York: Oxford University Press, 1984); reproduced below as Chapter 13.

16 Michael Cooke, 'Naming, Being, and Black Experience', *The Yale Review*, 68 (1978), p. 172.

17 Eldridge Cleaver, *Soul on Ice* (New York: McGraw-Hill, 1968).

18 Cf. Pryse's (op. cit., pp. 108–42) and Cooke's (op. cit., pp. 172–5) analyses of Faulkner's Joe Christmas.

19 Richard Wright, *Black Boy* (New York and London: Harper, 1945) chapter 5.

20 Wright seems to have begun his agon with the grandfather as a boy, as if sensing immediately that the elder would be what he elsewhere in the book calls a 'warning, not an example': 'And I would read him the letter – reading slowly and pronouncing each word with extreme care'; it is as if the act of reading in a precisely enunciated fashion is designed to call attention to the grandfather's problematic inabilities to *read* and *pronounce*. The grandfather is, in fact, a veritable master of *oral* artistry, the inadequacy of which in modern 'civilization' is pointed to by Wright throughout *Black Boy*. Cf. Robert B. Stepto's analysis of Wright's relation to his *father*, in *From Behind the Veil: A Study of Afro-American Narrative* (Urbana, Ill.: University of Illinois Press, 1979).

21 The quotations in this and the following paragraph are from Ellison's essay 'Hidden Name and Complex Fate', in *Shadow and Act* (New York: Signet, 1966), pp. 148–68.

22 Cf. Gates's analysis of Ellison's title, which he cleverly situates between Wright's 'Native Son' and Reed's 'Mumbo Jumbo'.

23 Ralph Ellison, *Invisible Man* (New York: Vintage Books, 1972), p. 43. Page numbers will subsequently be given in parentheses in the text.

24 Most of the etymological and allegorical ideas of these names are clear (Bledsoe as a drained or draining soul, Wrestrum as restroom, Hambro as a false brother, etc.). Tod Clifton may require more particular explication: 'Tod' is German for death, while 'Clifton' suggests an adhering to (from Middle English *clif* and Anglo-Saxon *clipian*).

25 See Ralph Ellison, 'Change the Joke and Slip the Yoke', in *Shadow and Act*, pp. 61–73.

26 Ellison explicated his allusion to Melville's *The Confidence Man* in 'The Art of Fiction: An Interview': 'Rinehart is my name for the personification of chaos. It is the old theme of *The Confidence Man*. He is a figure in a country with no solid past or stable class lines; therefore he is able to move about easily from one to the other' (*Shadow and Act*, pp. 181–2). This may help explain Rinehart's constant association in *Invisible Man* with Ras, Ellison's catachresis of Melville's Ahab, the spear-throwing, whiteness-hating man of revenge.

27 'In the South everyone knew you, but coming North was a jump into the unknown. How many days could you walk the streets of the big city without encountering anyone who knew you' (*Invisible Man*, pp. 487–8).

28 This is Ellison's famous definition of the blues' tragicomic status. See 'Richard Wright's Blues', in *Shadow and Act*, p. 94.

29 Here the sense of 'blood' as a blessed or sacramental wound (from the Anglo-Saxon *blod*) becomes relevant.

30 To Douglass's inspiration that there 'was a magic in spoken words' (*Invisible Man*, p. 372) we may compare the hero's idea of Trueblood as 'one who told the old stories with . . . a magic that made them come alive' (p. 46).

31 One is reminded in this regard of Rilke, who, in *The Notebooks of Malte Laurids Brigge*, said that whenever one's name is spoken too often and by everyone it is time to take another – any other – in order to be free and to do one's work again.

32 Robert C. Elliott, in *The Power of Satire: Magic, Ritual, Art* (Princeton, NJ: Princeton University Press, 1960), discusses several instances of such magical cursing in Celtic, Greek and Norse lore, and relates these practices to those of Renaissance satirists such as Molière and Jonson.

33 Paul de Man, 'Intentional Structure of the Romantic Image', in Harold Bloom (ed.), *Romanticism and Consciousness* (New York: Norton, 1970), pp. 65–77.

34 This religious and mythical system has been expounded in a series of works by Marcel Griaule, most notably *Conversations with Ogotemmêli* (London: Oxford University Press (for the International African Institute), 1965), a profound influence on Wright.
35 Wright tells us in a note to his poem that 'Nanī is an ancestor, made at the completion of a funeral rite.'
36 This connection between salvation and vocation provides a vital link between Wright and his basic source in Afro-American tradition, Frederick Douglass. The final thrust into history for Douglass, we remember, comes at the time of his first public oration. On the last page of his narrative, Douglass writes:

> While attending an anti-slavery convention at Nantucket, on the 11th of August, 1841, I felt strongly moved to speak. . . . It was a severe cross and I took it up reluctantly. The truth was, I felt myself a slave, and the idea of speaking to white people weighed me down. I spoke but a few moments, when I felt a degree of freedom, and said what I desired with considerable ease. From that time until now, I have been engaged in pleading the cause of my brethren.

Part II

Practice

7

Robert B. Stepto

Storytelling in early Afro-American fiction: Frederick Douglass's 'The Heroic Slave'

In 1847 Frederick Douglass finally decided to close the chapter of his 'semi-exile' in England and Ireland and to return to the United States. Upon his return, he soon discovered that many of his old friends and supporters were skeptical about and even hostile toward his plans for the creation of an anti-slavery newspaper. Instead of contributing to the funds freely given in England for the purchase of a press and printing materials, they offered advice of a most discouraging sort. According to the account Douglass provides in *My Bondage and My Freedom*, they opposed his venture not only because they thought 'the paper was not needed' and could not succeed but also because Douglass himself was, in their estimation, more useful as a lecturer and 'better fitted to speak than to write'.[1] One notices in these arguments – especially the latter two – a distinct echo of the dispiriting admonition Douglass had heard time and again during the years just after he was 'discovered' by William Lloyd Garrison and other Massachusetts abolitionists in the fall of 1841. In those days, whenever Douglass strayed from narrating wrongs to denouncing them, Garrison would gently correct him by whispering, 'Tell your story Frederick', and John Collins would remark more directly, 'Give us the facts, . . . we will take care of the philosophy' (*Bondage*, p. 361).

After two years abroad, Douglass returned to America only to discover that the arguments often used to limit his speech at anti-slavery meetings would be revived – indeed, they were ready and waiting – for the purpose of shutting down his newspaper before it began. Years later, well after the tumultuous split with Garrison, Douglass would write that he had decided to go ahead with his newspaper and to publish it in Rochester, New York, not Boston, 'from motives of peace': hundreds of miles away from 'New England friends' and 'among strangers', the circulation of the *North Star* (for so the newspaper would be named) 'could not interfere with the local circulation of the Liberator and the Standard' (*Bondage*, p. 395). Douglass's preference to be among 'strangers' in 'Western New York' rather than with 'New England friends' tells us in no uncertain terms that, when faced with opposition to his newspaper *and* his full development not just as an anti-slavery agent but also as a human being, he chose to embark upon another 'semi-exile'. In a special sense, it can thus be said that Douglass's move to Rochester was at least a third expatriation in a persistent quest for greater freedom and literacy.

By 1852 Douglass's newspaper was five years old and generally on its way to attaining the circulation figure of 3000 that he reports in *Bondage*. However, it is also true that the newspaper was going through a bit of a crisis. In May of the previous year, at the annual convention of the American Anti-Slavery Society, Douglass had formally proclaimed his dissociation from the cardinal tenets of Garrisonian abolitionism, and Garrison had responded by removing the *North Star* from the list (in truth, Garrison's list) of approved abolitionist publications. Of course, Garrison's move had great effect: supporters of the cause were no longer directed to the pages of the *North Star*, and Garrisonians who had subscribed to the *North Star* in the past were not likely to do so again. Part of Douglass's counter-response was to rename the newspaper *Frederick Douglass' Paper*, and more than a few of his detractors would suggest that such a name was the inevitable issue of an arrogance they had seen and deplored before. It can be said, however, that the newspaper's new name was an expression not so much of his arrogance as of his exile and solitude: while not alone in his opposition to Garrison, Douglass was nevertheless in the relatively unique and harrowing position of being the editor of a newspaper that was more dependent than ever upon its editor's resources.

In a sense, Douglass's chief resource was his name, but of course he knew that to keep his newspaper alive his bank checks would have to be worth more than his signature. Various fund-raising activities were pursued, among these being the publication in 1853 of *Autographs for Freedom*, a collection of anti-slavery writings edited for the Rochester Ladies' Anti-Slavery Society so that they might assist in raising funds for *Frederick Douglass' Paper*. While not often cited, *Autographs for Freedom* is worthy of the attention of scholars of Afro-American literature for at least three reasons. First, as a fund-raising mechanism for Douglass's paper, commissioned by women abolitionists, it stands as remarkable evidence of the alliance Douglass was able to strike with various women's organizations, especially after he had been the 'only man to take a prominent part in the proceedings of the Equal Rights for Women Convention' in July of 1848.[2] Second, the list of contributors to *Autographs for Freedom* provides us with a roster of those individuals, black and white, who presumably were willing – or at least not afraid – to align themselves with Douglass and his newspaper even after both had been in some sense 'blacklisted' by the Garrisonians. The contributors included William H. Seward, Harriet Beecher Stowe, Horace Mann, Richard Hildreth, John Greenleaf Whittier, James M. Whitfield, James McClure Smith, Lewis Tappan, Horace Greeley and James G. Birney. Finally, the volume is worthy of interest because Douglass's own contribution to it is not an extract from a famous speech (such as 'What to the Slave is the Fourth of July?' or 'The Nature of Slavery' – both of which were written and available for inclusion at the time) but a novella entitled 'The Heroic Slave',[3] a new work in what was for Douglass a new form. Why and how Douglass wrote this novella are questions well worth pursuing, for the answers tell us much about the beginnings of Afro-American fiction.

One reason why Douglass wrote 'The Heroic Slave' is easy to come by. In 1845, in response to the taunting cries that he had never been a slave, Douglass was 'induced', as he put it, 'to write out the leading facts connected with [his] experience in slavery, giving names of persons, places, and dates – thus putting it in the power of any who doubted, to ascertain the truth or falsehood of [his] story of being a fugitive slave' (*Bondage*, p. 363). Thus the *Narrative of the Life of Frederick Douglass, An American Slave, Written by Himself* came to life. And in 1847, while harassed by suggestions that his place was to speak, not write, Douglass began the *North Star*, his mission being to demonstrate that a 'tolerably well conducted press, in the hands of persons of the despised race', could prove to be a 'most powerful means of removing prejudice, and of awakening an interest in them' (*Bondage*, p. 389). Then, in 1852, Douglass took a logical next step: he wrote a historical fiction about a heroic slave named Madison Washington who had led a slave revolt aboard a slave ship in 1841. All these writing activities, as opposed to speaking duties, are of a piece, each one bolder than the one preceding it, each a measure of Douglass's remove from acts of literacy involving merely spoken renditions of what Garrison and company alternately called Douglass's 'facts' or 'story' or 'simple narrative'. This suggests something of why Douglass would attempt a novella at this time, but we must also ask why he chose Madison Washington's story for his subject matter.

The ship upon which Washington and his fellow slaves revolted was known as the *Creole*. The revolt occurred while the *Creole* was *en route* from Hampton, Virginia (in 'The Heroic Slave' it is Richmond, not Hampton), to New Orleans. After the takeover, the *Creole*'s course was altered for Nassau, where the British set the former slaves free. A revealing feature of the American response to the episode was that some of the prominent individuals who had argued so strenuously in favor of freedom for the Spanish slaves (who had revolted aboard the *Amistad* in 1839) soon became outraged by what they saw to be British interference. Daniel Webster, for example, cried out, 'The British Government cannot but see that their case is one calling loudly for redress. . . . What duty or power, according to the principles of national intercourse, had they to inquire at all [into the status of the slaves]?'[4] Webster's 'double talk' – and that of many others – regarding the *Amistad* case on the one hand and the *Creole* case on the other undoubtedly had much to do with Douglass's interest in the literary possibilities of Madison Washington's story. The Word and the contradiction of the Word, to paraphrase Ralph Ellison, is, to a substantial degree, Douglass's primary theme and, quite understandably, his obsession.

To be sure, Douglass was also attracted to other features of the *Creole* affair, one such feature being the heroic role played by the British government in Nassau when it freed *American* slaves who had revolted. This was of use to Douglass in at least three ways, for here was an example of a government upholding the Word rather than contradicting it; here was an example as well of successful anti-slavery agitation on the part of British abolitionists; and here, on a more personal level, was an opportunity for Douglass to salute those same British abolitionists, many of whom had hosted him in England and given generously to the creation and support of his newspaper when 'New England friends' had not.

Another attractive feature of the episode for Douglass was the militancy of the slaves as a group and the militant heroism of Madison Washington as the group's stalwart leader. The opportunity to retell Washington's story was also one for making clear to all that he had indeed broken from the Garrisonian policies condemning agitation and armed force, and that he believed more than ever that 'the sable arms which had been engaged in beautifying and adorning the South' should not shrink from the increasingly necessary chore of 'spreading death and devastation there'.[5] Moreover, Douglass might very possibly have been attracted to Washington's story because it in some measure revises his own story. Both Washington and Douglass began their escape attempts in 1835, and both gained public attention as free men in the fall of 1841. However, while Douglass caulked ships in Baltimore (including, perhaps a slaver or two such as the *Creole*), Washington led black slaves in a ship's revolt. Similarly, while Douglass escaped from slavery wearing a sailor's suit, Washington was, in both a literal and a figurative sense, a truer and more heroic sailor. Douglass was a good man, and it would be wrong to suggest that he thought that Washington was a better man than himself, or that Washington's story was altogether better than his own. Nevertheless Douglass was embattled and open to self-doubt, and he was more than willing to review his own history and present circumstances by way of writing a novella about a personal hero.

'The Heroic Slave' is not an altogether extraordinary piece of work. I'm not about to argue that it should take a place beside, say, *Benito Cereno* as a major short fiction of the day. Still, after dismissing the florid soliloquies which unfortunately besmirch this and too many other anti-slavery writings, we find that the novella is full of craft, especially of the sort that combines artfulness with a certain fabulistic usefulness. Appropriately enough, evidence of Douglass's craft is available in the novella's attention to both theme and character. In Part I of 'The Heroic Slave' we are told of the 'double state' of Virginia and introduced not only to Madison Washington but also to Mr Listwell, who figures as the model abolitionist in the story. The meticulous development of the Virginia theme and of the portrait of Mr Listwell, much more than the portrayal of Washington as a hero, is the stuff of useful art-making in Douglass's novella.

The theme of the duality or 'doubleness' of Virginia begins in the novella's very first sentence: 'The State of Virginia is famous in American annals for the multitudinous array of her statesmen and heroes.' The rest of the paragraph continues as follows:

> She has been dignified by some the mother of statesmen. History has not been sparing in recording their names, or in blazoning their deeds. Her high position in this respect, has given her an enviable distinction among her sister States. With Virginia for his birth-place, even a man of ordinary parts, on account of the general partiality for her sons, easily rises to eminent stations. Men, not great enough to attract special attention in their native States, have, like a certain distinguished citizen in the State of New York, sighed and repined that they were not born in Virginia. Yet not all the great ones of the Old Dominion have, by the fact of their birthplace, escaped undeserved obscurity. By some strange neglect, one of the truest, manliest, and bravest of her children, – one who, in after years, will, I think, command the pen of genius to set his merits forth – holds now no higher place in the records of that grand old Commonwealth than is held by a horse or an ox. Let those account for it who can, but there stands the fact, that a man who loved liberty as well as did Patrick Henry – who deserved it as much as Thomas Jefferson – and who fought for it with a valor as high, an arm as strong, and against odds as great as he who led all the armies of the American colonies through the great war for freedom and independence, lives now only in the chattel records of his native state.[6]

At least two features here are worthy of note. The paragraph as a whole, but especially its initial sentences, can be seen as a significant revoicing of the conventional opening of a slave narrative. Slave narratives usually begin with the phrase 'I was born'; this is true of Douglass's 1845 *Narrative* and true also, as James Olney reminds us, of the narratives of Henry Bibb, Henry 'Box' Brown, William Wells Brown, John Thompson, Samuel Ringgold Ward, James W. C. Pennington, Austin Steward, James Roberts, and many, many other former slaves.[7] In 'The Heroic Slave', however, Douglass transforms 'I was born' into the broader assertion that in Virginia many heroes have been born. After that, he then works his way to the central point that a certain one – an unknown hero who lives now only in the chattel records and not the history books – has been born. Douglass knows the slave-narrative convention, partly because he has used it himself; but, more to the point, he seems to have an understanding of how to exploit its rhetorical usefulness in terms of proclaiming the existence and identity of an individual without merely employing it verbatim. This is clear evidence, I think, of a first step, albeit a small one, toward the creation of an Afro-American fiction based upon the conventions of the slave narratives. That Douglass himself was quite possibly thinking in these terms while writing is suggested by his persistent reference to the 'chattel records' which must, in effect, be transformed by 'the pen of genius' so that his hero's merits may be set forth – indeed, set free. If by this Douglass means that his hero's story must be liberated from the realm – the text – of brutal fact and, more, that texts must be created to compete with other texts, then it's safe to say that he brought to the creation of 'The Heroic Slave' all the intentions, if not all the skills, of the self-conscious *writer*.

The other key feature of the paragraph pertains more directly to the novella's Virginia theme. I refer here to the small yet delightfully artful riddle which permits a certain ingenious closure of the paragraph. After declaring that his hero loved liberty as much as did Patrick Henry, and deserved it as much as Thomas Jefferson, Douglass refuses to name the third famous son of Virginia with whom his hero is to be compared. He speaks only of 'he who led all the armies of the American colonies through the great war for freedom and independence'. Of course, as any schoolboy or schoolgirl knows, the mystery man is Washington. And that is the answer – and point – to Douglass's funny-sad joke about the 'double state' of Virginia as well: his mystery man is also a hero named Washington. Thus Douglass advances his comparison of heroic statesmen and heroic chattel, and does so quite ingeniously by both naming and *not* naming them in such a way that we are led to discover that statesmen and slaves may share the same name and be heroes and Virginians alike. Rhetoric and meaning conjoin in a very sophisticated way in this passage, thus providing us with an indication of how seriously and ambitiously Douglass will take the task of composing the rest of the novella.

'The Heroic Slave' is divided into four parts, and in each Virginia becomes less and less of a setting (especially of a demographic or even historical sort) and more of a ritual ground – a 'charged field', as Victor Turner would say – for symbolic encounters between slaves and abolitionists or Virginians and Virginians. For example, in Part I, the encounter between Mr Listwell, our soon-to-be abolitionist, and Madison Washington, our soon-to-be fugitive slave, takes place in a magnificent Virginia forest. In accord with many familiar notions regarding the transformational powers of nature in its purest state, both men leave the sylvan glen determined and resolved to become an abolitionist and a free man respectively. Thus the Virginia forest is established as a very particular space within the figurative geography of the novella, one which will receive further definition as we encounter other spaces which necessarily involve very different rituals for slave and abolitionist alike, and one to which we'll return precisely because, as the point of departure, it is the only known point of return.

Part II of 'The Heroic Slave' takes place in Ohio. Listwell lives there and has the opportunity to aid an escaping slave who turns out to be none other than Madison Washington. This change in setting from Virginia to Ohio assists in the development of the Virginia theme chiefly because it gives Douglass the opportunity to stress the point that something truly happened to each man in that 'sacred' forest, one happy result being that their paths did cross once again in the cause of freedom. As Listwell and Washington converse with each other before Listwell's hearth, and each man tells his story of self-transformation in the forest and what happened thereafter, we are transported back to the forest, however briefly and indirectly. By the end of Part II, it becomes clear in the context of the emerging novella that Ohio, as a free state, is an increasingly symbolic state to be achieved through acts of fellowship initiated however indirectly before. Ohio and that part of Virginia which we know only as 'the forest' become separate but one, much as our heroic slave and model abolitionist become separate but one as they talk and truly hear each other.[8]

In Part III the return to Virginia and the forest is far more direct and in keeping with the brutal realities of life in the ante-bellum south. Listwell is back in Virginia on business, and so is Washington, who has come surreptitiously in quest of his wife still in slavery. Having portrayed Virginia's heaven – the forest replete with pathways to freedom – Douglass now offers Virginia's hell. As one might imagine, given Douglass's zeal for temperance and the abolition of slavery, hell is a tavern full of drunkards, knaves and traders of human flesh. Hell's first circle is the yard adjacent to the tavern where slaves on their way to market are 'stabled' while the soul-driver drinks a dram. Its second circle is the remaining fifteen miles to Richmond where a slave auction awaits. The third circle may be sale to a new Virginia master and a long walk to a new plantation, or it may be a horrific re-encounter with Middle Passage, in the form of a 'cruise' aboard a Baltimore-built slaver bound for New Orleans. If the latter, many other circles of hell await, for there will be another auction, another sale, another master, another long walk, and perhaps yet another auction.

The point to Part III is that, while Washington has returned to Virginia, lost his wife in their escape attempt and been re-enslaved, Listwell is also there and able to provide the means by which Washington may free himself – and others. The suggestion is that it is quite one thing to aid an escaping slave in Ohio and quite another to assist one in deepest, darkest Virginia. Listwell rises to the occasion and, immediately after the slave auction in Richmond, slips Washington several files for the chains binding him. What Washington and the rest do once on board the Creole is, of course, a matter of historical record.

One might think that the fourth and last part of 'The Heroic Slave' would be totally devoted to a vivid narration of swashbuckling valor aboard the high seas. This is not the case. The scene is once again Virginia; the time is set some time after the revolt on the Creole; the place is a 'Marine Coffee-house' in Richmond; and the conversation is quite provocatively between two white Virginia sailors, obviously neither statesmen nor slaves.[9] One of the sailors had shipped on the Creole, the other had not. The conversation takes a sharp turn when the latter sailor, Jack Williams, makes it clear that

For my part I feel ashamed to have the idea go abroad, that a ship load of slaves can't be safely taken from Richmond to New Orleans. I should like, merely to redeem the character of Virginia sailors, to take charge of a ship load of 'em to-morrow. (p. 186)

Tom Grant, who had been on the Creole, soon replies, 'I dare say here what many men feel, but dare not speak, that this whole slave-trading business is a disgrace and scandal to Old Virginia' (pp. 186–7). The conversation goes on and, before it's done, Tom Grant has indeed told the story of the revolt led by Madison Washington.[10] The point is, however, that Tom Grant, not the narrator, tells this story, and he does so in such a way that it is clear that he has become a transformed man as a result of living through the episode.

Thus Douglass ends his novella by creating the dialogue between Virginians about the 'state' of Virginia which was effectively prefigured in the novella's first paragraph. The duality or doubleness of Virginia (and indeed of America) first offered as an assertion and then in the form of a riddle now assumes a full-blown literary form. More to the point, perhaps, is the fact that Tom Grant – the sailor who was forced to listen, if you will, to both the speech and action of Madison Washington – has become something of an abolitionist (though he bristles at the suggestion) and, most certainly, something of a white southern storyteller of a tale of black freedom. This particular aspect of Grant's transformation is in keeping with what happens to our white northerner, Mr Listwell. What we see here, then, is an expression within Douglass's narrative design of the signal idea that freedom for slaves can transform the south and the north and hence the nation.

This brings us to Mr Listwell, whose creation is possibly the most important polemical and literary achievement of the novella. In many ways, his name is his story and his story his name. He is indeed a 'Listwell' in that he enlists as an abolitionist and does well by the cause – in fact, he does magnificently. He is also a 'Listwell' in that he listens well; he is, in the context of his relations with Madison Washington and in accord with the aesthetics of storytelling, a model story-listener and hence an agent, in many senses of the term, for the continuing performance of the story he and Washington increasingly share and 'tell' together. Of course, Douglass's point is that both features of Listwell's 'listing' are connected and, ideally, inextricably bound: one cannot be a good abolitionist without being a good listener, with the reverse often being true as well.

Douglass's elaborate presentation of these ideas begins in Part I of 'The Heroic Slave' when Washington apostrophizes in the Virginia forest on his plight as an abject slave and unknowingly is overheard by Listwell. At the end of his speech, the storyteller slave vows to gain freedom and the story-listener white northerner vows to become an abolitionist so that he might aid slaves such as the one he has just overheard. This is storytelling of a sort conducted at a distance. Both storyteller and story-listener are present, and closure of a kind occurs in that both performers resolve to embark on new journeys or careers. But, of course, the teller (slave) doesn't know yet that he has a listener (abolitionist, brother in the cause), and the listener doesn't know yet what role he will play in telling the story that has just begun. In this way, Douglass spins three primary narrative threads: one is the storyteller/slave's journey to freedom; another is the story-listener/abolitionist's journey to service; the third is the resolution or con-summation of purposeful human brotherhood between slave and abolitionist, as it may be most particularly achieved through the communal aesthetic of storytelling.

In Part II the three primary threads reappear in an advanced state. Washington has escaped and is indeed journeying to freedom; Listwell is now a confirmed abolitionist whose references to conversations with other abolitionists suggest that he is actively involved; and Washington and Listwell are indeed in the process of becoming brothers in the struggle, both because they befriend each other on a cold night and because, once settled before Listwell's fire, they engage for long hours in storytelling. Several features of their storytelling are worth remarking upon. One is that Washington, as the storyteller, actually tells two stories about his adventures in the Virginia forest, one about a thwarted escape attempt and the resulting limbo he enters while neither slave nor free, and the other about how he finally breaks out of limbo, reasserting his desire for freedom.[11] The importance of this feature is that it occasions a repetition of the novella's 'primary' forest episode which creates in turn a narrative rhythm that we commonly associate with oral storytelling. While it would be stretching things to say that this is an African residual in the novella, we are on safe ground, however, in suggesting that in creating this particular episode Douglass is drawing deeply on his knowledge of storytelling among slaves.

Another pertinent feature is that Listwell, as the story-listener, is both a good listener and, increasingly, a good prompter of Washington's stories. Early on, Listwell says, 'But this was five years ago; where have you been since?' Washington replies, 'I will try to tell you', and to be sure storytelling ensues. Other examples of this abound. In one notable instance, in response to Washington's explanation of why he stole food while in flight, Listwell asserts:

And just there you were right. . . . I once had doubts on this point myself, but a conversation with Gerrit Smith, (a man, by the way, that I wish you could see, for he is a devoted friend of your race, and I know he would receive you gladly,) put an end to all my doubts on this point. But do not let me interrupt you. (p. 160)

Listwell interrupts, but his is what we might call a good interruption, for he *authenticates* the slave's rationale for stealing instead of questioning it. In this way, Listwell's remarks advance both story *and* cause, which is exactly what he's supposed to do now that he's an abolitionist.[12]

Resolution of this episode takes the form of a letter from Washington to

Listwell, written in Canada a few days after both men have told stories into the night. It begins, 'My dear Friend, – for such you truly are: – . . . Madison is out of the woods at last.' The language here takes us back to the initial encounter in the Virginia forest between Washington and Listwell, back to a time when they weren't acquaintances, let alone friends – nor on their respective journeys to freedom and service. In examining the essential differences between Washington's apostrophe to no apparent listener and his warm letter to a dear friend, we are drawn to the fact that in each case a simple voice cries out, but in the second instance a listener is not only addressed but remembered and hence re-created. The great effect is that a former slave's conventional token of freedom and literacy bound and found in Canada takes on certain indelible storytelling properties.

From this point on in 'The Heroic Slave' little more needs to be established between Washington and Listwell, either as fugitive slave and abolitionist or as storyteller and listener, except the all important point that their bond is true and that Listwell will indeed come to Washington's aid in Virginia just as promptly as he did before in the north. In a sense their story is over, but in another respect it isn't: there remains the issue, endemic to both oral and written art, of how their story will live on with full flavor and purpose. On one hand, the story told by Washington and Listwell lives on in a direct, apparent way in the rebellion aboard the Creole, the resulting dialogue between the two Virginia sailors who debate the state of their state, and the transformation of one of the sailors, Tom Grant, into a teller of the story. On the other, the story lives on in another way which draws the seemingly distant narrator into the communal bonds of storytelling and the cause.

Late in the novella, in Part III, the narrator employs the phrase 'Mr Listwell says' and soon thereafter refers to Listwell as 'our informant'. These phrases suggest rather clearly that Listwell has told his shared tale to the narrator and that he has thus been a storyteller as well as a story-listener all along. The other point to be made is, of course, that the narrator has been at some earlier point a good story-listener, meaning in part that he can now tell a slave's tale well because he was willing to hear it before making it his own tale to tell. What's remarkable about this narrative strategy is how it serves Douglass's needs both as a novelist and as a black public figure under pressure. Here was a theory of narrative distilled from the relations between tellers and listeners in the black and white worlds Douglass knew best; here was an answer to all who cried, 'Frederick, tell your story' – and then couldn't or wouldn't hear him.

Notes

1 Frederick Douglass, My Bondage and My Freedom (1855; repr. New York: Dover, 1969), p. 393. Hereafter cited as Bondage.

2 Benjamin Quarles, 'Chronology of Frederick Douglass, 1817?–1895', in Quarles (ed.), *Narrative of the Life of Frederick Douglass, An American Slave, Written by Himself* (Cambridge, Mass.: Harvard University Press, 1960), pp. xxv–xxvi.

3 Frederick Douglass, 'The Heroic Slave', in *Autographs for Freedom* (Boston, Mass.: John P. Jewett, 1853), pp. 174–239. The novella is more readily available to the contemporary reader as a volume in the Mnemosyne Press reprint series (Miami, Fla., 1969) and as a selection in Abraham Chapman (ed.), *Steal Away: Stories of the Runaway Slaves* (New York: Praeger, 1971), pp. 145–93.

4 Cited in Mary Cable, *Black Odyssey: The Case of the Slave Ship 'Amistad'* (New York: Penguin, 1977), p. 151. For further discussion of comparisons made between the *Amistad* and *Creole* affairs, see Howard Jones, 'The Peculiar Institution and National Honor: The Case of the *Creole* Slave Revolt', *Civil War History*, 21 (March 1975), pp. 34 ff.

5 Frederick Douglass in the *North Star*, 15 June 1849; cited in Leon F. Litwack, *North of Slavery: The Negro in the Free States, 1790–1860* (Chicago, Ill.: University of Chicago Press, 1961), p. 246. The same language may be found in Douglass's 'Slavery, The Slumbering Volcano', an address delivered in New York City on 23 April 1849. Texts of the address appear in the *National Anti-Slavery Standard* (3 May 1849), the *Liberator* (11 May 1849) and the *North Star* (11 May 1849). The address pertains to this discussion in that it concludes with a spirited telling of the story of Madison Washington and the *Creole* revolt. I am indebted to John W. Blassingame and the staff of the Frederick Douglass Papers Project for providing me with a copy of their annotated text of this address.

6 Douglass, 'The Heroic Slave', in Chapman (ed.), op. cit., p. 146. All future page references are to this republication of the novella.

7 James Olney, 'I Was Born: Slave Narratives, Their Status as Autobiography and as Literature'. An unpublished manuscript.

8 Listwell's role as host and story-listener in Part II suggests that he may be, at least in this section of the novella, a fictive portrait of abolitionist Joseph Gurney. Douglass himself plants this idea when he remarks in 'Slavery, The Slumbering Volcano' that Washington debated with Gurney how advisable it would be to attempt to rescue his wife from slavery.

9 Placing the sailors in a 'Marine Coffee-house' is possibly both an awkward and a revealing touch. To be sure, such establishments existed, but one cannot help but feel that a tavern would be a more 'natural' setting. The braggadocio and general belligerence of Jack Williams, for example, suggest the behavior of a man whose cup contains a headier brew than coffee or tea. Of course, the problem for Douglass was that, given his advocacy of temperance, he could not easily situate Tom Grant, the reformed sailor and a voice of reason, in one of the Devil's haunts. This is quite likely an instance where Douglass's politics and penchant for realism conflicted in a way he had not encountered before he attempted prose fiction.

10 Early in Part IV, Tom Grant is referred to as 'our first mate' (p. 185). This suggests that Grant is loosely modeled upon Zephaniah Gifford, the actual first mate of the *Creole*. Gifford gave many depositions on the revolt and hence told Washington's story many times. See Jones, op. cit., pp. 29–33.

11 These two stories of immersion in and ascent from a kind of limbo are central to the history of Afro-American letters, chiefly because they so conspicuously prefigure the trope of hibernation most accessible to the modern reader in Ralph Ellison's *Invisible Man*, published almost exactly one hundred years later. Madison Washington's cave in the realm between the plantation and the world beyond – 'In the dismal swamps I lived, sir, five long years – a cave for my home during the day. I wandered at night with the wolf and the bear, – sustained by the promise that my good Susan would meet me in the pine woods, at least once a week' – anticipates the Invisible Man's hole in the

region between black and white Manhattan. Once Washington's wolf and bear become, in the mind's eye, Brer Wolf and Brer Bear, this particular contour in Afro-American literary history is visible and complete.

12 This brief and seemingly utilitarian passage in the novella becomes remarkable when one realizes that Douglass is also about the task of composing a salute or 'praise song' for a new but fast friend in the cause, Gerrit Smith. 'The Heroic Slave', we must recall, was Douglass's contribution to an anthology collected for the purpose of raising funds for the newly established Frederick Douglass' Paper. The Paper was created when Douglass's North Star merged with Gerrit Smith's Liberty Party Paper and Smith committed himself to subsidizing the new publication. Listwell's praise of Smith in the novella is, in effect, both a tribute and a 'thank-you note' from Douglass to his new business partner. And it is something else as well: praise for Smith and not, say, Garrison is a clear signal from Douglass that he has broken with the Garrisonian abolitionists and aligned himself with new friends. His praise for Smith took an even grander form when Douglass dedicated My Bondage and My Freedom:

> To Honorable Gerrit Smith, as a slight token of esteem for his character, admiration for his genius and benevolence, affection for his person, and gratitude for his friendship, and as a small but most sincere acknowledgement of his pre-eminent services in behalf of the rights and liberties of an afflicted, despised and deeply outraged people, by ranking slavery with piracy and murder, and by denying it either a legal or constitutional existence, this volume is respectfully dedicated, by his faithful and firmly attached friend, Frederick Douglass.

The doffing of the cap in 'The Heroic Slave' became, within two years, a full and reverent bow.

8   Barbara E. Bowen

Untroubled voice:
call and response in *Cane*

If there is a single gesture which characterizes Jean Toomer's *Cane* – a book even its most vigorous supporter called a 'chaos'[1] – it is the gesture of listening for a voice. *Cane* begins with the word 'Oracular',[2] a call for voice from 'deep-rooted cane', and enacts again and again the same scene of calling for voice. The most powerful version of the scene comes in 'Esther', where it appears in doubled form: first a kind of silent call, a crowd's hushed anticipation of speech, then a story of calling and responding. The sketch begins with the crowd's gathering to listen to King Barlo:

> A clean-muscled, magnificent, black-skinned Negro, whom she had heard her father mention as King Barlo, suddenly drops to his knees on a spot called the Spittoon. . . . Soon, people notice him, and gather round. His eyes are rapturous upon the heavens. Lips and nostrils quiver. Barlo is in a religious trance. Town folks know it. They are not startled. They are not afraid. They gather round. Some beg boxes from the grocery stores. From old McGregor's notion shop. A coffin case is pressed into use. Folks line the curb-stones. Business men close shop. And Banker Warply parks his car close by. Silently, all await the prophet's voice. (p. 20)

The first words Barlo speaks are an announcement of an answer to his call; it is the answer that makes him a prophet. 'Jesus', he begins, 'has been awhisperin strange words deep down, O way down deep, deep in my ears.' Twice more he tells the crowd that Jesus has been awhisperin in his ears before he will let them hear what Jesus said. While he is heightening their eagerness for Jesus's words, he is at the same time focusing attention relentlessly on his own voice. It is

Barlo's voice that turns Jesus's message into an event, an intimate drama of father and son – 'He called me to His side an said, "Git down on your knees beside me, son, Ise gwine t whisper in your ears" ' – and Barlo's voice that releases us from the tautness of the narrator's prose. Listen to the freeing of rhythm as Barlo begins to speak:

> The crowd is hushed and expectant. Barlo's under jaw relaxes, and his lips begin to move.
> 'Jesus has been awhisperin strange words deep down, O way down deep, deep in my ears.' (p. 20)

And, finally, it is Barlo's voice that enables the crowd to speak. Silent until he speaks, the crowd finds voice in response to him. An 'old sister' interrupts with 'Ah, Lord', and later, 'Ah, Lord. Amen. Amen', while someone else shouts, 'Preach it, preacher, preach it!' (p. 21).

Barlo, too, has found voice after hearing a response to his call.[3] Jesus's message is for him not a chance revelation but an *answer* to his own voice. He inserts himself into the story of Jesus's message and shapes the message as a response to his readiness to hear; only after Barlo says 'Thy will be done on earth as it is in heaven' does Jesus speak. And the 'strange good words', when at last we hear them, are nothing more, or less, than instructions on how to speak. 'Tell 'em', Jesus says to Barlo, 'till you feel your throat on fire.' Barlo does not need to ask what he is to 'tell 'em'; he knows he has been enfranchised to preach. That a voice responds to his call suddenly confirms his own ability to speak.

The real event, then, in the drama Barlo narrates is not his hearing of Jesus's message but his own discovery of voice. Jesus's words are almost forgotten as Barlo's sermon becomes the center of the crowd's attention. By the end of the scene, the shift of voice from Jesus to Barlo is complete; despite Barlo's emphasis on hearing Jesus speak, it is his own voice that is finally compelling. And the sermon he preaches is testimony to what affirmation of voice means. Watch what happens the moment Barlo is authorized to speak:

> 'An He said, "Tell em till you feel your throat on fire." I saw a vision. I saw a man arise, an he was big an black an powerful – ' (p. 21)

Suddenly he is able to imagine a past; for the first time, Barlo sees himself not as an actor in a private drama but as a member of a community. The vision he sees connects him with Africa and provides a symbolic ancestor for the whole Afro-American community. 'He was big an black an powerful', Barlo tells us,

> ' – but his head was caught up in the clouds. An while he was agazin at the heavens, heart filled up with the Lord, some little white-ant biddies came an tied his feet to chains.'

For Barlo, affirmation of voice is affirmation of presence and release from what Geoffrey Hartman calls 'the terror of discontinuity'.[4] Barlo no longer needs a responding voice to establish continuity with his world; he has created his own continuity by envisioning a shared history.

His language bears lively witness to his faith in continuity, for it enacts the process of affirming continuity with a group. As Barlo tells the story of the captured African – 'They led him t the coast, they led him t th sea . . .' – his words begin to shape themselves into a perfect blues stanza:

> 'They led him t the coast,
> They led him t th sea,
> They led him across the ocean,
> An they didnt set him free.
>
> The old coast didnt miss him,
> An th new coast wasnt free,
> He left the old-coast brothers,
> T give birth t you an me.
>
> O Lord, great God Almighty,
> T give birth to you an me.'

The statement–variation–response sequence which is the essence of the blues is a development of the call-and-response pattern of collective work-songs and spirituals.[5] For the blues singer, the importance of the call-and-response pattern is its continual affirmation of collective voice. As antiphonal phrases repeat and respond to each other, the singers are assenting to membership in a group and affirming that their experience is shared. When Barlo slips easily into the blues, he is giving rhetorical expression to the continuity he discovered with assurance of voice.

More important, though, than Barlo's sense of continuity with the past is the promise of a future it implies. The crowd hears his vision of the past as a vision of the future; they turn his story of oppression into a prophecy of regeneration. As Barlo preaches, he is transformed for them into the African he describes: 'Barlo rises to his full height. He is immense. To the people he assumes the outlines of his visioned African.' Barlo has made the past present for his audience and embodied it in himself. That he can imagine continuity with the past enables them to imagine regeneration in the future, and their belief in regeneration takes the form it always has for Toomer: prophecy of a black messiah. As its narrators long for sexual consummation and search unsuccessfully for a black madonna, *Cane* is registering the struggle for belief in renewal. Barlo is a figure of such magnetism because he enacts the assurance of renewal as he teaches his people to hear a response to their call. Their response, too, comes from deep, deep down when Barlo enjoins them, 'Open your ears':

Years afterwards Esther was told that at that very moment a great, heavy, rumbling voice actually was heard. That hosts of angels and of demons paraded up and down the streets all night. That King Barlo rode out of town astride a pitch-black bull that had a glowing gold ring in its nose. . . . This much is certain: an inspired Negress, of wide reputation for being sanctified, drew a portrait of a black madonna on the courthouse wall. (p. 21)

This is the same portrait that appears in 'Fern', and there the connection with depth and the earth is even stronger. 'I felt strange,' the northern visitor observes,

> as I always do in Georgia, particularly at dusk. I felt that things unseen to men were tangibly immediate. It would not have surprised me had I had a vision. People have them in Georgia more often than you would suppose. A black woman once saw the mother of Christ and drew her in charcoal on the courthouse wall. . . . When one is on the soil of one's ancestors, most anything can come to one. (p. 17)

Kabnis, too, standing on the soil of his ancestors, is moved to comment: 'Things are so immediate in Georgia' (p. 84). As his characters locate the source of visions and voices in the soil, Toomer is subtly shifting the source of the messiah. While voices come to white prophets from the heavens, they come to black prophets from the earth. And specifically the Georgia earth, where the name of the state comes from the word for 'earth'. If the white messiah descends from heaven, the black messiah rises from the earth; and the earth takes on its enormous significance in *Cane*, reminding us of fertility, birth and the womb.

Over and over, Toomer's narrators hear the empowering response to their calls from deep, deep down and figure the response as the birth of a black messiah. In 'Box Seat', where the narrator is perhaps closest to Toomer himself, there are two striking moments of confidence in rebirth. First, as Dan Moore waits for Muriel, he resolves to stop merely watching – 'I'll never peep' – and begin actively listening:

> I'll listen. I like to listen.
>
> Dan goes to the wall and places his ear against it. A passing street car and something vibrant from the earth sends a rumble to him. That rumble comes from the earth's deep core. It is the mutter of powerful underground races. Dan has a picture of all the people rushing to put their ears against walls, to listen to it. The next world-savior is coming up that way. Coming up. A continent sinks down. The new-world Christ will need consummate skill to walk upon the waters where huge bubbles burst. (p. 57)

Dan's sense of the earth is a southerner's – and also a poet's – sense; when a streetcar rumbles beneath him he hears not the sounds of northern technology but the stirrings of a fertile earth. Without hesitation he declares the noise to be 'the mutter of powerful underground races'. By transforming the streetcar rumble into speech, he has given the earth voice; and in the process found his

own voice. That he can make the earth speak to him confirms his own authority
to speak and gives him the same assurance of renewal that was charcoaled on the
courthouse wall.

In his essay on apostrophe, Jonathan Culler suggests why response from
nature is crucial to the poet's authority to speak. 'The vocative of apostrophe', he
writes,

> is a device which the poetic voice uses to establish with an object a
> relationship which helps to constitute him. The object is treated as an *I* which
> implies a certain kind of *you* in its turn. One who successfully invokes nature is
> one to whom nature might, in its turn, speak. He makes himself poet,
> visionary.[6]

For Dan, as for Barlo's audience, hearing a response so strongly confirms the self
that it denies discontinuity and allows a vision of lasting renewal.

Dan's second vision of renewal is again centered in the earth; it is his
realization of what it means to stand on the soil of one's ancestors. Sitting in the
theater, he catches 'the soil-soaked fragrance' of the Negress next to him, and
suddenly the whole theater comes to life in a scene of intense eroticism:

> Through the cement floor her strong roots sink down. They spread under the
> asphalt streets. Dreaming, the streets roll over on their bellies, and suck their
> glossy health from them. Her strong roots sink down and spread under the
> river and disappear in blood-lines that waver south. Her roots shoot down.
> Dan's hands follow them. Roots throb. Dan's heart beats violently. He places
> his palms upon the earth to cool them. Earth throbs. Dan's heart beats
> violently. He sees all the people in the house rush to the walls to listen to the
> rumble. A new-world Christ is coming up. (p. 62)

Hearing a voice from deep in the earth allows Dan a fantasy of the sexual
consummation he never achieves in reality. The throbbing of the earth beneath
him is for Dan the evidence of a responding voice, and again the voice carries a
promise of renewal through a black messiah.

Here, the promise is intensified because Dan feels as well as hears nature's
response to him. In one of the transformations of image which animate this
section of *Cane* – think of the house in 'Rhobert' or the street in 'Seventh Street' –
the woman's fragrance changes from roots under a city to a network of roots
under a river and finally to blood-lines. By turning roots into blood-lines,
Toomer suddenly invests blood-lines with new meaning; they become literally
lines of blood: like roots, tangible lines of sustenance and connection with the
sources of regeneration. Evocative of soil and the sugar-cane plant, roots appear
throughout *Cane* and are one of the persistent figurations of the rebirth it
constantly seeks. What is important about Toomer's choice of roots as an image
of rebirth is that they are a specifically Afro-American symbol, part of the vitality
of southern black life that *Cane* celebrates.

Perhaps the most daring instance of Toomer's insistence on an *Afro-American* renewal is his revision of the standard Romantic image of mist or smoke. The first section of *Cane* could almost be a manifesto for a new literary tradition, based on community and belief rather than alienation and doubt. 'Karintha' takes one of the most celebrated Anglo-American poems of its day and pointedly rewrites a central image. Here is the famous beginning of T. S. Eliot's 'The Love Song of J. Alfred Prufrock':

> Let us go then, you and I,
> When the evening is spread out against the sky
> Like a patient etherised upon a table;
> Let us go, through certain half-deserted streets,
> The muttering retreats
> Of restless nights in one-night cheap hotels
> And sawdust restaurants with oyster-shells:
> Streets that follow like a tedious argument
> Of insidious intent
> To lead you to an overwhelming question . . .
> Oh, do not ask, 'What is it?'
> Let us go and make our visit.
>
> In the room the women come and go
> Talking of Michelangelo.
>
> The yellow fog that rubs its back upon the window-panes,
> The yellow smoke that rubs its muzzle on the window-panes,
> Licked its tongue into the corners of the evening,
> Lingered upon the pools that stand in drains,
> Let fall upon its back the soot that falls from chimneys,
> Slipped by the terrace, made a sudden leap,
> And seeing that it was a soft October night,
> Curled once about the house, and fell asleep.[7]

Now Toomer's 'Karintha':

At sunset, when there was no wind, and the pine-smoke from over by the sawmill hugged the earth, and you couldnt see more than a few feet in front, her sudden darting past you was a bit of vivid color, like a black bird that flashes in light. . . . A sawmill was nearby. Its pyramidal sawdust pile smouldered. It is a year before one completely burns. Meanwhile, the smoke curls up and hangs in old wraiths about the trees, curls up, and spreads itself out over the valley. . . . Weeks after Karintha returned home the smoke was so heavy you tasted it in water. Some one made a song:

> Smoke is on the hills. Rise up.
> Smoke is on the hills. O rise
> And take my soul to Jesus. (pp. 1–2)

Toomer has learned from Eliot how to personify smoke, and he calls attention to his source with the phrase 'spreads itself out' and the repetition of 'curls up' – both echoes from Eliot's opening lines. But if Eliot's fog, like the winding streets of his city, is an emblem for Prufrock's endless uncertainties, Toomer's pine-smoke is a physical sign of continuity between earth and heaven, a straightforward answer to the problem of reaching Jesus. The final brilliant stroke in the passage from 'Karintha' is to turn Eliot's urbane and intellectual fog into the smoke of a southern spiritual. The primitive prayer to lift the smoke from the valley is also an expression of belief in a personal, fatherly Jesus; 'Rise up' is as much a statement of the simple belief that Prufrock could never share as it is an exhortation to the heavy smoke. The pine-smoke wreathes throughout the first section of *Cane*, always as a symbol of the belief in renewal expressed in 'Karintha''s spiritual. In 'Becky', for instance, the trees themselves are given voice, and the phrase 'The pines whispered to Jesus' becomes a kind of refrain, promising regeneration with Jesus despite Becky's failure to bear the black messiah. Or in 'Georgia Dusk' we hear that 'the pine trees are guitars' and 'the chorus of the cane / Is caroling a vesper to the stars' (p. 13). Finally, in 'Song of the Sun' the pine-smoke is entrusted to carry the last vestige of a disappearing culture.

> Pour O pour that parting soul in song,
> O pour it in the sawdust glow of night,
> Into the velvet pine-smoke air tonight,
> And let the valley carry it along.
> And let the valley carry it along. (p. 12)

Cane's most dazzling moment of regeneration is enabled by another image of connection: the tongue. Like roots and curls of smoke, the tongue can be pictured as a winding line, and it is in this form that it becomes the center of 'Her Lips Are Copper Wire', a poem which must be *Cane*'s most stunning single piece:

> whisper of yellow globes
> gleaming on lamp-posts that sway
> like bootleg licker drinkers in the fog
>
> and let your breath be moist against me
> like bright beads on yellow globes
>
> telephone the power-house
> that the main wires are insulate
>
> (her words play softly up and down
> dewy corridors of billboards)
>
> then with your tongue remove the tape
> and press your lips to mine
> till they are incandescent. (p. 54)

This in Toomer's display of real virtuosity. His control of assonance and rhythm – in the third and last lines, for instance – produces a poem that is at once startling and seductive. Toomer has learned from the Metaphysical poets how to transform a technological instrument into an image for emotion or eroticism; his sensuous telephone wires owe much to Donne's 'stiff twin compasses'.[8] At the same time, the image of copper-wire lips unites the northern and southern sections of the book, combining technology and sexuality. With the union of north and south comes the only true possibility of sexual consummation in the book. The 'incandescence' of the poem's last stanza is the regenerating sexual union – and perhaps the promise of a black messiah – that *Cane's* narrators can never achieve. And the union, if it is possible, will be enabled by voice: lips and tongue. 'Then with your tongue remove the tape', the speaker urges, 'and press your lips to mine.' If in 'Esther' and 'Box Seat' the discovery of voice produced a vision of renewal, in 'Her Lips Are Copper Wire' it provides the renewal itself. The final stanza, then, with its deep eroticism, is a description of finding voice. Like Barlo and Dan, the poet is listening for a response; he asks the woman literally to empower his voice by removing the tape which keeps him silent. Thus the confidence and power of the closing line is as much a display of new-found voice as an expression of sexual fulfillment.

What is at stake for Toomer in hearing a response to his voice is perhaps clearest when we consider the source for his dilemma, the Romantic lyric. The Romantic poets sought oneness with nature, at least in part because they wanted to reverse the dualism and discontinuity imposed on us by the Fall. It is because Adam's naming of the animals in the Garden is our image of perfect continuity – man and nature, word and thing – that it becomes the Romantics' model for an unfallen poetry. The Adamic model informs Romanticism in America even more than in England, and perhaps most explicitly in the work of Walt Whitman. In poems such as 'To the Garden the World', 'As Adam Early in the Morning' and 'There Was a Child Went Forth', Whitman's project is to pose a new Adam, 'peering and penetrating' in perfect communion with nature.[9] One version of the new Adam is the child who becomes the world he observes:

> There was a child went forth every day,
> And the first object he look'd upon, that object he became,
> And that object became part of him for the day or a certain part of the day,
> Or for many years or stretching cycles of years.[10]

When Whitman made his poet a new Adam in the Garden, he was giving expression to what R. W. B. Lewis calls an 'emergent American myth'.[11] The myth is crucial for Toomer, because it is against this myth that *Cane* defines itself. The 'American Adam', Lewis writes, was an individual emancipated from history, happily bereft of ancestry, untouched and undefiled by the usual inheritances of family and race; an individual standing alone, self-reliant and self-propelling, ready to confront whatever awaited him with the aid of his own unique and inherent resources. It was not surprising, in a Bible-reading generation, that the new hero . . . was most easily identified with Adam before the Fall. Adam was the first, the archetypal, man. . . . And he was the type of the creator, the poet par excellence, creating language itself by naming the elements of the scene about him.[12]

If the figure for the American myth is Adam, the figure for the Afro-American myth is Cain.[13] In Genesis, God tells Cain, 'And now art thou cursed from the earth, which hath opened her mouth to receive thy brother's blood from thy hand . . . a fugitive and a vagabond shalt thou be in the earth.'[14] Cain is the first fugitive, the archetypal wanderer. As self-consciously as Whitman in his Adam poems, Toomer in *Cane* is offering a new cultural myth. While the American poet seeks the authority to speak by trying to recover an unfallen continuity of language and nature, the Afro-American poet seeks authority by trying to recover an unexiled continuity of speaker and listener. As Toomer's narrators listen for a responding voice and figure their response as pine-smoke, cane-roots, copper-wire lips and a black messiah, Toomer is posing an emphatically Afro-American solution to the essential Romantic problem: finding authority to speak in a discontinuous, dualistic world. For Romantic poets, response from nature assures the continuity that empowers voice; for Afro-American poets, the empowering response is from their people. *Cane* is the record of Toomer's discovery that call and response – the drama of finding authority through communal voice – has enabled the creation of a distinctively Afro-American literary form.

That *Cane* records the discovery of a literary form helps to explain Toomer's notoriously cryptic statement about its structure. Writing to Waldo Frank in December 1922, Toomer claimed:

> From three angles, *Cane*'s design is a circle. Aesthetically, from simple forms to complex ones, and back to simple forms. Regionally, from the South up to the North, and back into the South again. Or, from the North down into the South, and then a return North. From the point of view of the spiritual entity behind the work, the curve really starts with Bona and Paul (awakening), plunges into Kabnis, emerges in Karintha, etc., swings upward into Theater and Box Seat, and ends (pauses) in Harvest Song.[15]

Toomer is suggesting that *Cane* contains a kind of counterpoint, a dialectic, between content and form. The literary form that Paul awakens to and Kabnis loses sight of is the form the book itself employs from the beginning. It is as if Toomer wants to display the resources of a distinctive Afro-American form in order to give meaning to his protagonists' discovery of it. What gives *Cane* its richness and subtlety is the tension between style and narrative: at the same time that the book is stretching a literary form to its utmost, its protagonists are questioning and finally realizing their distance from the same form.

From its opening moments, *Cane* displays a restlessness with conventional forms. 'Karintha' defies classification as either prose or poetry; it alternates from Joycean verbal density to peasant diction, and combines complex patterns of imagery with unsophisticated spirituals. Toomer seems to share the impatience with convention, the sense that the Anglo-American tradition cannot contain what he has to say, that moved Ralph Ellison to remark: 'I became gradually aware that the forms of so many of the works which impressed me were too restricted to contain the experience which I knew. . . . [*Invisible Man* attempts] to burst such neatly understated forms of the novel asunder.'[16] For Toomer, the way to burst asunder the forms of the Anglo-American novel was to turn to the form he discovered in the black south: the spiritual. If *Cane* is an elegy, it is an elegy for a form; what moved Toomer to write was the sense that the spiritual would soon be lost to us. 'There was a valley,' he recalls in an autobiography,

> the valley of 'Cane', with smoke-wreaths during the day and mist at night. A family of back-country Negroes had only recently moved into a shack not too far away. They sang. And this was the first time I'd ever heard the folk-songs and spirituals. They were rich and sad and joyous and beautiful. . . . I realized, with deep regret, that the spirituals, meeting ridicule, would be certain to die out. With Negroes also the trend was towards the small town and then towards the city – and industry and commerce and machines. The folk-spirit was walking in to die on the modern desert. That spirit was so beautiful. Its death was so tragic. Just this seemed to sum life for me. And this was the feeling I put into 'Cane'. 'Cane' was a swan-song. It was a song of an end.[17]

Barlo's invocation of the blues, then, with its pattern of call and response, is emblematic of Toomer's impulse in *Cane*. From the moment he finds voice, his project is to shape his message through the forms of call and response. There are moments in *Cane* of straightforward spiritual or work-song – in 'Rhobert' or 'Cotton Song', for instance – but what distinguishes Toomer's work is that he is as demanding of his form as the Anglo-American novelists are of theirs. Toomer pushes the form of call and response as hard as Joyce pushes the form of the novel. And *Cane*'s most successful moments come when Toomer opens up for us what it means to turn the call-and-response pattern into a literary form.

In 'Blood-Burning Moon' Toomer takes one of the basic elements of the pattern and explores how it can generate a new narrative structure. The story forms the culmination of *Cane*'s first section, and the lynching it dramatizes is, in a sense, the event towards which the whole first section has been leading. What Toomer discovers in repetition is a way to wrench the story out of sequential time and give its central event the weight of inevitability. Tom Burwell dies figuratively so many times that his real death seems more a fulfillment of prefigurations than an event which results from the mob's violence. Toomer suggests the source of his narrative structure in the blues stanza that occurs three times in the story:

> Red nigger moon. Sinner!
> Blood-burning moon. Sinner!
> Come out that fact'ry door.   (p. 29)

The stanza follows what Sherley Williams identifies as the classic blues pattern of statement, variation and response, in which both variation and response intensify the meaning of the statement and place its situation 'in stark relief as an object for discussion'.[18] As the second and third lines repeat and respond to the first line, they force our attention back to it and become meditations on its significance. Ralph Ellison talks in *Shadow and Act* about the impulse in the blues 'to keep the painful details and episodes of a brutal experience alive in one's aching consciousness, to finger its jagged grain, to transcend it, not by the consolation of philosophy but by squeezing from it a near-comic, near-tragic lyricism',[19] and it is in the dwelling on the first line of a stanza that we can locate the impulse. For Toomer, the blues structure means that a single event can become isolated and intensified until all other events seem merely to prefigure or repeat it. In 'Blood-Burning Moon' the lynching of Tom Burwell acquires a kind of terrifying inevitability as every scene becomes charged with the significance of an omen. Even the mob's chilling plan of 'Two deaths for a godam nigger' (p. 34) cannot compare with the horror of a death that happens figuratively over and over before it at last actually takes place.

The lynching is so intensely foreshadowed that it seems to have happened even before the story begins. 'Portrait in Georgia', the poem that precedes 'Blood-Burning Moon', invokes the Petrarchan device of cataloguing a woman's features, but turns it into a grotesque description of a charred body:

> Hair – braided chestnut,
>   coiled like a lyncher's rope,
> Eyes – fagots,
> Lips – old scars, or the first red blisters,
> Breath – the last sweet scent of cane,
> And her slim body, white as the ash
>   of black flesh after flame.   (p. 27)

Thus when 'Blood-Burning Moon' begins with this incantatory paragraph the meaning of its omens is already clear:

> Up from the skeleton stone walls, up from the rotting floor boards and the solid hand-hewn beams of oak of the pre-war cotton factory, dusk came. Up from the dusk the full moon came. Glowing like a fired pine-knot, it illumined the great door and soft showered the Negro shanties aligned along the single

street of factory town. The full moon in the great door was an omen. Negro women improvised songs against its spell. (p. 28)

Skeleton stone walls, rotting floor boards, a fired pine-knot, a full moon in the great door, and finally the songs the women improvise: all these are foreshadowings of Tom's death. As the story continues, the omens take on more and more meaning and the lynching seems to be enacted in every passage. Thus, when Toomer lavishes attention on a description of the smoke from burning sugarcane, we sense that he is also describing the smoke from Tom's lynching:

Up from the deep dusk of a cleared spot on the edge of the forest a mellow glow arose and spread fan-wise into the low-hanging heavens. And all around the air was heavy with the scent of boiling cane. . . . The scent of cane came from the copper pan and drenched the forest and the hill that sloped to factory town, beneath its fragrance. . . . One tasted it in factory town. And from factory town one could see the soft haze thrown by the glowing stove upon the low-hanging heavens. (p. 29)

Or here, as an old woman draws water from a well, Toomer seems to be giving us a description of the fight which is to come:

The old woman lifted the well-lid, took hold the chain, and began drawing up the heavy bucket. As she did so, she sang. Figures shifted, restlesslike, between lamp and window in the front rooms of the shanties. Shadows of the figures fought each other on the gray dust of the road. (p. 31)

By the time the lynching occurs it seems outside of sequential causality and part of a larger scheme of prefiguration and repetition. Toomer has used the call-and-response patterns of the blues to defeat conventional time schemes and give a single event a stark, unmistakable significance. The final scene of 'Blood-Burning Moon' has the intensity of a blues statement, every word almost unbearably charged with meaning. When the blues stanza appears for the last time, it is finally an explicit call for a response; Louisa is asking Tom to come out that fact'ry door:

Louisa, upon the step before her home, did not hear [the yell], but her eyes opened slowly. . . . Where were they, these people? She'd sing, and perhaps they'd come out and join her. Perhaps Tom Burwell would come. At any rate, the full moon in the great door was an omen which she must sing to:

Red nigger moon. Sinner!
Blood-burning moon. Sinner!
Come out that fact'ry door.   (p. 35)

From the beginning, then, the song has been a plea to undo the lynching which becomes inevitable. The strength of 'Blood-Burning Moon' is the allusive, self-affirmative quality of its prose, and it is Toomer's development of the call-and-response pattern as a literary form that earns him the right to his style.

The pattern of call and response empowers, too, some of Toomer's most searing social criticism. Toomer finds in the spirituals, another form that originated in the call and response of collective work-groups, a demonstration of the way language can become an alternative source of political power. While the slaves singing in the fields were not in control of conventional sources of power, they were in control of language; they turned the words of their oppressors' own songs against them with what DuBois calls 'veiled and half-articulate' messages.[20] 'Kabnis', a play about violence which remains literally and figuratively underground, begins with a demonstration of how language can be turned against itself in a fine counterpoint of overt and covert meaning. 'Whiteman's land. / Niggers, sing' (p. 81), urges the first spiritual in 'Kabnis', and it could almost be a motto for the whole play. That white men own the land, the song suggests, will not change; all blacks can do is sing, but their singing is their resistance and finally their victory.

The version of 'Rock-a-by baby' that Kabnis imagines dramatizes the struggle to gain power through language. Kabnis has just leapt out of bed to kill a chicken in the coop where he sleeps, when his violence is interrupted by this passage of strange lyricism:

With his fingers about [the chicken's] neck, he thrusts open the outside door and steps out into the serene loveliness of Georgian autumn moonlight. Some distance off, down in the valley, a band of pine-smoke, silvered gauze, drifts steadily. The half-moon is a white child that sleeps upon the tree-tops of the forest. White winds croon its sleep-song:

> rock a-by baby . . .
> Black mother sways, holding a white child on her bosom.
> when the bough bends . . .
> Her breath hums through the pine-cones.
> cradle will fall . . .
> Teat moon-children at your breasts,
> down will come baby. . .
> Black mother.

Kabnis whirls the chicken by its neck, and throws the head away. Picks up the hopping body, warm, sticky, and hides it in a clump of bushes. He wipes blood from his hands onto the coarse scant grass. (p. 82)

The act of violence that frames the song provides a guide to its meaning. Kabnis's killing of the chicken acts out the violence against a small helpless creature that lies behind the song. The black nurse croons a white sleep-song, but she gradually wrests the song away from her white masters and gives it her own meaning. What begins as a lullaby ends as a wish to kill the white child she suckles. In the lines of narration between the lines of the song, Toomer gives us the process by which the slaves invested the spirituals with veiled messages: the collective experience underlying the call-and-response pattern allows them to share a meaning inaccessible to whites. The story of the black nurse becomes the subtext which decodes the song and establishes membership in the community. Kabnis's 'Rock-a-by baby' dramatizes the creation of a literary form which allows words to subvert themselves and a calm linguistic surface to express violent meanings. The black mother who remains at the end of the song achieves through language a triumph over her oppressors that makes her perhaps the only real black madonna of the book. And Kabnis's victory suddenly shrinks beside hers.

Crucial for the play between surface and hidden meaning is an assumption of a shared perspective among the audience. In his 'Rock-a-by baby' Toomer creates the shared situation, the kind of context the spirituals take for granted, in the story of the black nurse. By giving us the sketch of the nurse suckling a white woman's children, he makes us the community for which the song has special meaning. Both the spirituals and the blues have an assurance of communal voice built into their form, and it is on this unique strength that Toomer draws in 'Kabnis'. The assurance of collective voice gives the speaker in the spirituals or the blues an untroubled authority to speak. Michael Harper puts the source of this authority succinctly when he notes that the blues audience hears 'we' when the speaker says 'I';[21] communal response for the blues singer, as for Barlo, confers the authority to speak.

But Toomer is not simply singing the blues or preaching the coming of a new messiah; he has learned from the Romantics that hearing a response to one's voice cannot be unproblematic. *Cane* brings to the call-and-response pattern it celebrates all the questioning of voice we find in Whitman; it invests an Afro-American form with the problematic of Romanticism. When Toomer tells us that 'the spiritual entity behind the work' awakens in 'Bona and Paul', plunges in 'Kabnis', emerges in 'Karintha', swings upward in 'Theater' and 'Box Seat' and ends (pauses) in 'Harvest Song', he is charting the discovery of the problematics of response. What Paul awakens to is the realization that he cannot elicit from his people the response that would confirm his own voice. Paul's moment of luminous vision is followed by a lack of response so complete as to be almost comic. ' "I came back to tell you" ', he declares passionately to an unconcerned doorman,

> 'That something beautiful is going to happen. . . . That dark faces are petals of dusk. That I am going out and gather petals. That I am going out and know her whom I brought here with me to these Gardens which are purple like a bed of roses would be at dusk.'
> Paul and the black man shook hands.
> When he reached the spot where they had been standing, Bona was gone.
>
> (p. 78)

For Toomer, the meaning of isolation from one's own people is intensified by his own racial isolation. Like Paul, he was of mixed race, and perhaps it is his own separation from a community that makes his narrators' failures to get a response particularly acute.

When Kabnis sets out for the south, then, he is taking Toomer's journey to find a way to participate in the literary form at the heart of *Cane*. *Cane* gives us first the form – as it appears in the spirituals, blues and variation-and-repetition patterns throughout the book – then the writer's sense of separation from the form he celebrates. Toomer's story of failed response begins in the middle of the book, and takes him back through all the narrators whose failure to consummate love is emblematic of their failure to hear a response. Muriel's analysis is finally the right one; frustrated with Dan's harangues, she accuses him of being a 'Timid lover, brave talker' (p. 58). By the end or, as Toomer puts it, the pause of the story, the narrators are afraid even to talk. 'Harvest Song' is a poem about failure to speak for a community.[22] Before hearing Toomer, let us recall Langston Hughes writing four years later on the same subject:

> I bathed in the Euphrates when the dawns were young.
> I built my hut near the Congo and it lulled me to sleep.
> I looked upon the Nile and raised the pyramids above it.
> I heard the singing of the Mississippi when Abe Lincoln went down to
>   New Orleans, and I've seen its muddy bosom turn all golden in the
>   sunset.[23]

Now Toomer:

> I am a reaper whose muscles set at sundown. All my oats are cradled.
> But I am too chilled, and too fatigued to bind them. And I hunger.
>
> I fear to call. What should they hear me, and offer me their grain, oats, or
>   wheat, or corn? I have been in the fields all day. I fear I could not taste
>   it. I fear knowledge of my hunger. (p. 69)

Both poets adopt the strategy of embodying a community in a single voice; but while Hughes can range freely over history and geography, absorbing all voices into his as he goes, Toomer feels that he is in trouble from the moment he speaks. Almost immediately he feels he must qualify his definition of himself as a reaper. If he is part of a harvest, it is a failed harvest. In the poem which marks the end of Toomer's own journey, he returns to the work-songs which generated the pattern of call and response, then insists over and over that he cannot respond.

Cane enacts the confrontation of Romanticism and Afro-American culture. The untroubled assumption of voice at the heart of the call-and-response pattern is no longer possible in a world altered by Romanticism. The distinctive Afro-American form cannot survive Romanticism unchanged any more than southern blacks can blend unchanged into northern society. *Cane* in the deepest sense is about a clash of traditions, and what such a clash will mean for Afro-American literature. Perhaps, though, there is a more profound confrontation being enacted in *Cane*, one that is inevitable in any meeting of self-consciousness with nostalgia for untroubled voice. When Toomer wrote that *Cane* was a 'swan-song', it was this confrontation that he seems to have had in mind. 'It was', he says,

> a song of an end. And why no one has seen and felt that, why people have expected me to write a second and a third and a fourth book like 'Cane', is one of the queer misunderstandings of my life.[24]

There can be no second or third *Cane* because the call-and-response form which *Cane* explores and celebrates is exactly the form it shows is no longer possible.

Notes

1 Waldo Frank, 'Foreword' to *Cane* (New York: Boni & Liveright, 1923), p. x.
2 Jean Toomer, *Cane* (New York: Liveright, 1975), title page. All subsequent quotations from *Cane* will be taken from this edition, and page references will appear in the text in parentheses.
3 For a sense of the importance of the call-and-response pattern to Afro-American literature, I am indebted to Robert B. Stepto's *From Behind the Veil: A Study of Afro-American Narrative* (Urbana, Ill.: University of Illinois Press, 1979). Stepto, however, uses the pattern to describe relations between texts, while I consider how the pattern itself appears as a rhetorical structure within texts.
4 Geoffrey Hartman, *Wordsworth's Poetry: 1787–1814* (New Haven, Conn.: Yale University Press, 1964), p. 274.
5 Sherley Anne Williams, 'The Blues Roots of Contemporary Afro-American Poetry', in Dexter Fisher and Robert B. Stepto (eds), *Afro-American Literature: The Reconstruction of Instruction* (New York: Modern Language Association of America, 1979), p. 73.
6 Jonathan Culler, 'Apostrophe', *Diacritics* (December 1977), p. 63.
7 T. S. Eliot, 'The Love Song of J. Alfred Prufrock', in *The Complete Poems and Plays: 1909–1950* (New York: Harcourt, Brace & World, 1971), p. 3–4.
8 John Donne, 'A Valediction: Forbidding Mourning', in *John Donne's Poetry*, ed. A. L. Clemens (New York: Norton, 1966), p. 28.
9 Walt Whitman, 'To the Garden the World', *Leaves of Grass* (New York: Signet, 1958), p. 97.
10 Walt Whitman, 'There Was a Child Went Forth', ibid., p. 290.
11 R. W. B. Lewis, *The American Adam* (Chicago, Ill.: University of Chicago Press, 1955), p. 4.
12 Ibid., p. 5.
13 Charles W. Scruggs, in his essay 'The Mark of Cain and the Redemption of Art: A Study in Theme and Structure of Jean Toomer's *Cane*', *American Literature*, 44 (May 1972), p. 290, makes a similar suggestion.
14 Genesis 4: 11–12.
15 Quoted by Charles T. Davis, 'Jean Toomer and the South: Region and Race as Elements within a Literary Imagination', *Studies in the Literary Imagination*, 7, 2 (Fall 1974), p. 32.
16 Ralph Ellison, 'Brave Words for a Startling Occasion', *Shadow and Act* (New York: Random House, 1953), pp. 103–4.

17   Quoted by Darwin T. Turner, 'Introduction' to *Cane* (New York: Liveright, 1975), p. xxii.

18   Williams, op. cit., p. 75.

19   Ralph Ellison, 'Richard Wright's Blues', *Shadow and Act*, p. 78.

20   W. E. B. DuBois, 'Of the Sorrow Songs', *The Souls of Black Folk* (New York: Signet, 1969), p. 270.

21   Quoted by Williams, op. cit., p. 74, from Michael Harper's liner notes to the album *John Coltrane*.

22   Davis, op. cit., p. 34, draws attention to the absence of response in this poem, but his interest lies in the poem's 'plea for human values' rather than its plea for voice.

23   Langston Hughes, 'The Negro Speaks of Rivers', *Selected Poems of Langston Hughes* (New York: Vintage Books, 1959), p. 4.

24   Quoted by Turner, op. cit., p. xxii.

9

Barbara Johnson

Metaphor, metonymy and voice in *Their Eyes Were Watching God*

Not so very long ago, metaphor and metonymy burst into prominence as the salt and pepper, the Laurel and Hardy, the Yin and Yang, and often the Scylla and Charybdis of literary theory. Then, just as quickly, this cosmic couple passed out of fashion again. How did it happen that such an arcane rhetorical opposition was able to acquire the brief but powerful privilege of dividing and naming the whole of human reality, from Mommy and Daddy or Symptom and Desire all the way to God and Country or Beautiful Lie and Sober Lucidity?[1]

The contemporary sense of the opposition between metaphor and metonymy was first formulated by Roman Jakobson in an article entitled 'Two Aspects of Language and Two Types of Aphasic Disturbances'.[2] That article, first published in English in 1956, derives much of its celebrity from the central place accorded by the French structuralists to the 1963 translation of a selection of Jakobson's work, entitled *Essais linguistiques*, which included the aphasia study. The words 'metaphor' and 'metonymy' are not, of course, of twentieth-century coinage: they are classical tropes traditionally defined as the substitution of a figurative expression for a literal or proper one. In metaphor, the substitution is based on resemblance or analogy; in metonymy, it is based on a relation or association other than that of similarity (cause and effect, container and contained, proper name and qualities or works associated with it, place and event or institution, instrument and user, etc.). The use of the name 'Camelot' to refer to John Kennedy's Washington is thus an example of metaphor, since it implies an analogy between Kennedy's world and King Arthur's, while the use of the word 'Watergate' to refer to the scandal that ended Richard Nixon's presidency is a metonymy, since it transfers the name of an arbitrary place of origin onto a whole sequence of subsequent events.

Jakobson's use of the two terms is an extension and polarization of their classical definitions. In studying patterns of aphasia (speech dysfunction), Jakobson found that they fell into two main categories: similarity disorders and contiguity disorders. In the former, grammatical contexture and lateral associations remain while synonymity drops out; in the latter, heaps of word substitutes are kept while grammar and connectedness vanish. Jakobson concludes:

> The development of a discourse may take place along two different semantic lines: one topic may lead to another either through their similarity or through their contiguity. The metaphoric way would be the most appropriate term for the first case and the metonymic way for the second, since they find their most condensed expression in metaphor and metonymy respectively. In aphasia one or the other of these two processes is restricted or totally blocked – an effect which makes the study of aphasia particularly illuminating for the linguist. In normal verbal behavior both processes are continually operative, but careful observation will reveal that under the influence of a cultural pattern, personality, and verbal style, preference is given to one of the two processes over the other.
>
> In a well-known psychological test, children are confronted with some noun and told to utter the first verbal response that comes into their heads. In this experiment two opposite linguistic predilections are invariably exhibited: the response is intended either as a substitute for, or as a complement to the stimulus. In the latter case the stimulus and the response together form a proper syntactic construction, most usually a sentence. These two types of reaction have been labeled substitutive and predicative.
>
> To the stimulus *hut* one response was *burnt out*; another, *is a poor little house*. Both reactions are predicative; but the first creates a purely narrative context, while in the second there is a double connection with the subject *hut*: on the one hand, a positional (namely, syntactic) contiguity, and on the other a semantic similarity.
>
> The same stimulus produced the following substitutive reactions: the tautology *hut*; the synonyms *cabin* and *hovel*; the antonym *palace*, and the metaphors *den* and *burrow*. The capacity of two words to replace one another is an instance of positional similarity, and, in addition, all these responses are linked to the stimulus by semantic similarity (or contrast). Metonymical responses to the same stimulus, such as *thatch*, *litter*, or *poverty*, combine and contrast the positional similarity with semantic contiguity.
>
> In manipulating these two kinds of connection (similarity and contiguity) in both their aspects (positional and semantic) – selecting, combining, and ranking them – an individual exhibits his personal style, his verbal predilections and preferences.[3]

Two problems immediately arise that render the opposition between metaphor and metonymy at once more interesting and more problematic than

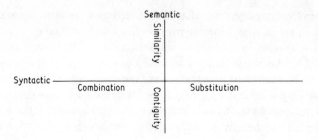

Figure 9.1

at first appears. The first is that there are not two poles here but four: similarity, contiguity, semantic connection and syntactic connection. A more adequate representation of these oppositions can be schematized as in Figure 9.1. Jakobson's contention that poetry is a syntactic extension of metaphor ('The poetic function projects the principle of equivalence from the axis of selection into the axis of combination'[4]), while realist narrative is an extension of metonymy, can be added to the graph as in Figure 9.2.

The second problem that arises in any attempt to apply the metaphor/metonymy distinction is that it is often very hard to tell the two apart. In Ronsard's poem 'Mignonne, allons voir si la rose . . .', the speaker invites the lady to go for a walk with him (the walk being an example of contiguity) to see a rose which, once beautiful (like the lady), is now withered (as the lady will eventually be): the day must therefore be seized. The metonymic proximity to the flower is designed solely to reveal the metaphoric point of the poem: enjoy life while you still bloom. The tendency of contiguity to become overlaid by similarity and vice versa may be summed up in the proverb, 'Birds of a feather flock together' – 'Qui se ressemble s'assemble'. One has only to think of the applicability of this proverb to the composition of neighborhoods in America to realize that the question of the separability of similarity from contiguity may have considerable political implications. The controversy surrounding the expression 'legionnaires' disease' provides a more comical example: while the name of the disease derives

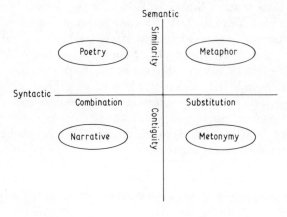

Figure 9.2

solely from the contingent fact that its first victims were at an American Legion Convention, and is thus a metonymy, the fear that it will take on a metaphoric color – that a belief in some natural connection or similarity may thereby be propagated between legionnaires and the disease – has led spokesmen for the legionnaires to attempt to have the malady renamed. And finally, in the sentence 'The White House denied the charges', one might ask whether the place name is a purely contiguous metonymy for the presidency, or whether the whiteness of the house isn't somehow metaphorically connected to the whiteness of its inhabitant.

One final prefatory remark about the metaphor/metonymy distinction: far from being a neutral opposition between equals, these two tropes have always stood in hierarchical relation to each other. From Aristotle to George Lakoff,[5] metaphor has always, in the Western tradition, had the privilege of revealing unexpected truth. As Aristotle puts it: 'Midway between the unintelligible and the commonplace, it is a metaphor which most produces knowledge.'[6] Paul de Man summarizes the preference for metaphor over metonymy by aligning analogy with necessity and contiguity with chance: 'The inference of identity and totality that is constitutive of metaphor is lacking in the purely relational metonymic contact: an element of truth is involved in taking Achilles for a lion but none in taking Mr Ford for a motor car.'[7] De Man then goes on to reveal this 'element of truth' as the product of a purely rhetorical – and ultimately metonymical – sleight of hand, thus overturning the traditional hierarchy and deconstructing the very basis for the seductiveness and privilege of metaphor.

I should like now to turn to the work of an author acutely conscious of, and superbly skilled in, the seductiveness and complexity of metaphor as privileged trope and trope of privilege. Zora Neale Hurston, novelist, folklorist, essayist, anthropologist and Harlem Renaissance personality, cut her teeth on figurative language during the tale-telling or 'lying' sessions that took place on a store porch in the all-black town of Eatonville, Florida, where she was born around 1901. She devoted her life to the task of recording, preserving, novelizing and analyzing the patterns of speech and thought of the rural black south and related cultures. At the same time, she deplored the appropriation, dilution and commodification of black culture (through spirituals, jazz, etc.) by the pre-Depression white world, and she constantly tried to explain the difference between a reified 'art' and a living culture in which the distinctions between spectator and spectacle, rehearsal and performance, experience and representation, are not fixed. 'Folklore', she wrote, 'is the arts of the people before they find out that there is such a thing as art.'

Folklore does not belong to any special area, time, nor people. It is a world and an ageless thing, so let us look at it from that viewpoint. It is the boiled down juice of human living and when one phase of it passes another begins which shall in turn give way before a successor.

Culture is a forced march on the near and the obvious. . . . The intelligent mind uses up a great part of its lifespan trying to awaken its consciousness sufficiently to comprehend that which is plainly there before it. Every generation or so some individual with extra keen perception grasps something of the obvious about us and hitches the human race forward slightly by a new 'law'. Millions of things had been falling on men for thousands of years before the falling apple hit Newton on the head and he saw the law of gravity.[8]

Through this strategic description of the folkloric heart of scientific law, Hurston dramatizes the predicament not only of the anthropologist but also of the novelist: both are caught between the (metaphorical) urge to universalize or totalize and the knowledge that it is precisely 'the near and the obvious' that will never be grasped once and for all but will only be (metonymically) named and renamed, as different things successively strike different heads. I shall return to this problem of universality at the end of this essay, but first I should like to take a close look at some of the figurative operations at work in Hurston's best-known novel, *Their Eyes Were Watching God*.[9]

The novel presents, in a combination of first- and third-person narration, the story of Janie Crawford and her three successive husbands. The first, Logan Killicks, is chosen by Janie's grandmother for his sixty acres and as a socially secure harbor for Janie's awakening sexuality. When Janie realizes that love does not automatically follow upon marriage and that Killicks completely lacks imagination, she decides to run off with ambitious, smart-talking, stylishly dressed Joe Starks, who is headed for a new all-black town where he hopes to become what he calls a 'big voice'. Later, as mayor and store owner of the town, he proudly raises Janie to a pedestal of property and propriety. Because this involves her submission to his idea of what a mayor's wife should be, Janie soon finds her pedestal to be a straitjacket, particularly when it involves her exclusion – both as speaker and as listener – from the tale-telling sessions on the store porch and at the mock funeral of a mule. Little by little, Janie begins to talk back to Joe, finally insulting him so profoundly that, in a sense, he dies of it. Some time later, into Janie's life walks Tea Cake Woods, whose first act is to teach Janie how to play checkers. 'Somebody wanted her to play,' says the text in free indirect discourse; 'Somebody thought it natural for her to play' (p. 146). Thus begins a joyous liberation from the rigidities of status, image and property – one of the most beautiful and convincing love stories in any literature. In a series of courtship dances, appearances and disappearances, Tea Cake succeeds in fulfilling Janie's dream of 'a bee for her blossom' (p. 161). Tea Cake, unlike Joe and Logan, regards money and work as worth only the amount of play and enjoyment they make possible. He gains and loses money unpredictably until he and Janie begin working side by side picking beans on 'the muck' in the Florida everglades. This idyll of pleasure, work and equality ends dramatically with a hurricane during which Tea Cake, while saving Janie's life, is bitten by a rabid dog. When Tea Cake's subsequent hydrophobia transforms him into a wild and violent animal, Janie is forced to shoot him in self-defense. Acquitted of murder by an all-white jury, Janie returns to Eatonville, where she tells her story to her friend Phoeby Watson.

The passage on which I should like to concentrate both describes and dramatizes, in its figurative structure, a crucial turning point in Janie's relation to Joe and to herself. The passage follows an argument over what Janie has done with a bill of lading, during which Janie shouts, 'You sho loves to tell me whut to do, but Ah can't tell you nothin' Ah see!'

'Dat's 'cause you need tellin',' he rejoined hotly. 'It would be pitiful if Ah didn't. Somebody got to think for women and chillun and chickens and cows. I god, they sho don't think none theirselves.'

'Ah knows uh few things, and womenfolks thinks sometimes too!'

'Aw naw they don't. They just think they's thinkin'. When Ah see one thing Ah understands ten. You see ten things and don't understand one.'

Times and scenes like that put Janie to thinking about the inside state of her marriage. Time came when she fought back with her tongue as best she could, but it didn't do her any good. It just made Joe do more. He wanted her submission and he'd keep on fighting until he felt he had it.

So gradually, she pressed her teeth together and learned how to hush. The spirit of the marriage left the bedroom and took to living in the parlor. It was there to shake hands whenever company came to visit, but it never went back inside the bedroom again. So she put something in there to represent the spirit like a Virgin Mary image in a church. The bed was no longer a daisy-field for her and Joe to play in. It was a place where she went and laid down when she was sleepy and tired.

She wasn't petal-open anymore with him. She was twenty-four and seven years married when she knew. She found that out one day when he slapped her face in the kitchen. It happened over one of those dinners that chasten all women sometimes. They plan and they fix and they do, and then some kitchen-dwelling fiend slips a scrochy, soggy, tasteless mess into their pots and pans. Janie was a good cook, and Joe had looked forward to his dinner as a refuge from other things. So when the bread didn't rise and the fish wasn't quite done at the bone, and the rice was scorched, he slapped Janie until she had a ringing sound in her ears and told her about her brains before he stalked on back to the store.

Janie stood where he left her for unmeasured time and thought. She stood there until something fell off the shelf inside her. Then she went inside there to see what it was. It was her image of Jody tumbled down and shattered. But looking at it she saw that it never was the flesh and blood figure of her dreams.

Just something she had grabbed up to drape her dreams over. In a way she turned her back upon the image where it lay and looked further. She had no more blossomy openings dusting pollen over her man, neither any glistening young fruit where the petals used to be. Şhe found that she had a host of thoughts she had never expressed to him, and numerous emotions she had never let Jody know about. Things packed up and put away in parts of her heart where he could never find them. She was saving up feelings for some man she had never seen. She had an inside and an outside now and suddenly she knew how not to mix them. (pp. 110–13)

This opposition between an inside and an outside is a standard way of describing the nature of a rhetorical figure. The vehicle, or surface meaning, is seen as enclosing an inner tenor, or figurative meaning. This relation can be pictured somewhat facetiously as a gilded carriage – the vehicle – containing Luciano Pavarotti, the tenor. Within the passage cited from *Their Eyes Were Watching God*, I should like to concentrate on the two paragraphs that begin respectively 'So gradually . . .' and 'Janie stood where he left her . . .' In these two paragraphs Hurston plays a number of interesting variations on the inside/outside opposition.

In both paragraphs, a relation is set up between an inner 'image' and outward, domestic space. The parlor, bedroom and store full of shelves already exist in the narrative space of the novel: they are figures drawn metonymically from the familiar contiguous surroundings. Each of these paragraphs recounts a little narrative of, and within, its own figurative terms. In the first, the inner spirit of the marriage moves outward from the bedroom to the parlor, cutting itself off from its proper place, and replacing itself with an image of virginity, the antithesis of marriage. Although Joe is constantly exclaiming, 'I god, Janie,' he will not be as successful as his namesake in uniting with the Virgin Mary. Indeed, it is his godlike self-image that forces Janie to retreat to virginity. The entire paragraph is an externalization of Janie's feelings onto the outer surroundings in the form of a narrative of movement from private to public space. While the whole of the figure relates metaphorically, analogically, to the marital situation it is designed to express, it reveals the marriage space to be metonymical, a movement through a series of contiguous rooms. It is a narrative not of union but of separation centered on an image not of conjugality but of virginity.

In the second passage, just after the slap, Janie is standing, thinking, until something 'fell off the shelf inside her'. Janie's 'inside' is here represented as a store that she then goes in to inspect. While the former paragraph was an externalization of the inner, here we find an internalization of the outer: Janie's inner self resembles a store. The material for this metaphor is drawn from the narrative world of contiguity: the store is the place where Joe has set himself up as lord, master and proprietor. But here Jody's image is broken, and reveals itself never to have been a metaphor but only a metonymy of Janie's dream: 'looking at it she saw that it never was the flesh and blood figure of her dreams. Just something she had grabbed up to drape her dreams over.'

What we find in juxtaposing these two figural mini-narratives is a kind of chiasmus, or cross-over, in which the first paragraph presents an externalization of the inner, a metaphorically grounded metonymy, while the second paragraph presents an internalization of the outer, or a metonymically grounded metaphor. In both cases, the quotient of the operation is the revelation of a false or discordant 'image'. Janie's image, as Virgin Mary, acquires a new intactness, while Joe's lies shattered on the floor. The reversals operated by the chiasmus map out a reversal of the power relations between Janie and Joe. Henceforth, Janie will grow in power and resistance, while Joe deteriorates both in his body and in his public image.

The moral of these two figural tales is rich with implications: 'She had an inside and an outside now and suddenly she knew how not to mix them.' On the one hand, this means that she knew how to keep the inside and the outside separate without trying to blend or merge them into one unified identity. On the other hand it means that she has stepped irrevocably into the necessity of figurative language, where inside and outside are never the same. It is from this point on in the novel that Janie, paradoxically, begins to speak. And it is by means of a devastating figure – 'You look like the change of life' – that she wounds Jody to the quick. Janie's acquisition of the power of voice thus grows not out of her identity but out of her division into inside and outside. Knowing how not to mix them is knowing that articulate language requires the co-presence of two distinct poles, not their collapse into oneness.

This, of course, is what Jakobson concludes in his discussion of metaphor and metonymy. For it must be remembered that what is at stake in the maintenance of both sides – metaphor and metonymy, inside and outside – is the very possibility of speaking at all. The reduction of a discourse to oneness, identity – in Janie's case, the reduction of woman to mayor's wife – has as its necessary consequence aphasia, silence, the loss of the ability to speak: 'she pressed her teeth together and learned how to hush.'

What has gone unnoticed in theoretical discussions of Jakobson's article is that behind the metaphor/metonymy distinction lies the much more serious distinction between speech and aphasia, between silence and the capacity to articulate one's own voice. To privilege *either* metaphor *or* metonymy is thus to run the risk of producing an increasingly aphasic *critical* discourse. If both, or all four, poles must be operative in order for speech to function fully, then the very notion of an 'authentic voice' must be redefined. Far from being an expression of Janie's new wholeness or identity as a character, Janie's increasing ability to speak grows out of her ability not to mix inside with outside, not to pretend that there is no difference, but to assume and articulate the incompatible forces involved in her own division. The sign of an authentic voice is thus not self-identity but self-difference.

The search for wholeness, oneness, universality and totalization can nevertheless never be put to rest. However rich, healthy or lucid fragmentation and division may be, narrative seems to have trouble resting content with it, as though a story could not recognize its own end as anything other than a moment of totalization – even when what is totalized is loss. The ending of *Their Eyes Were Watching God* is no exception:

> Of course [Tea Cake] wasn't dead. He could never be dead until she herself had finished feeling and thinking. The kiss of his memory made pictures of love and light against the wall. Here was peace. She pulled in her horizon like a great fish-net. Pulled it from around the waist of the world and draped it over her shoulder. So much of life in its meshes! She called in her soul to come and see.

The horizon, with all of life caught in its meshes, is here pulled into the self as a gesture of total recuperation and peace. It is as though self-division could be healed over at last, but only at the cost of a radical loss of the other.

This hope for some ultimate unity and peace seems to structure the very sense of an ending as such, whether that of a novel or that of a work of literary criticism. At the opposite end of the 'canonical' scale, one finds it, for example, in the last chapter of Erich Auerbach's *Mimesis*, perhaps the greatest of modern monuments to the European literary canon. That final chapter, entitled 'The Brown Stocking' after the stocking that Virginia Woolf's Mrs Ramsay is knitting in *To the Lighthouse*, is a description of certain narrative tendencies in the modern novel: 'multipersonal representation of consciousness, time strata, disintegration of the continuity of exterior events, shifting of narrative viewpoint', etc.

> Let us begin with a tendency which is particularly striking in our text from Virginia Woolf. She holds to minor, unimpressive, random events: measuring the stocking, a fragment of a conversation with the maid, a telephone call. Great changes, exterior turning points, let alone catastrophes, do not occur.

Auerbach concludes his discussion of the modernists' preoccupation with the minor, the trivial and the marginal by saying:

> It is precisely the random moment which is comparatively independent of the controversial and unstable orders over which men fight and despair. . . . The more numerous, varied, and simple the people are who appear as subjects of such random moments, the more effectively must what they have in common shine forth. . . . So the complicated process of dissolution which led to fragmentation of the exterior action, to reflection of consciousness, and to stratification of time seems to be tending toward a very simple solution. Perhaps it will be too simple to please those who, despite all its dangers and catastrophes, admire and love our epoch for the sake of its abundance of life and the incomparable historical vantage point which it affords. But they are

few in number, and probably they will not live to see much more than the first forewarnings of the approaching unification and simplication.[10]

Never has the desire to transform fragmentation into unity been expressed so succinctly and authoritatively – indeed, almost prophetically. One cannot help but wonder, though, whether the force of this desire has not been provoked by the fact that the primary text it wishes to unify and simplify was written by a woman. What Auerbach calls 'minor, unimpressive, random events' – measuring a stocking, conversing with the maid, answering the phone – can all be identified as conventional women's activities. 'Great changes', 'exterior turning points' and 'catastrophes' have been the stuff of heroic male literature. Even plot itself – up until Madame Bovary, at least – has been conceived as the doings of those who do not stay at home, i.e. men. Auerbach's urge to unify and simplify is an urge to re-subsume female difference under the category of the universal, which has always been unavowedly male. The random, the trivial and the marginal will simply be added to the list of things all men have in common.

If 'unification and simplification' is the privilege and province of the male, it is also, in America, the privilege and province of the white. If the woman's voice, to be authentic, must incorporate and articulate division and self-difference, so, too, has Afro-American literature always had to assume its double-voicedness. As Henry Louis Gates, Jr, puts it in 'Criticism in the Jungle':

> In the instance of the writer of African descent, her or his texts occupy spaces in at least two traditions – the individual's European or American literary tradition, and one of the three related but distinct black traditions. The 'heritage' of each black text written in a Western language, then, is a double heritage, two-toned, as it were. . . . Each utterance, then, is double-voiced.[11]

This is a reformulation of W. E. B. DuBois's famous image of the 'veil' that divides the black American in two:

> The Negro is a sort of seventh son, born with a veil, and gifted with second sight in this American world, – a world which yields him no true self-consciousness, but only lets him see himself through the revelation of the other world. It is a peculiar sensation, this double-consciousness, this sense of always looking at one's self through the eyes of others, of measuring one's soul by the tape of a world that looks on in amused contempt and pity. One ever feels his twoness – an American, a Negro; two souls, two thoughts, two unreconciled strivings; two warring ideals in one dark body, whose dogged strength alone keeps it from being torn asunder.
>
> The history of the American Negro is the history of this strife, – this longing to attain self-conscious manhood, to merge his double self into a better and truer self.[12]

James Weldon Johnson, in his Autobiography of an Ex-Colored Man, puts it this way:

This is the dwarfing, warping, distorting influence which operates upon each and every colored man in the United States. He is forced to take his outlook on all things, not from the view-point of a citizen, or a man, or even a human being, but from the view-point of a *colored* man. . . . This gives to every colored man, in proportion to his intellectuality, a sort of dual personality.[13]

What is striking about the above two quotations is that they both assume without question that the black subject is male. The black woman is totally invisible in these descriptions of the black dilemma. Richard Wright, in his review of *Their Eyes Were Watching God*, makes it plain that for him, too, the black female experience is nonexistent. The novel, says Wright, lacks

a basic idea or theme that lends itself to significant interpretation. . . . [Hurston's] dialogue manages to catch the psychological movements of the Negro folk-mind in their pure simplicity, but that's as far as it goes. . . . The sensory sweep of her novel carries no theme, no message, no thought.[14]

No message, no theme, no thought: the full range of questions and experiences of Janie's life are as invisible to a mind steeped in maleness as Ellison's Invisible Man is to minds steeped in whiteness. If the black *man's* soul is divided in two, what can be said of the black woman's? Here again, what is constantly seen exclusively in terms of a binary opposition – black versus white, man versus woman – must be redrawn at least as a tetrapolar structure (see Figure 9.3). What happens in the case of a black woman is that the four quadrants are constantly being collapsed into two. Hurston's work is often called non-political simply because readers of Afro-American literature tend to look for confrontational *racial* politics, not sexual politics. If the black woman voices opposition to male domination, she is often seen as a traitor to the cause of racial justice. But, if she sides with black men against white oppression, she often winds up having to accept her position within the Black Power movement as, in Stokely Carmichael's words, 'prone'. This impossible position between two oppositions is what I think Hurston intends when, at the end of the novel, she represents Janie as acquitted of the murder of Tea Cake by an all-white jury but condemned by her fellow blacks. This is not out of a 'lack of bitterness toward whites', as one

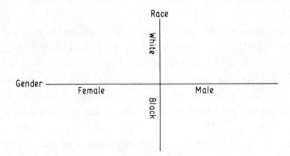

Figure 9.3

reader[15] would have it, but rather out of a knowledge of the standards of male dominance that pervade both the black and the white worlds. The black crowd at the trial murmurs, 'Tea Cake was a good boy. He had been good to that woman. No nigger woman ain't never been treated no better' (p. 276). As Janie's grandmother puts it early in the novel:

> 'Honey, de white man is de ruler of everything as fur as Ah been able tuh find out. Maybe it's some place way off in de ocean where de black man is in power, but we don't know nothin' but what we see. So de white man throw down de load and tell de nigger man tuh pick it up. He pick it up because he have to, but he don't tote it. He hand it to his womenfolks. De nigger woman is de mule uh de world so fur as Ah can see.' (p. 29)

In a very persuasive book on black women and feminism entitled *Ain't I a Woman*, Bell Hooks (Gloria Watkins) discusses the ways in which black women suffer from both sexism and racism within the very movements whose ostensible purpose is to set them free. Watkins argues that 'black woman' has never been considered a separate, distinct category with a history and complexity of its own. When a president appoints a black woman to a cabinet post, for example, he does not feel he is appointing a person belonging to the category 'black woman'; he is appointing a person who belongs *both* to the category 'black' *and* to the category 'woman', and is thus killing two birds with one stone. Watkins says of the analogy often drawn – particularly by white feminists – between blacks and women:

> Since analogies derive their power, their appeal, and their very reason for being from the sense of two disparate phenomena having been brought closer together, for white women to acknowledge the overlap between the terms 'blacks' and 'women' (that is, the existence of black women) would render this analogy unnecessary. By continuously making this analogy, they unwittingly suggest that to them the term 'women' is synonymous with 'white women' and the term 'blacks' synonymous with 'black men'.[16]

The very existence of black women thus disappears from an analogical discourse designed to express the types of oppression from which black women have the most to suffer.

In the current hierarchical view of things, this tetrapolar graph can be filled in as in Figure 9.4. The black woman is both invisible and ubiquitous: never seen in her own right but forever appropriated by the others for their own ends.

Ultimately, though, this mapping of tetrapolar differences is itself a fantasy of universality. Are all the members of each quadrant the same? Where are the nations, the regions, the religions, the classes, the professions? Where are the other races, the interracial subdivisions? How can the human world be totalized, even as a field of divisions? In the following quotation from Zora Neale

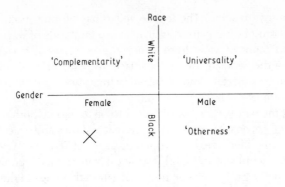

Figure 9.4

Hurston's autobiography, we see that even the *same* black woman can express self-division in two completely different ways:

> Work was to be all of me, so I said. . . . I had finished that phase of research and was considering writing my first book, when I met the man who was really to lay me by the heels. . . .
>
> He was tall, dark brown, magnificently built, with a beautifully modeled back head. His profile was strong and good. The nose and lips were especially good front and side. But his looks only drew my eyes in the beginning. I did not fall in love with him just for that. He had a fine mind and that intrigued me. When a man keeps beating me to the draw mentally, he begins to get glamorous. . . . His intellect got me first for I am the kind of woman that likes to move on mentally from point to point, and I like for my man to be there way ahead of me. . . .
>
> His great desire was to do for me. *Please* let him be a *man!* . . .
>
> That very manliness, sweet as it was, made us both suffer. My career balked the completeness of his ideal. I really wanted to conform, but it was impossible. To me there was no conflict. My work was one thing, and he was all the rest. But I could not make him see that. Nothing must be in my life but himself. . . . We could not leave each other alone, and we could not shield each other from hurt. . . . In the midst of this, I received my Guggenheim Fellowship. This was my chance to release him, and fight myself free from my obsession. He would get over me in a few months and go on to be a very big man. So I sailed off to Jamaica [and] pitched in to work hard on my research to smother my feelings. But the thing would not down. The plot was far from the circumstances, but I tried to embalm all the tenderness of my passion for him in *Their Eyes Were Watching God.*[17]

The plot is indeed far from the circumstances, and, what is even more striking, it is lived by what seems to be a completely different woman. While Janie struggles to attain equal respect within a relation to a man, Zora readily submits to the pleasures of submission yet struggles to establish the legitimacy of a professional life *outside* the love relation. The female voice may be universally described as divided, but it must be recognized as divided in a multitude of ways.

There is no point of view from which the universal characteristics of the human, or of the woman, or of the black woman, or even of Zora Neale Hurston, can be selected and totalized. Unification and simplification are fantasies of domination, not understanding.

The task of the writer, then, would seem to be to narrate both the appeal and the injustice of universalization, in a voice that assumes and articulates its own, ever differing self-difference. In the opening pages of *Their Eyes Were Watching God* we find, indeed, a brilliant and subtle transition from the seduction of a universal language through a progressive de-universalization that ends in the exclusion of the very protagonist herself. The book begins:

> Ships at a distance have every man's wish on board. For some they come in with the tide. For others they sail forever on the horizon, never out of sight, never landing until the Watcher turns his eyes away in resignation, his dreams mocked to death by Time. That is the life of men.
>
> Now, women forget all those things they don't want to remember, and remember everything they don't want to forget. The dream is the truth. Then they act and do things accordingly.
>
> So the beginning of this was a woman, and she had come back from burying the dead. Not the dead of sick and ailing with friends at the pillow and the feet. She had come back from the sodden and the bloated; the sudden dead, their eyes flung wide open in judgment.
>
> The people all saw her come because it was sundown . . . (p. 9)

At this point Janie crosses center stage and goes out, while the people, the 'bander log', pass judgment on her. The viewpoint has moved from 'every man' to 'men' to 'women' to 'a woman' to an absence commented on by 'words without masters', the gossip of the front porch. When Janie begins to speak, even the universalizing category of 'standard English' gives way to the careful representation of dialect. The narrative voice in this novel expresses its own self-division by shifts between first and third person, standard English and dialect. This self-division culminates in the frequent use of free indirect discourse, in which, as Henry Louis Gates, Jr, points out,[18] the inside/outside boundaries between narrator and character, between standard and individual, are both transgressed and preserved, making it impossible to identify and totalize either the subject or the nature of discourse.

Narrative, it seems, is an endless fishing expedition with the horizon as both the net and the fish, the big one that always gets away. The meshes continually enclose and let escape, tear open and mend up again. Mrs Ramsay never finishes the brown stocking.[19] A woman's work is never done. Penelope's weaving is nightly re-unraveled. The porch never stops passing the world through its mouth. The process of de-universalization can never, universally, be completed.

Notes

1 For an excellent discussion of the importance of the metaphor/metonymy distinction, see Maria Ruegg, 'Metaphor and Metonymy: the Logic of Structuralist Rhetoric', *Glyph*, 6 (1979).
2 In Roman Jakobson and Morris Halle, *Fundamentals of Language* ('S-Gravenhage:.Mouton, 1956).
3 Ibid., pp. 76–7.
4 Roman Jakobson, 'Linguistics and Poetics', in *The Structuralists from Marx to Lévi-Strauss* (Garden City, NY: Doubleday Anchor, 1972), p. 95.
5 See George Lakoff and Mark Johnson, *Metaphors We Live By* (Chicago, Ill.: University of Chicago Press, 1980).
6 Aristotle, *Rhetoric*, III. 1410.
7 Paul de Man, *Allegories of Reading* (New Haven, Conn.: Yale University Press, 1979), p. 14.
8 'Folklore Field Notes from Zora Neale Hurston', introduced by Robert Hemenway, *The Black Scholar*, 7, 7 (1976), pp. 41–2.
9 First published in 1937; all page references are to the Illini Book Edition (Urbana, Ill.: University of Illinois Press, 1978).
10 Erich Auerbach, *Mimesis* (New York: Doubleday Anchor, 1957), pp. 482–3, 488.
11 In *Black American Literature Forum*, 15, 4 (1981), pp. 123, 125.
12 W. E. B. DuBois, *The Souls of Black Folk*, repr. in *Three Negro Classics* (New York: Avon, 1965), pp. 214–15.
13 James Weldon Johnson, *The Autobiography of an Ex-Colored Man*, repr. in ibid., p. 403.
14 Richard Wright, 'Between Laughter and Tears', *New Masses*, 5 October 1937, pp. 25–6.
15 Arthur P. Davis, *From the Dark Tower* (Washington, DC: Howard University Press, 1974), p. 116.
16 Bell Hooks, *Ain't I a Woman* (Boston, Mass.: South End Press, 1981), p. 8.
17 Zora Neale Hurston, *Dust Tracks on a Road* (Philadelphia, Pa.: Lippincott, 1942), pp. 260–88.
18 See Gates's discussion of *Their Eyes Were Watching God* as what he calls (à la Barthes) a 'speakerly text', in *The Signifying Monkey* (New York: Oxford University Press, 1985).
19 I wish to thank Patti Joplin of Stanford University for calling my attention to this fact.

10

Houston A. Baker, Jr

To move without moving: creativity and commerce in Ralph Ellison's Trueblood episode

'Them boss quails is like a good man, what he got to do he *do*.'
(Trueblood)

In his essay 'Richard Wright's Blues',[1] Ralph Ellison states one of his cherished distinctions:

> The function, the psychology, of artistic selectivity is to eliminate from art form all those elements of experience which contain no compelling significance. Life is as the sea, art a ship in which man conquers life's crushing formlessness, reducing it to a course, a series of swells, tides and wind currents inscribed on a chart. (p. 94)

The distinction between non-significant *life* experiences and inscribed, artistic significance (i.e. meaning that is *form-induced*) leads Ellison to concur with André Malraux that artistic significance alone 'enables man to conquer chaos and to master destiny' (p. 94).

Artistic 'technique', according to Ellison, is the agency through which artistic meaning and form are achieved. 'It is a matter of outrageous irony, perhaps,' he writes in 'Hidden Name and Complex Fate',[2]

> but in literature the great social clashes of history no less than the painful experience of the individual are secondary to the meaning which they take on through the skill, the talent, the imagination and personal vision of the writer who transforms them into art. Here they are reduced to more manageable proportions; here they are imbued with humane value; here, injustice and catastrophe become less important in themselves than what the writer makes of them. (pp. 148–9)

Even the 'thing-in-itself' of lived, historical experience is thus seen as devoid of 'humane value' prior to its sea change under the artist's transforming technique.

Since Ellison's interest centers on the literary, the *inscribed*, work of art, he regards even folklore as part of that realm of life – 'elements . . . which contain no compelling significance' in themselves. In 'Change the Joke and Slip the Yoke',[3] he asserts:

> the Negro American writer is also an heir to the human experience which is literature, and this might well be more important to him than his living folk tradition. For me, at least, in the discontinuous, swiftly changing and diverse American culture, the stability of the Negro folk tradition became precious as a result of an act of *literary* discovery. . . . For those who are able to translate . . . [the folk tradition's] meanings into *wider, more precise vocabularies* it has much to offer indeed. (pp. 72–3; my italics)

Afro-American folklore thus appears to be coextensive with lived experience prior to its translation into 'more precise vocabularies'. Art and chaos in Ellison's criticism are homologous, I believe, with literature and folklore.

But to state this homology by inference from one or two critical remarks is to risk the abyss of 'false distinction' when faced with a canon as rich as Ellison's. For it is certainly true that the apparent disparagement of the folk in the critical instances cited can be qualified by the high praise of folklore characterizing Ellison's assertion that expressive folk projections represent symbolically 'profound' attempts by a group to 'humanize' the world.[4] Such projections, according to the entry in *Shadow and Act* entitled 'The Art of Fiction: An Interview', even in their crudest forms, constitute the 'humble base' on which 'great literature' is erected (p. 172).

It does seem accurate, however, to say that Ellison implies, time and again in his critical utterances, that there is an extant, identifiable tradition of *written, Western, literary* art – a tradition consisting of masters of literary form and technique who must be read, studied, emulated and (if one is very lucky and very eloquent) equalled. This tradition stands as the signal, vital repository of 'humane value'. And for Ellison the sphere that it describes is equivalent to the *primum mobile*, lending force and significance to all actions of the descending heavens and earth.

Hence, while one might suggest that the division between the 'folk' and the 'artistic' is only a discursive assignment bearing no more weight in 'factual' reality than other such divisions, the assignment does seem to matter to Ellison, who, as far as I know, never refers to himself as a 'folk' artist. Moreover, in our era of sophisticated 'folkloristics', it seems mere evasion to shy away from the assertion that Ellison's criticism makes an evaluative judgment on folklore and art in which the former is ranked lower in a total scale of value. What I shall suggest in the following essay is that the distinction between folklore and art that is legitimately inferable from Ellison's critical practice is a distinction that collapses in his creative practice in the Trueblood episode of *Invisible Man*. Further, I shall suggest that an exacting analysis of the narrative episode is an enabling condition for comprehending the relationship not only between Ellison's critical and creative practices but also between what might be called the public and private commerce of black art in America.

The Trueblood episode occupies chapter 2 of Ellison's novel. Its main character is both Ellison's depiction of the country blues singer *par excellence* (a tenor-voiced man of 'crude, high, plaintively animal sounds') and his portrait of the virtuoso prose narrator. In order to understand the disjunction between Ellison's somewhat disparaging critical pronouncements on 'raw' folklore and his striking, fictional representation of the folk character Trueblood, one must first comprehend, I think, the sharecropper's dual manifestation as trickster and merchant, as both creative and commercial man. Blues and narration, as modes of expression, conjoin and divide in harmony with this duality. And the episode in its entirety is – as I shall demonstrate in the following discussion – a meta-expressive commentary on the incumbencies of the Afro-American artist and the effects of his distinctive modes of expression.

In his essay 'Deep Play: Notes on the Balinese Cockfight'[5] the symbolic anthropologist Clifford Geertz asserts, after a brilliant ethnographic 'reading' of the Balinese cockfight, that:

Like any art form – for that, finally, is what we are dealing with – the cockfight renders ordinary, everyday experience comprehensible by presenting it in terms of acts and objects which have had their practical consequences removed and been reduced (or, if you prefer, raised) to the level of sheer appearances, where their meaning can be more powerfully articulated and more exactly perceived. (p. 443)

Catching up the *themes* of Balinese society in symbolic form, the cockfight thus represents, in Geertz's words, 'a metasocial commentary . . . a Balinese reading of Balinese experience, a story they tell themselves about themselves' (p. 448). The anthropologist's claims imply that the various symbolic (or 'semiotic') systems of a culture – religion, politics, economics – can themselves be 'raised' to a metasymbolic level by the orderings and processes of 'ritual interactions' like the Balinese cockfight.

The coming together of semiotic systems in ways that enlarge and enhance the world of human meanings is the subject of Professor Barbara Babcock's insightful essay 'The Novel and the Carnival World'.[6] Babcock, following the lead of Julia Kristeva, asserts that a 'metalanguage' is a symbolic system that treats of symbolic systems; for example, *Don Quixote* 'openly discusses other works of literature and takes the writing and reading of literature as its subject' (p. 912). The capacity of both social rituals and of novels to 'embed' other semiotic systems within their 'texture' makes both novels and rituals 'multivocal', 'polyvalent' or 'polysemous' – i.e. capable of speaking in a variety of mutually reflexive voices at once.

The narrative frames and 'voices' operative in Ellison's Trueblood episode are multiple and include: the novel *Invisible Man*, the protagonist's fictive autobiographical account, Norton's story recalled as part of the fictive autobiography, Trueblood's story as framed by the fictive autobiography, the sharecropper's own autobiographical recall, and his 'dream' narrative within that autobiographical recall. All of these 'stories' reflect, or 'objectify', each other in ways that complicate their individual and composite meanings. Further, the symbolic systems suggested by the stories are not confined to (though they do not exclude implicit comment upon) such familiar social configurations as education, economics, politics, religion, and so on. Subsuming these familiar manifests is, first, the 'outer' symbolic enterprise constituted by the novel itself. Additionally, within the novel (and heightening its 'multivocalic' character), the Trueblood episode acts as a metacommentary on the literary and artistic system out of which the novel itself is generated. Enriching the burden of meanings even further in Ellison's episode is Sigmund Freud's mythic 'narrative' concerning incest and the Christian myth of the Fall of Man, which the episode both connotes ('summons as a signifier', in Professor Babcock's terms) and parodies or inverts. I shall analyze the text's play on these myths later in the present discussion.

For the moment, I am interested primarily in suggesting that the Trueblood episode, like other systematic symbolic phenomena, both gains and generates its meanings in a dialogic relationship with various systems of signs. The logic of Ellison's sharecropper chapter *as a text* derives from its *intertextual* relationship with surrounding and encompassing texts, which, in turn, are complicated in their meanings by the farmer's episode. The Balinese cockfight, according to Geertz, can tell a 'metastory' only because it is intertextually implicated in a world that is itself constituted by a repertoire of 'stories' (those of 'economics' and 'politics', for example) that the Balinese tell themselves.

Functioning as a reflexive story that the author of *Invisible Man* tells himself about his own practice, the Trueblood episode serves to clarify distinctions that must be made between Ralph Ellison as critic and artist. In order to clarify the meta-expressive character of the sharecropper episode, it is necessary to summon analytical instruments from areas that Ellison sharply debunks in his own criticism.

For example, two of the three questions that begin the first part of his masterfully instructive essay on the criticism of Afro-American creativity entitled 'The World and the Jug'[7] are stated in the following terms:

> Why is it so often true that when critics confront the American as Negro they suddenly drop their advanced critical armament and revert with an air of confident superiority to quite primitive modes of analysis? Why is it that

sociology-oriented critics seem to rate literature so far below politics and ideology that they would rather kill a novel than modify their presumptions concerning a given reality which it seeks in its own terms to project? (pp. 115–16)

What I take Ellison's questions to imply is that a 'given' artistic reality designed to represent 'Negro American' experience should properly be analyzed in terms other than 'primitive' ones, which, in their lack of specificity in his utterance, stand in a significantly observable proximity to sociological, ideological and political modes of analysis. I hope to demonstrate in the following discussion that sociology, anthropology, economics, politics and ideology all provide models essential for the explication of the Trueblood episode. The first step, however, is to evoke the theater of Trueblood's performance.

The arena in which Trueblood's narration occurs is marked in chapter 2 by an unusual audience, but its physical setting is as familiar to the farmer and his Afro-American cohorts as train whistles in the Alabama night. The sharecropper, a white millionaire and a naïve undergraduate from a nearby black college have arranged themselves in a semicircle of camp chairs in the sharecropper's yard. They occupy a swath of shade cast by the enduring porch of a log cabin that has survived the hard times of slavery and the ravages of climate since emancipation. The millionaire queries: 'How are you faring now? . . . Perhaps I could help.'[8] The sharecropper responds: 'We ain't doing so bad, suh. 'Fore they heard 'bout what happen to us out here I couldn't get no help from nobody. Now lotta folks is curious and go outta their way to help' (p. 52). What has occurred 'out here' – in what the millionaire Mr Norton refers to as 'new territory for me' (p. 45) and what the narrator describes as 'a desert' (p. 45) that 'almost took my breath away' – is Jim Trueblood's impregnation of both his wife and his daughter. The event has brought disgrace on the sharecropper and has mightily embarrassed officials at the nearby black college.

White people in the proximate town and country, however, are scarcely outraged or perturbed by Trueblood's situation. Rather, they ensure the share-cropper's permanence among them, warning the college officials not to harass him or his family, and providing money, provisions and an abundance of work. 'White folks', says Trueblood, even 'took to coming out here to see us and talk with us. Some of 'em was big white folks, too, from the big school way cross the State. Asked me lots 'bout what I thought 'bout things, and 'bout my folks and the kids, and wrote it all down in a book' (p. 53). Hence, when the farmer begins to recount the story of his incestuous act with his daughter Matty Lou, he does so as a man who has thoroughly rehearsed his tale and who has carefully refined his knowledge of his audience: 'He cleared his throat, his eyes gleaming and his voice taking on a deep, incantatory quality, as though he had told the story many, many times' (p. 53).

The art of storytelling is not a recent gift for Trueblood. When he is introduced in *Invisible Man*, he is characterized as one who 'told the old stories with a sense of humor and a magic that made them come alive' (p. 46). The master storyteller thus recounts his provocative exploits to an audience that is, by turns, shamed, indignant, envious, humiliated and enthralled.

The tale begins on a cold, winter evening in the sharecropper's cabin. The smell of fat meat hangs in the air, and the last kindling crackles in the dying flames of the stove. Trueblood's daughter, in bed between him and his wife, sleepily whispers, 'Daddy.' At the story's close, the sharecropper reports his resolution to prevent Aunt Cloe the midwife from aborting his incestuous issue. At the conclusion of his tale, the narrator also reiterates his judgment that he and his family 'ain't doing so bad' in the wake of their ordeal.

Certainly the content and mode of narration chosen by the sharecropper are functions of his knowledge of white audience expectations regarding the Afro-American. Mr Norton is not only a 'teller of polite Negro stories' (p. 37) but also a man who responds to the fact that a pregnant Matty Lou does not have a husband by saying: 'But that shouldn't be so strange' (p. 49). The white man's belief in the promiscuity of blacks is further suggested when Mr Broadnax, a figure who appears in Trueblood's dream, looks at the sharecropper and his daughter engaged in incest and says: 'They just nigguhs, leave 'em do it' (p. 58). In conformity with audience expectations, the sharecropper's narrative is aggressively sexual in its representations.

Beginning with an account of the feel of his daughter's naked arm pressed against him in bed, the farmer proceeds to reminisce about bygone days in Mobile when he would lie in bed in the evenings with a woman named Margaret and listen to the music from steamboats passing on the river. Next, he introduces the metaphor of the woman in a red dress 'goin' past you down a lane . . . and kinda switchin' her tail 'cause she knows you watchin' ' (p. 56). From this evocative picture, he turns to a detailed account of his dream on the night of his incestuous act.

The dream is a type of parodic allegory in which the narrator goes in quest of 'fat meat'. The 'general concepts' that mark any narrative as allegory are captured in the Trueblood episode by the name 'Mr Broadnax' (Mr Broad-in-acts). The man whose house is on the hill is a philanthropist who dispenses sustaining gifts to poor blacks (True Bloods) as 'fat meat'. The model implied by this conceptualization certainly fits one turn-of-the-century American typology, recalling in its features the structural arrangement by which black southern colleges were able to sustain themselves. In one sense, the entire Trueblood episode can be read as a pejorative commentary on the castrating effects of white philanthropy. Trueblood's 'dream narrative' is *parodic* because it reveals the crippling assumptions (the castrating import) of the philanthropic model suggested in 'Broadnax'. The man who is broad-in-acts in the dream is one who suggests that the sharecropper and his daughter are 'just nigguhs'. Further, his philanthropy – like that of Mr Norton – is dangerously and confusingly connected with the sexuality of 'Mrs Broadnax'. What he dispenses as sustaining 'fat meat' may only be the temporarily satisfying thrill of sexual gratification. The 'pilgrim' or quester in Trueblood's dream allegory flees from the dangers and limitations of such deceptive philanthropy. And the general exposé effected by the narrative offers a devastating critique of that typography that saw white men on the hill (northern industrialists) as genuinely and philanthropically responsive to the needs of those in the valley (southern blacks).

Instructed to inquire at Mr Broadnax's house, Trueblood finds himself violating a series of southern taboos and fleeing for his life. He enters the front door of the home, wanders into a woman's bedroom, and winds up trapped in the embraces of a scantily clad white woman. The culinary and sexual appetites surely converge at this juncture, and the phrase 'fat meat' takes on a dangerous burden of significance. The dreamer breaks free, however, and escapes into the darkness and machinery of a grandfather clock. He runs until a bright, electrical light bursts over him, and he awakens to find himself engaged in sexual intercourse with his own daughter.

In *Totem and Taboo*, Freud advances the hypothesis that the two taboos of totemism – the interdictions on slaying the totem animal and on incest – result from events in human prehistory.[9] Following Darwin's speculations, Freud claims that men first lived in small hordes where one strong, jealous male took all women to himself, exiling the sons in order to protect his own exclusive sexual privileges. On one occasion, however, Freud suggests, the exiled sons arose, slayed and ate the father, and then, in remorse, established the taboo against such slaughter. To prevent discord among themselves and to ensure their newly achieved form of social organization, they also established a taboo on sexual intercourse with the women of their own clan. Exogamy, Freud concludes, is based on a prehistorical advance from a lower to a higher stage of social organization.

Trueblood's dream and subsequent incest seem to represent, where Freud's speculations are concerned, a historical regression. The sharecropper's dreamed violations of southern social and sexual taboos are equivalent to a slaughter of the white patriarch represented by Mr Broadnax, who does, indeed, control the 'fat' and 'fat meat' of the land. To eat 'fat meat' is to partake of the totemic animal. And, having run backward in time through the grandfather clock, Trueblood becomes the primal father, assuming all sexual prerogatives unto himself. He has warned away 'the boy' (representing the tumultous mob of exiled sons) who wanted to take away his daughter, and, as the sexual partner for Matty Lou as well as Kate, he reveals his own firm possession of all his 'womenfolks' – his status, that is to say, as a creative, sexual producer secure against the wrath of his displaced 'sons'. Insofar as Freud's notions of totemism represent a myth of progressive, social evolution, the farmer's story acts as a *counter-myth* of inversive, social dissolution. It breaks society down into componential elements and reveals man in what might be called his 'pre-social' and unaccommodated state.

One reason for the sharecropper's singular, sexual prerogatives is the fact that those Afro-Americans who surround him are either so constrained or so battered by their encounters with society that they are incapable of a legitimate and productive sexuality. The sharecropper's territory is bounded on one side, for example, by the black college where the 'sons' are indoctrinated in a course of instruction that leaves them impotent. On the other side, his domain is marked by the insane asylum and the veterans' home, residences of black men driven mad or, at least, rendered psychologically and physically crippled by their encounters with America. These 'disabled veterans' are scarcely 'family men' like Trueblood. Rather, they are listless souls who visit the whores in 'the sun-shrunk shacks at the railroad crossing . . . hobbling down the tracks on crutches and canes; sometimes pushing the legless, thighless one in a red wheelchair' (p. 35). Among such male company, Trueblood seems the only person capable of ensuring an authentic Afro-American lineage. When he finds himself atop Matty Lou, therefore, both the survival of the clan and the sharecropper's aversion to pain require him to reject the fate that has been physically or psychologically imposed on his male cohorts. He says:

> 'There was only one way I can figger that I could git out: that was with a knife. But I didn't have no knife, and if you'all ever seen them geld them young boar pigs in the fall, you know I knowed that was too much to pay to keep from sinnin'.' (p. 59)

In this reflection, he brings forward one of the dominant themes of Invisible Man. This theme – one frequently slighted, or omitted, in discussions of the novel – is black male sexuality.

Perhaps it is critical prudery that prevents commentators from acknowledging that the black male phallus is a dominant symbol in much of the ritual interaction of Invisible Man. In The Forest of Symbols: Aspects of Ndembu Ritual,[10] the symbolic anthropologist Victor Turner provides suggestive definitions of both 'ritual' and dominant symbols. He describes ritual as:

> prescribed formal behavior for occasions not given over to technological routine, having reference to beliefs in mystical beings or powers. The symbol is the smallest unit of ritual which still retains the specific properties of ritual behavior; it is the ultimate unit of specific structure in a ritual context. (p. 19)

For Turner, the most prominent – the 'senior', as it were – symbols in any ritual are 'dominant symbols' (p. 20); they fall into a class of their own. The important characteristic of such symbols is that they bring together, as a kind of condensed semiotic shorthand, disparate meanings. Further, they are able to refer both ideologically and sensibly: for example, the mudyi tree of Ndembu ritual refers both to the breast-milk of the mother and to the axiomatic values of the matrilineal Ndembu society (p. 28).

Ellison's Invisible Man is certainly an instance of 'prescribed formal behavior' insofar as it is governed by the conventions of the artistic system in which it is situated, a system that resides ludically outside 'technological routine' and promotes the cognitive exploration of all systems of 'being' and 'power', whether mystical or not. The black phallus as a dominant symbol in the novel's 'formal' patterns of behavior can be verified by observing its manifold recurrence. In 'The Art of Fiction: An Interview' Ellison writes:

> People rationalize what they shun or are incapable of dealing with; these superstitions and their rationalizations become rituals as they govern behavior. The rituals become social forms, and it is one of the functions of the artist to recognize them and raise them to the level of art. (p. 175)

Stated in slightly different terms, Ellison's comment suggests that an *intertextual* (indeed, a 'connoted') relationship exists between the 'prescribed' formal social behaviors of American race relations and the text of the novelist. Insofar as Jim Crow social laws and the desperate mob-exorcism of lynchings (with their attendant castrations) describe a 'formal' pattern of Anglo-American behavior *vis-à-vis* black men, this pattern offers an instance of ritual in which the black phallus gathers an extraordinary burden of disparate meanings and, surely, refers both sensibly and ideologically. It should come as no surprise that, in the world of an artist as perceptive as Ellison, the black phallus will be *recognized* as a dominant symbol of the sometimes bizarre social rituals of America, and incorporated into the text of a novel. In 'The Art of Fiction' Ellison, in fact, calls the 'battle royal' episode of *Invisible Man* 'a ritual in preservation of caste lines, a keeping of taboo to appease the gods and ward off back luck' (p. 175). He asserts that he did not have to 'invent' the ritual. All he had to do with the patterns represented by the episode was to 'present them in a broader context of meaning'.

The black phallus, then, does seem implicit in Ellison's text as a major symbol, and, prudery aside, there are venerable precedents for the discussion of male sexual symbols in ritual. For example, in his essay 'Deep Play', which I have previously cited, Geertz writes:

> To anyone who has been in Bali any length of time, the deep psychological identification of Balinese men with their cocks is unmistakable. The double entendre here is deliberate. It works in exactly the same way in Balinese as it does in English, even to producing the same tired jokes, strained puns, and uninventive obscenities. [Gregory] Bateson and [Margaret] Mead have even suggested that, in line with the Balinese conception of the body as a set of separately animated parts, cocks are viewed as detachable, self-operating penises, ambulent genitals with a life of their own. (p. 417)

The notion of 'ambulent genitals with a life of their own' is surely one that appears in tales of the roguish trickster as recorded in Paul Radin's classic work *The Trickster*.[11] In tale 16 of the Winnebago trickster cycle, Wakdjunkaga the trickster sends his penis across the waters of a lake to have intercourse with a chief's daughter.

The black phallus as a symbol of unconstrained force that white men contradictorily envy and seek to destroy appears first in the opening chapter of *Invisible Man*. The influential white men of the protagonist's home town force him and his fellow black boxers in the 'battle royal' to gaze on 'a magnificent blonde – stark naked' (p. 18). The boys are threatened both for looking and for not looking, and the white men smile at their obvious fear and discomfiture. The boys know the bizarre consequences that accompany the white men's ascription of an animal-like and voracious sexuality to black males. Hence they respond in biologically normal, but socially fearful (and justifiably embarrassed) ways. One boy strives to hide his erection with his boxing gloves, pleading desperately to go home. In this opening scene, the white woman as a parodic version of American ideals ('a small American flag tattooed upon her belly'; p. 19) is forced into tantalizing interaction with the mythically potent force of the black phallus. But the total control of the situation exercised by the town's white males makes the scene akin to a castration, excision or lynching.

Castration is one function of the elaborate glass box wired with electricity that incarcerates the protagonist in the Factory Hospital episode: ' "Why not castration, doctor?" a voice asked waggishly' (p. 231). In the Brotherhood, the class struggle is rather devastatingly transformed into the 'ass struggle' when the protagonist's voice and oratory are displaced as ideological agents by his penis. A white woman who hears him deliver a speech, and invites him home, passionately seizes the protagonist's biceps and says: 'Teach me, talk to me. Teach me the beautiful ideology of Brotherhood' (p. 405). And the protagonist admits that suddenly he 'was lost' as 'the conflict between the ideological and the biological, duty and desire' became too subtly confused (p. 406). Finally, in the concluding nightmare of the novel's text, the Invisible Man sees his own bloody testes, like those of the castrated Uranus of Greek myth, floating above the waters underneath a bridge's high arc (p. 557). In the nightmare, he tells his inquisitors that his castrated testes dripping blood on the black waters are not only his 'generations wasting upon the water' but also the 'sun' and the 'moon' and, indeed, the very 'world' of their own human existence (p. 558). The black phallus – in its creative, ambulent, generative power, even under conditions of castration – is like the cosmos itself, a self-sustaining and self-renewing source of life, provoking both envy and fear in Anglo-American society.

While a number of episodes in *Invisible Man* (including Trueblood's own dream) suggest the illusory freedoms and taboo-induced fears accompanying interaction between the black phallus and white women, only the Trueblood encounter reveals the phallus as indeed producing Afro-American 'generations' rather than wasting its seed 'upon the waters'. The cosmic force of the phallus thus becomes, in the ritual action of the Trueblood episode, symbolic of a type of royal paternity, an aristocratic procreativity turned inward to ensure the royalty (the 'truth', 'legitimacy' or 'authenticity') of an enduring black line of descent. In his outgoing phallic energy, therefore, the sharecropper is (as we learn on his first introduction in Invisible Man), indeed, a 'hard worker' who takes care of 'his family's needs' (p. 46). His family may, in a very real sense, be construed as the entire clan or 'tribe' that comprises Afro-America.

Like the Winnebago trickster, Trueblood, as a cosmic creator, is not bound by ordinary codes of social restraint. He is a being who ventures chaos in an outrageously sexual manner – and survives. As such, he, like Wakdjunkaga, offers an inversive play on social norms. He is the violator of boundaries who – unlike the scapegoat – eludes banishment.[12] Indeed, the sharecropper is so essential to whites in his sexual role that he and his family wear new clothes and shoes, have an abundance of food and work, purchase eyeglasses that have been needed for a long time, and even secure the means to reshingle their cabin after Trueblood has demonstrated his enviable sexual ability to survive chaos. 'I looks up at the mornin' sun,' says the farmer of his reaction to his incestuous act, 'and expects somehow for it to thunder. But it's already bright and clear. . . . I yells, "Have mercy, Lawd!" and waits. And there's nothin' but the clear bright mornin' sun' (p. 64–5).

Noting that 'most tricksters have an uncertain sexual status', the symbolic anthropologist Victor Turner points out that on some occasions

> tricksters appear with exaggerated phallic characteristics: Hermes is symbol-
> ized by the herm or pillar, the club, and the ithyphallic statue; Wakdjunkaga
> has a very long penis which has to be wrapped around him and put over his
> shoulder in a box; Eshu is represented in sculpture as having a long curved
> hairdress carved as a phallus.[13]

Such phallic figures are, for Turner, representatives par excellence of what he calls 'liminality'.[14] Liminality describes that 'betwixt and between' phase of rites of passage when an individual has left one fixed social status and has not yet been incorporated into another status in society. When African boys are secluded in the forest during circumcision rites, for example, they are in a liminal phase between childhood and adult statuses. They receive, during this seclusion, mythic instruction in the origin and structures of their society. And this instruction serves not only to 'deconstruct' the component elements of the ordered social world they have left behind but also to reveal these elements recombined into new and powerful composites. The duality of this process of mythic instruction is aptly represented by the phallic trickster. For he is radically antinomian in his activities; his transgressions include destruction of sacred property, murder and incest. In these acts, he symbolically captures what Turner describes as the 'amoral and nonlogical' rhythms and outcomes of human biology and of meteorological climate: i.e. the uncontrollable rhythms of nature.[15] But the trickster is also a cultural gift-bearer. Turner emphasizes the fact that 'the Winnebago trickster transforms the pieces of his broken phallus into plants and flowers for men.'[16] Hermes enriches human culture with dreams and music. In a sense, therefore, one may regard the phallic trickster as a force that is, paradoxically, both anti-conventional and culturally benevolent. The paradox is dissolved in the definition of the trickster as the 'prima materia – as undifferentiated raw material' from which all things derive.[17] Trueblood's sexual energies, antinomian acts, productive issue and resonant expressivity make him – in his incestuous, liminal moments and their immediate aftermath – a trickster par excellence.

In his sexual manifestation, Ellison's sharecropper challenges not only the mundane restraints of his environment but also the fundamental Judeo-Christian categories on which such restraints are founded. He has, as I have already noted, quickly abandoned the notion of the knife – of casting out, in Mr Norton's indignant (and wonderfully ironic) phrase, 'the offending eye'. His virtual parodies of the notions of sin and sacrifice lend comic point to his latitudinarian challenge to Christian orthodoxy. When his wife brings the sharpened axe down on his head, Trueblood recalls: 'I sees, it, Lawd, yes! I sees it and seein' it I twists my head aside. Couldn't help it . . . I moves. Though I meant to keep still, I moves! Anybody but Jesus Christ hisself woulda moved' (p. 63). So much for repentance and salvation through the bloody sacrifice of one's own life! But Trueblood goes on to indicate why such sacrifice may not have been called for in his case. His self-justification consists of distinguishing, with all the skill of a revisionist theologian, between 'blood-sin' and 'dream-sin' (p. 62). In essence, he claims, with unshakable human certainty, that only the dream of his encounter at the Broadnax household led to his sexual arousal and subsequent incest.

But while this casuistic claim suffices in the farmer's interaction with the social world around him, his own earlier appraisal of his act seems more in harmony with his role as a cosmically rebellious trickster. He says that, when he discovered his position atop Matty Lou, he felt that, since it 'happened when I was asleep', it might not be sinful. But then he adds: 'although maybe sometimes a man can look at a little old pigtail gal and see him a whore' (p. 59). The 'naturalness' and natural unpredictability of sexual arousal implied by the 'although' seem more in keeping with the sharecropper's manifestation as black, phallic energy.

The sharecropper's sexual energies are not without complement in the arid regions where he and his family eke out a living. Trueblood's wife Kate is an awesome force of both new life and outgoing socio-religious fury. His yard is filled with children borne by Kate, and his oldest child, Matty Lou, is Kate's double – a woman who looks just like her mother and who is fully grown and sexually mature. Kate and Matty Lou – both moving with the 'full-fronted motions of far-gone pregnancy' (p. 47) – are the first human figures seen by Mr Norton as he approaches the Trueblood property. Both woman are bearers of new black life, and they are engaged in a rite of purification, a workaday ritual of washing clothes in a huge, boiling cauldron that takes on significance as the camp-chair-encircled men situate themselves in a space near the porch where the 'earth . . . was hard and white from where wash water had long been thrown' (p. 51). In a sense, the two women (who flee behind the house at Norton's approach) are present, by ironical implication, as the sharecropper once more confessionally purges himself – as he, in vernacular terms, again 'washes his dirty laundry' before a white audience. Further, Matty Lou, as the object of True-blood's incestuous desire, and Kate, as the irate agent of his punishment for fulfilling his desire, assume significant roles in the farmer's narrative.

The reversal of a traditional Freudian typology represented by Trueblood's dream encounter at the Broadnax Big House is reinforced, in its inversive significations, by an implied parody on the Christian myth of the Fall of Man.[18] For, if the white Mrs Broadnax serves as the temptress Eve of the sharecropper's dream, then his daughter Matty Lou becomes an ersatz Eve who, paradoxically, is the receptor of the farmer's lust. Similarly, if Mr Broadnax – an inhabitant of the sanctuary-like precincts of a house of 'lighted candles and shiny furniture, and pictures on the walls, and soft stuff on the floor' – is the avenging 'Father', or patriarch, of the dream, then a matriarchal Kate is his substitute in actual vengeance. The 'fall' of Trueblood is thus enacted on two planes – a dream level of Christian myth, and a quotidian level of black, southern actuality. In its most intensely conscious and sexual interpretation, the sharecropper's incestuous act is a rank violation that drives Kate to blind and murderous rage:

'I heard Kate scream. It was a scream to make your blood run cold. It sounds like a woman who was watching a team of wild horses run down her baby chile and she caint move. . . . She screams and starts to pickin' up the first thing that comes to her hand and throwin' it.' (p. 61)

The 'doubleness' of Kate and Matty Lou is felt in the older woman's destructive and avenging energies which elevate her to almost legendary proportions. Her fully woman's wrath at the sharecropper's illicit violation of 'my chile!' spirals and inflates Kate to the metaphorical stature of implacable executioner:

'Then I sees her right up on me, big. She's swingin' her arms like a man swingin' a ten-pound sledge and I sees the knuckles of her hand is bruised and bleedin' . . . and I sees her swing and I smells her sweat and . . . I sees that ax.'
(p. 63)

Trueblood describes the effect of his attempt to forestall Kate's punishing blow in the following terms: 'I might as well been pleadin' with a switch engine' (p. 63). The axe falls, and the farmer receives the wound whose blood spills on Matty Lou. The wound becomes the 'raw and moist' scar the protagonist perceives when he first moves 'up close' on the sharecropper (p. 50).

Kate becomes not only an awesome agent of vengeance in the sharecropper's account, but also the prime mover of the parodic, ritual drama enacted in the chilly, southern cabin. It is Kate's secular rage that results in the substitute castration/crucifixion represented by Trueblood's wound. She is the priestess who bestows the scarifying lines of passage, of initiation – the marks that forever brand the farmer as a 'dirty lowdown wicked dog' (p. 66). At her most severe, Kate is the moral or socio-religious agent both of Trueblood's 'marking' and of his exile. She banishes him from the community that rallies to support her in her sorrow. In keeping with her role as purifier – as supervisor of the wash – she cleans up the pollution, the dirt and danger represented by Trueblood's taboo act.

It is important to bear in mind, however, that, while Kate is a figure of moral outrage, she is also a fertile woman who, like her husband, provides 'cultural gifts' in the form of new life. In her black, family manifestation, she is less a secular agent of moral justice than a sensitive, practical parent who turns away in sick disgust at the wound she inflicts upon Trueblood. And, though she first banishes the farmer, she also accepts his return, obeys his interdiction against abortions for herself and Matty Lou, and welcomes the material gains that ironically accrue after Trueblood's incestuous fall from grace. The sharecropper says:

> 'Except that my wife an' daughter won't speak to me, I'm better off than I ever been before. And even if Kate won't speak to me she took the new clothes I brought her from up in town and now she's gettin' some eyeglasses made what she been needin' for so long.' (p. 67)

Kate as a woman possessed of a practical (one might say a 'blues') sensibility knows that men are, indeed, sometimes 'dirty lowdown wicked' dogs who can perceive a whore in a pigtailed girl. Although she is scarcely resigned to such a state of affairs where her own daughter is concerned, Kate, like the black mother so aptly described in Carolyn Rodgers's poem 'It is Deep', knows that being 'religiously girdled in her god' will not pay the bills. She thus brings together the sacred and the secular, the religious and secular, the moral and the practical in a manner that makes her both a complement for Trueblood and (again in the words of Rodgers) a woman who, 'having waded through a storm, is very obviously, a sturdy Black bridge.'[19]

To freight Trueblood's sexual manifestation, or its complement in Kate, with more weight than they can legitimately bear would be as much a critical disservice as previous failures, or refusals, even to acknowledge such manifestations. For, while it is true that sexuality burdens the content of the sharecropper's narrative, it is also true that he himself metaphorically transforms his incestuous act into but a single, symbolic instance of his total life situation.

> 'There I was [atop Matty Lou], trying to git away with all my might, yet having to move without movin'. I flew in but I had to walk out. I had to move without movin'. I done thought 'bout it since a heap, and when you think right hard

you see that that's the way things is always been with me. That's just about been my life.' (p. 59)

Like the formidable task of the Invisible Man's grandfather, who gave up his gun during the Reconstruction but still had to fight a war, Trueblood's problem is that of making progress and getting out of a 'tight spot' without undue motion – without perceptibly moving. The strategy adopted by the grandfather was one of extrication by indirection. He pretended to affirm the designs of the dominant white society around him. Having relinquished his gun, he became 'a spy in the enemy's country', a man overcoming his adversaries with 'yeses'. He represents the trickster as subtle deceiver. Trueblood, by contrast, claims that to 'move without movin' ' means to take a refractory situation uncomprisingly in hand: 'You got holt to it,' he says, 'and you caint let go even though you want to' (p. 60). He conceives of himself in the throes of his incestuous ecstasies as 'like that fellow . . . down in Birmingham. That one what locked hisself in his house and shot [with a gun that he had refused to give up] at them police until they set fire to the house and burned him up. I was lost' (p. 60). An energetic, compulsive, even ecstatically expressive response is required:

> 'Like that fellow [in Birmingham], I stayed. . . . He mighta died, but I suspects now that he got a heapa satisfaction before he went. I know there ain't nothin' like what I went through, I caint tell how it was. It's like when a real drinkin' man gets drunk, or like a real sanctified religious woman gits so worked up she jumps outta her clothes, or when a real gamblin' man keeps on gamblin' when he's losing.' (p. 60)

In his energetic response, Trueblood says a resounding 'no' to all the castratingly tight spots of his existence as a poor black farmer in the undemocratic south.[20]

The most discursively developed, expressive form of this 'no' is, of course, the narrative that he relates. But he has come to this narrative by way of music. After fasting and reflecting on his guilt or innocence 'until I thinks my brain go'n bust', the farmer recalls that

> 'Finally, one night, way early in the mornin', I looks up and sees the stars and I starts singin'. I don't know what it was, some kinda church song, I guess. All I know is I ends up singin' the blues. I sings me some blues that night ain't never been sang before . . .' (pp. 65–6)

The first unpremeditated expression that Trueblood summons is a religious song. But the religious system that gives birth to the song is, presumably, one in which the sign 'incest' carries pejorative force. Hence, the sharecropper moves on, spontaneously, to the blues.

In *The Legacy of the Blues* Samuel Charters writes:

Whatever else the blues was it was a language; a rich, vital, expressive language that stripped away the misconception that the black society in the United States was simply a poor, discouraged version of the white. It was impossible not to hear the differences. No one could listen to the blues without realizing that there are two Americas.[21]

The blues singer Booker White has said of the origins of this 'blues' language:

You want to know where did the blues come from. The blues come from behind the mule. Well now, you can have the blues sitting at the table eating. But the foundation of the blues is walking behind the mule way back in slavery time.[22]

The language that Trueblood summons to contain his act is a language that grows out of the soil he works, a soil that has witnessed the unconscionable labor of many thousand blacks walking 'behind the mule', realizing as they went the absurdity of working from 'can-to-caint' for the profit of others.

Born on a farm in Alabama and working, at the time of his incestuous act, as an impoverished, cold and poorly provisioned sharecropper, Trueblood shares the inherent blues capacity of a songster like Lightnin' Hopkins who asserts: 'I had the one thing you need to be a blues singer. I was born with the blues.'[23] Originating in the field hollers and work-songs of the black agrarian south and becoming codified as stable forms by the second decade of the twentieth century, the blues offer a *language* that connotes a world of transience, instability, hard luck, brutalizing work, lost love, minimal security, and enduring human wit and resourcefulness in the face of such discouragements. Blues language enjoins one to accept hard luck, because without it there is 'no luck at all'. The lyrics of the blues are metaphorically charged with a surreal humor that wonders if 'a match box will hold my clothes'. In short, the 'other America' signaled by blues is a world of common labor, spare circumstances and grimly lusty lyrical challenges to a bleak fate.

Trueblood finds, in the system of the blues, the meet symbolic code for expressing the negativity of his own act. Since he is both a magical storyteller *and* a blues singer *par excellence*, he is able to incorporate the lean economics and fateful intransience of the blues world into his autobiographical, narrative account of his actions. The metaphorical talent that transforms a steamboat's musicians into a boss quail's whistle, and then points to the quail's actions as analogous to a good man who 'do' what he 'got to do', is surely that of a narrator who has more than a modicum of understanding regarding the earthy resonances of the blues. He says of his evenings listening to boats in Mobile:

'They used to have musicianers on them boats, and sometimes I used to wake her [Margaret] up to hear the music when they come up the river. I'd be layin' there and it would be quiet and I could hear it comin' from way, way off. Like when you quail huntin' and it's getting dark and you can hear the boss bird whistlin' tryin' to get the covey together again, and he's coming toward you slow and whistlin' soft, 'cause he knows you somewhere around with your gun. Still he got to round them up, so he keeps on comin'. Them boss quails is like a good man, what he got to do he do.' (p. 55)

Further, the farmer begins his story with a description of his desperate economic straits, like those frequently recorded in blues – i.e. no wood for fuel, and no work or aid to be found (p. 53) – and then traces the outcomes of these dire straits. Matty Lou is in bed with her mother and father because it is freezing: 'It was so cold all of us had to sleep together; me, the ole lady and the gal. That's how it started' (p. 53). It seems appropriate – even 'natural' – that the act resulting from such bitter, black agrarian circumstances should be expressively framed by the blues. The blues' affirmation of human identity in the face of dehumanizing circumstance thus resonates through the sharecropper's triumphant, penultimate utterance: 'I make up my mind that I ain't nobody but myself and ain't nothin' I can do but let whatever is gonna happen, happen' (p. 66). This is not an expression of 'transcendence'. It is, instead, an affirmation of a still-recognizable humanity by a singer who has incorporated his disaster into a system of blues meanings emanating from an unpredictably chaotic world. In the process of incorporating his tragedy into the vocabulary and semantics of the blues and, subsequently, into the electrifying expression of his narrative, Trueblood realizes that he is not so changed by disaster that he must condemn, mortify or redefine his essential character. This self, as I have sought to indicate in the preceding discussion, is in many ways the obverse of the stable, predictable, puritanical, productive, law-abiding ideal self of American industrial-capitalist society.

The words that the sharecropper issues from 'behind the mule' provide a moral opposition (if not a moral corrective) to the confident expressions of control emanating from the world of the machines. From a pluralistic perspective, the counteractive patterns represented by the sharecropper and the millionaire Mr Norton suggest a positive homeostasis in American life. The duty-bound but enfeebled rationalist of northern industry – this oppositional model suggests – can always achieve renewal and a kind of shamanistic cure for the ills of civilization in the southern regions of Trueblood. But, in truth, the millionaire hardly appears to represent a rejuvenated Fisher King at the close of the sharecropper's story. Rather, he seems paralyzed by the kind of ghostly torpor that characterizes a stunned Benito Cereno, or a horrified Mr Kurtz. The pluralistic model that projects a revivifying opposition between the sharecropper and the millionaire, therefore, will not provide an adequate explanation for the Norton–Trueblood relationship. Some of the more significant implications of the episode, in fact, seem to reside not in the opposition between the industrial technocrat and the agrarian farmer but in the commercial consensus they reach where Afro-American expressive culture is concerned. Esu and Hermes are not only figures of powerful creative instinct. They are also gods of the market-place. A consideration of analytical reflections on the study of literature and ideology by Fredric Jameson and Hayden White serves to elucidate the commercial consensus achieved between the farmer and the millionaire.

In his essay 'The Symbolic Inference; or, Kenneth Burke and Ideological Analysis' Fredric Jameson writes:

> The term 'ideology' stands as the sign for a problem yet to be solved, a mental operation which remains to be executed. It does not presuppose cut-and-dried sociological stereotypes like the notion of the 'bourgeois' or the 'petty bourgeois' but is rather a mediatory concept: that is, it is an imperative to re-invent a relationship between the linguistic or aesthetic or conceptual fact in question and its social ground. . . . Ideological analysis may . . . be described as the rewriting of a particular narrative trait or seme as a function of its social, historical, or political context.[24]

Jameson's interest in a 're-invented' relationship between linguistic fact and social ground is a function of his conviction that all acts of narration contain, within their very form, the inscription of social ideologies. Stated differently, one might say that there is always a historical, or ideological, 'subtext' inscribed in the literary work of art. For, since history is accessible to us only through texts, the literary work of art has either to 'rewrite' the historical texts of its time or to 'textualize' the uninscribed events of its day in order to *contextualize* itself. What Jameson calls the 'ideology of form' is denoted by Hayden White in his essay 'Literature and Social Action' as a 'reflection theory'.[25] If, indeed, literary art can be said to reflect, through inscription, the social ground from which it originates, at what level of a specifically social domain, asks White, does such reflection occur? How may we most appropriately view literary works of art as distinctively 'social' entities?

White's answer is that ideological analysis must begin at the level of a society's *exchange system*, regarding the literary work as 'merely one *commodity* among others and moreover as a commodity that has to be considered as not different in kind from any other' (pp. 376–7; my italics). To adopt such an analytical strategy, according to White, is to comprehend

> not only the alienation of the artist which the representation of the value of his product in terms of money alone might foster, but also the tendency of the artist to fetishize his own produce as being itself the universal sign and incarnation of value in a given social system. (p. 378)

White could justifiably summon Ellison's remarks on the transformative powers of art quoted earlier as an instance of the 'fetishizing' of art as the incarnation of value. In Ellison's view, however, 'artistic value' is not a 'sign' or 'incarnation' in a 'given social system', but rather a sign of 'humane value' *in toto*. What is pertinent about White's remarks for the present discussion, however, is that the relation-ship that Jameson would 're-invent' is, for White, an economic one involving challenging questions of axiology.

The application of Jameson's and White's reflections in an analysis of the Trueblood episode begins with the recognition that the sharecropper's achieve-ment of expressive *narrative* form is immediately bracketed by the exchange system of Anglo-American society. Recalling his first narration of his story to a group of whites, the sharecropper remembers that Sheriff Barbour asked him to tell

> 'What happen, and I tole him and he called in some more men and they made me tell it again. They wanted to hear about the gal lots of times and they gimme somethin' to eat and drink and some tobacco. Surprised me, 'cause I was scared and spectin' somethin' different. Why, I guess there ain't a colored man in the county who ever got to take so much of the white folkses' time as I did.' (p. 52)

Food, drink, tobacco and audience time are commodities the sharecropper receives in barter for the commodity that he delivers: i.e. his story. The narrative of incest, after its first telling, accrues an ever-spiraling exchange value. The Truebloods receive all of the items enumerated earlier in the present discussion, as well as a 100-dollar bill from the Moroccan-leather wallet of Mr Norton. The story thus moves from its exchange status in a system of barter to commodifica-tion in a money economy overseen by northern industrialists. The status of the farmer's story *as a commodity* cannot be ignored.

As an artistic form containing within its inscriptions the historical and ideological 'subtexts' of American industrial society, the sharecropper's tale represents a supreme capitalist fantasy. The family, as the fundamental social unit of middle-class society, is governed by the property relationship. Men marry – take wives as their exclusive 'property' – in order to produce legitimate heirs who will keep their father's wealth (i.e. their property) 'in the family'. In royal or aristocratic circumstances, such marriages may describe an exclusive circle of exchange. Only certain women are eligible as royal or aristocratic wives. And, in the tightest of all circumstances, incest may be justified as the sole available means of preserving intact the family heritage – the nobleman's or aristocrat's private property. The dream of an unfettered, incestuous procreativity that results not only in new and legitimate heirs but also in a marked increase in property (e.g. Trueblood's situation) can be viewed as a fine reverie of capital-ism. And, if such a dreamed procreativity can be effected without fear of holy sanction, then procreation assumes the character of an intense, secular feat of 'human engineering'.

Mr Norton reflects that his 'real life's work' has not been his banking or his researches but his 'first-hand organizing of human life' (p. 42). What more exacting control could this millionaire New Englander exercise than the incestuous domination of his own human family as a productive unit, eternally giving birth to new profits? Only terror of dreadful, heavenly retribution has prevented Norton from attempting such a construction of life with his deceased, and pathetically idealized, only child. Part of his stupefaction at the conclusion of the sharecropper's narrative results from his realization that he might have *safely* effected such a productive arrangement of life when his daughter was living. One need not belabor the capitalist-fantasy aspect of Trueblood's narrative, however, in order to comprehend his story's commodification and positioning in an industrial-capitalist system of exchange. What the farmer is ultimately merchandizing is an image of himself that is itself a *product*; it is a bizarre product, in fact, of the *commodification* that made industrial America possible.

Africans became slaves through what the West Indian novelist George Lamming describes as an act of 'commercial deportation' overseen by the white West.[26] In America, Africans were *commodified* as 'chattel personal'. To forestall the moral guilt associated with this aberrant mercantile transformation, white Americans conceptualized a degraded, subhuman animal as substitute for the actual African. This categorical parody effected by the Anglo-American mind found its public, physical embodiment in the mask of the minstrel theatrical. The African in America was thus reduced, in Ellison's phrase, to a 'negative sign'.[27] In 'Change the Joke and Slip the Yoke' he writes:

> the [minstrel] mask was the thing (the 'thing' in more ways than one) and its function was to veil the humanity of Negroes thus reduced to a sign, and to repress the white audience's awareness of its moral identification with its own acts and with the human ambiguities pushed behind the mask. (p. 64)

Following the lead of Constance Rourke, Ellison asserts that the minstrel show is, in fact, a 'ritual of exorcism' (p. 64). But what of the minstrel performance given by the Afro-American who dons the mask? In such performances, writes Ellison:

> Motives of race, status, economics and guilt are always clustered. . . . The comic point is inseparable from the racial identity of the performer . . . who by assuming the group-debasing role for gain not only substantiates the audience's belief in the 'blackness' of things black, but relieves it, with dreamlike efficiency, of its guilt by accepting the very profit motive that was involved in the designation of the Negro as national scapegoat in the first place. There are all kinds of comedy; here one is reminded of the tribesman in *Green Hills of Africa* who hid his laughing face in shame at the sight of a gut-shot hyena jerking out its own intestines and eating them, in Hemingway's words, 'with relish'. (pp. 64–5)

Trueblood, who assumes the minstrel mask to the utter chagrin of the Invisible Man ('How can he tell this to white men, I thought, when he knows they'll say that all Negroes do such things?'), has, indeed, accepted the 'profit motive' which gave birth to that mask 'in the first place'. He tells his tale with relish: 'He talked willingly now, with a kind of satisfaction and no trace of hesitancy or shame' (p. 53). The firm lines of capitalist economics are, therefore, not the only ideological inscriptions in the sharecropper's narrative. The story also contains the distorting contours of the mask that the directors of such an economic system conceptualized to subsume their guilt. The rambunctiously sexual, lyrical and sin-adoring 'darky' is an image dear to the hearts of white America.

Ideologically, then, there is every reason to regard the sharecropper's story as a commodity in harmony with its social ground – with the system of exchange sanctioned by the dominant Anglo-American society. For, though Trueblood has been denied 'book learning' by the nearby black college, he has not failed to garner some knowledge of marketing. Just as the college officials peddle the sharecropper's 'primitive spirituals' to spring's seasonally descended white millionaires, so Trueblood sells his own expressive product – a carefully constructed narrative, framed to fit market demands. His actions as a merchant seem to compromise his status as a blues artist, as a character of undeniable folk authenticity. And his delineation as an untrammeled and energetic prime mover singing a deep blues 'no' to social constraints seems to collapse under the impress of ideological analysis. The complexities of American culture, however, function in a way that enables the sharecropper to reconcile his merchandizing role as oral storyteller and his position as the antinomian trickster.

For the Afro-American blues manifest an effective, expressive duality that has been captured by Samuel Charters in the following terms:

> The blues has always had a duality to it. One of its sides is its personal creativity – the consciousness of a creative individual using it as a form of expression. The other side is the blues as entertainment. Someone like Memphis Slim is a professional blues entertainer. But the blues is a style of music that emphasizes integrity – so how does a singer change his style without losing his credibility as a blues artist?[28]

As 'entertainment', the blues, whether classic or country, according to Ellison, were sung professionally in theaters.[29] This public theatricality of the blues shares a relationship of identity with the Afro-American's donning of the minstrel mask. There is, perhaps, something obscenely – though profitably – gut-wrenching about an Afro-American man or woman delivering up carefully modified versions of the essential, expressive self for the entertainment of his or her Anglo-American oppressors. And the question of 'integrity' does, indeed, loom large. But the most apt query that arises in the wake of Charter's comment is: 'Integrity, *as what?*'

To deliver the blues as entertainment – if you are an *entertainer* – is to maintain a fidelity to your role. Again, if the performance required is that of a minstrel and you are a genuine *performer*, then to don the mask is an act consistent with your status. There are always fundamental economic questions involved in such uneasy, Afro-American public postures. As Ellison implies, the Afro-American, in his public guise as entertainer, seasons the possum of black expressive culture to the taste of his Anglo-American audience, maintaining, in the process, his integrity as a *performer*. But in private sessions – in the closed circle of his own community – everybody knows that the punchline to the recipe, and the proper response to the performer's constrictive dilemma, is: 'Damn the possum! That sho' is some good gravy!' It is just possible that 'the gravy' is the inimitable *technique* of the Afro-American artist, a technique (derived from lived, blues experience) that is as capable of 'playing possum' as of presenting one.

A further question arises at this point, however, and it has to do with the affective response that commodification is supposed to produce on the part of the artist. With this query, the global descriptiveness of White's and Jameson's formulations proves less valuable than a closer inspection of the self-reflexive expressivity of Afro-American spokespersons themselves. Ellison's Trueblood episode, for example, suggests that the *Angst* assumed to accompany artistic commodification is sharply ameliorated when such commodification constitutes the sole means of securing power in a hegemonic system.

In the sharecropper episode, blacks who inhabit the southern college's terrain assume they have transcended the 'peasant' status marked by Trueblood and his cohorts. In fact, both the college's inhabitants and Trueblood's agrarian fellows are but respective constituencies in a single black underclass. When the college authorities threaten the sharecropper with exile or arrest, he has only to turn to the white Mr Buchanan ('the boss man') in order to secure immunity and a favorable audience before the white law represented by Sheriff Barbour (p. 52). In the face of the imperious fiats of whites, all blacks are relegated to an underclass. Trueblood states the situation as follows: 'no matter how biggity a nigguh gits, the white folks can always cut him down' (p. 53). The sole means of negotiating passage beyond this underclass status, Ellison's episode implies, is expressive representation.

Dr Bledsoe, for example, endorses 'lying' as an effective strategy of interaction with Mr Norton and other college trustees. And Trueblood himself adopts tale-telling as a mode of expression which allows him a degree of dignity and freedom within the confines of a severe white hegemony. The expressive 'mask', one might say, is as indispensable for college blacks as it is for those beyond the school's boundaries. The protagonist reports the initial meeting between Mr Norton and the sharecropper in the following terms:

I hurried behind him [Mr Norton], seeing him stop when he reached the man and the children. They became silent, their faces clouding over, their features becoming soft and negative, their eyes bland and deceptive. They were crouching behind their eyes waiting for him to speak – just as I recognized that I was trembling behind my own. (p. 50)

The evasive silence of the farmer and of the other blacks present is as expressive of power relationships in the south as the expressive strategy advocated by Dr Bledsoe.

When the protagonist returns from his ill-fated encounters with Trueblood and with the crew at the Golden Day, the school's principal asks him if he is unaware that blacks have 'lied enough decent homes and drives [from white coffers] for you to show him [Mr Norton]' (p. 136). When the protagonist responds that he was obeying Mr Norton's orders by showing the millionaire the 'slum' regions of Trueblood rather than 'decent homes and drives', Bledsoe exclaims: 'He *ordered* you. Dammit, white folk are always giving orders, it's a habit with them. . . . My God, boy! You're black and living in the South – did you forget how to lie?' (p. 136).

Artful evasion and expressive illusion are equally traditional black expressive modes in interracial exchange in America. Such modes, Ellison's episode implies, are the only resources that blacks, at any level, can barter as tokens for a semblance of control and decency in their lives. The act of 'commodifying' expressiveness for blacks, therefore, is not simply a gesture in a bourgeois economics of art. Rather, it is a crucial move in a somewhat limited repertoire of black survival motions in the United States. To examine the status of black expressiveness as a commodity, then, is to do more than observe, within the constraints of an institutional theory of art, that the 'art world' is a function of economics. In a very real sense, the entire sum of Afro-America's exchange power has always been coextensive with its stock of expressive resources. What is implicit, then, in an analysis of commodification and black expressiveness is not a limited history of the 'clerks' but rather an *histoire totale* (a total history) of Afro-American cultural interaction in the United States.

In his brilliant study *When Harlem was in Vogue*, which treats the black artistic awakening of the 1920s known as the 'Harlem Renaissance', for example, David Levering Lewis captures the essential juxtaposition between white hegemony and the negotiable power of exchange of black creativity in the following terms. Writing of Charles Johnson, the energetic black editor of *Opportunity* magazine during the twenties, Lewis says that Johnson

> gauged more accurately than perhaps any other Afro-American intellectual the scope and depth of the national drive to 'put the nigger in his place' after the war, to keep him out of the officer corps, out of labor unions and skilled jobs, out of the North and quaking for his very existence in the South – and out of politics everywhere. Johnson found that one area alone – probably because of its very implausibility – had not been proscribed. No exclusionary rules had been laid down regarding a place in the arts. Here was a small crack in the wall of racism, a fissure that was worth trying to widen.[30]

'Exclusionary rules' were certainly implicit in the arts during the 1920s, but what Lewis suggests is that the rules of domains other than art in America were far more rigid and explicit than those of the creative arena. Blacks thus sought to widen the 'fissure', to gain what power of determination over their own lives they could through a 'renaissance' of black expressiveness.

Ideological analysis of expressive commodification should take adequate account of the defining variables of the culture in which such commodification occurs. In the instance of Afro-American culture, exchanging words for safety and profit is scarcely an 'alienating' act. It is, instead, a defining act in aesthetics. Further, such commodification lies at the heart of Afro-American politics conceived in terms of who gets what, when and how. Black expressive commodification, as I shall seek to make clear in the concluding section of my present discussion, does entail the inscription of an identifying economics. But the aggressively positive character of its manifestations (despite the dualism entailed) results from a self-reflexive acknowledgement that only the 'economics of slavery' give valuable and specifically black resonance to Afro-American works of art.

The critic George Kent has observed that there is a 'mathematical consistency between Ellison's critical pronouncements and his creative performance.'[31] Insofar as Ellison provides insightful critical interpretations of his own novel and its characters, Kent's judgment is correct. But the 'critical pronouncements' in Ellison's canon that imply his devaluing of Afro-American folklore hardly seem consistent with the meanings implicit in his Trueblood episode. Such utterances may be regarded, I believe, as public statements by Ellison 'the merchant' rather than as incisive, affective remarks by Ralph Ellison the creative genius.

Trueblood's duality is, finally, also that of his creator. For Ellison knows that his work as an *Afro-American* artist derives from those 'economics of slavery' which provided conditions of existence for Afro-American folklore. Black folk expression is a product of the actual impoverishment of blacks in America. The blues, as a case in point, are unthinkable in well-endowed circumstances.

Yet, if the folk artist is to turn a profit from his monumental creative energies (which are often counteractive, or inversive, vis-à-vis Anglo-American culture), he must take a lesson from the boss quail and 'move without moving'. He must, in essence, sufficiently modify his folk forms (and amply advertise himself) to merchandize such forms as commodities on the *artistic* market. The folk artist may even have to don a mask that distorts what he knows is his genuine self in order to make his product commensurate with a capitalistic market-place. Ralph Ellison is a master of such strategies.

Ellison reconciles the trickster's manifestations as untrammeled creator and as god of the market-place by providing critical advertisements for himself as a novelist that carefully bracket the impoverishing economics of Afro-America. For example, he writes:

I use folklore in my work not because I am a Negro, but because writers like Eliot and Joyce made me conscious of the literary value of my folk inheritance. My cultural background, like that of most Americans, is dual (my middle name, sadly enough, is Waldo).[32]

What is designated in this quotation as 'literary value' is, in reality, *market value*. Joyce and Eliot taught Ellison that, if he was a skillful enough strategist and spokesman, he could market his own folklore. What is bracketed, of course, are the economics that dictated that if Ellison wished to be an *Afro-American* artist he could *only* turn to Afro-American folklore as a traditional, authenticating source for his art. Like his sharecropper, Ellison is wont to make 'literary value' out of socio-economic necessity. But he is also an artist who recognizes the value of Afro-American folk forms, *in themselves*, suggesting in 'The Art of Fiction' that such forms 'have named human situations so well that a whole corps of writers could not exhaust their universality' (p. 173). What Ellison achieves in the Trueblood episode is a dizzying hall of mirrors, a redundancy of structure, that enables him to extend the value of Afro-American folk forms by combining them with an array of Western narrative forms and tropes. Written novel and sung blues, polysyllabic autobiography and vernacular personal narrative, a Christian Fall of Man and an inversive triumph of the black trickster are conjoined in a magnificently embedded manner.

I have tried to suggest in the foregoing analysis that it is in such creative instances that one discovers Ellison's *artistic* genius, a genius that links him in inextricably positive ways to his invented sharecropper. For in the Trueblood episode, conceived as a chapter in a novel, one finds not only the same kind of meta-expressive commentary that marks the represented farmer's narration to Norton but also the identical type of self-reflexive artist implied by the share-cropper's recitation – an artist who is fully aware of the contours and limitations, the rewards and dilemmas of the Afro-American's uniquely expressive craft.

In the expository, critical moment, by contrast, one often finds a quite different Ralph Ellison. Instead of the *reflexive* artist, one finds the *reflective* spokesman. Paraphrasing Barbara Babcock, who uses a 'failed' Narcissus to illustrate the difference between the 'reflective' and the 'reflexive', one might say that in his criticism Ralph Ellison is 'not narcissistic enough'.[33] His reflections in *Shadow and Act* seem to define Afro-American folk-expressiveness in art as a sign of 'identity', a sign that marks its creator as unequivocally Afro-American and, hence, *other*. I have sought to demonstrate, however, that Ellison's folk-expressiveness is, in fact, 'identity with a difference'. While the critic experiences alienation, the artist is able to detach himself from, survive and even laugh at his initial experience of otherness. Like Velázquez in his *Las Meninas*, or the Van Eyck of *Giovanni Arnolfini and His Bride*, the creator of Trueblood is 'conscious of being self-conscious of himself' as artist.[34] Rather than solacing himself with critical distinctions, he employs reflexively mirroring narratives to multiply distinctions and to move ludically across categorical boundaries. Like his invented share-cropper, he knows indisputably that his most meaningful self is his Afro-American self imaged in acts of expressive creativity.

Ellison's bracketings as a 'public' critic thus do not forestall his private, artistic recognition that he 'ain't nobody but himself'. And it is out of this realization that a magnificent folk creation like Trueblood emerges. Both the creator and his character possess the wisdom that informs them that they are resourceful 'whistlers' for the tribe. They know that their principal grounding as artists is not coextensive with a capitalistic society. Rather, it finds its origin in material circumstances like those implied by Howling Wolf's lament:

> Well I'm a po' boy, long way from home.
> Well I'm a po' boy, long way from home.
> No spendin' money in my pocket, no spare meat on my bone.[35]

One might say that, in the brilliant reflexivity of the Trueblood encounter, we hear the blues whistle among the high-comic thickets. We glimpse Ellison's creative genius beneath his Western critical mask. And, while we stand awaiting the next high-cultural 'pronouncement' from the critic, we are startled by the captivating sound of flattened thirds and sevenths – the private artist's blues-filled flight.

Notes

1 Ralph Ellison, 'Richard Wright's Blues', *Shadow and Act* (New York: Signet, 1966), pp. 89–104. All quotations from *Shadow and Act* are taken from the Signet edition; page numbers for this essay subsequently appear in the text in parentheses.
   Ellison's essays in *Shadow and Act* comprise the bulk of his critical canon. Certainly my references to his critical canon in the present discussion are confined to *Shadow and Act*.
2 Ralph Ellison, 'Hidden Name and Complex Fate', *Shadow and Act*, pp. 148–68. Subsequent page references to this essay appear in the text in parentheses.
3 Ralph Ellison, 'Change the Joke and Slip the Yoke', *Shadow and Act*, pp. 61–73. Subsequent page references to this essay appear in the text in parentheses.
4 Ralph Ellison, 'The Art of Fiction: An Interview', *Shadow and Act*, p. 172. Subsequent page references appear in the text in parentheses.
5 Clifford Geertz, *The Interpretation of Cultures* (New York: Basic Books, 1973), pp. 412–53. All page numbers refer to this edition and subsequently appear in the text in parentheses.
6 Barbara Babcock, 'The Novel and the Carnival World', *Modern Language Notes*, 89 (1974), pp. 911–37. Page numbers subsequently appear in the text in parentheses.
7 Ralph Ellison, 'The World and the Jug', *Shadow and Act*, pp. 115–47. Page references subsequently appear in the text in parentheses.
8 Ralph Ellison, *Invisible Man* (New York: Vintage Books, 1972), p. 52. All quotations from *Invisible Man* are taken from this edition, and page numbers subsequently appear in the text in parentheses.
9 Sigmund Freud, *Totem and Taboo*, trans. James Strachey (New York: Norton, 1950). The general statement of hypothesis to which I refer in this present discussion occupies pages 141–6. One of the general questions provoking Freud's inquiry into totemism is: 'What is the ultimate source of the horror of incest which must be recognized as the root of exogamy?' (p. 122).

10 Victor Turner, *The Forest of Symbols: Aspects of Ndembu Ritual* (Ithaca, NY: Cornell University Press, 1967). All page references are to this edition and appear in the text in parentheses.

11 Paul Radin, *The Trickster* (London: Routledge & Kegan Paul, 1955).

12 For a stimulating discussion of the trickster in his various literary and non-literary guises, one might consult Professor Barbara Babcock's provocative essay ' "A Tolerated Margin of Mess": The Trickster and His Tales Reconsidered', *Journal of the Folklore Institute*, 2 (1975), pp. 147–86. Professor Babcock writes: 'In contrast to the scapegoat or tragic victim, trickster belongs to the comic modality or marginality where violation is generally the precondition for laughter and communitas, and there tends to be an incorporation of the outsider, a levelling of hierarchy, a reversal of statuses' (p. 153).

13 Victor Turner, 'Myth and Symbol', in *International Encyclopedia of the Social Sciences* (New York: Macmillan and Free Press, 1968), vol. 10, p. 580.

14 Victor Turner, 'Betwixt and Between: The Liminal Period in *Rites de Passage*', in *The Forest of Symbols*, pp. 93–112.

15 Turner, 'Myth and Symbol', p. 577.

16 Ibid., p. 580.

17 Turner, 'Betwixt and Between', p. 98.

18 Conversations with Professor Kimberly Benston were quite enlightening on the Trueblood episode's parodic representation of the Fall of Man. Professor Benston explores these representations at some length in a critical work in progress. I am grateful for his generous help.

19 Carolyn Rodgers, *how i got ovah: New and Selected Poems* (New York: Doubleday, 1975), pp. 11–12.

20 The sharecropper's incestuous progeny may be said to carry the same weight of significance as that possessed by the broken link of leg chain Brother Tarp presents to the Invisible Man during his early days in the Brotherhood. 'I don't think of it in terms of but two words,' says Tarp, 'yes and no; but it signifies a heap more' (*Invisible Man*, p. 379).

21 Samuel Charters, *The Legacy of the Blues* (New York: Da Capo, 1977), p. 22.

22 Quoted in Giles Oakley, *The Devil's Music: A History of the Blues* (New York: Harvest, 1976), p. 7.

23 Quoted in Charters, op. cit., p. 183.

24 Fredric Jameson, 'The Symbolic Inference; or, Kenneth Burke and Ideological Analysis', *Critical Inquiry*, 4 (1978), pp. 510–11.

25 Hayden White, 'Literature and Social Action: Reflections on the Reflection Theory of Literary Art', *New Literary History*, 12 (1980), pp. 363–80. Further page references to White's work appear in the text in parentheses.

26 George Lamming, *Season of Adventure* (London: Allison & Busby, 1979), p. 93.

27 Ellison, 'Change the Joke and Slip the Yoke', p. 63.

28 Charters, op. cit., p. 168.

29 Ellison, 'Blues People', *Shadow and Act*, p. 249. Ellison introduces his own claim in contradiction to the assertions on blues of LeRoi Jones, whose book *Blues People* he is reviewing in his essay.

30 David Levering Lewis, *When Harlem was in Vogue* (New York: Knopf, 1981), p. 48.

31 George Kent, *Blackness and the Adventure of Western Culture* (Chicago, Ill.: Third World, 1972), p. 161.

32 Ellison, 'Change the Joke and Slip the Yoke', p. 72. The implicit 'trickiness' of Ellison's claim – its use of words to 'signify' quite other than what they seem to intend on the surface – is an aspect of the Afro-American 'critic as trickster'. Professor Henry Louis Gates, Jr, began an analysis – in quite suggestive terms – of the trickster's 'semiotic' manifestation in a paper delivered at the Modern Language Association convention in

December 1981. In Gates's terms, the Afro-American folk figure of the 'signifying monkey' becomes an archetype of the Afro-American critic. In the essays 'Change the Joke and Slip the Yoke' and 'The World and the Jug', one can certainly think of Ellison demonstrating an elegant mastery of what might be termed the 'exacerbating strategies' of the monkey. Perhaps one also hears his low, Afro-American voice directing a *sotto voce* 'Yo' Mamma!' at heavyweights of the Anglo-American critical establishment.

33 Barbara Babcock, 'Reflexivity: Definitions and Discriminations', *Semiotica*, 30 (1980), p. 4.
34 Ibid. One of the most intriguing recent discussions of the Velázquez painting is that of Michel Foucault in *The Order of Things* (New York: Random House, 1973). The Van Eyck is briefly discussed in the introduction to Jay Ruby (ed.), *A Crack in the Mirror: Reflexive Perspectives in Anthropology* (Philadelphia, Pa.: University of Pennsylvania Press, 1982).
35 Quoted from A. S. Nicholas (ed.), *Woke Up This Mornin': Poetry of the Blues* (New York: Bantam, 1973), p. 85.

11

Mary Helen Washington

'Taming all that anger down': rage and silence in Gwendolyn Brooks's *Maud Martha*

> Then emotionally aware
> Of the black and boisterous hair,
> Taming all that anger down.
> (Gwendolyn Brooks)

When Gwendolyn Brooks's autobiographical first novel, *Maud Martha*, was published in 1953,[1] it was given the kind of ladylike treatment that assured its dismissal. Reviewers invariably chose to describe the novel in words that reflected what they considered to be the novel's appropriate feminine values. The young black woman heroine was called a 'spunky Negro girl', as though the novel were a piece of juvenile fiction. Reviewers, in brief notices of the novel, insisted on its optimism and faith: Maud's life is made up of 'moments she loved', she has 'disturbances', but she 'struggles against jealousy' for the sake of her marriage; there is, of course, 'the delicate pressure of the color line', but Maud has the remarkable 'ability to turn unhappiness and anger into a joke'. Brooks's style was likened to the exquisite delicacy of a lyric poem. The *New York Times* reviewer said the novel reminded him of imagist poems or 'clusters of ideograms from which one recreates connected experience'.

In 1953 no one seemed prepared to call *Maud Martha* a novel about bitterness, rage, self-hatred and the silence that results from suppressed anger. No one recognized it as a novel dealing with the very sexism and racism that these reviews enshrined. What the reviewers saw as exquisite lyricism was actually the truncated stutterings of a woman whose rage makes her literally unable to speak.

This autobiographical novel[2] is about silences. Maud Martha rarely speaks aloud to anyone else. She has learned to conceal her feelings behind a mask of gentility, to make her hate silent and cold, expressed only in the most manipulative and deceptive ways. When she is irritated with her husband, Paul, who pinches her on the buttocks, trying to interest her in the activities of the book he is reading, *Sex in the Married Life*, she rises from the bed as though she is at a garden party, and says, 'pleasantly', 'Shall I make some cocoa? . . . And toast some sandwiches?' (p. 67). That she is aware of this pattern and its destructiveness, and her need to change, is clearly part of the novel's design: 'There were these scraps of baffled hate in her, hate with no eyes, no smile, and – this she especially regretted, called her hungriest lack – not much voice' (p. 176). But the silences of *Maud Martha* are also Brooks's silences. The short vignetted chapters enact Maud Martha's silence. Ranging in length from one and a half pages to eighteen pages, these tightly controlled chapters withhold information about Maud, just as she withholds her feelings; they leave her frozen in an arrested moment so that we are left without the reactions that are crucial to our understanding of her. With no continuity between one chapter and the next, the flow of Maud's life is checked just as powerfully as she checks her own anger. The short, declarative sentences, with few modifiers and little elaboration, are as stiff, unyielding and tight-lipped as Maud Martha herself.

An example of Brooks's tendency to check Maud's activity (and thus her growth) is chapter 5, ironically entitled 'you're being so good so kind'. As the teenage Maud awaits a visit from a white schoolmate named Charles, she begins to feel embarrassed by the shabbiness of her home and worried that her house may have the unpleasant smell that 'colored people's houses necessarily had'. It is a moment of pure terror. She is the whole 'colored' race and 'Charles was the personalization of the entire Caucasian plan' (p. 18) about to sit in judgment on her. Charles never actually materializes. The chapter ends with a freeze frame of Maud hiding in the bathroom, experiencing an emotion worse than fear:

> What was this she was feeling now? Not fear, not fear. A sort of gratitude! It sickened her to realize it. As though Charles in coming gave her a gift. Recipient and benefactor. It's so good of you. You're being so good. (p. 18)

These last few lines, set off from the rest of the text, are a commentary by a black consciousness more aware and more removed from the event than the teenage Maud. While the commentator's indignation is reassuring, we can only imagine how the visit would have affected Maud: whether Charles continues to have such power when he appears, or whether Maud is as truly defeated in the encounter as her position behind closed doors intimates.

In all the chapters covering Maud's girlhood on the south side of Chicago in the 1930s and 1940s, there are powerful oppositions to her freedom. In chapter 1, for example, 'description of Maud Martha', she decides on a personal metaphor for herself: she is a dandelion, a sturdy flower of demure prettiness, but, just as a puff of wind can destroy it, so her belief in its – and her – power to allure is easily shaken, for 'it was hard to believe that a thing of only ordinary allurements – if the allurements of any flower could be said to be ordinary – was as easy to love as a thing of heart-catching beauty' (p. 2). Maud's wish to be alluring is dashed in the last two sentences of this chapter by a sudden shift to a description of her prettier sister, Helen, who is described in a gasp of pure pleasure at the thought: 'her sister Helen! who was only two years past her own age of seven, and was almost her own height and weight and thickness. But oh, the long lashes, the grace, the little ways with the hands and feet' (p. 3). Once, at the age of 10, when she is trying to appear more daring than she feels, she calls out 'Hi handsome' to the little boy Emmanuel riding by in his wagon. He scowls back: 'I don't mean you, old black gal' (p. 34), and he offers the ride to her sister Helen. In this chapter Maud tries to account for the mysterious, implacable design which has determined her inferior status and the greater worthiness of light-skinned beauties like Helen. In the short, staccato sentences that charac-terize much of the novel's narration, she tries to be nobly superior about her family's preference for Helen: 'It was not their fault. She understood. They could not help it. They were enslaved, were fascinated, and they were not at all to blame' (p. 35). Yet it is not her problem that we feel in these sentences but her anger. These broken utterances, as Anna Julia Cooper called them,[3] are evidence of a woman denied expression of powerful feelings.

The painful awareness of herself as an undesirable object whose worth cannot be gauged by eyes accustomed to dismissing the commonplace mystifies the child Maud. She is disdainful of her family's failure to see that she is smarter than Helen, that she reads more, that old folks like to talk to her, that she washes as much and has longer and thicker (if nappier) hair. But from the age of 17 to the birth of her first child (chapters 10–19) her own self-perception is dismissed while she abandons herself to the obligatory quest for a man. When she is finally chosen by one of 'them', or, in her words, when she 'hooks' Paul, her language and attitude shift. She now sees herself entirely through Paul's eyes. In the chapter called 'low yellow' Maud engages in a grotesque act of double-consciousness in which she fantasizes about Paul's negative view of her:

He wonders as we walk in the street, about the thoughts of the people who look at us. Are they thinking that he could do no better than – me? Then he thinks, Well, hmp! All the little good-lookin' dolls that have wanted him – all the little sweet high yellows that have ambled slowly past his front door – What he would like to tell those secretly snickering ones! – That any day out of the week he can do better than this black gal. (p. 53)

Rewarded for her pains with marriage, Maud settles down to 'being wife to him, salving him, in every way considering and replenishing him.' In chapter 16, 'the young couple at home', we perceive how Maud is the one who's been 'hooked', who feels hemmed in, cramped and 'unexpressed' in this marriage. Although she is as disappointed as he in their life together, she evades her feelings. Once, in a classic example of self-abnegation, she worries that *he* is tired of *her*:

> She knew that he was tired of his wife, tired of his living quarters, tired of working at Sam's, tired of his two suits. . . . He had no money, no car, no clothes, and he had not been put up for membership in the Foxy Cats Club. . . . He was not on show. . . . Something should happen. . . . She knew that he believed he had been born to invade, to occur, to confront, to inspire the flapping of flags, to panic people. (p. 147)

Maud's lack of voice and her indirection become more troubling for us when, as a grown woman confined to a small apartment and to being Mrs Paul Phillips, she seems to have become an accomplice to her own impotence. Maud's passivity in the face of the persecutory actions of others[4] inhibits her growth and reflects her resistance to facing her anger. When Maud and Paul are invited to the Foxy Cats Club Ball, where acceptance requires sophistication and good looks, Maud is once again up against the image of the 'little yellow dream girl'. Thinking about how she will forestall her old feelings of inferiority, she prepares for the event in language that we know will defeat her:

> 'I'll settle', decided Maud Martha, 'on a plain white princess-style thing and some blue and black satin ribbon. I'll go to my mother's. I'll work miracles at the sewing machine.'
> 'On that night, I'll wave my hair. I'll smell faintly of lily of the valley.' (p. 95)

The words she uses to refashion herself – *white, princess, wave, lily* – all suggest how complete a transformation she imagines she needs in order to be accepted. At the club, Paul goes off with the beautiful, 'white-looking', curvy Maella, leaving Maud on a bench by the wall. Maud imagines how she might handle the interloper: 'I could . . . go over there and scratch her upsweep down. I could spit on her back. I could scream. "Listen," I could scream, "I'm making a baby for this man and I mean to do it in peace" ' (p. 88).

Instead of asserting herself, however, Maud chooses to say nothing. The scraps of rage and baffled hate accumulate while she resists the words of power as though she has subjected her language to the same perverted standards by which she judges her physical beauty. In one of the early chapters she describes the 'graceful' life as one where people glide over floors in softly glowing rooms, smile correctly over trays of silver, cinnamon and cream, and retire in quiet elegance. She imagines herself happy and caressed in these cool, elegant (white) places, and she aspires to the jeweled, polished, calm lives the people live there. This life, as she imagines it, is like a piece of silver, silent and remote and behind bright glass. The black world, as symbolized by the Foxy Cats Ball, is, by comparison, hot, steamy, sweaty and crowded. Far from caressing her, this real world batters her until she retreats into her imagination, refusing to speak in it because it does not match the world of her fantasies. She conceals her real self behind the bright glass of her strained gentility.

All of this pretense, this muted rage, this determination to achieve housewifely eminence – the feminine mystique of the 1950s – the desire to protect herself, 'to keep herself to herself', masks so much of Maud's real feelings that we are compelled to consider what is missing in *Maud Martha*. Are there places in the novel where the real meaning of the character's quest is disguised? Are there 'hollows, centers, caverns within the work – places where activity that one might expect is missing . . . or deceptively coded'?[5]

Something is missing in *Maud Martha*, something besides the opportunity to speak, something we have the right to expect in Maud's life because Maud herself expects it. She has already – in the first chapters – begun to chafe at the domestic role, and yet Brooks suggests that Maud has no aspirations beyond it. When Maud asks in the last chapter 'What, *what*, am I to do with all this life?', she is expressing the same sense of perplexity that her readers have been feeling throughout the novel. How is this extraordinary woman going to express herself? She claims not to want to be a star because she once saw a singer named Howie Joe Jones parade himself before an audience foolishly 'exhibiting his precious private identity', and she has vowed that she will never be like that: 'she was going to keep herself to herself' (p. 21). The artist's role, she says, is not for her. But the fact that she has considered and dismissed the possibility is revealing:

> To create . . . a role, a poem, a picture, music, a rapture in stone: great. But not for her. What she wanted was to donate to the world a good Maud Martha. That was the offering, the bit of art, that could not come from any other. She would polish and hone that. (p. 22)

Everywhere in the novel, however, Maud's artistic intentions are indirectly revealed. She perceives the world sensuously; she responds to the complexity of beauty: 'What she wanted to dream, and dreamed, was her affair. It pleased her to dwell upon color and soft bready textures and light, on a complex beauty, on gem-like surfaces. *What was the matter with that?*' (p. 51; my italics). What indeed is the matter with a woman having some subversive ideas? In an article on the sexist images of woman in modernist texts, Joyce Carol Oates maintains that, by aspiring to art, women violate the deeply conservative and stereotypical images of men. The autonomy of the artist is considered unnatural for women, unfeminine and threatening.[6] Maud uses the language of the artist as she surrenders her claim to be an artist; her language betrays her. Maud's gifts are words, insight, imagination. She has the artist's eye, the writer's memory, that unsparing honesty which does not put a light gauze across little miseries and monotonies but exposes them, leaving the audience as ungauzed as the creator (p. 20).

It is natural to wonder why Brooks, in her 'autobiographical novel', did not allow Maud the same independence and creative expression that she herself had as a writer. After all, Brooks was her own model of a black woman artist in the 1950s. In her autobiography, *Report from Part One* (1972), she describes the exuberance she felt as she waited for books she would review to arrive in the mail, the 'sassy brass' that enabled her to chide Richard Wright for his clumsy prose, and her eager sense of taking on the responsibility of a writer. But Maud, who *craves* something 'elaborate, immutable, and sacred', who wants to express herself in 'shimmering form', 'warm, but hard as stone and as difficult to break', is never allowed to fulfill these cravings.

The novelist Paule Marshall has pointed out that women writers often make their first woman protagonist a homebody, as if to expiate their own 'deviance' in succeeding in the world of men. There is, she says, some need to satisfy the domestic role, and so they let their characters live it. *Maud Martha* ends with a pregnancy, not a poem; but, if Maud has no life outside marriage, she has a child, through whom she begins to hear her own voice.

The pregnancy actually becomes a form of rebellion against the dominance of both her mother and her husband. She screams at Paul in the midst of her labor pains: 'DON'T YOU GO OUT OF HERE AND LEAVE ME ALONE! Damn! Damn!' When her mother, who is prone to faint over blood, comes in the door, Maud sets her straight about who's important in this drama: 'Listen, if you're going to make a fuss, go on out. I'm having enough trouble without you making a fuss over everything.' In that one vital moment of pulling life out of herself, Maud experiences her own birth and hears in the cries of her daughter Paulette something of her own voice: 'a bright delight had flooded through her upon first hearing that part of Maud Martha Brown Phillips expressing herself *with a voice of its own*' (p. 99; my italics). Shortly after the birth of her child, Maud speaks aloud the longest set of consecutive sentences she has so far uttered. For a woman who has hardly said more than a dozen words at one time, this is quite a speech:

> 'Hello, Mrs Barksdale!' she hailed. 'Did you hear the news? I just had a baby, and I feel strong enough to go out and shovel coal! Having a baby is *nothing*, Mrs Barksdale. Nothing at all.'(p. 82)

Pregnancy and the birth of a child connect Maud to some power in herself, some power to speak, to be heard, to articulate feelings.

Yet, however powerful the reproductive act is, it is not the same as the creative process: a child is a separate, independent, individualized human being, not a sample of one's creative work. Without the means to satisfy her deeper cravings for her own inner life, Maud's life remains painfully ambiguous. Brooks must have felt this ambiguity, for when she imagined a sequel to *Maud Martha* she immediately secured some important work for Maud and dispensed with the role of housewife. In a 1975 interview, Brooks was asked to bring *Maud Martha* up to the present day. With obvious relish, Brooks eliminates Maud's husband:

Well, she has that child, and she has another child and then her husband dies in the bus fire that happened in Chicago in the fifties. One of those flammable trucks with a load of oil ran into a street car and about thirty-six people burned right out on Sixty-third and State Streets. *So I put her husband in that fire.* Wasn't that nice of me? I had taken him as far as I could. He certainly wasn't going to change. I could see that.[7]

Brooks insists that Maud feels some regret at the loss of her husband, but returning from the funeral Maud is 'thinking passionately about the cake that's going to be at the wake and how good it's going to be'. Having safely buried Paul, Brooks proceeds to explain how Maud Martha will get on with her own adventures. She will be chosen as a guide to accompany some children on a trip to Africa, and will use her slender resources to help them. She will live her life with herself at the center of it.

Brooks's tone as she describes the sequel to *Maud Martha* – so freewheeling and aggressive and self-assured – reveals by comparison the uncertainties and tensions of the 1953 version. Maud needs a language powerful enough to confront life's abuses. Maud's polite, precious and prim little rhetoric is no match for the uncouth realities she faces as a poor black woman. Rhetoric and setting seem to be at odds with each other, just as they are in Brooks's 1949 epic poem *Annie Allen*, in which, using the language of the tradition of courtly love, she tries to tell the tragic love story of a poor black woman named Annie Allen. There is power in yoking together the diction of chivalric, religious and classical traditions and that of a woman born into a world of 'old peach cans and old jelly jars', but the power of *Annie Allen* derives from the poet's ironic perspective. Maud's life is told in her own words and thoughts, and so the poet's perspective is not available. Maud needs more access to the vernacular.

One wonders if Brooks also denies Maud a more dynamic role in the novel by her own ambivalence (understandable in view of the restrictions on women in the 1950s) towards women as heroic figures. In her poetry all the heroes are men. From the dapper hustler Satin-Legs Smith to the renegade Way-out Morgan or the soldier in 'Negro Hero' or the armed man defending his family against a white mob, Brooks selects the heroic strategies of men and the ritual grounds on which men typically perform. Even a plain man like Rudolph Reed has a moment of glory as he runs out into the street 'with a thirty-four / And a beastly butcher knife'. He dies in defense of his family, while his wife, who has been passive throughout the entire ballad, stands by mutely and does nothing 'But change the bloody gauze'.

Brooks, in her poetry, seldom endows women with the power, integrity or magnificence of her male figures. The passive and vulnerable Annie Allen, the heroine of her Pulitzer-Prize-winning poem, is deserted by her soldier husband and left pathetically mourning her fate in her little kitchenette, 'thoroughly / Derelict and dim and done.' Sometimes Brooks's women manage to be 'decently wild' as girls, but they grow up to be worried and fearful, or fretful over the loss of a man. They wither in back yards, afraid to tackle life; they are done in by dark skin; and, like 'estimable Mable', they are often incapable of estimating their worth without the tape measure of a man's interest in them.[8]

Brooks does allow Maud to grow in some ways, to become more in control of her life and to speak out against the racist violence of her life. When Maud moves away from the domestic sphere of her little kitchenette apartment and out into a larger social and political world, she feels more urgently the need to speak. There are three racial encounters leading up to Maud's self-affirmation. Each encounter involves a change in the language Maud has available to her; each moves her closer to experiencing and expressing her rage. In the last of these three encounters Maud makes the longest speech of the novel: she tries to explain to her child, Paulette, that Santa Claus loves her as much as any white child.

A large downtown department store in the 1940s – a place where black women were generally allowed to work only as 'stock girls' or kitchen helps – is fundamentally alien territory for Maud, and yet it is on this hostile ground that Maud finally asserts herself. On the traditional Christmas visit to see Santa Claus with Paulette, Maud notices that Santa is merry and affectionate with the white children but distant and unresponsive with Paulette, looking vaguely away from her as though she is not there. As Maud sees her own child learning the lessons of inferiority and invisibility, she speaks up to him in a clear and uncompromising statement that forces him to recognize Paulette: ' "Mister," said Maud Martha, "my little girl is talking to you" ' (p. 173). Maud suddenly experiences her anger as powerful enough to lead to physical violence. She yearns to 'jerk trimming scissors from purse and jab jab jab that evading eye' (p. 175). Now there is no desire to cover up her rage, to feign cold indifference: 'She could neither resolve nor dismiss. There were these scraps of baffled hate in her, hate with no eyes, no smile, and – this she especially regretted, called her hungriest lack – not much voice' (p. 176).

Ironically this chapter, where Maud regrets her lack of voice, is the one where she does the most talking. In the longest speech of the entire novel she has to make Paulette believe that Santa Claus did like her:

> 'Listen, child. People don't have to kiss you to show they like you. Now you know Santa Claus liked you. What have I been telling you? Santa Claus loves every child, and on the night before Christmas he brings them swell presents. Don't you remember, when you told Santa Claus you wanted the ball and bear and tricycle and doll he said "Um-hm"? That meant he's going to bring you all those. You watch and see. Christmas'll be here in a few days. You'll wake up Christmas morning and find them and then you'll know Santa Claus loved you too.' (p. 175)

From Maud Martha, this is a veritable torrent of words, but the problem with her words is that they are still part of her subterfuge. She denies Santa Claus's rejection of Paulette and insists that Paulette deny her own perception of Santa's cold indifference.

The honest voice in this chapter is Paulette's:

'Why didn't Santa Claus like me?
  'Baby, of course he liked you.'
  'He didn't like me. Why didn't he like me?'
  'It maybe seemed that way to you. He has a lot on his mind, of course.'
  'He liked the other children. He smiled at them and shook their hands.'
  'He maybe got tired of smiling. Sometimes even I get – '
  'He didn't look at me, he didn't shake my hand.' (p. 174)

In the chapter 'a birth', Maud has said that her daughter's voice is part of her own. Mother and child are locked in a conversation that forces Maud out from behind the bright glass of her pretense. Now Maud admits rage, laments her lack of voice, speaks aloud and bites back the tears as she looks down at her child's trusting face, knowing she cannot keep for her a fairy-tale land where no Santa Claus ever hates a black child. Brooks does not leave Maud frozen in this chapter; we do see her acting and speaking. But perhaps the most important change is that Maud is given her most aggressive role when she confronts the racism of that cool, elegant, white, fantasy world.

If Brooks's novel seems fragmentary and incomplete, undoubtedly it is because the knowledge of one's self as a black woman was fragmented by a society that could not imagine her. I am thinking specifically of the 1940s and 1950s, those post-war decades which enshrined the Great American Domestic Dream of a housewife and a Hoover in every home. If the housewife in that dream was a white woman, the servant was always a black woman – simple and unsophisticated, as the reviews called Maud Martha. The leading black magazines of those years – Ebony, Negro Digest, Crisis – contributed their share of images of black women as idealized, childlike creatures and assumed that their basic role was to satisfy the male imagination. The magazine Crisis alternated pictures of cute babies and 'cute' women on its covers, while the covers of Negro Digest featured bathing beauties, tennis beauties, homecoming queens, and pin-ups in various stages of undress. In contrast to these pictures of black women, the back page of the Digest spotlighted 'Men of Achievement', so that back to back with the smiling faces and exposed bodies of black women were mini-stories about the first black man to enter a prestigious college, to excel in athletics or to perform valiantly in some war. The August 1947 issue of the Digest featured on its back page the bravery of Negro volunteers (all men) during the Civil War; on the front cover there is a picture of a fan 'girl' whose partially nude body is coyly hidden behind a polka-dot umbrella. Beneath the fan girl's picture is the title of the opening article by Era Bell Thompson, 'What's Wonderful about Negro Men'.

The articles about black women in these magazines range from the condescending to the obscene. The titles themselves reveal extreme hostility: 'What's

Wrong with Negro Women?', 'Are Black Women Beautiful?', 'The Care and Feeding of Negro Women'. This last article, based on the metaphor of cultivating a really fine pet, claims that a properly trained female will develop the loyalty of a German shepherd dog and the cleverness of a Siamese cat, and will provide many hours of diversion and relaxation for her owner. The article 'What's Wrong with Negro Women?' lists among the many shortcomings of black women their lack of cultural interests, their sense of inferiority to white women and their lack of militancy: 'Where are the Negro women of self-sacrifice and courage in the cause of the race?' the writer Roi Ottley wonders. 'There is not one woman to rank with the distinguished Harriet Tubman.'[9]

If we consider the way *Maud Martha* was received in 1953 by the literary community (black and white males), then we can clearly see another example of how black women were silenced in the 1950s. Despite Brooks's stature as a Pulitzer-Prize-winning poet, no one in 1953 had more than 600 words to say about the novel. The reviewers of Ralph Ellison's *Invisible Man* (published just the year before, when Ellison was relatively unknown), suffering no such taciturnity, devoted as many as 2100 words to Ellison's novel. *The New Republic, The Nation, The New Yorker* and *Atlantic* magazine contained lengthy and signed reviews of *Invisible Man*. Wright Morris and Irving Howe were called in to write serious critical assessments of it for the *New York Times* and *The Nation*.[10] In contrast, the *New Yorker* review of *Maud Martha* was unsigned, suggesting that the real 'invisible man' of the 1950s was the black woman. Brooks's character was never held up for comparison with any other literary character. Ellison's nameless hero was considered not only 'the embodiment of the Negro race' but the 'conscience of all races'; the titles of the reviews – 'Black & Blue', 'Underground Notes', 'A Brother Betrayed', 'Black Man's Burden' – indicated the universality of the Invisible Man's struggles. The title of Brooks's reviews – 'Young Girl Growing Up' and 'Daydreams in Flight' – deny any relationship between the protagonist's personal experiences and the historical experiences of her people. Ellison himself was compared to Richard Wright, Dostoevsky and Faulkner; Brooks only to unspecified 'imagists'. Questions about narrative strategy, voice and methods of characterization that were asked of *Invisible Man* were obviously considered irrelevant to an understanding of *Maud Martha*, since they were not posed. Most critically, Ellison's work was placed in a tradition; it was described as an example of the 'picaresque' tradition and the pilgrim/journey tradition by all reviews. *Maud Martha*, the reviewers said, 'stood alone'. Not one of these reviewers could place *Maud Martha* in the tradition of Zora Neale Hurston's *Their Eyes Were Watching God* (1937), Dorothy West's *The Living is Easy* (1948) or Nella Larsen's *Quicksand* (1928). Is this because no one in 1953 could picture the questing figure, the hero with a thousand faces, the powerful, articulate voice, as a plain, dark-skinned woman living in a kitchenette building on the south side of Chicago?[11]

The supreme confidence of Ellison's text – its epic sweep, its eloquent flow of words, its historical significance – invites its greater critical acceptance. By comparison the Maud Martha text is hesitant, self-doubting, mute, retentive. Maud is restricted, for the most part, to a domestic life that seems limited and narrow. At the end of the novel, poised on the edge of self-creation, at the moment we expect the 'illumination of her gold', she announces that she is pregnant again, and happy.

My initial reaction to this ending was critical of Brooks for precluding any growth beyond the domestic life. But that disappointment ignores the novel's insistence that we read Maud's life in tone, in images and in gestures. Released from an incapacitating anger, Maud becomes exhilarated and full of energy. In the last chapter she is out of doors with her daughter on a glorious day. She is outside all the spaces that have enclosed her – the bedrooms, the kitchens, the male clubs, the doctors' offices, the movie theatres, the white women's houses, the dress shops, the beauty parlors; out of the psychic confines that left her preoccupied with her 'allurements' and presumed deficiencies. Free from destructive self-concern, Maud thinks of the people around her, of the glory and bravery in their ability to continue life amid the reality of city streets, lynchings in Mississippi and Georgia, and the grim reminder of death as the soldiers, back from war, march by with arms, legs and parts of faces missing. Maud says she is ready for anything. So this catalog of evils (including the Negro press's preoccupation with pale and pompadoured beauties) has to be seen as Maud's growing sense of relation to the social and political problems of her world. Even Maud's pregnancy can be seen as a powerful way of being in the world. For, in the midst of destruction and death, she will bring forth life.

Brooks then reintroduces the raised arm image of the first chapter when Maud at the age of 7 longed to fling her arms rapturously up to the sky. In the final chapter the raised arms are like 'wings cutting away all the higher layers of air'. There is the suggestion of flight and transcendence, her arms, purposeful and powerful, directing her up out of a dark valley. In sharp contrast to the child whose dearest wish was 'to be cherished' as a yellow-jeweled, demurely pretty dandelion, this Maud thinks of the common flower as an image of survival and self-possession: 'for would its kind (like her) come up again in the spring? come up, if necessary, among, between, or out of – the smashed corpses lying in strict composures, in that hush infallible and sincere' (p. 173).

Still, in spite of all the victorious imagery in this last chapter, there is a sense of incompleteness about Maud's quest; some exploration not undertaken, some constriction of the blood. Brooks does not solve the problem of Maud's anger or her silence. Part of this lies in the privateness of Maud's story. Her constant self-analysis and self-consciousness emphasize her solitariness. She lives alien-ated from the two blood-related women in her life – the fussy, domineering mother and the vain sister. She has no women friends. Although she succeeds through heroic individual effort in rejecting others' definitions of her, she is still unable to express the full meaning of her growth. True, the presence of another 'woman-in-embryo' allows her her first move towards freedom, but she does not have the advantage of Zora Neale Hurston's Janie of telling her story to an eager, loving listener whose life is changed by hearing Janie's tale.[12] I only wish Brooks had found a way for Maud to know that someone in the community had grown ten feet higher from listening to her story.

Rereading *Maud Martha* is a necessary step in revising the male-dominated Afro-American canon not only because this unusual text requires a different set of interpretative strategies but because it suggests a different set of rituals and symbols for Afro-American literature and a different set of progenitors. Current feminist theories which insist that we have to learn how to read the coded messages in women's texts – the silences, the evasions, the repression of female creativity[13] – have helped me to reread *Maud Martha*, to read interiority in this text as one of the masks Maud uses to defend herself against rage. But if she cannot rely on the spoken word for help, she certainly appropriates power in more concealed ways – she writes her husband out of the text mid-way, she reduces her mother to a vain, pretentious fool, and she assigns her beautiful sister to a static end in a compromising marriage – thus the victim becomes superior to her victimizers.[14] The reconstruction of scenes in which condescending others (white women and black and white men) are shown dominating Maud, while the reader is aware of her internal resistance, is another indirect way of giving Maud power. However oblique Maud's methods might seem, they are effective, for her manipulation of power in the narrative finally erupts into speech when she confronts the white Santa Claus.

If *Maud Martha* is considered an integral part of the Afro-American canon, we will have to revise our conception of power and powerlessness, of heroism, of symbolic landscapes and ritual grounds. With his access to middle-class aspirations, to a public life and to male privilege, is the Invisible Man as easily defined out of existence as the physically vulnerable and speechless Maud? Yet, in spite of her greater powerlessness, she is not at the end of her text submerged in a dark hole, contemplating her invisibility in isolation. She is outside, in the light, with her daughter by the hand, exhilarated by the prospect of new life. Her ritual grounds are domestic enclosures, where we have rarely looked for heroic gestures; her most heroic act is one defiant declarative sentence; and yet she has changed in enough small ways for us to hope that 'these little promises, just under cover' may, as she says earlier in the novel, in time, fulfill themselves.

The real significance of *Maud Martha* for the literary canon is that its discontinuous and truncated chapters, its short, angry sentences, its lack of ornamentation and freeze-frame endings represent structurally the entrapment of women expressed thematically in the earlier narratives of black women like Nella Larsen, Zora Hurston, Ann Petry, Dorothy West and Harriet Jacobs. Helga Crane's thwarted creativity, Janie Starks's concealed inner self, Lutie Johnson's checked rage, Cleo Judson's frustrated maneuverings, Linda Brent's self-effacement are literally enacted in *Maud Martha*. While the novel looks back to the past, it also prefigures the themes of silence, repressed creativity and alienation from language in the more articulate novels of Alice Walker, and Toni Morrison. Paule Marshall has said that *Maud Martha* is the first novel she read which permitted a black woman a rich interior life, and it provided the inspiration for her own writing about black women. Perhaps these 'little promises, just under cover' are, in fact, fulfilling themselves in the vibrant novels of contemporary black women.

Notes

1 Gwendolyn Brooks, *Maud Martha* (Boston, Mass.: Atlantic Monthly Press, 1953). All page references are to this edition and appear in the text in parentheses.

2 In her 'autobiographical statement' *Report from Part One* (Detroit, Mich.: Broadside Press, 1972), Brooks says openly that *Maud Martha* is an autobiographical novel, though not in the usual sense. 'Much that has happened to Maud Martha has not happened to me – and she is a nicer and a better coordinated creature than I am. But it is true that much in the story was taken out of my own life, and twisted, highlighted or dulled, dressed up or down.' All of Maud Martha's experiences, though 'much juggled', are based on Brooks's own experiences; see pp. 191–3.

3 Anna Julia Cooper, *A Voice from the South by a Black Woman of the South* (Xenia, Ohio: Aldine Printing House, 1892), p. 133.

4 Roy Schafer, 'Narration in the Psychoanalytic Dialogue', in W. J. T. Mitchell (ed.), *On Narrative* (Chicago, Ill.: University of Chicago Press, 1980), pp. 25–49. Schafer says that in the psychoanalytic process, as the analysand begins to become more responsible, he/she 'comes to construct narratives of personal agency ever more readily' and to de-emphasize narratives that highlight the persecutory actions of others. This seems to me to be appropriate to all forms of narrative, for we do emphasize our own responsibility as we feel more powerful and in control.

5 Sandra M. Gilbert and Susan Gubar, *The Madwomen in the Attic: The Woman Writer and the Nineteenth-Century Literary Imagination* (New Haven, Conn.: Yale University Press, 1979), p. 75. In this passage the authors are referring to ideas in Patricia Spacks's *The Female Imagination* and to discussions of women's literature by Carolyn Heilbrun and Catherine Stimpson.

6 Joyce Carol Oates, ' "At Least I Have Made a Woman of Her": Images of Women in Twentieth-Century Literature', *Georgia Review*, 38 (Spring 1983), pp. 7–30.

7 'Update on *Part One*: An Interview with Gwendolyn Brooks', *CLA Journal*, 21 (1977), p. 26; my italics.

8 These references to Brooks's poetry are from the following poems in *The World of Gwendolyn Brooks* (New York: Harper & Row, 1971): 'The Ballad of Rudolph Reed', p. 12; 'The Anniad', p. 84; 'obituary for a living lady', p. 18; 'a song in the front yard', p. 12. 'Estimable Mable' is from *Family Pictures* (Detroit, Mich.: Broadside Press, 1970), p. 20.

9 Roi Ottley, 'What's Wrong with Negro Women?', *Negro Digest*, 8 (December 1950), pp. 71–5; E. Simms Campbell, 'Are Black Women Beautiful?', *Negro Digest*, 9 (June 1951), pp. 16–20; Louie Robinson, 'The Care and Feeding of Negro Women', *Negro Digest*, 10 (September 1951), pp. 9–12.

10 Reviews of *Invisible Man* in 1952 include: George Mayberry, 'Underground Notes', *The New Republic*, 21 April 1952 (600 words); Irving Howe, 'A Negro in America', *The Nation*, 10 May 1952 (950 words); Anthony West, 'Black Man's Burden', The New Yorker, 31 May 1952 (2100 words); C. J. Rolo, 'Candide in Harlem', *Atlantic* (July 1952) (450 words); Wright Morris, 'The World Below', *New York Times Book Review*, 13 April 1952 (900 words); 'Black & Blue', *Time*, 14 April 1952 (850 words); J. E. Cassidy, 'A Brother Betrayed', *Commonweal*, 2 May 1952 (850 words).

11 The most egregious example of the condescension towards black women in the 1950s was the *Negro Digest's* August 1950 article covering Brooks's winning of the Pulitzer Prize. The entire piece is an act of sabotage. It begins with a list of all the people who didn't believe Brooks had won the prize. It catalogs all the negative experiences Brooks had after winning the prize. It mentions her husband briefly – as a poet who cannot devote time to writing because he feels 'no one family can support two poets'. The article includes a poem written by the poet's 9-year-old son (but not a line from the poet who has just won the Pulitzer Prize!) and ends with the son's complaint that his mother's fame has upset his life so much that he is glad the attention is wearing off so that he can have some peace. The article focuses entirely on the negativity of Brooks's literary achievement, and it so absolutely ignores the work of the poet that one can only infer that the writer had little respect for the achievement. A similar article on Ralph Ellison, written in *Crisis* in March 1953, focuses on the professional achievement of the writer.

12 Janie is the main character in Zora Neale Hurston's 1937 novel, *Their Eyes Were Watching God*.

13 Although many feminist critics have dealt with these topics, the most instructive is Margaret Homans's '"Her Very Own Howl": the ambiguities of representation in recent women's fiction', *Signs*, 9 (1983), pp. 186–205. Homans deals specifically with the double marginality of black women writers.

14 Nancy K. Miller, 'Emphasis added: plots and plausibilities in women's fiction', *PMLA*, 96 (January 1981), p. 41.

12

Susan Willis

Eruptions of funk:
historicizing Toni Morrison

I begin to feel those little bits of color floating up into me – deep in me. That streak of green from the june-bug light, the purple from the berries trickling along my thighs, Mama's lemonade yellow runs sweet in me. Then I feel like I'm laughing between my legs, and the laughing gets all mixed up with the colors, and I'm afraid I'll come, and afraid I won't. But I know I will. And I do. And it be rainbow all inside.[1]

This is how Polly Breedlove remembers the experience of orgasm. Remembers it, because, in the grim and shabby reality of her present, orgasm (which we might take as a metaphor for any deeply pleasurable experience) is no longer possible.[2] Living in a storefront, her husband fluctuating between brutality and apathy, her son estranged, her daughter just plain scared, Polly has no language to describe the memory of a past pleasure, except one drawn from her distant childhood.

The power of this passage is not just related to the fact that it evokes one of the most intense female experiences possible. Much of its impact is produced by the way it describes. Morrison defamiliarizes the portrayal of sensual experience. Adjectives become substantives, giving taste to color and making it possible for colors to trickle and flow and, finally, be internalized like the semen of an orgasmic epiphany.

As often happens in Morrison's writing, sexuality converges with history and functions as a register for the experience of change, i.e. historical transition. Polly's remembrance of childhood sensuality coincides with her girlhood in the rural south. Both are metaphorically condensed and juxtaposed with the alienation she experiences as a black emigrant and social lumpen in a northern industrial city. The author's metaphoric language produces an estrangement of alienation. While her metaphors are less bold in their form and content, they neverthless achieve an effect very similar to that of the negritude poets. Indeed, the image of an internal rainbow evokes the poetics of surrealism, but in a language less disjunctive because prose reveals the historical and artistic process through which the image is produced.[3]

When Polly Breedlove reminisces, her present collides with her past and spans her family's migration from the hills of Alabama to a small Kentucky town, and her own subsequent journey as the wife of one of the many black men who, in the late 1930s and early 1940s, sought factory jobs in the industrial north. The rural homeland is the source of the raw material of experience and praxis, which in the border-state small town is abstracted to colors, tastes and tactile sensations. Ohio is, then, the site where images are produced out of the discontinuity between past and present.

If metaphor, and much of Morrison's writing in general, represents a return to origins, it is not rooted in a nostalgia for the past. Rather, it represents a process for coming to grips with historical transition. Migration to the north signifies more than a confrontation with (and contagion of) the white world. It implies a transition in social class. Throughout Morrison's writing, the white world is equated with the bourgeois class – its ideology and lifestyle. This is true of *Song of Solomon*, where Macon Dead's attitudes toward rents and property make him more 'white' than 'black'. It is true of *Tar Baby*, where notions of bourgeois morality and attitudes concerning the proper education and role of women have created a contemporary 'tar baby': a black woman in cultural limbo. And it is made dramatically clear in *The Bluest Eye*, whose epigrammatic introduction and subsequent chapter headings are drawn from a white middle-class 'Dick and Jane' reader. In giving voice to the experience of growing up black in a society dominated by white, middle-class ideology, Morrison is writing against the privatized world of suburban house and nuclear family, whose social and psychological fragmentation does not need her authorial intervention but is aptly portrayed in the language of the reader: 'Here is the family. Mother, Father, Dick, and Jane live in the green-and-white house. They are very happy.'[4]

The problem at the center of Morrison's writing is how to maintain an Afro-American cultural heritage once the relationship to the black rural south has been stretched thin over distance and generations. While a number of black Americans will criticize her problematizing of Afro-American culture, seeing in it a symptom of Morrison's own relationship to white bourgeois society as a successful writer and editor, there are a number of social and historical factors that argue in support of her position. These include the dramatic social changes produced by recent wide-scale migration of industry to the south which has transformed much of the rural population into wage laborers; the development, particularly in the northern cities, of a black bourgeoisie; and the coming into being, under late capitalism, of a full-blown consumer society capable of homogenizing society by recuperating cultural difference. The temporal focus of each of Morrison's novels pinpoints strategic moments in black American history, during which social and cultural forms underwent disruption and transformation. Both The Bluest Eye and Sula focus on the forties, a period of heavy black migration to the cities, when, particularly in the Midwest, black 'neighborhoods' came into being in relation to towns that had never before had a sizable black population. Sula expands the period of the forties by looking back to the First World War, when blacks as a social group were first incorporated in a modern capitalist system as soldiers; and it looks ahead to the sixties, when cultural identity seems to flatten out and, as Helene observes, all young people tend to look like the 'Deweys'. Song of Solomon focuses on the sixties, when neighborhoods are perceived from the outside and called ghettos, a time of urban black political activism and general counter-cultural awareness. And Tar Baby, Morrison's most recent book, is best characterized as a novel of the eighties, where the route back to cultural origins is very long and tenuous, making many individuals cultural exiles.

With this as an outline of modern black history in the United States, Morrison develops the social and psychological aspects that characterize the lived experience of historical transition. For the black emigrant to the north, the first of these is alienation. As Morrison defines it, alienation is not simply the result of an individual's separation from his or her cultural center. This is a contributory factor which reinforces the alienation produced by the transition to wage labor. For the black man, incorporated into the wartime labor pool (as for many white Appalachians[5]), selling one's labor for the creation of surplus value was only half of an alienation whose brutal second half was the grim reality of unemployment once war production was no longer necessary. The situation for the black woman was somewhat different. Usually employed as a maid and therefore only marginally incorporated as a wage laborer, her alienation was the result of striving to achieve the white bourgeois social model (in which she worked but did not live) which is itself produced by the system of wage labor under capitalism. As housemaid in a prosperous lakeshore home, Polly Breedlove lives a form of schizophrenia, where her marginality is constantly confronted with a world of Hollywood movies, white sheets and tender blond children. When at work or at the movies, she separates herself from her own kinky hair and decayed tooth. The tragedy of a woman's alienation is its effect on her role as mother. Her emotions split, she showers tenderness and love on her employer's child, and rains violence and disdain on her own.

Morrison's aim in writing is very often to disrupt alienation with what she calls 'eruptions of funk'. Dismayed by the tremendous influence of bourgeois society on young black women newly arrived from deep-south cities like 'Meridian, Mobile, Aiken, and Baton Rouge', Morrison decries their loss of spontaneity and sensuality. They learn how to behave. The careful development of thrift, patience, high morals, and good manners. In short, how to get rid of the funkiness. The dreadful funkiness of passion, the funkiness of nature, the funkiness of the wide range of human emotions.[6]

For Polly Breedlove, alienation is the inability ever again to experience pleasure – orgasm or otherwise. While for the 'thin brown girls from Mobile', whose husbands are more successful and, therefore, better assimilated to bourgeois society, alienation is the purposeful denial of pleasure. Once again Morrison translates the loss of history and culture into sexual terms and demonstrates the connection between bourgeois society and repression:

He must enter her surreptitiously, lifting the hem of her nightgown only to her navel. He must rest his weight on his elbows when they make love, ostensibly to avoid hurting her breasts but actually to keep her from having to touch or feel too much of him.

While he moves inside her, she will wonder why they didn't put the necessary but private parts of the body in some more convenient place – like the armpit, for example, or the palm of the hand. Someplace one could get to easily, and quickly, without undressing. She stiffens when she feels one of her paper curlers coming undone from the activity of love; imprints in her mind which one it is that is coming loose so she can quickly secure it once he is through. She hopes he will not sweat – the damp may get into her hair; and that she will remain dry between her legs – she hates the glucking sound they make when she is moist. When she senses some spasm about to grip him, she will make rapid movements with her hips, press her fingernails into his back, suck in her breath, and pretend she is having an orgasm.[7]

At a sexual level, alienation is the denial of the body, produced when sensuality is redefined as indecent. Sounds and tactile sensations which might otherwise have precipitated or highlighted pleasure instead provoke annoyance or disdain. Repression manifests itself in the fastidious attention given to tomorrow's Caucasian-inspired coiffure and the decathexis of erogenous stimulation. While repression inhibits sexual pleasure, it does not liberate a woman from sexuality. In faking an orgasm, the woman negates her pleasure for the sake of her husband's satisfaction, thus defining herself as a tool for his sexual gratification.

To break through repressed female sexuality, Morrison contrasts images of stifled womanhood with girlhood sensuality. In *The Bluest Eye*, the author's childhood alter ego, Claudia, is fascinated by all bodily functions and the physical residues of living in the world. She rebels at being washed, finding her scrubbed body obscene because of 'the dreadful and humiliating absence of dirt'.[8] Even puke is interesting for its color and consistency as it 'swaddles down the pillow onto the sheet'.[9] In wondering how anything can be 'so neat and nasty at the same time',[10] Claudia shows a resistance toward the overdetermination of sensual experience, which, as Morrison sees it, is the first step toward repression. Openness to a full range of sensual experience may be equated with polymorphous sexuality, typified by the refusal of many young children to be thought of as either a boy or a girl. As my own four-year-old daughter sees it, 'Little girls grow up to be big boys', and because there is no firm distinction between the sexes her teddy is 'both a boy and a girl'. The refusal to categorize sensual experience – and likewise sex – captures the essence of unrepressed childhood, which Morrison evokes as a mode of existence prior to assimilation by bourgeois society.

The ultimate horror of bourgeois society against which Morrison writes, and the end result of both alienation and repression, is reification.[11] None of Morrison's black characters actually accedes to the upper reaches of bourgeois reification, but there are some who come close. They are saved only because they remain marginal to the bourgeois class and are imperfectly assimilated to bourgeois values. In *Song of Solomon*, Hagar offers a good example. Rejected by her lover, she falls into a state of near catatonia, oblivious to all around her. However, chancing to look in a mirror, she is horrified by her appearance and marvels that anyone could love a woman with her looks. Thus roused from her withdrawal, Hagar embarks on a day-long shopping spree, driven by the desire to be the delightful image promised by her brand-name purchases.

> She bought a Playtex garter belt, I. Miller No Color hose, Fruit of the Loom panties, and two nylon slips – one white, one pink – one pair of Joyce Fancy Free and one of Con Brio ('Thank heaven for little Joyce heels'). . . .
> The cosmetics department enfolded her in perfume, and she read hungrily the labels and the promise. Myrurgia for primeval woman who creates for him a world of tender privacy where the only occupant is you, mixed with Nina Ricci's L'Air du Temps. Yardley's Flair with Tuvaché's Nectaroma and D'Orsay's Intoxication.[12]

Hagar's shopping spree culminates in a drenching downpour. Her shopping bags soaked, everything – her 'Sunny Glow' and 'fawn-trimmed-in-sea-foam shortie nightgown' – her wished-for identity and future, falls into the wet and muddy street. Returning home, Hagar collapses with fever and dies after days of delirium.

Hagar's hysteria and death mark the limits of her assimilation to bourgeois culture. Neither through withdrawal nor through commodity consumption can Hagar transform herself into an object. Her marginality, by reason of race and lumpen background, is the basis for her inalienable human dimension. As Morrison might have put it, she is simply too black, too passionate, too human ever to become reified.

Reification, while never attained by any of Morrison's characters – not even those drawn from the white world[13] – is, instead, embodied in a number of figural images. These are the celluloid images of Shirley Temple or her 'cu-ute' face on a blue-and-white china cup, and the candy-wrapper images of Mary Jane. Most of all, reification is the plastic smile and moronic blue eyes of a white Christmas baby doll. When Claudia destroys these – dismembering them and poking their eyes out – her rebellion is not just aimed at the idea of beauty incarnated in a white model. She is also striking out against the horrifying dehumanization that acceptance of the model implies – both for the black who wears it as a mask and for the white who creates commodified images of the self.

If Morrison's highly sensual descriptions explode the effects of alienation and repression and stave off the advent of reification, they do so because sensuality is embedded in a past which is inaccessible to sexual repression and bourgeois culture. The retrieval of sensuality allows an alternative social mode and historical period to be envisioned. When, again in The Bluest Eye, the prostitute, Marie, remembers the succulent taste and crunch of fried fish, her memories bring forth tastes and textures which are not separate from the moment of their production but integral with praxis. Her memory summons up her specific past – her boyfriend and free-spirited youth – and makes these concrete for the reader and for the child, Pecola, who in the depths of fearful alienation perceives a very different image of the world, where adolescence, petty outlawry and economic marginality constitute a form of freedom.

In Morrison, everything is historical. Objects, too, are embedded in history and are the bearers of the past. For those characters closest to the white bourgeois world, objects contain the residues of repressed and unrealized desires. For Ruth Foster in Song of Solomon, the daughter of the town's first black doctor and wife of the slumlord, Macon Dead, a water mark on a table is the stubborn and ever-present reminder of her husband's remorseless rejection. The bowl of flowers around which their hatred crystallized is no longer present; only its sign remains, an opaque residue indelibly written into the table. If, for the bourgeois world, experience is capable of being abstracted to the level of sign, this is not the case for the world of the marginal characters. To cite an example from the same novel, Pilate, Ruth Foster's sister-in-law and in every way her antithesis, enjoys a special relationship to all levels of natural experience – including a specific shade of blue sky. Now, color does not function as a sign in the way that the water mark on the table does. While it bears a concrete relationship to a real object (the blue ribbons on Pilate's mother's hat), it is not an abstract relationship in the way that the water mark stands for the bowl of flowers. For Ruth Foster, the water mark is an 'anchor' to the mental and sexual anguish imprisoned in the sign. In contrast, when Pilate points to a patch of sky and remarks that it is the same color as her mother's bonnet ribbons, she enables her nephew, Milkman (Ruth Foster's overly sheltered son), to experience a unique moment of sensual perception. The experience is liberational because Pilate is not referring to a specific bonnet – or even to a specific mother; rather, the color blue triggers the whole range of emotions associated with maternal love, which Pilate offers to anyone who will share the experience of color with her.

In contrast to the liberational aspect of *Song of Solomon*, Morrison's most recent novel, *Tar Baby*, registers a deep sense of pessimism. Here, cultural exiles – both white and black – come together on a Caribbean island where they live out their lives in neatly compartmentalized bourgeois fashion: the candy magnate, Valerian Street,[14] in his stereophonic-equipped greenhouse; his wife, cloistered in her bedroom; and the servants, Odine and Sydney, ensconced in their comfortable quarters. Daily life precludes the 'eruption of funk', a lesson poignantly taught when Margaret Lenore discovers the bedraggled wild man, Son, in her closet. While Son's appearance suggests Rastafarianism and outlawry, any shock value stirred by his discovery is cancelled when he, too, proves to be just another exile. Except for one brief incident, when Odine kills a chicken and in plucking it recalls a moment from her distant past when she worked for a poultry butcher, there are no smells, tastes or tactile experiences to summon up the past. Rather, there is a surfeit of foods whose only quality is the calories they contain.

In contrast with Morrison's earlier novels, the past in *Tar Baby* is never brought to metaphoric juxtaposition with the present. Rather, it is held separate and bracketed by dream. When Valerian Street, sipping a brandy in his greenhouse, lapses into daydream, his recollection of the past, which in essence contrasts entrepreneurial capitalism to modern corporate capitalism, does not intrude upon his present retirement. The past is past, and the significant historical transition evoked is perceived as inaccessible and natural.

The past is made more remote when it informs a nighttime dream. This is the case for Sydney, who every night dreams of his boyhood in Baltimore. 'It was a tiny dream he had each night that he would never recollect from morning to morning. So he never knew what it was exactly that refreshed him.'[15] For the black man hanging to the coattails of the white upper bourgeoisie, who thinks of himself as a 'Philadelphia Negro', the backstreets of Baltimore are a social debit. His desire for assimilation to white bourgeois culture and the many years spent in service to the bourgeois class negate his ever experiencing the deep sensual and emotional pleasure that Pilate has whenever she beholds a blue sky or bites into a vine-ripe tomato.

With every dreamer dreaming a separate dream, there are no bridges to the past and no possibility of sharing an individual experience as part of a group's social history. While a reminiscence like Marie's account of eating fried fish can be communicated, a dream, as Son finds out, cannot be pressed into another dreamer's head. Son's dream of 'yellow houses with white doors' and 'fat black ladies in white dresses minding the pie table in the basement of the church'[16] is an image of a wish-fulfillment, rooted in private nostalgia. It bears no resemblance to his real past as we later come to understand it out of what the book shows us of Eloe, Florida, where tough black women with little time for pie tables have built their own rough-hewn, unpainted homes.

For the tar baby, Jadine, fashioned out of the rich white man's indulgence and the notions of culture most appealing to bourgeois America (European education and Paris *haute couture*), the past is irretrievable and no longer perceived as desirable. As the individual whose cultural exile is the most profound, Jadine is haunted by waking visions, born out of guilt and fear. In her most terrifying vision, a mob of black women – some familiar, some known only by their names – crowds into her room. Revealing, then waving their breasts at her, they condemn Jadine for having abandoned the traditional, maternal role of black women.

While Jadine lives her separation from the past and rejection of traditional cultural roles with tormented uncertainty and frenzied activity, Milkman, in Morrison's previous novel, experiences his alienation from black culture as a hollow daily monotony. Jadine, whose desire to find self and be free leads to jet hops between Paris, the Caribbean and New York, has not had the benefit of a powerful culture mentor like Pilate, who awoke Milkman's desire to know his past. In contrast, all of Jadine's possible culture heroes are bracketed by her rupture with the past and her class position. Jadine rejects family – her Aunt Odine, for her homey ways and maternal nature – and culture: the black islanders, so remote from Jadine's trajectory into the future that she never even bothers to learn their names.

Milkman, on the other hand, has been born and raised in the ghetto, albeit in the biggest house. He has never been to college, but he has had the benefit of teachers – both the 'streetwise' Guitar and the 'folkwise' Pilate. If Milkman's present is a meaningless void of bourgeois alienation, the possibility of a past opens out to him like a great adventure. A quest for gold initiates Milkman's journey into the past – and into the self – but gold is not the novel's real object. Imagining that gold will free him from his father's domination and his family's emotional blackmail, Milkman comes to realize that only by knowing the past can he hope to have a future.

There is a sense of urgency in Morrison's writing, produced by the realization that a great deal is at stake. The novels may focus on individual characters like Milkman and Jadine, but the salvation of individuals is not the point. Rather, these individuals, struggling to reclaim or redefine themselves, are portrayed as epiphenomenal to community and culture; and it is the strength and continuity of the black cultural heritage as a whole which is at stake and being tested.

As Morrison sees it, the most serious threat to black culture is the obliterating influence of social change. The opening line from *Sula* might well have been the novel's conclusion, so complete is the destruction it records: 'In that place, where they tore the nightshade and blackberry patches from their roots to make room for the Medallion City Golf Course, there was once a neighborhood.'[17] This is the community Morrison is writing to reclaim. Its history, terminated and dramatically obliterated, is condensed in a single sentence whose content spans from rural south to urban redevelopment. As throughout Morrison's writing, natural imagery refers to the past, the rural south, the reservoir of culture which has been uprooted – like the blackberry bushes – to make way for moderniza-tion. In contrast, the future is perceived as an amorphous, institutionalized power embodied in the notion of 'Medallion City', which suggests neither nature nor a people. Joining the past to the future is the neighborhood, which occupies a very different temporal moment (which history has shown to be transitional), and defines a very different social mode, as distinct from its rural origins as it is from the amorphous urban future.

It is impossible to read Morrison's four novels without coming to see the neighborhood as a concept crucial to her understanding of history. It defines a northern social mode rather than a southern one, for it describes the rela-tionship of an economic satellite, contiguous to a larger metropolis, rather than separate, subsistence economies like the southern rural towns of Shalimar and Eloe. It is a Midwestern phenomenon rather than a northeast, big-city category, because it defines the birth of principally first-generation, northern working-class black communities. It is a mode of the forties rather than the sixties or the eighties and evokes the many locally specific black populations in the north before these became assimilated to a larger, more generalized and less regionally specific sense of black culture, which we today refer to as the 'black community'.

The fact that Milkman embarks on a quest for his past is itself symptomatic of the difference between the forties neighborhood and the sixties community. In contrast with Milkman, the black youth of the forties had no need to uncover and decipher the past simply because enough of it was still present, borne on successive waves of southern black immigrants. For Milkman the past is a riddle, a reality locked in the verses of a children's song (the song of Solomon) whose meaning is no longer explicit because time has separated the words from their historical content. Childhood and the way children perceive the world is again a figure for a mode of existence prior to the advent of capitalism and bourgeois society. And in *Song of Solomon* it coincides with the function of song in all marginal cultures as the unwritten text of history and culture.

Milkman's quest is a journey through geographic space in which the juxtaposi-tion of the city to the countryside represents the relationship of the present to the past. In tracing his roots from the Detroit ghetto, where he was familiar with Pilate's version of the Solomon song; to Danville, Pennsylvania, where his father grew up; and then to Shalimar, West Virginia, where his grandfather was born and children still sing of Solomon, Milkman deciphers the twin texts of history: song and genealogy. In so doing, he reconstructs a dialectic of historical transition, where individual genealogy evokes the history of black migration and the chain of economic expropriation from hinterland to village, and village to metropolis. The end point of Milkman's journey is the starting point of his race's history in this country: slavery. The confrontation with the reality of slavery, coming at the end of Milkman's penetration into historical process, is liberational because slavery is not portrayed as the origin of history and culture. Instead, the novel opens out to Africa, the source, and takes flight on the wings of Milkman's great-grandfather, the original Solomon. With the myth of the 'flying Africans', Morrison transforms the moment of coming to grips with slavery as an allegory of liberation.

The fact that geographic space functions for history is symptomatic of a time when a people's past no longer forms a continuity with the present. It is one of the features that differentiates literary modernism from realism, where people's lives are portrayed as integral to the flow of history. Because the past is perceived as problematical and historical transition is represented by the relationship between countryside, village and city, Song of Solomon is very similar to the great modernist novels of the Latin American 'Boom'. In Morrison's novel, as in the Peruvian Mario Vargos Llosa's La casa verde, the synchronic relationship defined in geographic space stands for a diachronic relationship. The most interesting feature about these modernist texts is that, in reading them, the reader, like Milkman, restores diachrony to the text; and, in so doing, realizes the historical dialectic which the text presents as inaccessible.

Milkman's journey into the past takes him out of consumer society, where he, Christmas shopping in the Rexall, practices the translation of human emotions into commodities, and thrusts him into the pre-industrial world of Shalimar, where for the first time in his life Milkman sees women with 'nothing in their hands'.[18] Stunned, Milkman realizes that he 'had never in his life seen a woman on the street without a purse slung over her shoulder, pressed under her arm, or dangling from her clenched fingers.'[19] The vision of women walking empty-handed produces an estrangement of Milkman's normal view of women who, conditioned by a market economy, haul about purses like grotesque bodily appendages.

The descent into the past means stepping out of reified and fetishized relationships. Milkman's sensitivities are abruptly awakened when, trudging through the woods, he is scratched by branches, bruised by rocks and soaked in a stream. As all his commodified possessions fall away – his watch, his Florsheim shoes and his three-piece suit – he comes to realize a full range of sensual perceptions (along with some human social practices – like sharing) he had never before experienced. Entering Solomon's General Store, Milkman is struck by its dramatic antithesis to the big-city department store, where money (rather than need or use) mediates the exchange of human identities for brand names.

For Macon Dead, Milkman's father, all human relationships have become fetishized by their being made equivalent to money. His wife is an acquisition; his son, an investment in the future; and his renters, dollar signs in the bank. The human sentiments he experienced as a boy have given way to the emotional blackmail he wages as an adult. Driven by the desire to own property – the basis of bourgeois class politics – Macon Dead uses property, like a true capitalist, for further accumulation through the collection of rents. When Milkman, echoing his father's words, refers to money as 'legal tender', he reveals how deeply fetishized and abstracted the concept of money itself has become. In this context, the search for gold takes on new meaning as a search for the only unfetishized form of value; and, in an allegorical sense, as the retrieval of unfetishized human relationships.

However, Macon Dead is not so totally integrated into the bourgeois class that he cannot sense the impoverishment of his life – 'his wife's narrow unyielding back; his daughters, boiled dry from years of yearning; his son, to whom he could speak only if his words held some command or criticism.'[20] A phantom in search of some vision of human fulfillment, Macon wanders one evening into the southside ghetto, his sister's neighborhood. There, drawn by her singing, he pauses to peer in her window. In every way Pilate is her brother's emotional and social antithesis. What Macon sees when he looks into her house is a totally alternative lifestyle, whose dramatic opposition to the spiritual impoverishment of Macon's world gives rise to a utopian moment:

he crept up to the side window where the candlelight flickered lowest, and peeped in. Reba was cutting her toenails with a kitchen knife or a switchblade, her long neck bent almost to her knees. The girl, Hagar, was braiding her hair, while Pilate, whose face he could not see because her back was to the window, was stirring something in a pot. Wine pulp, perhaps. Macon knew it was not food she was stirring, for she and her daughters ate like children. Whatever they had a taste for. No meal was ever planned or balanced or served. Nor was there any gathering at the table. Pilate might bake hot bread and each one of them would eat it with butter whenever she felt like it. Or there might be grapes, left over from the winemaking, or peaches for days on end. If one of them bought a gallon of milk they drank it until it was gone. If another got a half bushel of tomatoes or a dozen ears of corn, they ate them until they were gone too. They ate what they had or came across or had a craving for. Profits from their wine-selling evaporated like sea water in a hot wind – going for junk jewelry for Hagar, Reba's gifts to men, and he didn't know what all.[21]

In its journey back to rural origins, the novel demonstrates that Pilate's household is not, as this passage tends to suggest, structured on infantile desires and relationships; but that the world of childhood is rooted in rural society, where reciprocity and the unmediated response to desire determine social life. The utopian aspect of Pilate's household is not contained within it, but generated out of its abrupt juxtaposition to the bourgeois mode of her brother's household. In contrast to Macon's world which is based on accumulation, Pilate's household is devoted in true 'potlatch' fashion to non-accumulation. With everyone working to separate berries from thorns, wine-making is not a means for creating surplus value but a communal social activity, whose natural raw material suggests, in Morrison's symbolic register, another link to rural agricultural society. Reba, who wins lotteries and department-store give-aways, enjoys a non-commodified relationship to objects, where value is defined not by an object's money equivalent but by the gratuity of its possession and the pleasure it renders in the giving. Finally, Pilate's only pretense to property ownership is purely symbolic: a bag of bones, which turn out to be her father's, and rocks, one gathered from every state she visited.

Throughout her writing Morrison defines and tests the limits of individual freedom. Unlike those characters who realize total freedom and as a result are incapable of living in society and maintaining human relationships, like Cholly Breedlove[22] and Sula, Pilate's unencumbered life is the basis for a social form of freedom, rich in human understanding and love, which is neither sexual nor familial. In the text, Pilate's freedom, which makes her different from everybody else, has a very curious explanation: namely, the lack of a navel.

Now, it would be wrong simply to see Pilate's lack as just one more example of the mutilated, deformed and stigmatized characters who tend to crop up in Morrison's writing. And it would be equally wrong to dismiss these forms of physical difference as nothing more than the author's obsession with freaks of nature. Rather, as Morrison herself indicates, Pilate's lack is to be read in social terms. It, like the other versions of physical deformity, functions as a metaphor, which allows the reader to perceive a unique personal relationship to society as a whole.

Born without a navel, Pilate is the product of an 'unnatural birth'. In social terms, her father dead and having never known her mother, she is an orphan. Her smooth, unbroken abdominal skin causes her to be shunned by everyone who either befriends her or comes to be her lover. Consequently, she has 'no people'. Because no clan claims her, she is outside all the potentially limiting aspects of blood relationships and traditional forms of social behavior. Apparently without a past and a place, Pilate embodies the 'mythic hero',[23] first portrayed by Faulkner's Thomas Sutpen. The difference between Faulkner and Morrison, conditioned by the intervening years which have brought black civil rights, counter-cultural politics and the feminist perspective, is that, while Morrison invests her 'mythic hero' with utopian aspirations, Faulkner does not. In making Sutpen and his 'design' for plantation and progeny the epitome of southern class society, Faulkner negates the utopian potential that his mythic outsider first represents in opposition to the stifled, small-town sensibilities of Jefferson, Mississippi.

Another dimension which Pilate's lack of a navel allows the reader to experience is the child's discovery of sexual difference. The metaphor of lack articulates the relationship between the advent of adult sexuality and the way it transforms the individual's relationship to others. As a child, having seen only her brother's and father's stomachs, Pilate imagines that navels, like penises, are something men have and women lack. Later, when others point to her lack as a form of freakishness, Pilate achieves adult sexuality only to have it denied her. Deprived of sex because of her unique body and the superstitious fear it creates,

Pilate's lack becomes the basis for her liberation from narrowly defined human relationships based on sexuality and the expansion of her social world to one based on human sensitivity. This is very different from the way Pilate's sister-in-law, Ruth Foster, lives her sexual deprivation. Shunned by her husband, she turns inward to necrophiliac fantasies of her father, a mildly obscene relationship with her son, and masturbation. Ruth, like many of Morrison's female characters dependent on a possessive and closed heterosexual relationship, never comes to see human relationships as anything but sexual. For her, the denial of sex simply means a more narrowly defined sexuality and the closure of her social world.

The only aspect of lack as a metaphor for social relationships which is not explicit but does, nevertheless, inform Morrison's treatment of Pilate is its function as a figure for the experience of racial otherness. This is not the case for other instances of lack, which, like Pecola's lack of blue eyes and Hagar's lack of copper-colored hair, capture the horror of seeing the self as 'other' and inferior. While Pilate, like many of Morrison's characters, does undergo a moment of looking at (and into) the self, during which she recognizes her lack (or difference), and as a consequence determines to live her life according to a very different set of values, her moment of self-recognition (unlike many of theirs) is not couched in racial terms. Because lack in every other instance is a figure for the experience of race, it would seem to be implicit – if not explicit – in the characterization of Pilate. There is just no need for Pilate to affirm herself through race as the shell-shocked Shadrack does when, amnesiac and terrified by his own body, he glimpses the reflection of his face and sees in it the bold reality of his 'unequivocal' blackness. For Pilate, blackness is already unequivocal. And pastlessness does not endanger identity, or separate her from society, as it does for Shadrack. Rather, it liberates the self into society.

As a literary figure for examining the lived experience of social difference, and testing the human potential for liberation, lack has its opposite in a full term: bodily stigma. In contrast to Pilate who has no mark, Sula possesses a striking birthmark above her eye. A patch of skin unlike that found on any other human, Sula's birthmark is thought to represent a tadpole, a flower or a snake, depending on the mood of the beholder. Stigma is the figural equivalent of Sula's role in the community. As a social pariah branded as different, she is the freedom against which others define themselves.

Bodily deformity is another metaphor for the experience of social difference. When Shadrack awakes in a hospital bed, he comes into a world so totally fragmented and sundered that he is unsure where his own hands might be; after all, 'anything could be anywhere'.[24] When he finally does behold his hands, he imagines that they are monstrously deformed – so terrifying that he cannot bear to look at them. Totally disoriented, his hands hidden behind his back, Shadrack is expelled from the hospital and pushed out into the world – a lone, cringing figure in an alien landscape.

For Morrison, the psychological, like the sensual and sexual, is also historical. In a novel whose opening describes the leveling of a neighborhood and its transformation into the Medallion City Golf Course, Shadrack's experience of bodily fragmentation is the psychological equivalent of annihilating social upheaval, which he, as an army draftee, has been subjected to (the army being the first of capitalism's modern industrial machines to incorporate black men). Shadrack's imagined physical deformity is a figure for the equally monstrous psychological and social transformations which capitalism in all its modes (slavery, the military and wage labor) has inflicted on the minds and bodies of black people.

Shadrack's affirmation of self, arising out of the moment he sees his image reflected in a toilet bowl and beholds the solid and profound reality of his blackness, ranks as one of the most powerful literary statements of racial affirmation. Race is the wellspring of Shadrack's inalienable identity. While all around him and within him may be subject to transformation, his blackness is forever. This sense of continuity in the face of chaos lies at the heart of Shadrack's cryptic, one-word message to the child, Sula: 'Always.' It is the basis for both Shadrack's and Sula's reinsertion into society as representations of freedom. As both messiah and pariah, Shadrack is marginal, accepted by, but never asssimilated to, the black community. He, like Sula and Morrison's other social pariah, Soaphead Church, provides a point of perspective on the community which is both interior and exterior; and he allows the community to define itself against a form of freedom, which it, being a social unit, cannot attain. When Morrison remarks that the black community tolerates difference while the white bourgeois world shuts difference out, she underscores the fact that for the white world, under capitalism, difference, because it articulates a form of freedom, is a threat and therefore must be institutionalized or jailed.

In *Tar Baby* bodily deformity takes a very different form. Because this novel describes an already sundered black community, whose exiles have neither the wish nor the capacity to rediscover the source of black culture, freedom cannot be articulated (as it was in the previous novels) by an individual's moment of self-affirmation and reinsertion into society. Having no possible embodiment in the real world – not even a pariah – freedom takes mythic form and defines the text's alternative, subterranean world, where, in sharp contrast with the bourgeois world of manor house and leisure, a centuries-old band of blind black horsemen rides the swamps.

Blindness is another way of giving metaphoric expression to social difference and freedom.[25] It overlaps with the function of lack in that the lack of sight, which in bourgeois society is the basis for an individual's alienation, is in the mythic world the basis for the group's cohesion and absolute alternality. This is because blindness is portrayed not as an individual's affliction but rather as a communally shared way of being in the world. Once again the figure of deformity evokes a historical reality. The myth of the blind horsemen has its roots in the many real maroon societies whose very existence depended upon seclusion and invisibility. This is the social reality for which blindness is its metaphoric reversal.

A final metaphor for social otherness is self-mutilation.[26] Unlike lack and deformity, self-mutilation represents the individual's direct confrontation with the oppressive social forces inherent in white domination. Because it functions as a literary figure, self-mutilation is liberational and contrasts sharply with all the other forms of violence done to the self portrayed in Morrison's writing. For instance, when Polly Breedlove lashes out at her child, Pecola, berating her and beating her for spilling a berry cobbler, and at the same time comforts and cuddles the white child in her charge, she internalizes her hate for white society and deflects the spontaneous eruption of violence away from its real object and towards a piece of herself. Unlike Polly Breedlove's violence toward the self, which locks her in profound self-hatred, self-mutilation is portrayed as a confrontational tactic which catapults the individual out of an oppressive situation. Because it involves severing a part of the body, self-mutilation coincides with the figure of lack and intensifies (by reason of its direct articulation) the potential for expressing freedom. In Morrison's writing, self-mutilation brings about the spontaneous redefinition of the individual, not as an alienated cripple – as would be the case in bourgeois society – but as a new and whole person, occupying a radically different social space.

When, as an adolescent, Sula is confronted by a band of teenage Irish bullies, she draws a knife. Instead of threatening the boys with it or plunging it into one of them, she whacks off the tip of her own finger. Sula's self-mutilation symbolizes castration and directly contests the white male sexual domination of black women which the taunting and threatening boys evoke. Her act, coupled with words of warning, 'If I can do that to myself, what you suppose I'll do to you?',[27] represents the refusal – no matter how high the cost – to accept and cower in the face of domination.

For its defiance of oppressive social norms as well as its symbolic nature, Sula's act of self-mutilation has its precedent in her grandmother's solution to a similar confrontation with bourgeois-dominated society. Abandoned by her husband, with three small children and nothing but five eggs and three beets between them, Eva Peace takes a truly radical course of action, which lifts her out of the expected role of an abandoned black mother *circa* 1921, who could do no more than live hand-to-mouth, and gives her a very different future. Leaving her children in the care of a neighbor, she sets out. 'Eighteen months later she swept down from a wagon with two crutches, a new black pocketbook, and one leg.'[28] Eva never confirms neighborhood speculation that she allowed a train to sever her leg, because how she lost it is not important. The real issue is what her self-mutilation enables her to achieve. As the juxtaposition between Eva's 'new black pocketbook' and 'one leg' suggests, monthly insurance checks make it possible for her to build a new life. The construction of a rambling, many-roomed house for family and boarders gives physical evidence for Eva's confrontation with and manipulation of the written laws of white society, whose unwritten laws would have condemned her to a life of poverty.

The most radical aspect of Eva's act is not the contestatory moment of self-mutilation but the subsequent lack, which allows a wholly new social collective to come into being around her. If the loss of a limb means that Eva practically never leaves her room, it does not signify withdrawal. Instead, Eva is 'sovereign' of an entire household, which includes three generations of Peace women as its nucleus, Eva, Hannah and Sula; their boarders, the young married couples and an alcoholic hillbilly; and their adopted outcasts, the three Deweys. For its fluid composition, openness to outsiders and organization upon a feminine principle, Eva's household represents a radical alternative to the bourgeois family model.

At one level, Morrison writes to awaken her reader's sensitivity, to shake up and disrupt the sensual numbing that accompanies social and psychological alienation. This is the function of her 'eruptions of funk', which include metaphors drawn from past moments of sensual fulfillment as well as the use of lack, deformity and self-mutilation as figures for liberation. At a deeper level, and as a consequence of these features, Morrison's writing often allows an alternative social world to come into being. When this happens, 'otherness' no longer functions as an extension of domination (as it does when blackness is beheld from the point of view of racist bourgeois society, or when the crippled, blind and deformed are compared to the terrorizing totality of a whole, and therefore 'perfect', body). Rather, the space created by otherness permits a reversal of domination and transforms what was once perceived from without as 'other' into the explosive image of a utopian mode. Morrison's most radical 'eruption of funk' is the vision of an alternative social world. It comes into view when Macon Dead peers into Pilate's window; when the child, Nel, the product of her mother's stifled bourgeois morality, scratches at Sula's screen door; and when the intimidated and fearful Pecola visits her upstairs neighbors, the three prostitutes.

It is not gratuitous that in all these cases the definition of social utopia is based on a three-woman household. This does not imply a lesbian orientation, because in all cases the women are decidedly heterosexual. Rather, these are societies that do not permit heterosexuality as it articulates male domination to be the determining principle for the living and working relationships of the group, as it is in capitalist society.

Morrison's three-woman utopian households contrast dramatically with an earlier literary version which occurs in, of all places, Faulkner's *Absalom! Absalom!* During the grinding culmination of the Civil War, their men all gone – siphoned off by the army – the economy reduced to bare subsistence, the novel brings together three women: Judith, Sutpen's daughter and heir; Clytie, Sutpen's black non-heir; and the young spinster, Miss Rosa, Sutpen's non-betrothed. Refuged in the shell of a once prosperous manor house, they eke out their survival on a day-to-day basis:

> So we waited for him. We led the busy eventless lives of three nuns in a barren and poverty-stricken convent: the walls we had were safe, impervious enough, even if it did not matter to the walls whether we ate or not. And amicably, not as two white women and a negress, not as three negroes or three whites, not even as three women, but merely as three creatures who still possessed the need to eat but took no pleasure in it, the need to sleep but from it no joy in weariness or regeneration, and in whom sex was some forgotten atrophy like the rudimentary gills we call the tonsils or the still-opposable thumbs for old climbing.[29]

In considering the cataclysm of the Civil War and its destruction of traditional southern society, Faulkner is led to imagine the basis for a potentially radical new form of social organization, based on subsistence rather than accumulation, and women rather than men. However, the incipient possibility of social utopia dies stillborn. This is because the male principle and the system of patrimony have not been transformed or refuted, but merely displaced. Sutpen, even in his absence, is still the center of the household. Race, too, is not confronted or transcended. Rather, it, like sex, is simply dismissed. And with it go all vestiges of humanity.

The tremendous differences between Faulkner and Morrison, which include historical period, race and sex, lie at the heart of their dramatically opposed images: the one, dystopian; the other, utopian. Rather than dwell on the social and historical factors that shape their fiction, I think it is more interesting in the study of literature to see how historical differences are manifested in the texts. Faulkner's dehumanized monads and the routinized lives they lead contrast sharply with Morrison's portrayal of Pilate's household, where individual differences between the three women function to test the social dynamic within the group and between it and society at large. Faulker's retrenched espousal of the male-dominated social model and his tenacious refusal to imagine anything else condition his bleak vision of society. On the other hand, Morrison's projection of a social utopia arises from its confrontation with and reversal of the male-dominated bourgeois social model. Rather than systematically leveling social problems, Morrison foregrounds them. The utopian aspect of her vision is produced by the totality of its opposition to society at large – not by its individual members. This makes her portrayal very different from classical literary utopias, whose individuals were presented as perfect and harmonious models. None of Morrison's individual characters in any of her three utopias is perfect. Rather than supplying answers to social problems, they give rise to questions about social relationships and society as a whole. Thus Pilate demonstrates the insufficiency of the agrarian social mode to provide for its members once they are transplanted to urban consumer society. Her strength and resourcefulness cannot be passed on to her daughter and granddaughter because each is more distant from the rural society in which Pilate worked and grew up. Their experience of insufficiency leads to hollow consumption (Reba's of sex and Hagar's of commodities) and demonstrates the way consumer society penetrates and impoverishes human relationships.

When 'funk' erupts as myth, its potential for estranging fetishized relationships is minimized because of its distance from the urban and suburban settings that condition the lives of more and more Americans – both black and white. Son's quest for the mythic community of blind maroon horsemen which ends *Tar Baby* may represent a dramatic departure from his previous endeavors, but it does not bring disruption into the heart of social practice, as occurs when the image of Pilate's household bursts upon Macon Dead's alienated and numbed sensibilities. Although *Song of Solomon* also has a mythic dimension, myth is not the novel's only form of 'funk'. Then, too, myth is integral to Milkman's concrete past, as he discovers by following his family's route back to slavery; while, for Son, it represents a very distant cultural source not directly linked to his present.

'Funk' is really nothing more than the intrusion of the past in the present. It is most oppositional when it juxtaposes a not so distant social mode to those evolved under bourgeois society. It remains to be seen what form 'funk' will take in Morrison's future work. Will it be mythic or social? Will it represent a wish-fulfillment or the challenging struggle for social change?

Notes

1 Toni Morrison, *The Bluest Eye* (New York: Pocket Books, 1972), pp. 103–4. Subsequent page references are to this edition.

2 Much of the criticism of Toni Morrison's work is done from a sociological point of view. See, for example: Joan Bischoff, 'The Novels of Toni Morrison: Studies in Thwarted Sensitivity', *Studies in Black Literature*, 6, 3 (1975), pp. 21–3; Phyllis Klotman, 'Dick-and-Jane and the Shirley Temple Sensibility in *The Bluest Eye*', *Black American Literature Forum*, 13 (1979), pp. 123–5; Barbara Lounsberry and Grace Anne Hovet, 'Principles of Perception in Toni Morrison's *Sula*', *Black American Literature Forum*, 13 (1979), pp. 126–9. These studies focus on the erosion of the individual's sensitivity by white cultural domination on the one hand, and ordering mechanisms within the black neighborhood on the other. The critics tend to agree that, while Morrison regrets the loss of sensitivity, she favors a practical and pragmatic point of view.

Without denying the objective social facts or the importance of literary studies which document the social in literature, I am more interested in how texts subvert the limitations within which they are written. The focus of this study is thus on those instances in Morrison's writing when the literature does something more than simply monitor and confirm social fact.

3 The surrealist metaphors of the negritude poets resist being read in the way we can read through Morrison's metaphors, progressively constructing their referents and meaning. A passage from Césaire's *Cahier d'un retour au pays natal* exemplifies the difference between

the poetics of negritude and Morrison's use of metaphor. Conjuring up the Congo, Césaire depicts a rich natural setting:

où l'eau fait
likouala – likouala

– 'where the water goes likouala – likouala'. This is followed by one of the most complex and condensed examples of surrealist metaphor:

où l'éclair de la colère lance sa hache verdâtre
et force les sangliers de la putréfaction dans
la belle orée violente des narines

Reading the metaphor produces something like this: 'where the lightning bolt of anger hurls its green axe and forces the wild boars of putrefaction over the beautiful and violent edge of the nostrils.'

Over all, the image evokes the powerful and driving force of nature and the hunt. Individual words are themselves metaphors, linked together to form a total metaphoric image, whose meaning does not reside in a particular referent but in the myriad cross-references pulled into the whole.

The 'lightning bolt of anger' captures the essence of the poem as a whole, for it voices the enraged outcry of black people and reverses the image of the meek, long-suffering 'poor old Negro' produced by colonialism. The image of 'wild boars pouring over the nostrils' (like snot) extends the notion of putrefaction, which is itself a code word for the effects of colonialism. This is developed at length in the poem's opening pages where the Antilles are portrayed not as a tropical island paradise but as a degraded, diseased and decayed speck of land:

Here the parade of contemptible and scrofulous bubos, the gluttony of very strange microbes, the poisons for which there are no known alexins, the pus of very ancient wounds, the unforeseeable fermentations of species destined to decay.

Bodily orifices, too, are in more than one instance related to the visage of colonialism. But these observations do not translate what the metaphor says. Rather, they are embraced by it. There is no single, comprehensive way to decipher Césaire's metaphor as there is for Morrison's. This is because, while history infuses the image, the metaphor resists being tied to any specific referent or set of referents. The effect is finally an explosion of meanings, created out of the convergence of many possible interpretations, as opposed to, in Morrison, the revelation of meaning, made possible by linking images to referents.

4 Morrison, *The Bluest Eye*, p. 7
5 Harriette Arnow's *The Dollmaker*, an account of an Appalachian family's migration to Detroit during the Second World War, is very similar to Morrison's portrayal of black southern migration. Notably, it documents the initial experience and assimilation to wage labor, the erosion of folk culture and the fragmentation of the family unit. In Arnow, as in Morrison, the individual's experience of alienation is portrayed in relation to fetishization under the commodity form. For a brief discussion of this novel, see my article, 'A Literary Lesson in Historical Thinking', *Social Text*, 3 (Fall 1980), p. 136.
6 Morrison, *The Bluest Eye*, p. 68.
7 Ibid., p. 69.
8 Ibid., p. 21.
9 Ibid., p. 13.
10 Ibid.

11 See Georg Lukács, 'Reification and the Consciousness of the Proletariat', *History and Class Consciousness* (London: Merlin Press, 1971), p. 83. According to Lukács, reification occurs when the 'commodity structure penetrates society in all its aspects and remoulds it in its own image'. This differentiates bourgeois society from previous social modes where the commodity form may have pertained to certain endeavors or may have been only partially developed. Reification means the transformation of all human functions and qualities into commodities 'and reveals in all its starkness the dehumanized and dehumanizing function of the commodity relation'.

12 Toni Morrison, *Song of Solomon* (New York: New American Library, 1978), pp. 314–15. Subsequent page references are to this edition.

13 Referred to as 'The Principal Beauty of Maine', Margaret Lenore from *Tar Baby* comes closest to embodying bourgeois reification. Her characterization may well be a literary allusion to another great beauty and bourgeois stereotype in contemporary fiction, 'The Most Beautiful Woman in the World', in Gabriel García Márquez's *One Hundred Years of Solitude*. Both Margaret Lenore and Márquez's 'Most Beautiful Women' are first beheld by their future husbands as beauty-contest winners, draped in ermine and in a parade. However, neither Margaret Lenore nor Márquez's Remedios defines total reification. First of all, neither is originally of the bourgeois class: Remedios is the sole survivor of a transplanted and bankrupt Spanish aristocracy, and Margaret Lenore is the daughter of struggling Italian immigrants. Both develop forms of hysteria as a result of the discontinuity between their pasts and presents and imperfect assimilation to bourgeois culture. Margaret Lenore abuses her infant son and Remedios develops a relationship with 'imaginary doctors', who she hopes will cure her bodily ailments through telepathic surgery (a situation not unlike Margaret Lenore's long-distance telephone conversations with her son, which, because no one witnesses or overhears them, appear to be imaginary).

14 In Morrison's writing, candy is often associated with capitalism. In *Song of Solomon* it is the symbolic payoff given by the boss's wife when Guitar's father is crushed in a mill accident. In *The Bluest Eye* it is a penny's worth of sweetness in the life of a little girl who will never find satisfaction in human terms. And in *Tar Baby* it is a metaphor for all of capitalist production. The association is not gratuitous, for the connection between candy and capitalism extends far beyond the current glut of sugary breakfast cereals and junk foods. As Immanuel Wallerstein explains in *The Modern World System* (New York: Academic Press, 1974), sugar production in the New World was essential to the rise of capitalism. Rather than simply satisfying luxury consumption, a lot of the sugar produced under slavery in the Caribbean found its way into the daily diet of the growing European proletariat. With many peasants leaving the countryside to seek jobs in the cities, there was an increased need for food production and a shrinking rural labor force. The need for more food was met neither by increased cereal production (which would have required substantial transformations in production techniques) nor by increasing meat production (which was basically intended for the bourgeoisie). Rather, sugar became – as it is today – a substitute for real food. Capable of providing increased energy output at the expense of long-term health, sugar is the opiate of the working class under capitalism.

15 Toni Morrison, *Tar Baby* (New York: Knopf, 1981), p. 61. Subsequent page references are to this edition.

16 Ibid., p. 119.

17 Toni Morrison, *Sula* (New York: Knopf, 1974), p. 3. Subsequent page references are to this edition.

18 Morrison, *Song of Solomon*, p. 262.

19 Ibid.

20 Ibid., p. 28.
21 Ibid., p. 29.
22 Abandoned at birth by his mother, rejected by his father for the sake of a poker game, and having experienced the ultimate moment of objectification when two white hunters catch him in his first sex act, Cholly Breedlove finds absolute freedom in the realization that he has nothing to lose. In many ways he is Pilate's antithesis – his freedom a barrier rather than a bridge to others. As opposed to Pilate, who similarly did not know her mother's name, who lost her father and also experienced the freezing 'look' of the other for her lack of a navel, Cholly can neither communicate nor share his freedom.
23 Many modernist novels from the Third World include 'mythic heroes' very similar to Faulkner's Thomas Sutpen. In Vargas Llosa's La casa verde, Don Anselmo abrupts upon a stodgy, backwater town, shrouded in mystery, apparently without a past or a name. Like Sutpen, he embarks upon an enterprise which the townspeople marvel at, and at first do not comprehend. What Don Anselmo builds symbolizes exploitation in the Third World: a brothel. The 'mythic hero' creates a distance from society, which enables its estrangement once it is revealed that what was first perceived as very different and foreign is nothing more than that society's ultimate representation.
24 Morrison, Sula, p. 8.
25 The otherness of blindness and the fear it instills in a repressive bourgeois society is developed in Sobre heroes y tumbas, the great historical novel by the Argentinian Ernesto Sabatú. Similar to Morrison's portrayal, Sabatú conjures up an underground society of the blind, whose otherness, perceived as grotesque from the point of view of the Peronist social model, is the basis for the group's solidarity and resistance to assimilation by the forces of domination.
26 The relationship between forms of mutilation and freedom is not unique to Morrison but recurs in the history of slavery and its literature. In his mythic account of the Haitian Revolution, Alejo Carpentier portrays the mutilation of Mackandal, an early slave leader, in terms that coincide with Morrison's treatment. His arm crushed in a cane mill, and amputated, Mackandal is unfit for most forms of plantation labor. Freed from the most grueling forms of toil, he wanders the countryside, watching over his master's livestock. There he discovers and studies plant and animal life, learning the secrets of science and voodoo. Mutilation is thus the means for Mackandal's liberation from labor and access to learning. Furthermore, because Mackandal, as voodoo priest, is capable of undergoing various metamorphoses, his human body and its mutilation are not perceived as permanently disabled but as one more manifestation of transitory and transitional matter. Mackandal's spiritual liberation – made possible by his mutilation – finally transcends his earthly form.
27 Morrison, Sula, pp. 54–5.
28 Ibid., p. 34.
29 William Faulkner, Absalom! Absalom! (1936; New York: Random House, 1972), p. 155.

neologism - word disapproved
of because of its newness
or barbarousness

homonym - one or two words
spelled or pronounced alike but
diff. in meaning

For Patti

With the deepest appreciation and affection.

Skip Gates

13 Henry Louis Gates, Jr

The blackness of blackness: a critique of the sign and the Signifying Monkey

> Signification is the nigger's occupation.
> (Traditional)[1]

> Be careful what you do,
> Or Mumbo-Jumbo, God of the Congo
> And all of the other
> Gods of the Congo,
> Mumbo-Jumbo will hoo-doo you,
> Mumbo-Jumbo will hoo-doo you,
> Mumbo-Jumbo will hoo-doo you.
> (Vachel Lindsay, 'The Congo')

I need not trace here the history of the concept of signification. Since Ferdinand de Saussure, at least, signification has become a crucial aspect of contemporary theory. It is curious to me that this neologism in the Western tradition is a homonym of a term in the black vernacular tradition that is approximately two centuries old. Tales of the Signifying Monkey had their origins in slavery; hundreds of these tales have been recorded since the nineteenth century. In black music, Jazz Gillum, Count Basie, Oscar Peterson, Oscar Brown, Jr, Little Willie Dixon, Nat King Cole, Otis Redding, Wilson Pickett and Johnny Otis – among others – have recorded songs called either 'The Signifying Monkey' or, simply, 'Signifyin(g)'. My theory of interpretation, arrived at from within the black cultural matrix, is a theory of formal revision; it is tropological; it is often characterized by pastiche; and, most crucially, it turns on repetition of formal structures, and their difference. Signification is a theory of reading that arises from Afro-American culture; learning how 'to signify' is often part of our adolescent education. I had to step outside my culture, had to defamiliarize the concept by translating it into a new mode of discourse, before I could see its potential in critical theory.[2]

Signifyin(g): definitions

Perhaps only Tar Baby is as enigmatic and compelling a figure from Afro-American mythic discourse as is that oxymoron, the Signifying Monkey.[3] The ironic reversal of a received racist image of the black as simianlike, the Signifying Monkey – he who dwells at the margins of discourse, ever punning, ever troping, ever embodying the ambiguities of language – is our trope for repetition and revision, indeed, is our trope of chiasmus itself, repeating and simul-taneously reversing in one deft, discursive act. If Vico and Burke, or Nietzsche, Paul de Man and Harold Bloom, are correct in identifying 'master tropes', then we might think of these as the 'master's tropes', and of *signifying* as the slave's trope, the trope of tropes, as Bloom characterizes metalepsis, 'a trope-reversing trope, a figure of a figure'. Signifying is a trope that subsumes other rhetorical tropes, including metaphor, metonymy, synecdoche and irony (the 'master' tropes), and also hyperbole, litotes and metalepsis (Bloom's supplement to Burke). To this list, we could easily add aporia, chiasmus and catachresis, all of which are used in the ritual of signifying.

The black tradition has its own subdivisions of signifying, which we could readily identify with the typology of figures received from classical and medieval rhetoric, as Bloom has done with his 'map of misprision'. In black discourse 'signifying' means modes of figuration itself. When one signifies, as Kimberly W. Benston puns, one 'tropes-a-dope'. The black rhetorical tropes subsumed under signifying would include 'marking', 'loud-talking', 'specifying', 'testifying', 'calling out' (of one's name), 'sounding', 'rapping' and 'playing the dozens'.[4]

Let us consider received definitions of the act of signifying and of black mythology's archetypal signifier, the Signifying Monkey. The Signifying Monkey is a trickster figure, of the order of the trickster figure of Yoruba mythology, Èṣù-Ẹlégbára in Nigeria, and Legba among the Fon in Dahomey, whose New World figurations – Exú in Brazil, Echu-Elegua in Cuba, Papa Legba in the pantheon of the loa of Vaudou in Haiti, and Papa La Bas in the loa of Hoodoo in the United States – speak eloquently of the unbroken arc of metaphysical pre-suppositions and patterns of figuration shared through space and time among black cultures in West Africa, South America, the Caribbean and the United States. These trickster figures, aspects of Èṣù, are primarily *mediators*: as tricksters they are mediators and their mediations are tricks.[5]

The versions of Èṣù are all messengers of the gods: he interprets the will of the gods to human beings; he carries the desires of human beings to the gods. He is known as the divine linguist, the keeper of àṣẹ ('logos') with which Olódùmarè created the universe. Èṣù is guardian of the crossroads, master of style and the stylus, phallic god of generation and fecundity, master of the mystical barrier that separates the divine from the profane world. In Yoruba mythology, Èṣù always limps, because his legs are of different lengths: one is anchored in the realm of the gods, the other rests in the human world. The closest Western relative of Èṣù is Hermes, of course; and, just as Hermes' role as interpreter lent his name readily to 'hermeneutics', the study of the process of interpretation, so too the figure of Èṣù can stand, for the critic of comparative black literature, as our metaphor for the act of interpretation itself. In African and Latin American mythologies, Èṣù is said to have taught Ifa how to read the signs formed by the sixteen sacred palm nuts which, when manipulated, configure into 'the signature of an Odù', 256 of which comprise the corpus of Ifá divination. The Ọpọ́n Ifá, the carved wooden divination tray used in the art of interpretation, is said to contain at the center of its upper perimeter a carved image of Èṣù, meant to signify his relation to the act of interpretation, which we can translate either as ìtúmọ̀ ('to untie or unknot knowledge') or as iyípadà ('to turn around' or 'to translate'). That which we call 'close reading' the Yoruba call Ọ̀dá fá ('reading the signs'). Above all else, Èṣù is the Black Interpreter, the Yoruba god of indeterminacy, the sheer plurality of meaning, or àriyèmuyè ('that which no sooner is held than slips through one's fingers'). As Hermes is to hermeneutics, Èṣù is to Èṣù-'túfunàalò ('bringing out the interstices of the riddle').[6]

The Èṣù figures, among the Yoruba systems of thought in Dahomey and Nigeria, in Brazil and in Cuba, in Haiti and in New Orleans, are divine: they are gods who function in sacred myths as do characters in a narrative. Èṣù's functional equivalent in Afro-American profane discourse is the Signifying Monkey, a figure who seems to be distinctly Afro-American, probably derived from Cuban mythology which generally depicts Echu-Elegua with a monkey at his side.[7] Unlike his Pan-African Èṣù cousins, the Signifying Monkey exists in the discourse of mythology not primarily as a character in a narrative but rather as a vehicle for narration itself. It is from this corpus of mythological narratives that signifying derives. The Afro-American rhetorical strategy of signifying is a rhetorical practice unengaged in information-giving. Signifying turns on the play and chain of signifiers, and not on some supposedly transcendent signified. Alan Dundes suggests that the origins of signifying could 'lie in African rhetoric'. As anthropologists demonstrate, the Signifying Monkey is often called 'the signifier', he who wreaks havoc upon 'the signified'. One is 'signified upon' by the signifier. The Signifying Monkey is indeed the 'signifier as such', in Julia Kristeva's phrase, 'a presence that precedes the signification of object or emotion'.[8]

Scholars have for some time commented upon the peculiar use of the word 'signifying' in black discourse. Though sharing some connotations with the standard English-language word, 'signifying' has its own definitions in black discourse. Roger D. Abrahams defines it this way:

Signifying seems to be a Negro term, in use if not in origin. It can mean any of a number of things; in the case of the toast about the signifying monkey, it certainly refers to the trickster's ability to talk with great innuendo, to carp, cajole, needle, and lie. It can mean in other instances the propensity to talk around a subject, never quite coming to the point. It can mean making fun of a person or situation. Also it can denote speaking with the hands and eyes, and in this respect encompasses a whole complex of expressions and gestures. Thus it is signifying to stir up a fight between neighbors by telling stories; it is signifying to make fun of a policeman by parodying his motions behind his back; it is signifying to ask for a piece of cake by saying, 'My brother needs a piece of cake.'[9]

Essentially, Abrahams concludes, signifying is a 'technique of indirect argument or persuasion', 'a language of implication', 'to imply, goad, beg, boast, by indirect verbal or gestural means'. 'The name "signifying" ', he concludes, 'shows the monkey to be a trickster, signifying being the language of trickery, that set of words or gestures achieving Hamlet's "direction through indirection".' The Monkey, in short, is not only 'a master of technique', as Abrahams concludes; he is technique, or style, or the literariness of literary language; he is the great Signifier. In this sense, one does not signify something; rather, one signifies in some way.[10]

There are thousands of 'toasts' of the Signifying Monkey, most of which commence with a variant of the following formulaic lines:

> Deep down in the jungle so they say
> There's a signifying monkey down the way.
> There hadn't been no disturbin' in the jungle for quite a bit,
> For up jumped the monkey in the tree one day and laughed,
> 'I guess I'll start some shit.'[11]

Endings, too, tend toward the formulaic, as in

> Monkey, said the Lion,
> Beat to his unbooted knees,
> You and all your signifying children
> Better stay up in them trees.
> Which is why today
> Monkey does his signifying
> A-way-up out of the way.[12]

In the narrative poems, the Signifying Monkey invariably 'repeats' to his friend, the Lion, some insult purportedly generated by their mutual friend, the Elephant. The Lion, indignant and outraged, demands an apology from the Elephant, who refuses and then trounces the Lion. The Lion, realizing that his mistake was to take the Monkey literally, returns to trounce the Monkey. Although anthropologists and socio-linguists have succeeded in establishing a fair sample of texts featuring the Signifying Monkey, they have been less successful at establishing a consensus of definitions of black 'signifying'.

In addition to Abrahams's definitions of 'signifying', those by Thomas Kochman, Claudia Mitchell-Kernan, Geneva Smitherman, Zora Neale Hurston and Ralph Ellison are of particular interest here for what they reveal about the nature of Afro-American narrative parody.[13] I shall attempt to explicate Afro-American narrative parody and then to employ it in reading Ishmael Reed's third novel, *Mumbo Jumbo*, as a signifying pastiche of the Afro-American narrative tradition itself. Kochman argues that signifying depends upon the signifier *repeating* what someone else has said about a third person in order to *reverse* the status of a relationship heretofore harmonious; signifying can also be employed to *reverse* or *undermine* pretense or even one's opinion about one's own status. The use of repetition and reversal (chiasmus) constitutes an implicit parody of a subject's own complicity in illusion. Mitchell-Kernan, in perhaps the most thorough study of the concept, compares the etymology of 'signifying' in black usage with usages from standard English:

> What is unique in Black English usage is the way in which signifying is extended to cover a range of meanings and events which are not covered in its Standard English usage. In the Black community it is possible to say, 'He is signifying' and 'Stop signifying' – sentences which would be anomalous elsewhere.[14]

Mitchell-Kernan points to the ironic, or dialectic, relation between 'identical' terms in standard and black English which have vastly different meanings:

> The Black concept of *signifying* incorporates essentially a folk notion that dictionary entries for words are not always sufficient for interpreting meanings or messages, or that meaning goes beyond such interpretations. Complimentary remarks may be delivered in a left-handed fashion. A particular utterance may be an insult in one context and not another. What pretends to be informative may intend to be persuasive. The hearer is thus constrained to attend to all potential meaning carrying symbolic systems in speech events – the total universe of discourse. ('Sig.', p. 314)

This is an excellent instance of the nature of signifying. Mitchell-Kernan refines these definitions somewhat by suggesting that the Signifying Monkey is able to signify upon the Lion only because the Lion does not understand the nature of the Monkey's discourse: 'There seems something of symbolic relevance from the perspective of language in this poem. The monkey and the lion do not speak the same language; the lion is not able to interpret the monkey's use of language' ('Sig.', p. 323). The Monkey speaks *figuratively*, in a symbolic code; the Lion interprets or 'reads' *literally* and suffers the consequences of his folly, which is a reversal of his status as King of the Jungle. The Monkey rarely acts in these narrative poems; he simply speaks. As the signifier, he determines the actions of the signified – the hapless Lion and the puzzled Elephant.

As Mitchell-Kernan and Hurston attest, signifying is not a gender-specific rhetorical game, despite the frequent use, in the 'masculine' versions, of expletives that connote intimate relations with one's mother. Hurston, in *Mules and Men* (1935), and Mitchell-Kernan, in her perceptive 'Signifying, Loud-talking, and Marking', are the first scholars to record and explicate female signifying rituals. Hurston is the first author of the tradition to represent signifying itself as a vehicle of liberation for an oppressed woman, and as a rhetorical strategy in the narration of fiction.[15]

Hurston, whose definitions of the term in *Mules and Men* is one of the earliest in the linguistic literature, has made *Their Eyes Were Watching God* (1937) into a paradigmatic signifying text, for this novel resolves that implicit tension between the literal and the figurative contained in standard English usages of the term 'signifying'. *Their Eyes* represents the black trope of signifying both as thematic matter and as a rhetorical strategy of the novel itself. Janie, the protagonist, gains her voice, as it were, in her husband's store not only by engaging with the assembled men in the ritual of signifying (which her husband had expressly forbidden her to do) but also by openly *signifying upon* her husband's impotency. His image wounded fatally, he soon dies of a displaced 'kidney' failure. Janie 'kills' her husband, rhetorically. Moreover, Hurston's masterful use of free indirect discourse (*style indirect libre*) allows her to signify upon the tension between the two voices of Jean Toomer's *Cane* (1923) by adding to direct and indirect speech a strategy through which she can privilege the black oral tradition, which Toomer had found to be problematic, and dying. The text of *Their Eyes*, therefore, is itself a signifying structure, a structure of intertextual revision, because it revises key tropes and rhetorical strategies received from such precursory texts as Toomer's *Cane* and W. E. B. DuBois's *The Quest of the Silver Fleece* (1911).

Afro-American literary history is characterized by such *tertiary* formal revision, by which I mean its authors seem to revise at least two antecedent texts, often taken from different generations or periods within the tradition. Hurston's opening of *Their Eyes* is a revision of *Narrative of the Life* (1845), Frederick Douglass's apostrophe to the ships at Chesapeake Bay; *Their Eyes* also revises the trope of the swamp in DuBois's *Quest*, as well as the relation of character to setting in Toomer's *Cane*. The example of Ellison is even richer: *Invisible Man* (1952) revises Richard Wright's *Native Son* (1940) and *Black Boy* (1945), along with DuBois's *The Souls of Black Folk* (1903) and Toomer's *Cane* (but it also revises Melville's *Confidence-Man* and Joyce's *Portrait of the Artist as a Young Man*, among others). Reed, in *Mumbo Jumbo* (1972), revises Hurston, Wright and Ellison.[16] It is clear that black writers read and critique other black texts as an act of rhetorical self-definition. Our literary tradition exists because of these precisely chartable formal literary relationships, relationships of signifying.

The key aspect of signifying for Mitchell-Kernan is 'its indirect intent or metaphorical reference', a rhetorical indirection which she says is 'almost purely stylistic': its art characteristics remain foregrounded. By 'indirection', Mitchell-Kernan means that

> the correct semantic (referential interpretation) or signification of the utterance cannot be arrived at by a consideration of the dictionary meaning of the lexical items involved and the syntactic rules for their combination alone. The apparent significance of the message differs from its real significance. The apparent meaning of the sentence signifies its actual meaning. ('Sig.', p. 325)

This rhetorical naming by indirection is, of course, central to our notions of figuration, troping and parody. This parody of forms, or pastiche, is in evidence when one writer repeats another's structure by one of several means, including a fairly exact repetition of a given narrative or rhetorical structure, filled incongruously with a ludicrous or incongruent content. T. Thomas Fortune's 'The Black Man's Burden' is an excellent example of this form of pastiche, signifying as it does upon Rudyard Kipling's 'The White Man's Burden':

> What is the Black Man's Burden,
> Ye hypocrites and vile,
> Ye whited sepulchres
> From th' Amazon to the Nile?
> What is the Black Man's Burden,
> Ye Gentile parasites,
> Who crush and rob your brother
> Of his manhood and his rights?

Dante Gabriel Rossetti's 'Uncle Ned', a dialect verse parody of Harriet Beecher Stowe's *Uncle Tom's Cabin*, provides a second example:

> Him tale dribble on and on widout a break,
> Till you hab no eyes for to see;
> When I reach Chapter 4 I had got a headache;
> So I had to let Chapter 4 be.

Another kind of formal parody suggests a given structure precisely by failing to coincide with it – that is, suggests it by dissemblance. Repeating a form and then inverting it through a process of variation is central to jazz – a stellar example is John Coltrane's rendition of 'My Favorite Things', compared to Julie Andrews's vapid version. Resemblance thus can be evoked cleverly by dissemblance. Aristophanes' *Frogs*, which parodies the styles of both Aeschylus and Euripides; Cervantes' relationship to the fiction of knight-errantry; Fielding's parody, in *Joseph Andrews*, of the Richardsonian novel of sentiment; and Lewis Carroll's double parody in 'Hiawatha's Photographing', which draws upon Longfellow's rhythms to parody the convention of the family photograph, all come readily to mind.

Ellison defines the parody aspect of signifying in several ways which I shall bring to bear on my discussion below of the formal parody strategies at work in Reed's Mumbo Jumbo. In his complex short story, 'And Hickman Arrives' (1960), Ellison's narrator defines 'signifying':

And the two men [Daddy Hickman and Deacon Wilhite] standing side by side, the one large and dark, the other slim and light brown; the other reverends rowed behind them, their faces staring grim with engrossed attention to the reading of the Word; like judges in their carved, high-backed chairs. And the two voices beginning their call and countercall as Daddy Hickman began spelling out the text which Deacon Wilhite read, playing variations on the verses just as he did with his trombone when he really felt like signifying on a tune the choir was singing.[17]

Following this introduction, the two ministers demonstrate this 'signifying', which in turn signifies upon the antiphonal structure of the Afro-American sermon. Ellison's parody of form here is of the same order as Richard Pryor's parody of that sermonic structure and Stevie Wonder's 'Living for the City', which he effects by speaking the lyrics of Wonder's song in the form of and with the intonation peculiar to the Afro-American sermon in his 'reading' of 'The Book of Wonder'. Pryor's parody is a signification of the second order, revealing simultaneously the received structure of the sermon (by its presence, de-mystified here by its incongruous content), the structure of Wonder's music (by the absence of its form and the presence of its lyrics) and the complex, yet direct, formal relationship between both the black sermon and Wonder's music specifically, and black sacred and secular narrative forms generally.

Ellison defines 'signifying' in other ways as well. In his essay on Charlie Parker, 'On Bird, Bird-Watching, and Jazz' (1962), Ellison defines the satirical aspect of signifying as one aspect of riffing in jazz.

But what kind of bird was Parker? Back during the thirties members of the old Blue Devils Orchestra celebrated a certain robin by playing a lugubrious little tune called 'They Picked Poor Robin'. It was a jazz community joke, musically an extended 'signifying riff' or melodic naming of a recurrent human situation, and was played to satirize some betrayal of faith or loss of love observed from the bandstand.[18]

Here again, the parody is twofold, involving a formal parody of the melody of 'They Picked Poor Robin' as well as a ritual naming, and therefore a troping, of an action 'observed from the bandstand'.

Ellison, of course, is our Great Signifier, naming things by indirection and troping throughout his works. In his well-known review of LeRoi Jones's Blues People, Ellison defines 'signifying' in yet a third sense, then signifies upon Jones's reading of Afro-American cultural history, which he argues is misdirected and wrongheaded: 'The tremendous burden of sociology which Jones would place upon this body of music', writes Ellison, 'is enough to give even the blues the blues.' Ellison writes that Lydia Maria Child's title, *An Appeal in Favor of that Class of Americans Called Africans,*

> sounds like a fine bit of contemporary ironic *signifying* – 'signifying' here meaning, in the unwritten dictionary of American Negro usage, 'rhetorical understatements'. It tells us much of the thinking of her opposition, and it reminds us that as late as the 1890s, a time when Negro composers, singers, dancers and comedians dominated the American musical stage, popular Negro songs (including James Weldon Johnson's 'Under the Bamboo Tree', now immortalized by T. S. Eliot) were commonly referred to as 'Ethiopian Airs'.[19]

Ellison's stress upon 'the unwritten dictionary of American Negro usage' reminds us of the problem of definitions, of signification itself, when one is translating between two languages. The Signifying Monkey, perhaps appropriately, seems to dwell in this space between two linguistic domains. One wonders, incidentally, about this Afro-American figure and a possible French connection between *signe* ('sign') and *singe* ('monkey').

Ellison's definition of the relation that his works bear to those of Wright constitutes a definition of 'narrative signification', 'pastiche' or 'critical parody', although Ellison employs none of these terms. His explanation of what might be called 'implicit formal criticism', however, comprises what is sometimes called 'troping' and offers a profound definition of 'critical signification' itself:

> I felt no need to attack what I considered the limitations of [Wright's] vision because I was quite impressed by what he had achieved. And in this, although I saw with the black vision of Ham, I was, I suppose, as pious as Shem and Japheth. Still I would write my own books and they would be in themselves, implicitly, criticisms of Wright's; just as all novels of a given historical moment form an argument over the nature of reality and are, to an extent, criticisms each of the other.[20]

Ellison in his fictions signifies upon Wright by parodying Wright's literary structures through repetition and difference. The complexities of the parodying I can readily suggest. The play of language, the signifying, starts with the titles: Wright's *Native Son* and *Black Boy*, titles connoting race, self and presence, Ellison tropes with *Invisible Man*, invisibility an ironic response, of absence, to the would-be presence of 'blacks' and 'natives', while 'man' suggests a more mature and stronger status than either 'son' or 'boy'. Wright's distinctive version of naturalism Ellison signifies upon with a complex rendering of modernism; Wright's reacting protagonist, voiceless to the last, Ellison signifies upon with a nameless protagonist. Ellison's protagonist is nothing but voice, since it is he who shapes, edits and narrates his own tale, thereby combining action with the representation of action to define 'reality' by its representation. This unity of presence and representation is perhaps Ellison's most subtle reversal of Wright's theory of the novel as exemplified in *Native Son*. Bigger's voicelessness and powerlessness to act (as opposed to react) signify an absence, despite the metaphor of presence found in the novel's title; the reverse obtains in *Invisible Man*, where the absence implied by invisibility is undermined by the presence of the narrator as the narrator of his own text.

There are other aspects of critical parody at play here, too, one of the funniest being Jack's glass eye plopping into his water glass before him. This is function-ally equivalent to the action of Wright's protagonist in 'The Man Who Lived Underground' as he stumbles over the body of a dead baby, deep down in the sewer. It is precisely at this point in the narrative that we know Fred Daniels to be 'dead, baby', in the heavy-handed way that Wright's naturalism was self-consciously 'symbolic'. If Daniels's fate is signified by the objects over which he stumbles in the darkness of the sewer, Ellison signifies upon Wright's novella by repeating this underground scene of discovery, but having his protagonist burn the bits of paper through which he had allowed himself to be defined by others. By explicitly repeating and reversing key figures of Wright's fictions, and by implicitly defining in the process of narration a sophisticated form more akin to Hurston's *Their Eyes Were Watching God*, Ellison exposed naturalism as merely a hardened conventional representation of 'the Negro problem', and perhaps part of 'the Negro problem' itself. I cannot emphasize enough the major import of this narrative gesture to the subsequent development of black narrative forms. Ellison recorded a new way of seeing and defined both a new manner of representation and its relation to the concept of presence.

The formal relationship that Ellison bears to Wright, Reed bears to both, though principally to Ellison. Not surprisingly, Ellison has formulated this type of complex and inherently polemical intertextual relationship of formal signify-ing. In a refutation of Irving Howe's critique of his work Ellison states:

> I agree with Howe that protest is an element of all art, though it does not necessarily take the form of speaking for a political or social program. It might appear in a novel as a *technical assault against the styles* which have gone before.[21]

This form of critical parody, of repetition and inversion, is what I define to be 'critical signification', or 'formal signifying', and is my metaphor for literary history.

I intend here to elicit the tertiary relationship in *Mumbo Jumbo* of Reed's signifying post-modernism to Wright's naturalism and Ellison's modernism. The set of intertextual relations that I chart through formal signification is related to what Mikhail Bakhtin labels 'double-voiced' discourse, which he subdivides into parodic narration and the hidden or internal polemic. These two types of double-voiced discourse can merge, as they do in *Mumbo Jumbo*. In hidden polemic the other speech act remains outside the bounds of the author's speech, but is implied or alluded to in that speech. The other speech act is not reproduced with a new intention, but shapes the author's speech while remaining outside its boundaries. Such is the nature of discourse in hidden polemic. . . .

In hidden polemic the author's discourse is oriented toward its referential object, as is any other discourse, but at the same time each assertion about that object is constructed in such a way that, besides its referential meaning, the author's discourse brings a polemical attack to bear against another speech act, another assertion, on the same topic. Here one utterance focused on its referential object clashes with another utterance on the grounds of the referent itself. That other utterance is not reproduced; it is understood only in its import.[22]

Ellison's definition of the formal relationship his works bear to Wright's is a salient example of the hidden polemic: Ellison's texts clash with Wright's 'on the grounds of the referent itself'. 'As a result,' Bakhtin continues, 'the latter begins to influence the author's speech from within.' In this double-voiced relationship, one speech act determines the internal structure of another, the second effecting the 'voice' of the first by absence, by difference.

Much of the Afro-American literary tradition can, in a real sense, be read as successive attempts to create a new narrative space for representing the recurring referent of Afro-American literature – the so-called black experience. Certainly, this is the way we read the relation of Sterling Brown's regionalism to Toomer's lyricism, Hurston's lyricism to Wright's naturalism and, equally, Ellison's modernism to Wright's naturalism. This set of relationships can be illustrated by the schematic representation in Figure 13.1, which I intend only to be suggestive.[23]

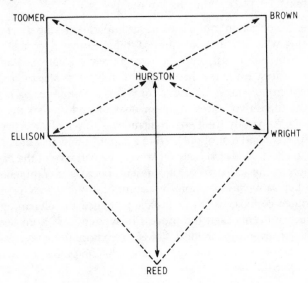

Figure 13.1

These relationships are reciprocal because we are free to read in critical time machines, to read backwards. The direct relation most important to my own theory of reading is that solid black line connecting Reed with Hurston. While Reed and Hurston seem to relish the play of the tradition, Reed's work seems to be a magnificently conceived play on the tradition. Both Hurston and Reed have written myths of Moses, both draw upon black sacred and secular mythic discourse as metaphorical and metaphysical systems, both write self-reflexive texts which comment upon the nature of writing itself, both make use of the frame to bracket their narratives-within-a-narrative, and both are authors of fictions which I characterize as 'speakerly texts'. Speakerly texts privilege the representation of the speaking black voice, of what the Russian Formalists called *skaz* and which Hurston and Reed have called 'an oral book, a talking book' (a figure which occurs, remarkably enough, in five of the first six slave narratives in the black tradition).[24]

Reed's relation to these authors in the tradition is double-voiced at all points, since he seems to be especially concerned with employing satire to utilize literature in what Northrop Frye calls 'a special function of analysis, of breaking up the lumber of stereotypes, fossilized beliefs, superstitious terrors, crank theories, pedantic dogmatisms, oppressive fashions, and all other things that impede the free movement . . . of society.'[25] Reed, of course, seems to be most concerned with the 'free movement' of writing itself. In his work, parody and hidden polemic overlap, in a process Bakhtin describes as follows:

> When parody becomes aware of substantial resistance, a certain forcefulness and profundity in the speech act it parodies, it takes on a new dimension of complexity via the tones of the hidden polemic. . . . A process of inner dialogization takes place within the parodic speech act.[26]

This 'inner dialogization' can have curious implications, the most interesting, perhaps, being what Bakhtin describes as 'the splitting of double-voiced discourse into two speech acts, into the two entirely separate and autonomous voices'. The clearest evidence that Reed is signifying in *Mumbo Jumbo* through parody-as-hidden-polemic is his use of these two autonomous narrative voices. Reed employs these two voices in the manner of, and renders them through, foregrounding, to parody the two simultaneous stories of detective narration (that of the present and that of the past) in a narrative flow that moves hurriedly from cause to effect. In *Mumbo Jumbo*, however, the narrative of the past bears an ironic relation to the narrative of the present, because it comments not only upon the other narrative but upon the nature of *its writing itself*. Frye describes this, in another context, as 'the constant tendency to self-parody in satiric rhetoric which prevents even the process of writing itself from becoming an oversimplified convention or ideal'.[27] Reed's rhetorical strategy assumes the form of the relation between the text and the criticism of that text, which serves as discourse upon that text.

Talking texts: signifying revisions

Consult the text!
(Ralph Ellison)[28]

With these definitions of narrative parody and critical signification as a frame, let me turn directly to Reed's *Mumbo Jumbo*. A close reading of Reed's works strongly suggests his concerns with the received form of the novel, with the precise rhetorical shape of the Afro-American literary tradition, and with the relation that the Afro-American tradition bears to the Western tradition.[29] Reed's concerns, as exemplified in his narrative forms, seem to be twofold: (1) the relation his own art bears to his black literary precursors, including Hurston, Wright, Ellison and James Baldwin; and (2) the process of willing-into-being a rhetorical structure, a literary language, replete with its own figures and tropes, but one that allows the black writer to posit a structure of feeling that simultaneously critiques both the metaphysical presuppositions inherent in Western ideas and forms of writing and the metaphorical system in which the 'blackness' of the writer and his experience have been valorized as a 'natural' absence. In six demanding novels, Reed has criticized, through signifying, what he perceives to be the conventional structures of feeling that he has received from the Afro-American tradition. He has proceeded almost as if the sheer process of the analysis can clear a narrative space for the next generation of writers as decidedly as Ellison's narrative response to Wright and naturalism cleared a space for Leon Forrest, Toni Morrison, Alice Walker, James Alan McPherson and especially for Reed himself.

By undertaking the difficult and subtle art of pastiche, Reed criticizes the Afro-American idealism of a transcendent black subject, integral and whole, self-sufficient and plentiful, the 'always already' black signified, available for literary representation in received Western forms as would be the water dippered from a deep and dark well. Water can be poured into glasses or cups or canisters, but it remains water just the same. Put simply, Reed's fictions argue that the so-called black experience cannot be thought of as a fluid content to be poured into received and static containers. For Reed, it is the signifier that both shapes and defines any discrete signified – and it is the signifiers of the Afro-American tradition with whom Reed is concerned.

Reed's first novel lends credence to this sort of reading and also serves to create a set of generic expectations for reading the rest of his works. *The Free-Lance Pallbearers* is, above all else, a parody of the confessional mode which is the fundamental, undergirding convention of Afro-American narrative, received, elaborated upon and transmitted in a chartable heritage from Briton Hammon's captivity narrative of 1760, through the ante-bellum slave narratives, to black autobiography, and into black fiction, especially the fictions of Hurston, Wright, Baldwin and Ellison.[30] The narrative of Reed's Bukka Doopeyduk is a pastiche of the classic black narrative of the questing protagonist's 'journey into the heart of whiteness'; but it parodies that narrative form by turning it inside out, exposing the character of the originals and thereby defining their formulaic closures and disclosures. Doopeyduk's tale ends with his own crucifixion; as the narrator of his own story, therefore, Doopeyduk articulates, literally, from among the dead, an irony implicit in all confessional and autobiographical modes, in which any author is forced by definition to imagine him- or herself to be dead. More specifically, Reed signifies upon *Black Boy* and *Go Tell It on the Mountain* in a foregrounded critique which can be read as an epigraph to the novel: 'read growing up in soulsville first of three installments – or what it means to be a backstage darky.'[31] Reed foregrounds the 'scat-singing voice' that introduces the novel against the 'other' voice of Doopeyduk, whose 'second' voice narrates the novel's plot. Here, Reed parodies both Hurston's use of free indirect discourse in *Their Eyes Were Watching God* and Ellison's use in *Invisible Man* of the foregrounded voice in the prologue and epilogue that frame his nameless protagonist's picaresque account of his own narrative. In his second novel, *Yellow Back Radio Broke-Down*, Reed more fully, and successfully, critiques both realism and modernism. The exchange between Bo Shmo and the Loop Garoo Kid is telling:

> It was Bo Shmo and the neo-social realist gang. They rode to this spot from their hideout in the hills. Bo Shmo leaned in his saddle and scowled at Loop, whom he considered a deliberate attempt to be obscure. A buffoon an outsider and frequenter of sideshows. . . .

> The trouble with you Loop is that you're too abstract, the part time autocrat monarchist and guru finally said. Crazy dada nigger that's what you are. You are given to fantasy and are off in matters of detail. Far out esoteric bullshit is where you're at. Why in those suffering books that I write about my old neighborhood and how hard it was every gumdrop machine is in place while your work is a blur and a doodle. I'll bet you can't create the difference between a German and a redskin.

> What's your beef with me Bo Shmo, what if I write circuses? No one says a novel has to be one thing. It can be anything it wants to be, a vaudeville show, the six o'clock news, the mumblings of wild men saddled by demons.

> All art must be for the end of liberating the masses. A landscape is only good when it shows the oppressor hanging from a tree.

> Right on! Right on, Bo, the henchmen chorused.

> Did you receive that in a vision or was it revealed to you?[32]

At several points in his first two novels, then, Reed deliberately reflects upon the history of the black tradition's debate over the nature and purpose of art.

Reed's third novel, *Mumbo Jumbo*, is a novel about writing itself – not only in the figurative sense of the post-modern, self-reflexive text but also in a literal sense: 'So Jes Grew is seeking its words. Its text. For what good is a liturgy without a text?'[33] Mumbo Jumbo is both a book about texts and a book of texts, a composite narrative composed of sub-texts, pre-texts, post-texts and narratives-within-narratives. It is both a definition of Afro-American culture and its deflation. 'The Big Lie concerning Afro-American culture', Mumbo Jumbo's dust jacket states, 'is that it lacks a tradition.' The 'Big Truth' of the novel, on the other hand, is that this very tradition is as rife with hardened convention and presupposition as is the rest of the Western tradition. Even this cryptic riddle of Jes Grew and its Text parodies Ellison: Invisible Man's plot is set in motion with a riddle, while the themes of the relation between words and texts echo a key passage from Ellison's short story 'And Hickman Arrives': 'Good. Don't talk like I talk; talk like I say talk. Words are your business, boy. Not just the Word. Words are everything. The key to the Rock, the answer to the Question.'[34]

Reed's signifying on tradition begins with his book's title. 'Mumbo jumbo' is the received and ethnocentric Western designation for the rituals of black religions as well as for all black languages themselves. A vulgarized Western 'translation' of a Swahili phrase, mambo, jambo, 'mumbo jumbo', according to Webster's Third New International Dictionary, connotes 'language that is unnecessarily involved and difficult to understand: GIBBERISH.' The Oxford English Dictionary cites its etymology as 'of unknown origin', implicitly serving here as the signified on which Reed's title signifies, recalling the myth of Topsy in Uncle Tom's Cabin who, with no antecedents, 'jes' grew' – a phrase with which James Weldon Johnson characterizes the creative process of black sacred music. Mumbo Jumbo, then, signifies upon Western etymology, abusive Western practices of deflation through misnaming, and Johnson's specious, albeit persistent, designation of black creativity as anonymous.

But there is even more parody in this title. Whereas Ellison tropes the myth of presence in Wright's titles of Native Son and Black Boy through his title of Invisible Man, Reed parodies all three titles by employing as his title the English-language parody of black language itself. Although the etymology of 'mumbo jumbo' has been problematic for Western lexicographers, any Swahili speaker knows that the phrase derives from the common greeting jambo and its plural, mambo, which loosely translated mean 'What's happening?' Reed is also echoing, and signifying upon, Vachel Lindsay's ironic poem, 'The Congo', which so (fatally) influenced the Harlem Renaissance poets, as Charles T. Davis has shown.[35] From its title on, Mumbo Jumbo serves as a critique of black and Western literary forms and conventions, and of the complex relations between the two.

On the book's cover, which Reed designed (with Allen Weinberg), repeated and reversed images of a crouching, sensuous Josephine Baker are superimposed upon a rose.[36] Counterposed to this image is a medallion depicting a horse with two riders. These signs, the rose and the medallion, adumbrate the two central oppositions of the novel's complicated plot. The rose and the double image of Baker together form a cryptic vé vé. A vé vé is a key sign in Haitian Vaudou, a sign drawn on the ground with sand, cornmeal, flour and coffee to represent the *loas*. The *loas* are the deities comprising the pantheon of *Vaudou* gods. The rose is a sign of Erzulie, goddess of love, as are the images of Baker, who became the French goddess of love in the late 1920s, in the Parisian version of the Jazz Age. The doubled image, as if mirrored, is meant to suggest the divine crossroads, where human beings meet their fate. At its center presides the *loa* Legba (Èṣù), guardian of the divine crossroads, messenger of the gods, the figure representing the interpreter and interpretation itself, the muse or *loa* of the critic. Legba is master of that mystical barrier separating the divine from the profane world. This complex yet cryptic *vé vé* is meant both to placate Legba himself and to summon his attention and integrity in a double act of criticism and interpretation: that of Reed in the process of his representation of the tradition, to be found between the covers of the book, and of the critic's interpretation of Reed's figured interpretation.

Located outside of the *vé vé*, as counterpoint, placed almost off the cover itself, is the medallion, the sign of the Knights Templar, representing the heart of the Western tradition. The opposition between the *vé vé* and the medallion represents two distinct warring forces, two mutually exclusive modes of reading. Already we are in the realm of doubles, but not the binary realm; rather, we are in the realm of doubled doubles. ('Doubled doubles' are central figures in Yoruba mythology, as is Èṣù.) Not only are two distinct and conflicting metaphysical systems here represented and invoked, but Reed's cover also serves as an overture to the critique of dualism and binary opposition which gives a major thrust to the text of *Mumbo Jumbo*. Reed parodies this dualism – which he thinks is exemplified in Ellison's *Invisible Man* – not just in *Mumbo Jumbo* but also in another text, his poem 'Dualism: in ralph ellison's invisible man'.

This critique of dualism is implicit in *Mumbo Jumbo*'s central *speaking* character, PaPa LaBas. I emphasize 'speaking' here because the novel's central character, of course, is Jes Grew itself, which never speaks and is never seen in its 'abstract essence', only in discrete manifestations, or 'outbreaks'. Jes Grew is the supra-force which sets the text of *Mumbo Jumbo* in motion, as Jes Grew and Reed seek their texts, as all characters and events define themselves against this omnipresent, compelling force. Jes Grew, here, is a clever and subtle parody of similar forces invoked in the black novel of naturalism, most notably in Wright's *Native Son*.

Unlike Jes Grew, PaPa LaBas does indeed speak. He is the chief detective in hard-and-fast pursuit of both Jes Grew and its Text. PaPa LaBas's name is a conflation of two of the several names of Èṣù, the Pan-African trickster. Called 'Papa Legba' as his Haitian honorific and invoked through the phrase 'eh là-bas' in New Orleans jazz recordings of the 1920s and 1930s, PaPa LaBas is the Afro-American trickster figure from black sacred tradition. His surname, of course, is French for 'over there', and his presence unites 'over there' (Africa) with 'right here'. He is indeed the messenger of the gods, the divine Pan-African interpreter, pursuing, in the language of the text, 'The Work', which is not only

Vaudou but also the very work (and play) of art itself. PaPa LaBas is the figure of the critic, in search of the text, decoding its telltale signs in the process. Even the four syllables of his name recall *Mumbo Jumbo*'s play of doubles. Chief sign reader, LaBas also in a sense is a sign himself. Indeed, PaPa LaBas's incessant and ingenious search for the Text of Jes Grew, culminating as it does in his recitation and revision of the myth of Thoth's gift of writing to civilization, constitutes an argument against the privileging in black discourse of what Reed elsewhere terms 'the so-called oral tradition' in favor of the primacy and priority of the written text. It is a brief for the permanence of the written text, for the need of criticism, for which LaBas's myth of origins also accounts ('Guides were initiated into the Book of Thoth, the 1st anthology written by the 1st choreographer'; MJ, p. 164).

Let us examine the text of *Mumbo Jumbo* as a textbook, complete with illustrations, footnotes and a bibliography. A prologue, an epilogue and an appended 'Partial Bibliography' frame the text proper, again in a parody of Ellison's framing devices in *Invisible Man*. (Reed supplements Ellison's epilogue with the bibliography, parodying the device both by its repeated presence and by the subsequent asymmetry of *Mumbo Jumbo*.) This documentary scheme of notes, illustrations and bibliography parodies the documentary conventions of black realism and naturalism, as does Reed's recurrent use of lists and catalogs. These 'separate' items Reed fails to separate with any sort of punctuation, thereby directing attention to their presence as literary conventions rather than as sources of information, particularly about the 'black experience'. Reed's text also includes dictionary definitions, epigraphs, epigrams, anagrams, photo-duplicated type from other texts, newspaper clips and headlines, signs (such as those that hang on doors), invitations to parties, telegrams, 'Situation Reports' (which come 'from the 8-tubed Radio'; MJ, p. 32), yin–yang symbols, quotations from other texts, poems, cartoons, drawings of mythic beasts, handbills, photographs, book-jacket copy, charts and graphs, playing cards, a representation of a Greek vase, and a four-page handwritten letter, among even other items. Just as our word 'satire' derives from *satura*, 'hash', so Reed's form of satire is a version of 'gumbo', a parody of form itself.[37]

Reed here parodies and underscores our notions of intertextuality, present in all texts. *Mumbo Jumbo* is the great black inter-text, replete with intra-texts referring to one another within the text of *Mumbo Jumbo* and also referring outside themselves to all those other named texts, as well as to those texts unnamed but invoked through concealed reference, repetition and reversal. The 'Partial Bibliography' is Reed's most brilliant stroke, since its unconcealed presence (along with the text's other undigested texts) parodies both the scholar's appeal to authority and all studied attempts to conceal literary antecedents and influence. All texts, claims *Mumbo Jumbo*, are inter-texts, full of intra-texts. Our notions of originality, Reed's critique suggests, are more related to convention and material relationships than to some supposedly transcendent truth. Reed lays bare that mode of concealment and the illusion of unity which characterize modernist texts. Coming as it does after the epilogue, Reed's 'Partial Bibliography' is an implicit parody of Ellison's ideas of craft and technique in the novel and suggests an image of Ellison's nameless protagonist, buried in his well-lighted hole, eating vanilla ice cream smothered by sloe gin, making annotations for his sequel to *Invisible Man*. The device, moreover, mimics the fictions of documentation and history which claim to order the ways societies live. The presence of the bibliography also recalls Ellison's remarks about the complex relationship between the 'writer's experience' and the writer's experiences with books.

Reed's parodic use of intertextuality demonstrates that *Mumbo Jumbo* is a post-modern text. But what is its parody of the Jazz Age and the Harlem Renaissance about, and for whom do the characters stand? Reed's novel is situated in the 1920s because, as the text explains, the Harlem Renaissance was the first full-scale, patronized attempt to capture the essence of Jes Grew in discrete *literary* texts. Jes Grew had made its first appearance in the 1890s, when 'the Dance' swept the country. Indeed, James Weldon Johnson appropriated the phrase 'jes' grew' to refer to the composition of the musical texts of Ragtime, which depended upon signifying riffs to transform black secular, and often vulgar, songs into formal, repeatable compositions. Ellison makes essentially the same statement about the 1890s by suggesting that signifying is implicit in the common designation of this music as 'Ethiopian Airs'. Ellison's pun could well serve as still another signified upon which *Mumbo Jumbo* signifies. The power of Jes Grew was allowed to peter out in the 1890s, Reed argues, because it found no literary texts to contain, define, interpret and thereby will it to subsequent black cultures.

Although the Harlem Renaissance did succeed in the creation of numerous texts of art and criticism, most critics agree that it failed to find its voice, which lay muffled beneath the dead weight of Romantic convention, which most black writers seemed not to question but to adopt eagerly. This is essentially the same critique rendered by Wallace Thurman in his *Infants of the Spring* (1932), a satirical novel about the Harlem Renaissance, written by one of its most thoughtful literary critics. Few of Reed's characters stand for historical personages; most are figures for types. Hinckle Von Vampton, however, suggests Carl Van Vechten, but his first name, from the German *hinken* ('to limp'), could suggest the German engraver Hermann Knackfuss, whose name translates as 'a person with a clubfoot'.[38] Abdul Sufi Hamid recalls a host of Black Muslims, most notably Duse Mohamed Ali, editor of the *African Times and Orient Review*, as well as Elijah Muhammad's shadowy mentor, W. D. Fard. The key figures in the action of the plot, however, are the Atonist Path and its military wing, the Wallflower Order, on one hand, and the Neo-HooDoo detectives, headed by PaPa LaBas, and its 'military' wing, the Mu'tafikah, on the other. 'Wallflower Order' is a two-term pun on 'Ivy League', while Mu'tafikah puns on a twelve-letter word which signifies chaos. Also, 'mu' is the twelfth letter of the Greek alphabet, suggesting 'the dozens', which forms a subdivision of the black ritual of signifying; the Mu'tafikah play the dozens on Western art museums. The painter Knackfuss created a heliogravure from Wilhelm II's allegorical drawing of the European authority to go to war against the Chinese. This heliogravure, *Völker Europas, wahrt eure heiligsten Güter* ('People of Europe, protect that which is most holy to you'), was completed in 1895. It appears in *Mumbo Jumbo* as part of a chapter in which members of the Wallflower Order plot against the Mu'tafikah (see MJ, p. 155). The pun on 'Knackfuss' and *hinken* is wonderfully consistent with Reed's multiple puns on the 'Wallflower Order' and 'Atonist'.

'Atonist' signifies multiply here. 'One who atones' is an Atonist; a follower of Aton, Pharoah Akhnaton's Supreme Being who 'reappears' as Jehovah, is an Atonist; but also one who lacks physiological tone, especially of a contractile organ, is an Atonist. On a wall at Atonist headquarters are the Order's symbols, 'the Flaming Disc, the # 1 and the creed':

> Look at them! Just look at them! throwing their hips this way, that way while I, my muscles, stone, the marrow of my spine, plaster, my back supported by decorated paper, stand here as goofy as a Dumb Dora. Lord, if I can't dance, no one shall (MJ, p. 65; original in italics, emphasis mine)

The Atonists and the Jes Grew Carriers ('JGC's') re-enact allegorically a primal, recurring battle between the forces of light and the forces of darkness, between forces of the Left Hand and forces of the Right Hand, between the descendants of Set and the descendants of Osiris, all symbolized in Knackfuss's heliogravure.

We learn of this war in *Mumbo Jumbo*'s marvelous parody of the scene of recognition so fundamental to the structure of detective fiction, which occurs in the library of a black-owned villa at Irvington-on-Hudson, called Villa Lewaro, 'an anagram', the text tells us, 'upon the Hostess' name, by famed tenor Enrico Caruso' (MJ, p. 156). Actually, 'Lewaro' is an anagram for 'we oral'. This recognition scene in which PaPa LaBas and his sidekick, Black Herman, arrest Hinckle Von Vampton and his sidekick, Hubert 'Safecracker' Gould, parodies its counterpart in the detective novel by its exaggerated frame. When forced to explain the charges against Von Vampton and Gould, LaBas replies, 'Well if you must know, it all began 1000s of years ago in Egypt, according to a high up member in the Haitian aristocracy' (MJ, p. 160). He then proceeds to narrate, before an assembled company of hundreds, the myth of Set and Osiris and its key subtext, the myth of the introduction of writing in Egypt by the god Thoth. The parody involved here is the length of the recapitulation of facts – of the decoded signs – which LaBas narrates in a thirty-one-page chapter, the longest in the book (see MJ, pp. 161–91). The myth, of course, recapitulates the action of the novel up to this point of the narrative, but by an *allegorical* representation through mythic discourse. By fits and turns, we realize that Von Vampton and the

Wallflower Order are the descendants of Set, by way of the story of Moses and Jethro and the birth of the Knights Templar in AD 1118. Von Vampton, we learn, was the Templar librarian, who found the sacred Book of Thoth, 'the 1st anthology written by the 1st choreographer', which is Jes Grew's sacred Text (MJ, p. 164). In the twentieth century, Von Vampton subdivided the Book of Thoth into fourteen sections, just as Set had dismembered his brother Osiris' body into fourteen segments. The fourteen sections of the anthology he mailed anonymously to fourteen black people, who are manipulated into mailing its parts to each other in a repeating circle, in the manner of a 'chain book' (MJ, p. 69). Abdul Sufi Hamid, one of these fourteen who, we learn, are unwitting Jes Grew Carriers, calls in the other thirteen chapters of the anthology, reassembles the Text, and even translates the Book of Thoth from the hieroglyphics. Sensing its restored Text, Jes Grew surfaces in New Orleans, as it had in the 1890s with the birth of Ragtime, and heads toward New York. Ignorant of the existence or nature of Jes Grew and of the true nature of the sacred Text, Abdul destroys the Book, and then, when he refuses to reveal its location, is murdered by the Wallflower Order. LaBas, Von Vampton's arch-foe, master of HooDoo, devout follower of Jes Grew ('PaPa LaBas carries Jes Grew in him like most other folk carry genes'; MJ, p. 23), chief decoder of signs, recapitulates this complex story, in elaborate detail, to the assembled guests at Villa Lewaro, thereby repeating, through the recited myth, the figures of Mumbo Jumbo's own plot, functioning as what Reed calls 'the shimmering Etheric Double of the 1920s. The thing that gives it its summary' (MJ, p. 20). Despite numerous murders and even the arrests of Von Vampton and Gould and their repatriation to Haiti for trial by the loas of Vaudou, neither the mystery of the nature of Jes Grew nor the identity of its Text is ever resolved. The epilogue presents PaPa LaBas in the 1960s, delivering his annual lecture to a college audience on the Harlem Renaissance and its unconsummated Jes Grew passion.

But just as we can define orders of multiple substitution and signification for Reed's types and caricatures, as is true of allegory generally (e.g. Von Vampton/Van Vechten, hinken/Knackfuss), so too we can find many levels of meaning which could provide a closure to the text. The first decade of readers of Mumbo Jumbo have attempted, with great energy, to find one-to-one correlations, decoding its allegorical structure by finding analogues between, for example, the Harlem Renaissance and the Black Arts Movement. As interesting as such parallel universes are, however, I am more concerned here with Mumbo Jumbo's status as a rhetorical structure, as a mode of narration, and with relating this mode of narration to a critique of traditional notions of closure in interpretation. Reed's most subtle achievement in Mumbo Jumbo is to parody, to signify upon, the notions of closure implicit in the key texts of the Afro-American canon. Mumbo Jumbo, in contrast to that canon, is a novel that figures and glorifies indeterminacy. In this sense, Mumbo Jumbo stands as a profound critique and elaboration upon the convention of closure, and its metaphysical implications, in the black novel.

In its stead, Reed posits the notion of aesthetic play: the play of the tradition, the play on the tradition, the sheer play of indeterminacy itself.

Indeterminacy and the Text of Blackness

The text of Mumbo Jumbo is framed by devices characteristic of film narration. The prologue, situated in New Orleans, functions as a 'false start' of the action: five pages of narration are followed by a second title page, a second copyright and acknowledgment page, and a second set of epigraphs, the first of which concludes the prologue. This prologue functions like the prologue of a film, with the title and credits appearing next, before the action continues. The novel's final words are 'Freeze frame' (MJ, p. 218). The relative fluidity of the narrative structure of film, compared with that of conventional prose narrative, announces here an emphasis upon figural multiplicity rather than singular referential correspondence, an emphasis that Reed recapitulates throughout the text by an imaginative play of doubles. The play of doubles extends from the title and the double-Erzulie image of Baker on the novel's cover ('Erzulie' means 'love of mirrors'; MJ, p. 162) to the double beginning implicit in every prologue, through all sorts of double images scattered in the text (such as the 'two heads' of PaPa LaBas (see MJ, pp. 24, 45) and the frequently repeated arabic numerals 4 and 22), all the way to the double ending of the novel implied by its epilogue and 'Partial Bibliography'. The double beginning and double ending frame the text of Mumbo Jumbo, a book of doubles, from its title on.

These thematic aspects of doubleness represent only its most obvious form of doubling; the novel's narrative structure, a brilliant elaboration upon that of the detective novel, is itself a rather complex doubling. Reed refers to this principle of 'structuration' as 'a doubleness, not just of language, but the idea of a double-image on form. A mystery-mystery, Erzulie-Erzulie.'[39] In Mumbo Jumbo, form and content, theme and structure, all are ordered upon this figure of the double; doubling is Reed's 'figure in the carpet'. The form the narration takes in Mumbo Jumbo replicates the tension of the two stories which grounds the form of the detective novel, defined by Tzvetan Todorov as 'the missing story of the crime, and the presented story of the investigation, the role justification of which is to make us discover the first story.' Todorov describes three forms of detective fiction – the whodunit, the série noire (the thriller, exemplified by Chester Himes's For Love of Imabelle) and the suspense novel, which combines the narrative features of the first two.[40] Let us consider Todorov's typology in relation to the narrative structure of Mumbo Jumbo.

The whodunit comprises two stories: the story of the crime and the story of the investigation. The first story, that of the crime, has ended by the time the second story, that of the investigation of the crime, begins. In the story of the investigation, the characters 'do not act, they learn'. The whodunit's structure, as in Agatha Christie's Murder on the Orient Express, is often framed by a prologue and an epilogue, 'that is, the discovery of the crime and the discovery of the killer' (PP, p. 45). The second story functions as an explanation not just of the investigation but also of how the book came to be written; indeed, 'it is precisely the story of that very book' (PP, p. 45). As Todorov concludes, these two stories are the same as those which the Russian Formalists isolated in every narrative, that of the *fable* (story) and that of the *subject* (or plot): 'The story is what has happened in life, the plot is the way the author presents it to us' (PP, p. 45). 'Story', here, describes the reality represented, while 'plot' describes the mode of narration, the literary convention and devices, used to represent. A detective novel merely renders these two principles of narrative *present* simultaneously. The story of the crime is a story of an absence, since the crime of the whodunit has occurred before the narrative begins; the second story, therefore, 'serves only as mediator between the reader and the story of the crime' (PP, p. 46). This second story, the plot, generally depends upon temporal inversions and sub-jective, shifting points of view. These two conventions figure prominently in the narrative structure of Mumbo Jumbo.

Todorov's second type of detective fiction, the *série noire*, or thriller, combines the two stories into one, suppressing the first and vitalizing the second. Whereas the whodunit proceeds from effect to cause, the thriller proceeds from cause to effect: the novel reveals at its outset the causes of the crime, the *données* (in Mumbo Jumbo, the Wallflower Order, the dialogue of whose members occupies 60 per cent of the prologue), and the narration sustains itself through sheer suspense, through the reader's expectation of what will happen next. Although Mumbo Jumbo's narrative strategy proceeds through the use of suspense, its two stories, as it were, are not fused; accordingly, neither of these categories fully describes it.

Mumbo Jumbo imitates and signifies upon the narrative strategy of the third type of detective novel, the suspense novel. According to Todorov, its defining principles are these: 'it keeps the mystery of the whodunit and also the two stories, that of the past and that of the present; but it refuses to reduce the second to a simple detection of the truth' (PP, p. 50). What *has* happened is only just as important to sustaining interest as what *shall* happen; the second story, then, the story of the present, is the focus of interest. Reed draws upon this type of narrative as his rhetorical structure in Mumbo Jumbo, with one important exception. We do find the two-stories structure intact. What's more, the mystery presented at the outset of the text, the double mystery of the suppression of both Jes Grew *and* its Text (neither of which is ever revealed nor their mysteries solved in the standard sense of the genre), is relayed through the dialogue of the *données*. This means that the movement of the narration is from cause to effect, from the New Orleans branch of the Wallflower Order and their plans to 'decode this coon mumbo jumbo' (MJ, p. 4) through their attempts to kill its Text and thereby dissipate its force. The detective of the tale, PaPa LaBas, moreover, is integrated solidly into the action and universe of the other characters, risking his life and systematically discovering the murdered corpses of his friends and colleagues as he proceeds to decode the signs of the mystery's solution, in the manner of 'the vulnerable detective', which Todorov identifies as a subtype of the suspense novel (PP, p. 51).

In these ways, the structure of Mumbo Jumbo conforms to that of the suspense novel. The crucial exception to the typology, however, whereby Reed is able to parody even the mode of the two stories themselves and transform the structure into a self-reflecting text or allegory upon the nature of writing itself, is Mumbo Jumbo's device of drawing upon the story of the past to reflect upon, analyze and philosophize about the story of the present. The story of the present is narrated from the limited but multiple points of view of the characters who people its sub-plots and sub-mysteries; the story of the past, however, is narrated in an omniscient voice, which 'reads' the story of the present, in the manner of a literary critic close reading a primary text. Mumbo Jumbo's double narrative, then, its narrative-within-a-narrative, is an allegory of the act of reading itself. Reed uses this second mode of ironic omniscient narration to signify upon the nature of the novel in general but especially upon Afro-American naturalism and modernism.

The mystery type of narrative discourse is characterized by plot inversions, which, of course, function as temporal inversions. Before discussing Reed's use of the narrative-within-a-narrative and its relation to the sort of indeterminacy the text seems to be upholding, it would be useful to chart his use of inversion as impediment. The summary of the fable, the essential causal-temporal relationships of the work which I have sketched above, is somewhat misleading, for the novel can be related in summary fashion only after we have read it. In the reading process we confront a collection of mysteries, mysteries-within-mysteries, all of which are resolved eventually except for the first two. We can list the following mysteries which unfold in this order as the subject, or the plot:[41]

1 The mystery of Jes Grew ('the Thing'). 2 The mystery of its Text.	These are basic mysteries. They frame the plot and remain unresolved.
3 The mystery of the Wallflower Order's history and its relation to that of the Knights Templar.	The mystery of the identity of these medieval orders, Jes Grew's antagonists, runs the length of the novel and is resolved only in the recognition scene at Villa Lewaro. Figured as antithetical dance metaphors.
4 The Mu'tafikah's raids on American art museums, especially the North Wing of the Center of Art Detention.	This partial mystery is resolved, but disastrously for LaBas's forces. It creates a series of imbalances between Earline and Berbe-

	lang, and between Berbelang and PaPa LaBas, which function as structural parts to the tension between the Wallflower Order and the Knights Templar.
5 Installation of the anti-Jes Grew President Warren Harding and mystery of his complex racial heritage.	Plot impediments.
6 The mystery of the Talking Android.	
7 Gang wars between Buddy Jackson and Schlitz, 'the Sarge of Yorktown'.	
8 Mystery of the US Marine invasion of Haiti.	Resolved midway; allows for ironic denouncement.
9 Mystery of PaPa LaBas's identity and Mumbo Jumbo Kathedral.	Resolved in epilogue.
10 Woodrow Wilson Jefferson and the mystery of the Talking Android.	Plot impediments; resolved, but ambiguously. Explanations resort to fantastic element.
11 Staged mystery of 'Charlotte's (Isis) Pick' (Doctor Peter Pick).	
12 Hinckle Von Vampton's identity.	This mystery is resolved and in the process resolves the mysteries of the Wallflower Order and the Atonist Path.
13 Mystery of the fourteen JGCs and the sacred anthology.	This resolves mystery 2, but only partially, superficially.
14 The mystery of Abdul Sufi Hamid's murder and his riddle, 'Epigram on American-Egyptian Cotton'.	These mysteries function in a curious way, seemingly to resolve the mystery of Jes Grew's Text.
15 Berbelang's murder and betrayal of the Mu'tafikah by Thor Wintergreen. Charlotte's murder.	Plot impediments.
16 Earline's possession by Erzulie and Yemanjá loas; Doctor Peter Pick's disappearance.	
17 Mystery of The Black Plume and Benoit Battraville, and the ring of the Dark Tower.	VooDoo/HooDoo exposition. Resolves Knights Templar mystery. Leads to capture of Von Vampton.

Most of these interwoven mysteries impede the plot in the manner of detective fiction by depicting, as does jazz, several simultaneous actions whose relationship is not apparent. These mysteries run parallel throughout the novel, only to be resolved in the scene of recognition in the library at the Villa Lewaro, where PaPa LaBas presents his decoded evidence through his elaborate recasting of the myth of Osiris and Set. This allegory recapitulates, combines and decodes the novel's several simultaneous sub-plots and also traces the novel's complex character interrelationships from ancient Egypt up to the very moment of LaBas's narration. The narration leads to the arrest of Gould and Von Vampton, but also to the antidiscovery of the sacred Book of Thoth, the would-be Text of Jes Grew. Recast myths serve the same function of plot impediment for the purpose of repeating the novel's events through metaphorical substitution in two other places: these are the allegories of Faust and of the *houngan*, Ti Bouton (see *MJ*, pp. 90–2, 132–9). These recast myths serve as the play of doubles, consistent with the 'double-image on form', which Reed sought to realize, and are implicit in the nature of allegory itself.

Plot impediment can be created in ways other than through temporal inversion; local-color description does as well. Local color, of course, came to be a standard feature in the social novel; in the Afro-American narrative, realism-as-local-color is perhaps the most consistent aspect of black rhetorical strategy from the slave narratives to *Invisible Man*. Reed uses and simultaneously parodies the convention of local color as plot impediment by employing unpunctuated lists and categories throughout the text. Local color is provided in the novel's first paragraph:

> A True Sport, the Mayor of New Orleans, spiffy in his patent-leather brown and white shoes, his plaid suit, the Rudolph Valentino parted-down-the-middle hair style, sits in his office. Sprawled upon his knees is Zuzu, local doo-wack-a-doo and voo-do-dee-odo-fizgig. A slatternly floozy, her green, sequined dress quivers. (*MJ*, p. 3)

The following sentence exemplifies Reed's undifferentiated catalogs: 'The dazzling parodying punning mischievous pre-Joycean style-play of your Cake-walking your Calinda your Minstrelsy give-and-take of the ultra-absurd' (*MJ*, p. 152). Viktor Šklovskij says that the mystery novel was drawn upon formally by the social novel; Reed's use of devices from the detective novel to parody the black social novel, then, reverses this process, appropriately and ironically enough.[42]

I have discussed how the tension of the two stories generally operates in the types of detective fiction. Reed's play of doubles assumes its most subtle form in his clever rhetorical strategy of using these two narratives, the story of the past and the story of the present. It is useful to think of these two as the narrative of *understanding* and the narrative of *truth*. The narrative of understanding is the presented narrative of the investigation of a mystery, in which a detective (reader) interprets or decodes 'clues'. Once these signs are sufficiently decoded, this narrative of understanding reconstitutes the missing story of the crime, which we can think of as the narrative of truth. The presented narrative, then, is implicitly a story of another, absent story and hence functions as an internal allegory.

The nature of this narrative of the investigation in Mumbo Jumbo can be easily characterized: the narrative remains close to the action with local-color description and dialogue as its two central aspects; character-as-description and extensive catalogs propel the narrative forward; the narrative remains essentially in the present tense, and the point of view is both in the third person and limited, as it must be if the reader's understanding of the nature of the mystery is to remain impeded until the novel's detective decodes all the clues, assembles all the suspects, interprets the signs and reveals the truth of the mystery. The detective makes his arrests, and then everyone left eats dinner.

Mumbo Jumbo's prologue opens in this narrative mode of the story of the present. Near the end of the prologue, however, a second narrative mode intrudes. It is separated from the first narrative by spacing and is further foregrounded by italic type (see MJ, p. 6). It not only interprets and comments upon characters and actions in the first story but does so in a third-person omniscient mode. In other words, it reads its counterpart narrative, of which it is a negation. Following its italic type are three other sorts of subtexts which comprise crucial aspects of this second, antithetical narration of past, present and future: a black-and-white photograph of people dancing; an epigraph on the nature of the 'second line', written by Louis Armstrong; and an etymology of the phrase 'mumbo jumbo', taken from the American Heritage Dictionary. That which the characters ponder or 'misunderstand', this foregrounded antithetical narration reads 'correctly' for the reader.

> But they did not understand that the Jes Grew epidemic was unlike physical plagues. Actually Jes Grew was an anti-plague. Some plagues caused the body to waste away; Jes Grew enlivened the host. . . . So Jes Grew is seeking its words. Its text. For what good is a liturgy without a text? In the 1890s the text was not available and Jes Grew was out there all alone. Perhaps the 1920s will also be a false alarm and Jes Grew will evaporate as quickly as it appeared again broken-hearted and double-crossed (+ +). (MJ, p. 6)

This second, anti-, narration consists of all of Mumbo Jumbo's motley subtexts which are not included in its first narration. Whereas the first story adheres to the present, the second roams remarkably freely through space and time, between myth and 'history', humorously employing the device of anachronism. It is discontinuous and fragmentary, not linear like its counterpart; it never contains dialogue; it contains all of the text's abstractions.

All of the novel's subtexts (illustrations, excerpts from other texts, Situation Reports, etc.) are parts of this second narration, which we might think of as an extended discourse on the history of Jes Grew. The only mysteries this antithetical narration does not address are the text's first two mysteries – what exactly Jes Grew is and what precisely its Text is. After chapter 8, the foregrounding of italics tends to disappear, for the narration manages to bracket or frame itself, functioning almost as the interior monologue of the first narrative mode. While the first story remains firmly in the tradition of the presented detective story, the second turns that convention inside out, functioning as an ironic double, a reversed mirror image like the cryptic *vé vé* on the novel's cover.

This second mode of narration allows for the 'allegorical double' of *Mumbo Jumbo*. As many critics have gone to great lengths to demonstrate, *Mumbo Jumbo* is a thematic allegory of the Black Arts Movement of the 1960s rendered through causal connections with the Harlem Renaissance of the 1920s. A more interesting allegory, however, is that found in the antithetical narrative, which is a discourse on the history and nature of writing itself, especially that of the Afro-American literary tradition. *Mumbo Jumbo*, then, is a text that directs attention to its own writing, to its status as a text, related to other texts which it signifies upon. Its second narration reads its first, as does discourse upon a text. It is Reed reading Reed and the tradition. A formal metaphor for Reed's mode of writing is perhaps the bebop mode of jazz, as exemplified in that great reedist, Charlie Parker, who sometimes played a chord on the alto saxophone, then repeated and reversed the same chord to hear, if I understand him correctly, what he had just played. Parker is a recurring figure in Reed's works: 'Parker, the houngan (a word derived from *n'gana gana*) for whom there was no master adept enough to award him the Asson, is born' (MJ, p. 16).[43] Just as Jes Grew, the novel's central 'character', in searching for its Text is seeking to actualize a desire, to 'find its Speaking or strangle upon its own ineloquence', so too is the search for a text replicated and referred to throughout the second, signifying narration (MJ, p. 34).

What is the status of this desired Text? How are we to read Reed? Jes Grew's desire would be actualized only by finding its Text. *Mumbo Jumbo*'s parodic use of the presented story of the detective novel states this desire; the solution of the novel's central mystery would be for Jes Grew to find its Text. This Text, PaPa LaBas's allegorical narrative at the Villa Lewaro tells us, is in fact the vast and terrible Text of Blackness itself, 'always already' there:

> the Book of Thoth, the sacred Work . . . of the Black Birdman, an assistant to Osiris. (If anyone thinks this is 'mystifying the past' [the narrative intrudes] kindly check out your local bird book and you will find the sacred Ibis' Ornithological name to be *Threskiornis aethiopicus*). (MJ, p. 188)

The irony of the mystery structure evident in *Mumbo Jumbo* is that this Text, Jes Grew's object of desire, is 'defined' only by its absence; it is never seen or found. At the climax of LaBas's amusingly detailed and long recapitulation of his process of reading the signs of the mystery (as well as the history of the dissemination of the Text itself), La Bas instructs his assistant, T Malice, to unveil the Text:

> Go get the Book T!
> T Malice goes out to the car and returns with a huge gleaming box covered with snakes and scorpions shaped of sparkling gems.

The ladies intake their breath at such a gorgeous display. On the top can be seen the Knights Templar seal; 2 Knights riding Beaseauh, the Templars' piebald horse. T Malice places the box down in the center of the floor and removes the 1st box, an iron box, and the 2nd box, which is bronze and shines so that they have to turn the ceiling lights down. And within this box is a sycamore box and under the sycamore, ebony, and under this ivory, then silver and finally gold and then . . . empty!! (MJ, p. 196)

The nature of the Text remains undetermined and, indeed, indeterminate, as it was at the novel's beginning. Once the signs of its presence have been read, the Text disappears, in what must be the most humorous anticlimax in the whole of Afro-American fiction.

We can read this anticlimax against the notion of indeterminacy. Geoffrey H. Hartman defines the function of indeterminacy as 'a bar separating understanding and truth'.[44] The 'bar' in Mumbo Jumbo is signified by that unbridgeable white space that separates the first narrative mode from the second, the narrative of truth. Mumbo Jumbo is a novel about indeterminacy in interpretation itself. The text repeats this theme again and again. In addition to the two narrative voices, the Atonist Path and its Wallflower Order are criticized severely for a foolish emphasis upon unity, upon the number 1, upon what the novel calls 'point'. One of the three symbols of the Atonist Order is 'the #1' (MJ, p. 65). Their leader is called 'Hierophant 1' (MJ, p. 63). A 'hierophant', of course, is an expositor. The Atonists are defined in the antithetical narrative as they who seek to interpret the world through one interpretation:

To some if you owned your own mind you were indeed sick but when you possessed an Atonist mind you were healthy. A mind which sought to interpret the world by using a single loa. Somewhat like filling a milk bottle with an ocean. (MJ, p. 24)

The novel defines the nature of this urge for the reduction of unity:

1st they intimidate the intellectuals by condemning work arising out of their own experience as being 1-dimensional, enraged, non-objective, preoccupied with hate and not universal, universal being a word co-opted by the Catholic Church when the Atonists took over Rome, as a way of measuring every 1 by their deals. (MJ, p. 133)

One is an Atonist, the novel maintains consistently, who attempts to tie the sheer plurality of signification to one, determinate meaning.

In contrast is the spirit of Jes Grew and PaPa LaBas. As I have shown, the name 'LaBas' is derived from Èṣù-Ẹlẹ́gbára. The Yoruba call Èṣù the god of indeterminacy (àriyèmuyè) and of uncertainty. PaPa LaBas, in contradistinction to Hierophant 1, has not one but two heads, like the face of the sign: 'PaPa LaBas, noonday HooDoo, fugitive-hermit, obeah-man, botanist, animal impersonator, 2-headed man, You-Name-It' (MJ, p. 45). Moreover, he functions, as the detective of Jes Grew, as a decoder, as a sign reader, the man who cracked de code, by using his two heads: 'Evidence? Woman, I dream about it, I feel it, I use my 2 heads. My Knockings' (MJ, p. 25). LaBas is the critic, engaged in The Work, the work of art, refusing to reduce it to a 'point':

People in the 60s said they couldn't follow him. (In Santa Cruz the students walked out.) What's your point? they asked in Seattle whose central point, the Space Needle, is invisible from time to time. What are you driving at? they would say in Detroit in the 1950s. In the 40s he haunted the stacks of a ghost library. (MJ, p. 218)

While arguing ironically with Abdul Sufi Hamid, the Black Muslim who subsequently burns the Book of Thoth, LaBas critiques Abdul's 'black aesthetic' in terms identical to his critique of the Atonists:

Where does that leave the ancient Vodun aesthetic: pantheistic, becoming, 1 which bountifully permits 1000s of spirits, as many as the imagination can hold. Infinite Spirits and Gods. So many that it would take a book larger than the Koran and the Bible, the Tibetan Book of the Dead and all of the holy books in the world to list, and still room would have to be made for more. (MJ, p. 35; see also Abdul's letter to LaBas, MJ, pp. 200–3)

It is indeterminacy, the sheer plurality of meaning, the very play of the signifier itself, which *Mumbo Jumbo* celebrates. *Mumbo Jumbo* addresses the *play* of the black literary tradition and, as a parody, is a *play* upon that same tradition. Its central character, Jes Grew, cannot be reduced by the Atonists, as they complain: 'It's nothing we can bring into focus or categorize; once we call it 1 thing it forms into something else' (MJ, p. 4). Just as LaBas the detective is the text's figure for indeterminacy (paradoxically because he is a detective), so too is Jes Grew's 'nature' indeterminate: its Text is never a presence, and it disappears when its Text disappears, as surely as does Charlotte when Doctor Peter Pick recites, during his reverse-minstrel plantation routine, an incantation from PaPa LaBas's *Blue Back: A Speller* (see MJ, pp. 104–5, 199).

Even the idea of one transcendent subject, Jes Grew's Text, the Text of Blackness itself, *Mumbo Jumbo* criticizes. When the poet, Nathan Brown, asks the Haitian *houngan* Benoit Battraville how to catch Jes Grew, Benoit replies: 'don't ask me how to catch Jes Grew. Ask Louis Armstrong, Bessie Smith, your poets, your painters, your musicians, ask them how to catch it' (MJ, p. 152). Jes Grew also manifests itself in more curious forms:

The Rhyming Fool who sits in Rē'-mote Mississippi and talks 'crazy' for hours. The dazzling parodying punning mischievous pre-Joycean style-play of your Cakewalking your Calinda your Minstrelsy give-and-take of the ultra-absurd. Ask the people who put wax paper over combs and breathe through them. In other words, Nathan, I am saying Open-Up-To-Right-Here and then you will have something coming from your experience that the whole world will admire and need. (MJ, p. 152)

Jes Grew's Text, in other words, is not a transcendent signified but must be *produced* in a dynamic process and manifested in discrete forms, as in black music and black speech acts: 'The Blues is a Jes Grew, as James Weldon Johnson surmised. Jazz was a Jes Grew which followed the Jes Grew of Ragtime. Slang is Jes Grew too,' PaPa LaBas tells his 1960s audience in his annual lecture on the Harlem Renaissance (MJ, p. 214).

'Is this the end of Jes Grew?' the narrative questions when we learn that its Text does not exist. 'Jes Grew has no end and no beginning,' the text replies (MJ, p. 204). The echoes here are intentional: Reed echoes Ellison or, rather, Ellison's echo of T. S. Eliot. 'In my end is my beginning,' writes Eliot in 'East Coker', 'In my beginning is my end.' The 'end', writes Ellison, 'is in the beginning and lies far ahead.'[45] Reed signifies upon Ellison's gesture of closure here, and that of the entire Afro-American literary tradition, by positing an open-endedness of interpretation, of the play of signifiers, just as his and Ellison's works both signify upon the idea of the transcendent signified of the black tradition, the Text of Blackness itself.

The tradition's classic text on the 'blackness of blackness' is found in the prologue of *Invisible Man*:

'Brothers and sisters, my text this morning is the "Blackness of Blackness".'
And a congregation of voices answered: 'That blackness is most black, brother, most black ...'
'In the beginning ...'
'At the very start,' they cried.
'... there was blackness ...'
'Preach it ...'
'... and the sun ...'
'The sun, Lawd ...'
'... was bloody red ...'
'Red ...'
'Now black is ...' the preacher shouted.
'Bloody ...'
'I said black is ...'
'Preach it, brother ...'
'... an' black ain't ...'
'Red, Lawd, red: He said it's red!'
'Amen, brother ...'
'Black will git you ...'
'Yes, it will ...'
'... an' black won't ...'
'Naw, it won't!'

'It do . . .'
'It do, Lawd . . .'
'. . . an' it don't'
'Halleluiah . . .'
'. . . It'll put you, glory, glory, Oh my Lawd, in the WHALE'S BELLY.'
'Preach it, dear brother . . .'
'. . . an' make you tempt . . .'
'Good God a-mighty!'
'Old Aunt Nelly!'
'Black will make you . . .'
'Black . . .'
'. . . or black will un-make you.'
'Ain't it the truth, Lawd?' (IM, pp. 12–13)

This sermon signifies on Melville's passage in *Moby-Dick* on 'the blackness of darkness' and on the sign of blackness, as represented by the algorithm $\frac{\text{signified}}{\text{signifier}}$.[46] As Ellison's text states, 'black is' and 'black ain't', 'It do, Lawd', 'an' it don't'. Ellison parodies here the notion of essence, of the supposedly natural relation between the symbol and the symbolized. The vast and terrible Text of Blackness, we realize, has no essence; rather, it is signified into being by a signifier. The trope of blackness in Western discourse has signified absence at least since Plato. Plato, in the *Phaedrus*, recounts the myth of Theuth (*Mumbo Jumbo*'s 'Thoth') and the introduction of writing into Egypt. Along the way, Plato has Socrates draw upon the figure of blackness as a metaphor for one of the three divisions of the soul, that of 'badness':

> The other is crooked of frame, a massive jumble of a creature, with thick short neck, snub nose, black skin, and gray eyes; hot-blooded, consorting with wantonness and vainglory; shaggy of ear, deaf, and hard to control with whip and goad.[47]

Reed's use of the myth of Thoth is, of course, not accidental or arbitrary: he repeats and inverts Plato's dialogue, salient point for salient point, even down to Socrates' discourse on the excesses of the dance, which is a theme of *Mumbo Jumbo*.[48] It is not too much to say that *Mumbo Jumbo* is one grand signifying riff on the *Phaedrus*, parodying it through the hidden polemic.

Both Ellison and Reed, then, critique the received idea of blackness as a negative essence, as a natural, transcendent signified; but implicit in such a critique is an equally thorough critique of blackness as a *presence*, which is merely another transcendent signified. Such a critique, therefore, is a critique of the structure of the sign itself and constitutes a profound critique. The Black Arts Movement's grand gesture was to make of the trope of blackness a trope of presence. That movement willed it to be, however, a transcendent presence. Ellison's 'text for today', 'the "Blackness of Blackness" ' (IM, p. 12), analyzes this gesture, just as surely as does Reed's Text of Blackness, the 'sacred Book of Thoth'. In literature, blackness is *produced* in the text only through a complex process of signification. There can be no transcendent blackness, for it cannot and does not exist beyond manifestations of it in specific figures. Put simply, Jes Grew cannot conjure its texts; 'texts', in the broadest sense of this term (Parker's music, Ellison's fictions, Romare Bearden's collages, etc.), conjure Jes Grew.

Reed has, in *Mumbo Jumbo*, signified upon Ellison's critique of the central pre-supposition of the Afro-American literary tradition, by drawing upon Ellison's trope as a central theme of the plot of *Mumbo Jumbo* and by making explicit Ellison's implicit critique of the nature of the sign itself, of a transcendent signified, an essence, which supposedly exists prior to its figuration. Their formal relationship can only be suggested by the relation of modernism to post-modernism, two overworked terms. Blackness exists, but 'only' as a function of its signifiers. Reed's open-ended structure, and his stress on the indeterminacy of the text, demands that we, as critics, in the act of reading, *produce* a text's signifying structure. For Reed, as for his great precursor, Ellison, figuration is indeed the 'nigger's occupation'.

Coda: the warp and the woof

Reed's signifying relation to Ellison is exemplified in his poem, 'Dualism: in ralph ellison's invisible man':

> i am outside of
> history. i wish
> i had some peanuts, it
> looks hungry there in
> its cage.

> i am inside of
> history. its
> hungrier than i
> thot.[49]

The figure of history, here, is the Signifying Monkey; the poem signifies upon that repeated trope of dualism figured initially in black discourse in DuBois's essay 'Of Our Spiritual Strivings', which forms the first chapter of *The Souls of Black Folk*. The dualism parodied by Reed's poem is that represented in the epilogue of *Invisible Man*: 'Now I know men are different and that all life is divided and that only in division is there true health' (IM, p. 499). For Reed, this belief in the 'reality' of dualism spells death. Ellison, here, had refigured DuBois's trope:

> After the Egyptian and Indian, the Greek and Roman, the Teuton and Mongolian, the Negro is a sort of seventh son, born with a veil, and gifted with second-sight in this American world, – a world which yields him no true

self-consciousness, but only lets him see himself through the revelation of the other world. It is a peculiar sensation, this double-consciousness, this sense of always looking at one's self through the eyes of others, of measuring one's soul by the tape of a world that looks on in amused contempt and pity. One ever feels his two-ness, – an American, a Negro; two souls, two thoughts, two unreconciled strivings; two warring ideals in one dark body, whose dogged strength alone keeps it from being torn asunder.

The history of the American Negro is the history of this strife, – this longing to attain self-conscious manhood, to merge his double self into a better and truer self. In this merging he wishes neither of the older selves to be lost.[50]

Reed's poem parodies, profoundly, both the figure of the black as outsider and the figure of the divided self. For, he tells us, even these are only tropes, figures of speech, rhetorical constructs like 'double-consciousness', and not some preordained reality or thing. To read these figures literally, Reed tells us, is to be duped by figuration, just like the signified Lion. Reed has secured his place in the canon precisely by his critique of the received, repeated tropes peculiar to that very canon. His works are the grand works of critical signification.

Notes

1 Quoted in Roger D. Abrahams, *Deep Down in the Jungle . . .: Negro Narrative Folklore from the Streets of Philadelphia* (Chicago, Ill.: Aldine, 1970), p. 53.

2 The present essay is extracted from my larger work, *The Signifying Monkey: Towards a Theory of Literary History* (New York: Oxford University Press, 1985).

3 On Tar Baby, see Ralph Ellison, 'Hidden Name and Complex Fate: A Writer's Experience in the United States', *Shadow and Act* (New York: Vintage Books, 1964), p. 147, and Toni Morrison, *Tar Baby* (New York: Knopf, 1981). On the black as quasi-simian, see Jean Bodin, *Method for the Easy Comprehension of History*, trans. Beatrice Reynolds (1945; New York: Octagon Books, 1966), p. 105; Aristotle, *Historia animalium*, 606b; Thomas Herbert, *Some Years Travels* (London, 1677), pp. 16–17; and John Locke, *An Essay Concerning Human Understanding*, 8th edn, 2 vols (London, 1721), vol. 2, p. 53.

4 Geneva Smitherman defines these and other black tropes and then traces their use in several black texts. Smitherman's work, like that of Claudia Mitchell-Kernan and Abrahams, is especially significant for literary theory. See Smitherman, *Talkin' and Testifyin': The Language of Black America* (Boston, Mass.: Houghton Mifflin, 1977), pp. 101–66. See also notes 13 and 14 below.

5 On versions of Èṣù, see Robert Farris Thompson, *Black Gods and Kings* (1971; Bloomington, Ind.: Indiana University Press, 1976), ch. 4, pp. 1–12, and *Flash of the Spirit* (New York: Random House, 1983); Pierre Verger, *Notes sur le culte des Orisa et Vodun* (Dakar: IFAN, 1957); Joan Westcott, 'The Sculputure and Myths of Eshu-Elegba, the Yoruba Trickster', *Africa*, 32 (October 1962), pp. 336–54; Leo Frobenius, *The Voice of Africa*, 2 vols (London, 1913); J. Melville and Frances Herskovits, *Dahomean Narrative* (Evanston, Ill.: Northwestern University Press, 1958); Wande Abimbola, *Sixteen Great Poems of Ifa* (New York: Unesco, 1975); William R. Bascom, *Ifa Divination: Communication between Gods and Men in West Africa* (Bloomington, Ind.: Indiana University Press, 1969); Ayodele Ogundipe, 'Esu Elegbara: The Yoruba God of Chance and Uncertainty', 2 vols (PhD dissertation, Indiana University, 1978); E. Bolaji Idowu, *Olódùmarè, God in Yoruba Belief* (London:

Longman, 1962), pp. 80–5; and Robert Pelton, *The Trickster in West Africa* (Los Angeles, Calif.: University of California Press, 1980).

6 On Èṣù and indeterminacy, see Robert Plant Armstrong, *The Powers of Presence: Consciousness, Myth, and Affecting Presence* (Philadelphia, Pa.: University of Pennsylvania Press, 1981), p. 4. See ibid., p. 43, for a drawing of the Ọpọn Ifá, and Thompson, *Black Gods and Kings*, ch. 5.

7 On Èṣù and the Monkey, see Lydia Cabrera, *El Monte: Notes sobre las religiones, la magia, las supersticiones y el folklore de los negros criollos y el pueblo de Cuba* (Miami, Fla.: Ediciones Universal, 1975), p. 84, and Alberto de Pozo, *Oricha* (Miami, Fla.: Oricha, 1982), p. 1. On the Signifying Monkey, see Abrahams, op. cit., pp. 51–3, 66, 113–19, 142–7, 153–6 and esp. 264; Bruce Jackson (comp.), *'Get Your Ass in the Water and Swim Like Me': Narrative Poetry from Black Oral Tradition* (Cambridge, Mass.: Harvard University Press, 1974), pp. 161–80; Daryl Cumber Dance, *Shuckin' and Jivin': Folklore from Contemporary Black Americans* (Bloomington, Ind.: Indiana University Press, 1978), pp. 197–9; Dennis Wepman, Ronald B. Newman and Murray B. Binderman (comps), *The Life: The Lore and Folk Poetry of the Black Hustler* (Philadelphia, Pa.: University of Pennsylvania Press, 1976), pp. 21–9; Lawrence W. Levine, *Black Culture and Black Consciousness: Afro-American Folk Thought from Slavery to Freedom* (New York: Oxford University Press, 1977), pp. 346, 378–80, 438; and Richard M. Dorson (comp.), *American Negro Folktales* (New York: Fawcett, 1967), pp. 98–9.

8 Julia Kristeva, *Desire in Language: A Semiotic Approach to Literature and Art*, ed. Leon S. Roudiez, trans. Thomas Gora, Alice Jardine and Leon S. Roudiez (New York: Columbia University Press, 1980), p. 31.

9 Abrahams, op. cit., pp. 51–2. See also Roger D. Abrahams, 'Playing the Dozens', *Journal of American Folklore*, 75 (July–September 1962), pp. 209–20; 'The Changing Concept of the Negro Hero', in Mody C. Boatright, Wilson M. Hudson and Allen Maxwell (eds), *The Golden Log*, Publications of the Texas Folklore Soceity, no. 31 (Dallas, Tex., 1962), pp. 125–34; and *Talking Black* (Rowley, Mass.: Newbury House, 1976).

10 Abrahams, *Deep Down in the Jungle*, pp. 52, 264, 66, 67; my emphasis. Abrahams's awareness of the need to define uniquely black significations is exemplary; as early as 1964, when he published the first edition of *Deep Down in the Jungle*, he saw fit to add a glossary, as an appendix of 'Unusual Terms and Expressions', a title that unfortunately suggests the social scientist's apologia.

11 Ibid., p. 113. In the second line of the stanza, 'motherfucker' is often substituted for 'monkey'.

12 'The Signifying Monkey', in *The Book of Negro Folklore*, ed. Langston Hughes and Arna Bontemps (New York: Dodd, Mead, 1958), pp. 365–6.

13 On signifying as a rhetorical trope, see Thomas Kochman (ed.), *Rappin' and Stylin' Out: Communication in Urban Black America* (Urbana, Ill.: University of Illinois Press, 1972) and ' "Rappin" in the Black Ghetto', *Trans-action*, 6 (February 1969), p. 32; Smitherman, op. cit., pp. 101–67; Alan Dundes (ed.), *Mother Wit from the Laughing Barrel* (Englewood Cliffs, NJ: Prentice-Hall, 1973), p. 310; and Ethel M. Albert, ' "Rhetoric", "Logic", and "Poetics" in Burundi: Culture Patterning of Speech Behavior', in John J. Gumperz and Dell Hymes (eds), *The Ethnography of Communication*, *American Anthropologist*, 66, pt 2 (December 1964), pp. 35–54.

One example of signifying can be gleaned from an anecdote. While writing this essay, I asked a colleague, Dwight Andrews, if as a child he had heard of the Signifying Monkey. 'Why, no,' he replied intently, 'I never heard of the Signifying Monkey until I came to Yale and read about him in a book.' I had been signified upon. If I had responded to Dwight Andrews, 'I know what you mean; your Momma read to me from that same book the last time I was in Detroit,' I would have signified upon him in return.

14 Claudia Mitchell-Kernan, 'Signifying', in Dundes (ed.), op. cit., p. 313; all further references to this work, abbreviated 'Sig.', will be included parenthetically in the text. See also her 'Signifying, Loud-talking, and Marking', in Kochman (ed.), op. cit., pp. 315–35.

15 See Mitchell-Kernan, 'Signifying, Loud-talking, and Marking', pp. 315–35. For Zora Neale Hurston's definition of 'signifying', see *Mules and Men: Negro Folktales and Voodoo Practices in the South* (1935; New York: Harper & Row, 1970), p. 161.

16 For a definitive study of revision and its relation to ideas of modernism, see Kimberly W. Benston, *Afro-American Modernism* (forthcoming). Benston's reading of Hurston's revision of Frederick Douglass has heavily informed my own.

17 Ralph Ellison, 'And Hickman Arrives', in *Black Writers of America: A Comprehensive Anthology*, ed. Richard Barksdale and Keneth Kinnamon (New York: Macmillan, 1972), p. 704.

18 Ellison, 'On Bird, Bird-Watching, and Jazz', *Shadow and Act*, p. 231.

19 Ellison, 'Blues People', *Shadow and Act*, pp. 249–50.

20 Ellison, 'The World and the Jug', *Shadow and Act*, p. 117.

21 Ibid., p. 137; my emphasis.

22 Mixhail Baxtin (Mikhail Bakhtin), 'Discourse Typology in Prose', in Ladislav Matejka and Krystyna Pomorska (eds), *Readings in Russian Poetics: Formalist and Structuralist Views* (Cambridge, Mass.: MIT Press, 1971), p. 187; see also pp. 176–96.

23 The use of interlocking triangles as a metaphor for the intertextual relationships of the tradition is not meant to suggest any form of concrete, inflexible reality. On the contrary, it is a systematic metaphor, as René Girard puts it, 'systematically pursued':

> The triangle is no *Gestalt*. The real structures are intersubjective. They cannot be localized anywhere; *the triangle has no reality whatever; it is a systematic metaphor, systematically pursued.* Because changes in size and shape do not destroy the identity of this figure, as we will see later, the diversity as well as the unity of the works can be simultaneously illustrated. The purpose and limitations of this structural geometry may become clearer through a reference to 'structural models'. The triangle is a model of a sort, or rather a whole family of models. But these models are not 'mechanical' like those of Claude Lévi-Strauss. They always allude to the mystery, transparent yet opaque, of human relations. All types of structural thinking assume that human reality is intelligible; it is a *logos* and, as such, it is an incipient logic, or it degrades itself into a logic. It can thus be systematized, at least up to a point, however unsystematic, irrational, and chaotic it may appear even to those, or rather especially to those who operate the system. (René Girard, *Deceit, Desire, and the Novel: Self and Other in Literary Structure*, trans. Yvonne Freccero (Baltimore, Md: Johns Hopkins University Press, 1965), pp. 2–3; my emphasis)

24 For Ishmael Reed on 'a talking book', see 'Ishmael Reed: A Self Interview', *Black World*, 23 (June 1974), p. 25. For the slave narratives in which this figure appears, see James Albert Ukawsaw Gronniosaw, *A Narrative of the Most Particular Particulars of the Life of James Albert Ukawsaw Gronniosaw, An African Prince* (Bath, 1770); John Marrant, *Narrative of the Lord's Wonderful Dealings with John Marrant, A Black* (London, 1785); Ottabah Cugoano, *Thoughts and Sentiments on the Evil and Wicked Traffic of the Slavery and Commerce of the Human Species* (London, 1787); Olaudah Equiano, *The Interesting Narrative of the Life of Olaudah Equiano, or Gustavus Vassa, The African. Written by Himself* (London, 1789); and John Jea, *The Life and Sufferings of John Jea, An African Preacher* (Swansea, 1806).

25 Northrop Frye, *Anatomy of Criticism: Four Essays* (Princeton, NJ: Princeton University Press, 1957), p. 233.

26 Baxtin (Bakhtin), op. cit., p. 190.

27 Frye, op. cit., p. 234.

28 Ellison, 'The World and the Jug', *Shadow and Act*, p. 140.
29 See Ishmael Reed, *The Free-Lance Pallbearers* (Garden City, NY: Doubleday, 1967), *Yellow Back Radio Broke-Down* (Garden City, NY: Doubleday, 1969), *Mumbo Jumbo* (Garden City, NY: Doubleday, 1972), *The Last Days of Louisiana Red* (New York: Random House, 1974), *Flight to Canada* (New York: Random House, 1976) and *The Terrible Twos* (New York: St Martin's/Marek, 1982).
30 See Neil Schmitz, 'Neo-HooDoo: The Experimental Fiction of Ishmael Reed', *Twentieth Century Literature*, 20 (April 1974), pp. 126–8. Schmitz's splendid reading is, I believe, the first to discuss the salient aspect of Reed's rhetorical strategy. This paragraph is heavily indebted to Schmitz's essay.
31 Reed. *The Free-Lance Pallbearers*, p. 107.
32 Reed, *Yellow Back Radio Broke-Down*, pp. 34–6. For an excellent close reading of *Yellow Back Radio Broke-Down*, see Michel Fabre, 'Postmodern Rhetoric in Ishmael Reed's *Yellow Back Radio Broke-Down*', in Peter Bruck and Wolfgang Karrer (eds), *The Afro-American Novel since 1960* (Amsterdam: B. R. Gruner, 1982), pp. 167–88.
33 Reed, *Mumbo Jumbo*, p. 6; all further references to this work, abbreviated MJ, will be included parenthetically in the text.
34 Ellison, 'And Hickman Arrives', p. 701.
35 See Charles T. Davis, *Black is the Color of the Cosmos: Essays on Black Literature and Culture, 1942–1981*, ed. Henry Louis Gates, Jr (New York: Garland, 1982), pp. 167–233.
36 My reading of the imagery on Reed's cover was inspired by a conversation with Robert Farris Thompson.
37 On Reed's definition of 'gombo' (gumbo), see his 'The Neo-HooDoo Aesthetic', *Conjure: Selected Poems, 1963–1970* (Amherst, Mass.: University of Massachusetts Press, 1972), p. 26.
38 This clever observation is James A. Snead's, for whose Yale seminar on parody I wrote the first draft of this essay.
39 Reed, interview by Calvin Curtis, 29 January 1979.
40 Tzvetan Todorov, 'The Two Principles of Narrative', trans. Philip E. Lewis, *Diacritics*, 1 (Fall 1971), p. 41. See his *The Poetics of Prose*, trans. Richard Howard (Ithaca, NY: Cornell University Press, 1977), pp. 42–52; all further references to this work, abbreviated PP, will be included parenthetically in the text.
41 For a wonderfully useful discussion of *fabula* ('fable') and *sjužet* ('subject'), see Victor Šklovskij, 'The Mystery Novel: Dickens's *Little Dorrit*', in Matejka and Pomorska (eds), op. cit., pp. 220–6. On use of typology, see p. 222.
42 See ibid., pp. 222, 226.
43 A *houngan* is a priest of *Vaudou*. On *Vaudou*, see Jean Price-Mars, *Ainsi parla l'Oncle* (Port-au-Prince: Imprimerie de Campiègne, 1928), and Alfred Métraux, *Le Vodou haitien* (Paris: Gallimard, 1958).
44 Geoffrey H. Hartman, *Criticism in the Wilderness: The Study of Literature Today* (New Haven, Conn.: Yale University Press, 1980), p. 272.
45 Ralph Ellison, *Invisible Man* (New York: Random House, 1952), p. 9; all further references to this work, abbreviated IM, will be included parenthetically in the text.

46 Melville's passage from *Moby-Dick* reads:

> It seemed the great Black Parliament sitting in Tophet. A hundred black faces turned
> round in their rows to peer; and beyond, a black Angel of Doom was beating a book
> in a pulpit. It was a negro church; and the preacher's text was about the blackness of
> darkness, and the weeping and wailing and teeth-gnashing there. Ha, Ishmael,
> muttered I, backing out, Wretched entertainment at the sign of 'The Trap'. (*Moby-Dick*
> (1851; New York: W. W. Norton, 1967), p. 18)

This curious figure also appears in James Pike's *The Prostrate State: South Carolina under Negro
Government* (New York, 1874), p. 62.

47 Plato, *Phaedrus*, 253d–254a. For the myth of Theuth, see 274c–275b.

48 See ibid., 259b–259e.

49 Ishmael Reed, 'Dualism: in ralph ellison's invisible man', *Conjure*, p. 50.

50 W. E. B. DuBois, *The Souls of Black Folk: Essays and Sketches* (1903; New York: Fawcett, 1961),
pp. 16–17.

Index

Freud, Sigmund, 21, 67; *Totem and Taboo*, 227–8, 246n.
Frye, Northrop, 296

Garrison, William Lloyd, 175, 176
Gates, Henry Louis Jr, 156, 218; 'Criticism in the Jungle', 214
Gaultier, Jules de, 8
Geertz, Clifford, 21; 'Deep Play: Notes on the Balinese Cockfight', 223, 224, 229
Georges, Robert A.: 'Structure in Folktales', 87
Guillén, Nicolás, 6
Gyekes, Kwame, 143

Hammon, Briton, 297
Haring, Lee, 86
Harlem Renaissance, 243, 302, 311
Harper, Michael, 152, 165–6, 200
Hartman, Geoffrey, 3, 4, 6, 188, 312
Hawthorne, Nathaniel, 154–5, 156, 170n.; *The Scarlet Letter*, 155
Hegel, Georg, 14, 72; on black culture, 62–4
hermeneutics, 83–4, 287
Hermes, 231, 232, 237–8, 287
history, 54, 65, 76–7n.; Afro-American, 151–2
Hitler, Adolf, 49
holism, 133
Horner, George, 87–8
Hughes, Langston, 201
humanism, revolutionary, 49
Hurston, Zora Neale, 18; *Dust Tracks on a Road*, 217; on folklore, 208–9; metaphor and, 208; relationship with Reed, 296, 297; signifying and, 290
Hurston, Zora Neale: *Their Eyes Were Watching God*, 19–20, 209, 215, 218, 258, 260n., 294; end of, 213, 215; inside/outside opposition, 210–12; metaphor and metonymy in, 211–12; plot of, 209–10; signifying text, 290; women and, 217–18
Husserl, Edmund, 116

Ibo, 44
idealism, 49
ideologies, 51, 54
Irele, Abiola, 105

Jahn, Janheinz, 108, 144
Jakobson, Roman, 105, 127, 135; *Essais de linguistics générales*, 136, 205; metaphor and metonymy, 205–8, 212; pattern of aphasia, 206; 'Two Aspects of Language and Two Types of Aphasic Disturbances', 20, 205
James, C. L. R.: *Mariners, Renegades and Castaways: The Story of Herman Melville and the World We Live In*, 1–2
Jameson, Fredric, 21; 'The Symbolic Inference', 238–9
Jason, Heda, 87

Jeyifo, Biodun, 45, 46; 'Soyinka Demythologized', 45
Johnson, Barbara, 14, 19–20, 22, 23
Johnson, Charles, 243
Johnson, James Weldon: *Autobiography of an ex-Colored Man*, 214–15
Jones, Elvin, 69
Joyce, James, 15, 74, 196, 245; *Portrait of the Artist . . .*, 290

Kent, George, 244
Kochman, Thomas, 289
Kristeva, Julia, 223, 287

Lacan, Jacques, 68
language, 28, 29, 32, 37, 40, 48, 49–50, 55, 130, 132; of alienation, 30, 37; of essentialization, 44; syntagmatic and paradigmatic features of, 1, 132–3
langue, 28–30, 36, 38, 42, 43, 54, 119, 128, 129, 133, 134
Larsen, Nella: *Quicksand*, 258
Leach, Edmund, 135
l'engage, 28, 32, 40, 55n.
leftocracy, 48, 54
Leftocratic Convention, 44, 56n.
Lévi-Strauss, Claude, 15, 82, 83, 88, 101, 102, 105, 106, 117, 119, 121, 135, 149n.; concept of the problematic, 106–7; myth analysis and, 89–91, 116–17, 136; structuralism of, 112–17
Lewis, David Levering: *When Harlem Was in Vogue*, 243
Lewis, R. W. B., 194–5
literature, African, 5, 105–6, 122–3; Asante Ananse tales, 84; oral literature, 83, 84; structuralism and, 105–6, 127
literature, 'black' (Afro-American), 295; Benston on, 18; 'blackness' and, 7, 156–7, 159; canon-formation, 19; figuration in, 6–7, 15; heritage of black texts, 4–5; influence of nineteenth-century American writers on, 154–6; literary criticism and, 3–4, 8–10; naming and rise of 'black consciousness', 165–9; narrative parody, 289, 291; negation and, 7; post-structural theory and, 20–1; relationship with Western literature, 3, 6, 10, 12–13; repetition in, 70–2; revision in, 290; structure of black texts, 5–6; trope of naming, 17; unnaming in, 152
literature, European, 44; literary criticism and, 3–4; relationship with 'black' literature, 3, 6, 10, 12–13
Lo Liyong, Taban, 11
love, 49

McPherson, James Alan, 297
Malcolm X, 151–2, 170n.
Man, Paul de, 208